FIDUCIARY LOYALTY

Fiduciary Loyalty presents a comprehensive analysis of the nature and function of fiduciary duties. The concept of loyalty, which lies at the heart of fiduciary doctrine, is a form of protection that is designed to enhance the likelihood of due performance of non-fiduciary duties, by seeking to avoid influences or temptations that may distract the fiduciary from providing such proper performance.

In developing this position, the book takes the novel approach of putting to one side the difficult question of when fiduciary duties arise in order to focus attention instead on what fiduciary duties do when they are owed. The issue of when fiduciary duties arise can then be returned to and considered more profitably, once a clear view has emerged of the function that such duties perform.

The analysis advanced in the book has both practical and theoretical implications for understanding fiduciary doctrine. For example, it provides a sound conceptual footing for understanding the relationship between fiduciary and non-fiduciary duties, highlighting the practical importance of analysing both forms of duties carefully when considering fiduciary claims. Further, it explains a number of tenets within fiduciary doctrine, such as the proscriptive nature of fiduciary duties and the need to obtain the principal's fully informed consent in order to avoid fiduciary liability. Understanding the relationship between fiduciary and non-fiduciary duties also provides a solid foundation for addressing issues concerning compensatory remedies for their breach and potential defences such as contributory fault. The distinctive purpose that fiduciary duties serve also provides a firm theoretical basis for maintaining their separation from other forms of civil obligation, such as those that arise under the law of contracts and of torts.

Fiduciary Loyalty

Protecting the Due Performance of Non-Fiduciary Duties

MATTHEW CONAGLEN

·HART·
PUBLISHING

OXFORD AND PORTLAND, OREGON
2011

Published in North America (US and Canada) by
Hart Publishing
c/o International Specialized Book Services
920 NE 58th Avenue, Suite 300
Portland, OR 97213–3786
USA
Tel: +1–503–287–3093 or toll-free: 1–800–944–6190
Fax: +1–503–280–8832
Email: orders@isbs.com
Website: http://www.isbs.com

Hart Publishing Ltd, 16C Worcester Place
Oxford OX1 2JW, United Kingdom
Tel: +44 (0)1865 517530
Fax: +44 (0)1865 510710
Email: mail@hartpub.co.uk
Website: http://www.hartpub.co.uk

British Library Cataloguing in Publication Data
Data Available

ISBN: 978-1-84113-583-0 (hardback)
978-1-84946-214-3 (paperback)

Typeset by Columns Design Ltd, Reading

Preface

Claimants regularly pursue allegations of breach of fiduciary duty in litigation because of the strict nature of such duties, which generates potential forensic advantages for claimants when compared with other private law claims, and because of the powerful remedies that can be obtained when a claimant succeeds in establishing such a breach. The circumstances that generate fiduciary duties and the content of those duties have consequently interested lawyers, myself included, for many years, and a rich literature has developed concerning those topics. However, several aspects of the debate about fiduciary doctrine remain unresolved. In particular, it remains unclear what function fiduciary doctrine serves and whether that justifies its separation from other, better known categories of legal doctrine. This book offers a response to those questions.

The core of the arguments contained in the book was originally formulated in the course of preparing my doctoral dissertation. Over many years since then, the arguments have been developed and refined through further investigation and deliberation. This book provides the opportunity to bring together the various strands of those arguments, and to develop and extend them in combination with others, in one coherent analysis.

The book is the culmination of around ten years of thinking, researching and writing about fiduciary doctrine. Over that space of time, numerous people have contributed to the writing of the book, through their various suggestions, support for and criticisms of my ideas about fiduciary doctrine, and conversations and correspondence with me about those ideas. They are too numerous to name individually. All of them contributed in their own ways to what follows, for which I am grateful.

Specific mention is, however, necessary in respect of a few people. David Fox, Richard Nolan and Peter Turner kindly read the manuscript in draft and offered helpful comments on its substance and presentation. David Wills, Peter Zawada, Kay Naylor and Kathy Wholley, at the Squire Law Library, helped with locating materials not present within that library or otherwise unavailable to me electronically, as did Robert Hollyman in New Zealand and Colin Campbell in Australia. And I am grateful to the trustees of the WM Tapp Scholarship fund at Gonville & Caius College, Cambridge for their decision to support my initial doctoral research on fiduciary duties.

Two people stand out as deserving especial thanks for their respective contributions to this book. My interest in equity generally and in the topic of fiduciary duties in particular was first excited as an undergraduate at the University of

Auckland in the early 1990s by Julie Maxton's teaching of the subject. And Richard Nolan's generous willingness to act as a critical foil, initially as my doctoral supervisor but over many years since then as a colleague and friend, has helped me to sharpen my thinking as I have sought to formulate, develop and defend my views.

Notwithstanding the contribution that all of these people have made, the usual disclaimer applies: I bear sole responsibility for the views presented in the book.

I have sought to advance certain aspects of the ideas presented here in my teaching at Cambridge (especially, but not exclusively, in graduate level classes concerning fiduciary duties) and at seminars held in a number of other forums, as well as in articles, the most important of which are 'Equitable Compensation for Breach of Fiduciary Dealing Rules' (2003) 119 *Law Quarterly Review* 246; 'The Nature and Function of Fiduciary Loyalty' (2005) 121 *Law Quarterly Review* 452; 'A Re-Appraisal of the Fiduciary Self-Dealing and Fair-Dealing Rules' [2006] *Cambridge Law Journal* 366; 'Fiduciary Regulation of Conflicts Between Duties' (2009) 125 *Law Quarterly Review* 111; and 'Remedial Ramifications of Conflicts between a Fiduciary's Duties' (2010) 126 *Law Quarterly Review* (forthcoming).

Finally, I thank Isabella and Katharine for their unwavering support.

The book endeavours to describe the state of the law at Easter 2009.

MDJC
Latham Court
Trinity Hall
Anzac Day 2009

Summary of Contents

Contents

Table of Cases

United Kingdom

Australia

Bermuda

Brunei Darussalam

Canada

Gibraltar

Hong Kong

Isle of Man

Jamaica

Jersey

Natal

New Zealand

Selangor

Singapore

South Africa

United States of America

West Indies

Table of Legislation

United Kingdom

Australia

Selangor

1

Prologue

The word 'fiduciary' recurs frequently in legal discussion, but the understanding of the meaning of the word is very confused. Anthony Mason famously described the fiduciary relationship as 'a concept in search of a principle'.[1] The clearest message to be taken from judicial pronouncements regarding the fiduciary concept is that it is concerned with the 'undivided loyalty' of the fiduciary:[2] as Millett LJ said in his judgment in *Bristol & West Building Society v Mothew*, which has been described as 'a masterly survey of the modern law of fiduciary duties',[3] the 'distinguishing obligation of a fiduciary is the obligation of loyalty'.[4] The concept of loyalty is now well established as the core—indeed the defining—concept of fiduciary doctrine.[5] The difficulty is that the precise meaning of the concept of loyalty remains unclear in the fiduciary context. It is that difficulty which this book seeks to address. In other words, the purpose of the book is to identify within equity's case law a more precise view as to the nature and function of the concept of fiduciary loyalty. Is the concept of fiduciary loyalty a helpful

---

[1] AF Mason, 'Themes and Prospects' in PD Finn (ed), *Essays in Equity* (Sydney, Law Book Co, 1985) 242, 246. See also *Frame v Smith* [1987] 2 SCR 99, 135; *Lac Minerals Ltd v International Corona Resources Ltd* [1989] 2 SCR 574, 643–44.

[2] *Boulting v Association of Cinematograph Television and Allied Technicians* [1963] 2 QB 606, 636 (CA). See also *Farrington v Rowe McBride & Partners* [1985] 1 NZLR 83, 90 (CA).

[3] *Johnson v EBS Pensioner Trustees Ltd* [2002] EWCA Civ 164 at [37], [2002] Lloyd's Rep PN 309. See also *Popek v National Westminster Bank plc* [2002] EWCA Civ 42 at [32].

[4] *Bristol & West Building Society v Mothew* [1998] Ch 1, 18.

[5] See, eg, *Hodgkinson v Simms* [1994] 3 SCR 377, 452; *Bank of New Zealand v New Zealand Guardian Trust Co Ltd* [1999] 1 NZLR 664, 680–81 and 687 (CA); *Williams v The Minister, Aboriginal Land Rights Act 1983* [1999] NSWSC 843 at [726]; *KLB v British Columbia* [2003] SCC 51 at [48], [2003] 2 SCR 403; *Chirnside v Fay* [2004] 3 NZLR 637 at [51]; *Hilton v Barker Booth & Eastwood (a firm)* [2005] UKHL 8, [2005] 1 WLR 567 at [30]; *Sinclair Investment Holdings SA v Versailles Trade Finance Ltd* [2005] EWCA Civ 722 at [20], [2006] 1 BCLC 60; *Ultraframe (UK) Ltd v Fielding* [2005] EWHC 1638 (Ch) at [1286]; *Southern Cross Mine Management Pty Ltd v Ensham Resources Pty Ltd* [2005] QSC 233 at [579]; *Gibson Motorsport Merchandise Pty Ltd v Forbes* [2006] FCAFC 44 at [11], (2006) 149 FCR 569; *P & V Industries Pty Ltd v Porto* [2006] VSC 131 at [23], (2006) 14 VR 1; *Take Ltd v BSM Marketing Ltd* [2006] EWHC 1085 (QB) at [93], not addressed on appeal: [2009] EWCA Civ 45; *Amaltal Corp Ltd v Maruha Corp* [2007] NZSC 40 at [21], [2007] 3 NZLR 192; *Australian Securities and Investments Commission v Citigroup Global Markets Australia Pty Ltd (No 4)* [2007] FCA 963 at [289], (2007) 160 FCR 35; *Hageman v Holmes* [2009] EWHC 50 (Ch) at [52]; *Premium Real Estate Ltd v Stevens* [2009] NZSC 15 at [67], [2009] 2 NZLR 384.

analytical tool, or is it empty rhetoric? What marks fiduciary duties out from other categories of legal duty such that they attract a different name and different remedies? Are they in fact a different kind of duty or rather merely another example of the kinds of duties that we recognise in the fields of contract law or the law of torts? If fiduciary duties are a different kind of duty, as their name suggests, how do they interact with the better known duties owed in contract and tort?

This analysis is important for several reasons. First, at a theoretical level, the proper classification of doctrines is important in understanding their interrelationship and, consequently, legal doctrine in general. While the historical origins of legal concepts and doctrines are undeniably important in understanding those concepts and doctrines, the ultimate goal of doctrinal legal analysis is to understand the doctrines themselves more fully. In that regard, the historical origins of doctrines are becoming less important than the substance of obligations.[6] Understanding the substance of obligations is further developed by reference to the differences between types of legal doctrine: those differences are much more than a matter of mere semantics.[7] Thus, there is merit in examining fiduciary doctrine, to seek to identify and analyse the theoretical similarities and differences between it and various other doctrines. Several law and economics scholars have argued that fiduciary duties are simply examples of implied, or default, contractual obligations.[8] Others have suggested that they are properly categorised as torts.[9] If fiduciary duties are to be distinguished from other kinds of duties by the fact that they demand loyalty, a more developed understanding of what that means is necessary.

Furthermore, the iterative nature of common law development means that a theoretical understanding of fiduciary doctrine is also important at the more practical level in indicating how we should approach the resolution of disputes about currently unsettled aspects of fiduciary doctrine. For example, as will be

---

[6] See, eg, *Mothew* (above n 4) 16; *Henderson v Merrett Syndicates Ltd* [1995] 2 AC 145, 205; *Aquaculture Corp v New Zealand Green Mussel Co Ltd* [1990] 3 NZLR 299, 301; *Lockwood Buildings Ltd v Trust Bank Canterbury Ltd* [1995] 1 NZLR 22, 26; *Bank of New Zealand* (above n 5) 686–87; AF Mason, 'The Place of Equity and Equitable Remedies in the Contemporary Common Law World' (1994) 110 *Law Quarterly Review* 238, 258; J Maxton, 'Equity and the Law of Civil Wrongs' in P Rishworth (ed), *The Struggle for Simplicity in the Law: Essays for Lord Cooke of Thorndon* (Wellington, Butterworths, 1997) 91, 94; A Tipping, 'Causation at Law and in Equity: Do We have Fusion?' (2000) 7 *Canterbury Law Review* 443, 448.

[7] *Mothew* (above n 4) 17.

[8] See, eg, H Butler and L Ribstein, 'Opting Out of Fiduciary Duties: A Response to the Anti-Contractarians' (1990) 65 *Washington Law Review* 1, 19, 30 and 32; F Easterbrook and D Fischel, 'Contract and Fiduciary Duty' (1993) 36 *Journal of Law and Economics* 425, 427 and 431; MJ Whincop, 'Of Fault and Default: Contractarianism as a Theory of Anglo-Australian Corporate Law' (1997) 21 *Melbourne University Law Review* 187, 189, 199–200 and 207.

[9] See, eg, PBH Birks 'Definition and Division: A Meditation on *Institute* 3.13' in PBH Birks (ed), *The Classification of Obligations* (Oxford, Oxford University Press, 1997) 1, 14 (referring to them as 'meta-torts'); PBH Birks, 'The Concept of a Civil Wrong' in D Owen (ed), *Philosophical Foundations of Tort Law* (Oxford, Oxford University Press, 1995) 31, 35; A Burrows, *Understanding the Law of Obligations: Essays on Contract, Tort and Restitution* (Oxford, Hart Publishing, 1998) 14 and 31.

seen, it is currently unclear whether and to what extent the remedy of equitable compensation might be available for a breach of fiduciary duty. 'The nature of the obligation determines the nature of the breach',[10] which in turn determines the nature and range of the remedies available in respect of that breach. A clearer understanding of the relationship between fiduciary duties and other types of duties where compensatory remedies clearly are available helps to resolve the question whether compensation ought to follow a breach of fiduciary duty. It also helps to answer questions about what types of loss can be said to flow from a breach of fiduciary duty, and whether a fiduciary should be able to rely on the principal's contributory fault to defend, in whole or in part, a claim for breach of fiduciary duty. Similarly, criticisms of the strictness of the duties imposed by fiduciary doctrine can only be evaluated properly in the light of an understanding of the purposes that fiduciary doctrine seeks to achieve.

The manner in which fiduciary doctrine operates also calls for elucidation. Why, for example, are fiduciary duties said to be proscriptive rather than prescriptive in nature?[11] Why does the scope of fiduciary duties depend upon the particular circumstances of each relationship?[12] How does that proposition correspond to the idea that fiduciary duties are inflexible in nature?[13] Why must a fiduciary get fully informed consent from his principal in order to act in a way that would otherwise be in breach of fiduciary duty, instead of merely needing to obtain an ordinary contractual consent?[14] Such questions cannot be answered adequately without resort to a proper understanding of the nature and function served by fiduciary doctrine. Similarly, a deeper understanding of what purpose is served by fiduciary duties provides some assistance in the practical determination of when the recognition of such duties is appropriate.[15]

The answers that the book provides to these sorts of questions are also timely, in the light of the recent global financial crisis and especially the recession in the United Kingdom. As Stephen Lennard has noted, 'the mass of claims that arose in the 1990s out of the previous market crash from 1989 to 1993 customarily alleged either negligence or fraud . . . and, in addition, cases against solicitors frequently included claims for equitable relief based on breaches of trust or fiduciary duty.'[16] There is a strong prospect that the earlier prevalence of such claims will be renewed in the current economic climate. It is time to take stock of the lessons about the nature of fiduciary liability that can be drawn from the case law.

---

[10] *Mothew* (above n 4) 18.

[11] See, eg, *Breen v Williams* (1996) 186 CLR 71, 113.

[12] See, eg, *New Zealand Netherlands Society 'Oranje' Inc v Kuys* [1973] 1 WLR 1126, 1130 (PC).

[13] See, eg, *Bray v Ford* [1896] AC 44, 51.

[14] See, eg, *Oranje* (above n 12) 1131–32.

[15] See also RP Austin, 'Moulding the Content of Fiduciary Duties' in AJ Oakley (ed), *Trends in Contemporary Trust Law* (Oxford, Oxford University Press, 1996) 153, 159; PBH Birks, 'The Content of Fiduciary Obligation' (2000) 34 *Israel Law Review* 3, 4 (republished at (2002) 16 *Trust Law International* 34).

[16] S Lennard, 'An Unwelcome Arrival?' (2008) 212 *Property Law Journal* 22, 22. See also M Willis and C Bending, 'A Damoclean Sword' (2008) 158 *New Law Journal* 83.

The central thesis advanced in this book is that the fiduciary concept of 'loyalty' is a convenient encapsulation of a series of legal principles, rather than a duty in its own right. These principles provide a subsidiary and prophylactic form of protection for non-fiduciary duties. The purpose of that protection is to enhance the chance of proper performance of those non-fiduciary duties by seeking to avoid influences or temptations that are likely to distract the fiduciary from providing such proper performance. It is frequently observed that fiduciary doctrine operates in a prophylactic manner, which is undoubtedly the case. However, the argument developed here is that fiduciary doctrine is prophylactic in its very nature, rather than simply in the methodology that it employs. It is designed to make breaches of non-fiduciary duties less likely by protecting them from inconsistent temptations that have a tendency to distract the fiduciary away from due performance of those non-fiduciary duties. This also indicates the subsidiary nature of fiduciary doctrine, in that it is designed to assist with ensuring proper performance of non-fiduciary duties. In that sense fiduciary duties are subsidiary to the protected non-fiduciary duties.

The clearest example of this prophylactic and subsidiary form of protection is found in the principle that prohibits fiduciaries from acting in situations in which their personal interest conflicts with the non-fiduciary duties that they have to perform. The existence of such a personal interest increases the risk that the fiduciary will be drawn away from, and so not deliver, proper performance of those non-fiduciary duties. Fiduciary doctrine therefore prohibits a fiduciary from acting in situations that involve conflicts of that nature, unless he makes full disclosure to the principal of all material facts and obtains the principal's fully informed consent. In other words, a fiduciary should only act in such a situation if his principal is made aware of the extraneous influences that are competing with the fiduciary's obligation to perform his non-fiduciary duties, and the principal has decided that he nonetheless wishes to proceed. The possibility of obtaining such consent also shows that fiduciary doctrine respects the autonomy of a *sui iuris* person, but only when the fiduciary has complied with safeguards designed to ensure that its protection is not inappropriately circumvented.

This protective conceptualisation of fiduciary doctrine is developed through-out the book, and it is argued that it provides an important reference point from which to answer the various questions raised above. It explains, for example, why the scope of fiduciary duties is moulded to the particular relationship in each case, and it provides a sound theoretical foundation for the proposition that fiduciary duties are proscriptive in nature rather than prescriptive. It is also important in understanding fully the relationship between fiduciary and non-fiduciary duties, and it emphasises the practical importance of careful consideration of *both* kinds of duties when addressing arguments about fiduciary liability. Such careful consideration is also fundamental when addressing currently unset-tled issues regarding remedies for breach of fiduciary duty, such as what loss might be said to flow from a breach of fiduciary duty and whether a fiduciary ought to be able to plead the principal's contributory fault in an attempt to reduce an award of equitable compensation for breach of fiduciary duty.

The book begins, in chapters two and three, by laying out the approach that will be taken in scrutinising fiduciary doctrine. This is important in that it makes clear what material forms the basis of the analysis offered in the rest of the book. Commentary concerning fiduciary doctrine is often unclear about the reference points from which the arguments are developed. In many instances, commentators talk past one another as their analyses arise out of different premises which are neither articulated nor defended. Thus, chapter two explains that the analysis is focused on duties that are peculiar to fiduciaries and justifies that approach, and chapter three seeks to isolate the duties that match that criterion. Having done so, in chapter four it is possible to explain how strong evidence can be found in the cases for the view that the fiduciary conflict principle is designed to provide a subsidiary and prophylactic form of protection for non-fiduciary duties. The remedies that are made available following a breach of that principle are also consistent with the protective function that fiduciary doctrine performs vis-à-vis non-fiduciary duties.

Chapter five then defends this instrumentalist understanding of fiduciary doctrine against an alternative view which suggests that fiduciary doctrine is concerned with exacting high moral standards of conduct from fiduciaries. Several doctrines that perhaps appear at first sight to support a moralistic understanding of fiduciary doctrine are considered in detail, as is an argument that the history of fiduciary doctrine supports a moralistic understanding of its nature and function. When they are considered carefully, the doctrines and the history are consistent with the instrumentalist understanding of fiduciary doctrine advanced in this book and thus provide no support for a moralistic understanding of the fiduciary concept of loyalty.

Chapter six considers further evidence for the protective view of fiduciary doctrine, focusing on the fiduciary rules applicable in situations in which a fiduciary acts for multiple principals and owes them inconsistent, or potentially inconsistent, non-fiduciary duties. Again, the fiduciary rules that apply in such situations are by and large consistent with and explained by the protective thesis, although one aspect of those rules is difficult to explain in that way. One cannot necessarily expect the common law—and equity is no different in this regard—to be perfectly conceptually pure, given the doctrines have been formed by numerous judges over hundreds of years. What is perhaps most impressive in that respect is the remarkable degree of conformity in purpose that one can identify in the cases that consider and apply fiduciary doctrine.

After analysis come the implications of that analysis. Chapter seven considers a number of important tenets within fiduciary doctrine concerning the relationship that fiduciary duties bear to non-fiduciary duties. It shows that the basis for these propositions can helpfully be located in the protective function that fiduciary doctrine serves as a whole. This emphasises the importance of paying close attention to both fiduciary and non-fiduciary duties when determining whether fiduciary liability has been made out. Chapter eight concentrates on more conceptual implications of the protective thesis, assessing the degree to which it provides helpful insights into the arguments advanced by other commentators about the similarities and differences between fiduciary doctrine on the one hand and contract and tort on the other. The unique protective function of fiduciary doctrine provides a good reason for it not to be lumped in with those other forms of legal doctrine. It is also possible to comment on whether other legal doctrines, whose categorisation is more contentious, should be treated as fiduciary doctrines. There are solid, albeit not irrefutable, reasons for treating undue influence and the doctrine of confidence as distinct from the fiduciary concept of loyalty.

Chapter nine then addresses the vexed question of when fiduciary duties arise. Although the protective conceptualisation of fiduciary loyalty does not directly answer that question, it is relevant in that fiduciary duties are often justified on the basis that it was legitimate to expect that they would be complied with in the circumstances of the case at hand. The legitimacy of such expectations is inherently linked to the content of and the function served by the duties generated by the expectation. Finally, chapter ten gathers together the main lessons to be drawn from the book, while also indicating areas where further research could profitably be developed in connection with the analysis that the book offers.

2

Points of Departure

I. Form of Analysis

Legal obligations are frequently analysed on the basis of a syllogism: where the circumstances are X, there is a duty of kind Y (the major premise); in a given factual scenario, the circumstances are (or are not) X (the minor premise); therefore, in that factual scenario, there is (or is not) a duty of kind Y (the conclusion). It is commonplace, therefore, when seeking to identify the function that legal obligations serve, to focus attention on the question of when duties of that kind arise: if one knows when they arise, one can determine why they arise in those circumstances and will therefore be able to ascertain the function that those duties serve. In other words, such analysis seeks to enhance understanding of the relevant kind of duty by treating the circumstances that are the trigger for the duty as the focal point for analysis. In contract law, for example, a contract arises when two parties agree on certain terms, or at least an objective assessment of the parties' conduct suggests that they have agreed on those terms, and consideration has been provided. Thus, attention can be focused on the parties' agreement, or on the outward (objective) appearance of agreement, and on the criterion of consideration, in an attempt to identify why those factors generate contractual obligations.

Unsurprisingly, much analysis of fiduciary doctrine follows this pattern. Commentators frequently focus their attention on the issue of when fiduciary duties arise, as the answer to that question should indicate the purpose of those duties. Thus, considerable attention has been focused on the concept of a 'fiduciary relationship' as the key to unlocking the function served by fiduciary duties: if one can identify when a fiduciary relationship arises, that will indicate when fiduciary duties arise, which in turn will indicate why those duties have arisen and so identify what purpose is served by those fiduciary duties.

That is not the approach adopted in this book. There are at least two difficulties with applying that mode of analysis to fiduciary duties. First, the circumstances in which a fiduciary relationship arises – the major premise in the syllogism – are far from clear. Secondly, it is not clear that the syllogistic mode of analysis that has been described above accurately represents the manner in which fiduciary doctrine operates. Each of these points merits expansion.

As to the first point, it is well established that certain categories of relationship are traditionally regarded as fiduciary in nature,[1] so that one of the parties in such relationships (the fiduciary) owes fiduciary duties to the other party (the principal[2]). The list of such traditional status-based fiduciary relationships includes trustee and beneficiary,[3] agent and principal,[4] director and company,[5] solicitor and client,[6] partners,[7] and Crown servants and the Crown.[8] When applied to those settled fiduciary relationships, the syllogistic analysis works reasonably well, in the sense that if one finds the facts constitute a relationship of that class (eg, a relationship of trustee and beneficiary, or of solicitor and client) it is clear that it is a fiduciary relationship and that the fiduciary will owe fiduciary duties to his principal.

However, there are two difficulties with extending this observation into the syllogistic form of analysis mentioned above. First, it is not clear from these settled categories of relationship *why* the relationships are recognised as fiduciary in nature, which makes it difficult to extract the data necessary for the sort of analysis described above. Secondly, it is clear that fiduciary relationships can arise in situations that do not fall within one of these settled classes.[9] In one sense, this could potentially assist with pursuit of the syllogistic analysis, because if fiduciary duties can arise in situations outside of the settled categories of fiduciary relationships then it might be possible to determine what it is about those ad hoc

---

[1] See, eg, *Hospital Products Ltd v United States Surgical Corp* (1984) 156 CLR 41, 96; *Lac Minerals Ltd v International Corona Resources Ltd* [1989] 2 SCR 574, 646–47; *Hodgkinson v Simms* [1994] 3 SCR 377, 409; DJ Hayton and C Mitchell, *Hayton & Marshall's Commentary and Cases on the Law of Trusts and Equitable Remedies*, 12th edn (London, Sweet & Maxwell, 2005) [6–12]; RP Meagher, JD Heydon and MJ Leeming, *Meagher, Gummow & Lehane's Equity: Doctrines and Remedies*, 4th edn (Chatswood, Butterworths LexisNexis, 2002) [5–005].

[2] In the paradigm fiduciary relationship between trustee and beneficiary, fiduciary duties are owed to the beneficiary. The term 'principal' is used throughout the book in an attempt to encompass all categories of fiduciary relationship.

[3] Eg, *Keech v Sandford* (1726) Sel Cas t King 61 (25 ER 223).

[4] Eg, *De Bussche v Alt* (1878) 8 ChD 286 (CA).

[5] Eg, *Regal (Hastings) Ltd v Gulliver* [1967] 2 AC 134n. The Companies Act 2006 (UK) creates a statutory code of duties for directors in place of the common law and equitable duties to which directors have hitherto been subject: see s 170(3). Technically, the result is that directors will no longer be subject to the duties discussed in this book, except insofar as the Act so provides. Cases regarding directors that were decided prior to the implementation of the 2006 Act are clearly still relevant here insofar as they state principles that are applicable to fiduciaries generally. Indeed, the 2006 Act provides that such cases are also relevant in interpreting the provisions of that Act: s 170(4). Furthermore, the civil consequences of directors acting in breach of the duties contained in the 2006 Act 'are the same as would apply if the corresponding common law rule or equitable principle applied': s 178(1).

[6] Eg, *Boardman v Phipps* [1967] 2 AC 46.

[7] Eg, *Aas v Benham* [1891] 2 Ch 244 (CA); *Chan v Zacharia* (1984) 154 CLR 178.

[8] Eg, *Reading v Attorney-General* [1951] AC 507; *Attorney-General for Hong Kong v Reid* [1994] 1 AC 324 (PC).

[9] *English v Dedham Vale Properties Ltd* [1978] 1 WLR 93, 110 (ChD); *Marr v Arabco Traders Ltd* (1987) 1 NZBLC 102,732, 102,743 (HC); *Schipp v Cameron* [1998] NSWSC 997 at [695], not questioned on appeal: *Harrison v Schipp* [2001] NSWCA 13; *Bell Group Ltd v Westpac Banking Corp (No 9)* [2008] WASC 239 at [4532]; *Hageman v Holmes* [2009] EWHC 50 (Ch) at [52].

fiduciary relationships that makes them fiduciary in nature. Unfortunately, that seems a vain hope. The question of when fiduciary duties arise has been described as a 'notoriously intractable problem',[10] and Donovan Waters has aptly observed that 'the subject has something of the fascination for equity lawyers . . . that the search for the Holy Grail had for the knights of antiquity.'[11]

Numerous commentators have offered definitions or descriptions of the fiduciary concept,[12] none of which has yet attracted uniform judicial acceptance.[13] To a large degree the problem here arises because courts have consistently declined to define when fiduciary duties arise outside of the settled categories of fiduciary relationship, preferring instead to develop the law from case to case. In *Lloyds Bank Ltd v Bundy*, Sir Eric Sachs said that 'it is neither feasible nor desirable to attempt closely to define the relationship, or its characteristics, or the demarcation line showing the exact transition point where a relationship that does not entail that duty passes into one that does.'[14] The consequence has been that 'the law has not, as yet, been able to formulate any precise or comprehensive definition of the circumstances in which a person is constituted a fiduciary in his or her relations with another.'[15] Without a clear idea of when fiduciary duties arise, it is misguided to attempt to develop a theory about the nature and function of those duties from the syllogistic point of view described above.

The second point that makes such a syllogistic approach unattractive is that it is not clear that it properly reflects the way that fiduciary doctrine operates. Paul Finn observed:

> It is not because a person is a 'fiduciary' or a 'confidant' that a rule applies to him. It is because a particular rule applies to him that he is a fiduciary or confidant for its purposes.[16]

In *Bristol & West Building Society v Mothew*, Millett LJ referred to Finn's observation and noted that a person 'is not subject to fiduciary obligations because he is a fiduciary; it is because he is subject to them that he is a

---

[10]   EJ Weinrib, 'The Fiduciary Obligation' (1975) 25 *University of Toronto Law Journal* 1, 5.
[11]   DWM Waters, 'Banks, Fiduciary Obligations and Unconscionable Transactions' (1986) 65 *Canadian Bar Review* 37, 56.
[12]   Famous contributions include: AW Scott, 'The Fiduciary Principle' (1949) 37 *California Law Review* 539, 540; LS Sealy, 'Fiduciary Relationships' [1962] *Cambridge Law Journal* 69, 72–79 (eschewing the search for a general definition in favour of a class-by-class analysis); Weinrib (above n 10) 4 and 15; PD Finn, *Fiduciary Obligations* (Sydney, Law Book Co, 1977) [467]; JC Shepherd, *The Law of Fiduciaries* (Toronto, Carswell, 1981) 96; JC Shepherd, 'Towards a Unified Concept of Fiduciary Relationships' (1981) 97 *Law Quarterly Review* 51, 74–76; PD Finn, 'The Fiduciary Principle' in TG Youdan (ed), *Equity, Fiduciaries and Trusts* (Toronto, Carswell, 1989) 1, 46 and 54; R Flannigan, 'The Fiduciary Obligation' (1989) 9 *Oxford Journal of Legal Studies* 285, 309–10.
[13]   *Maclean v Arklow Investments Ltd* [1998] 3 NZLR 680, 691 (CA).
[14]   *Lloyds Bank Ltd v Bundy* [1975] QB 326, 341. See also *Hospital Products* (above n 1) 96 and 141; *Maclean v Arklow* (*ibid*) 691.
[15]   *Breen v Williams* (1996) 186 CLR 71, 92.
[16]   Finn, *Fiduciary Obligations* (above n 12) [3].

fiduciary'.[17] Thus, as the Privy Council said in *Arklow Investments Ltd v Maclean*, 'it is the obligation and duty which makes the obligor a fiduciary.'[18]

This all suggests that the syllogism does not work for fiduciary duties in the way that was identified above: rather than fiduciary duties arising (*Y*) because there is a fiduciary relationship (*X*), the connection between these two propositions is inverted so that there is a fiduciary relationship (*X*) because fiduciary duties are owed (*Y*). Indeed, it may be the case that the syllogism is not reversed but rather that there is no syllogistic relationship between the two propositions at all: it is perhaps more accurate to view the two propositions as equivalent statements ($X \equiv Y$) rather than as related to one another by a syllogism ($X \to Y$). As Jay Shepherd put it, 'the terms fiduciary relationship and duty of loyalty are so much co-extensive as to be, in effect, alternate descriptions of the same thing.'[19] In other words, the statement that one owes fiduciary duties is equivalent to the statement that one is in a fiduciary relationship. So, the traditional syllogistic approach is either the reverse of what the case law indicates or is irrelevant to the way fiduciary duties are applied and so entirely uninformative.

The syllogistic approach is therefore not followed in this book. Instead, an alternative form of analysis is adopted, which focuses attention on the fiduciary duties themselves in order to evaluate their nature and function. In other words, rather than attempting to identify a principle that triggers the application of fiduciary duties so that one can endeavour to understand the nature of such duties from that principle, the analysis offered in this book concentrates instead on what it means to owe fiduciary duties. As Peter Birks pointed out:

> Among the many questions that can be asked of any legal obligation, or its correlative right, two are especially important. The first goes to content. What does the obligation require? The second seeks the causative event. From what facts does it arise? *It is often difficult to formulate a crisp answer to the second question unless one has a firm grip on the answer to the first.* That is certainly true of fiduciary obligations (emphasis added).[20]

Birks proceeded to offer a view on that first question, to which it will be necessary to return later. The point for present purposes is that, in methodological terms, a similar course is adopted in this book: the book represents an attempt to identify the nature and function of fiduciary duties by reference to their content, rather than an attempt to provide a universal principle that might resolve the question of when fiduciary duties arise.

This approach is feasible because of the point made earlier—that certain classes of relationship are traditionally regarded as fiduciary in nature.[21] In other

---

[17] *Bristol & West Building Society v Mothew* [1998] Ch 1, 18. See also *Chirnside v Fay* [2006] NZSC 68 at [72], [2007] 1 NZLR 433.

[18] *Arklow Investments Ltd v Maclean* [2000] 1 WLR 594, 600.

[19] Shepherd, *The Law of Fiduciaries* (above n 12) 48.

[20] PBH Birks, 'The Content of Fiduciary Obligation' (2000) 34 *Israel Law Review* 3, 4 (republished at (2002) 16 *Trust Law International* 34).

[21] See text accompanying nn 1–8 above.

words, it is clear that fiduciary duties are owed in such relationships. This permits analysis of the fiduciary obligations owed by persons in such relationships, without needing to develop a theory as to what factual circumstances might lead to such obligations being owed in other situations. One can analyse a concept based on a set of paradigm cases or instances of that concept, even if there is not universal agreement as to criteria of application of the concept.[22] Thus, for example, one can focus on the fiduciary duties owed by solicitors, trustees, company directors and other recognised fiduciary actors, and analyse the nature and function of those fiduciary duties, without needing first to develop a principle that is capable of identifying all cases in which fiduciary duties apply.[23] Once such analysis has been conducted, one can return to the question of when fiduciary duties may be owed. That is therefore considered in chapter nine.

II. Subject Matter of Analysis

The question that does naturally call for an answer, before an analysis of fiduciary duties is possible, is which of the duties owed by a fiduciary are his fiduciary duties? Obviously enough, one must identify the subject matter of the analysis—in this case, fiduciary duties—before one can begin that analysis.

A. Historical Analogies

One possible answer to that question, which holds considerable sway in North America and would permit the analysis to begin immediately, is to treat *all* of the duties that a fiduciary owes as fiduciary duties. In other words, if someone is a fiduciary, all of the duties that the person owes can be analysed as fiduciary duties. Thus, for example, in an approach that is widespread in the United States,[24] Dennis Block, Nancy Barton and Stephen Radin treat directors' duties of

---

[22] JL Coleman, *The Practice of Principle* (Oxford, Oxford University Press, 2001) 157; R Dworkin, *Law's Empire* (Cambridge, Belknap Press, 1986) 72; R Dworkin, 'Thirty Years On' (2002) 115 *Harvard Law Review* 1655, 1683–84.

[23] See also RP Austin, 'Moulding the Content of Fiduciary Duties' in AJ Oakley (ed), *Trends in Contemporary Trust Law* (Oxford, Oxford University Press, 1996) 153, 153–54.

[24] See, eg, *Corpus Juris Secundum*, vol 19: *Corporations* (Thomson West, 2007) [564]; T Frankel, 'Fiduciary Duties as Default Rules' (1995) 74 *Oregon Law Review* 1209, 1213; JH Langbein, 'The Contractarian Basis of the Law of Trusts' (1995) 105 *Yale Law Journal* 625, 642, 643 and 655; H Hansmann and U Mattei, 'The Functions of Trust Law: A Comparative Legal and Economic Analysis' (1998) 73 *New York University Law Review* 434, 447; DG Smith, 'The Critical Resource Theory of Fiduciary Duty' (2002) 55 *Vanderbilt Law Review* 1399, 1453; V Brudney, 'Contract and Fiduciary Duty in Corporate Law' (1997) 38 *Boston College Law Review* 595, 599 (fn 9); JD Cox, TL Hazen and FH O'Neal, *Corporations*, vol 1 (New York, Aspen Law & Business, Loose leaf edn) [10.19] (fn 1); CR Taylor, 'The Inadequacy of Fiduciary Duty Doctrine: Why Corporate Managers have Little to Fear and What Might be Done about It' (2006) 85 *Oregon Law Review* 993, 1007–8; DA DeMott, 'The Texture of Loyalty' in JJ Norton, J Rickford and J Klineman (eds), *Corporate Governance Post-Enron:*

care, duties of loyalty and duties of candour as all subsumed within an overarch-
ing category of fiduciary duties.[25]

This approach reflects the function that the fiduciary concept appears to have
served, particularly historically, in exporting the legal incidents from one form of
relationship to other relationships that are different from that original relationship but sufficiently similar to justify the imposition of similar duties. The classic
fiduciary relationship from which fiduciary duties were exported in this fashion
is the paradigm fiduciary relationship between trustee and beneficiary. Thus, in
Re West of England & South Wales District Bank, Fry J observed:

> What is a fiduciary relationship? It is one in respect of which if a wrong arises, the same
> remedy exists against the wrong-doer on behalf of the principal as would exist against a
> trustee on behalf of the *cestui que trust*.[26]

Hence, the question whether a given actor owed fiduciary duties was considered
by asking whether the actor occupied a position sufficiently similar to that of a
trustee to justify the imposition of duties like those owed by trustees. 'The
archetype of a fiduciary is . . . the trustee';[27] and the 'fiduciary relationship has
developed by analogy from the trust relationship.'[28]

That reasoning process—analogical development of doctrine by reference to
other recognised fiduciary relationships—can be seen at work in numerous
cases.[29] In *Foley v Hill*, for example, the appellant argued that an account should
be taken in equity rather than at law because the relationship between banker and
customer was a fiduciary relationship. The House of Lords rejected that argument. In doing so, Lord Cottenham LC addressed the question whether the
relationship between banker and customer was sufficiently analogous to other
fiduciary relationships to justify such a conclusion:

Comparative and International Perspectives (London, BICL, 2006) 23, 24; AB Laby, 'The Fiduciary
Obligation as the Adoption of Ends' (2008) 56 *Buffalo Law Review* 99, 105–6; T Frankel, *Fiduciary
Law* (Anchorage, Fathom Publishing, 2008) 98. The approach described in the text does not, however,
enjoy universal support in the United States: see, eg, LE Ribstein, 'Are Partners Fiduciaries?' [2005]
University of Illinois Law Review 209, 220; WA Gregory, 'The Fiduciary Duty of Care: A Perversion of
Words' (2005) 38 *Akron Law Review* 181; DA DeMott, 'Disloyal Agents' (2007) 58 *Alabama Law
Review* 1049, 1052.

[25] DJ Block, NE Barton, SA Radin, *The Business Judgment Rule: Fiduciary Duties of Corporate
Directors*, 5th edn (New York, Aspen Law & Business, 1998).

[26] *Re West of England & South Wales District Bank, ex parte Dale & Co* (1879) 11 ChD 772, 778.

[27] *Hospital Products* (above n 1) 68.

[28] *Gwembe Valley Devt Co Ltd v Koshy (No 3)* [2003] EWCA Civ 1048 at [89], [2004] 1 BCLC 131.
See also *Girardet v Crease & Co* (1987) 11 BCLC (2d) 361, 362 (BCSC).

[29] In addition to the cases discussed in the text, see also the analogical analysis in *Spackman v
Evans* (1868) LR 3 HL 171, 189–90; *Re Gresham Life Assurance Society* (1872) LR 8 Ch App 446, 449;
Huntington Copper & Sulphur Co (Ltd) v Henderson (1877) 4 SC (4th Series) 294, 299–300 (OH); *Re
Lands Allotment Co* [1894] 1 Ch 616, 631 and 638 (CA); *New Lambton Land and Coal Co Ltd v London
Bank of Australia Ltd* (1904) 1 CLR 524, 541–42; *Selangor United Rubber Estates Ltd v Cradock (No 3)*
[1968] 1 WLR 1555, 1575 (ChD); *Wallersteiner v Moir (No 2)* [1975] 1 QB 373, 397–98 (CA). And see
Liverpool & District Hospital for Diseases of the Heart v Attorney-General [1981] Ch 193, 209;
Commissioner of Taxation v Linter Textiles Australia Ltd [2005] HCA 20 at [48], (2005) 220 CLR 592.

[A factor is] within the jurisdiction of a Court of Equity, because the party *partakes of the character of a trustee*. . . So it is with regard to an agent dealing with any property; he obtains no interest himself in the subject-matter beyond his remuneration; he is dealing throughout for another, and *though he is not a trustee according to the strict technical meaning of the word, he is* quasi *a trustee* for that particular transaction for which he is engaged . . . But the *analogy* entirely fails, as it seems to me, when you come to consider the relative situation of a banker and his customer (emphasis added).[30]

Applying the same approach but reaching the opposite conclusion, the courts held that company directors owed fiduciary duties like the duties owed by trustees, because their control over the management of the company's property was akin to the control a trustee has over the trust fund: 'it is ... the actual control of assets belonging beneficially to a company which causes the law to treat directors as analogous to trustees of those assets.'[31] Thus, for example, in *Charitable Corp v Sutton*, Lord Hardwicke LC held the directors of a charitable company liable because their position was like that of trustees: 'by accepting a trust of this sort, a person is obliged to execute it with fidelity and reasonable diligence ... and therefore they are within the case of common trustees.'[32] Similarly, in *Land Credit Co of Ireland v Fermoy*, Lord Hatherley LC noted that the directors of a company had power to delegate their functions but that they 'must be tried as any other trustees accused of neglecting their duty'[33] when the appointed delegates acted inappropriately. And in *Overend Gurney & Co v Gurney*, he observed that directors would have been liable 'as trustees to their *cestuis que trust*'[34] had they conducted themselves in a grossly negligent way when buying ordinary property for the company. In *Re Oxford Benefit Building and Investment Society*, Kay J held that directors had committed a 'deliberate ... breach of trust'[35] by paying dividends out of capital with no thought as to whether this was permitted by the company's articles, which it was not. Analogies were also drawn with other fiduciary relationships, such as agency, to the same effect. Thus, in *Great Eastern Railway Co v Turner*, Lord Selborne LC said that 'the directors are the mere trustees or agents of the company—trustees of the company's money and property—agents in the transactions which they enter into on behalf of the company.'[36]

While the statements in these cases are not completely accurate, because directors do not own the company's property and so are not strictly speaking

---

[30] *Foley v Hill* (1848) 2 HLC 28, 35–36 (9 ER 1002).

[31] *Ultraframe (UK) Ltd v Fielding* [2005] EWHC 1638 (Ch) at [1253]. See also *Re the French Protestant Hospital* [1951] Ch 567, 570.

[32] *Charitable Corporation v Sutton* (1742) 2 Atk 400, 406 (26 ER 642).

[33] *Land Credit Co of Ireland v Fermoy* (1870) LR 5 Ch App 763, 771.

[34] *Overend Gurney & Co v Gurney* (1869) LR 4 Ch App 701, 715. See also, eg, Companies Act 1862, s 165 and Companies Act 2006, s 260(3).

[35] *Re Oxford Benefit Building and Investment Society* (1886) 35 ChD 502, 514.

[36] *Great Eastern Railway Co v Turner* (1872) LR 8 Ch App 149, 152. See also *Re European Central Railway Co* (1872) LR 13 Eq 255, 258–59. And see *Great Luxembourg Railway Co v Magnay (No 2)* (1858) 25 Beav 586, 592 (53 ER 761), although it is unclear whether this company was incorporated.

trustees of that property,[37] the important point is the process of reasoning by which directors were subjected to rules and duties akin to those owed by trustees because of their similar situations. Hence, Jessel MR referred to directors as '*quasi trustees for the company*' in *Flitcroft's Case*,[38] and Page Wood VC said in *Fraser v Whalley*:

> I cannot look upon these directors otherwise than as trustees for a public company, and I must judge of the propriety of their conduct in this matter on the ordinary principle applicable to cases of trustee and *cestui que trust*.[39]

Kay LJ described the position in *Re Lands Allotment Co*:

> [C]ase after case has decided that directors of trading companies are not for all purposes trustees or in the position of trustees, or *quasi* trustees, or to be treated as trustees in every sense; but if they deal with the funds of a company, although those funds are not absolutely vested in them, but funds which are under their control, and deal with those funds in a manner which is beyond their powers, then as to that dealing they are treated as having committed a breach of trust.[40]

The extension of duties by analogy can be seen in other contexts as well. Thus, for example, in *Sidny v Ranger*, Shadwell VC held that a solicitor who had undertaken to sell an estate could not purchase it for himself because '*persons standing in the situation of trustees* cannot buy for themselves' (emphasis added).[41] And in *Re Hallett's Estate*, Jessel MR described a bailee of bonds who was agent to receive the dividends on the bonds as occupying a fiduciary position.[42] The importance of that description was that it justified the application of equitable rules for the tracing of trust property: 'the moment you establish the fiduciary relation, the modern rules of Equity, as regards following trust property, apply.'[43]

It is that extension of duties by reference to other analogous fiduciary relationships that Len Sealy and Paul Finn noted[44] and that Peter Birks more

---

[37] *Smith v Anderson* (1880) 15 ChD 247, 275–76 (CA); *Re Faure Electric Accumulator Co* (1888) 40 ChD 141, 150; *Re Lands Allotment Co* (above n 29) 631 and 638; *Belmont Finance Corp v Williams Furniture Ltd (No 2)* [1980] 1 All ER 393, 405 (CA). The company's separate legal personality enables it to own property directly: *Salomon v Salomon & Co* [1897] AC 22.

[38] *Re Exchange Banking Co (Flitcroft's Case)* (1882) 21 ChD 519, 534 (CA).

[39] *Fraser v Whalley* (1864) 2 H & M 10, 28 (71 ER 361).

[40] *Re Lands Allotment Co* (above n 29) 638; see also p 631 *per* Lindley LJ. And see *JJ Harrison (Properties) Ltd v Harrison* [2001] EWCA Civ 1467 at [26], [2002] 1 BCLC 162.

[41] *Sidny v Ranger* (1841) 12 Sim 118, 120 (59 ER 1076). See also *Re Hindmarsh* (1860) 1 Dr & Sm 129, 132 (62 ER 327) (VC).

[42] *Re Hallett's Estate* (1879) 13 ChD 696, 708 and 710 (CA).

[43] *Ibid*, 710; see also p 721 *per* Baggallay LJ. And see *New Zealand & Australian Land Co v Watson* (1881) 7 QBD 374, 383–84 (CA).

[44] LS Sealy, 'The Director as Trustee' [1967] *Cambridge Law Journal* 83, 85–86 and 91–103; Sealy, 'Fiduciary Relationships' (above n 12) 71–73; Finn, *Fiduciary Obligations* (above n 12) [7]; Finn, 'The Fiduciary Principle' (above n 12) 34–35.

recently described as 'exporting incidents of the express trust by analogy'.[45] Counsel's argument before the House of Lords in *York Buildings Co v Mackenzie* reflects this well:

> He is a trustee (in technical style) who is vested with property in trust for others; but every man has a trust, to whom a business is committed by another, or the charge and care of any concern is confided or delegated by commission. He that is employed by one either to sell or to buy land for him, is in that instance his trustee, and has a trust reposed in him.[46]

In more modern terms, 'fiduciary duties are equitable extensions of trustee duties.'[47]

It is also worth emphasising that this process of analogising did not necessarily mean that the duties that were exported would apply in exactly the same fashion as they did to trustees or to other fiduciaries. Thus, for example, directors may be *analogous* to trustees, but that does not mean that they occupy an *identical* position.[48] Indeed, the very point of analogical analysis is that it is needed, and most helpful, when two things are not identical but are nonetheless similar in important respects. Hence, it was said that 'directors are *effectively* trustees of the company's assets' (emphasis added)[49] or '*quasi* trustees'.[50] Although a director's position was analogous to that of a trustee and so attracted a duty of care, the degree of care required was set at a different level to reflect the more speculative nature of business: 'their negligence must be not the omission to take all possible care; it must be much more blameable than that: it must be in a business sense culpable or gross.'[51]

The point here is not to enter into a detailed history of the development of directors' duties of care but rather to notice the way in which the courts allowed duties owed by one kind of fiduciary to be exported to other fiduciary relationships, modified as necessary to make those duties appropriate to their new context.

---

[45] Birks, 'The Content of Fiduciary Obligation' (above n 20) 3; see also pp 8–9.

[46] *York Buildings Co v Mackenzie* (1795) 8 Bro PC 42, 64 (3 ER 432); see also p 66, where counsel went on to argue: 'It is upon the same principle that the general doctrine of the law of Scotland stands with regard to all the acts of tutors and guardians, factors, trustees, and *all who are akin to a trust by any connection of character or office*' (emphasis added).

[47] *Swindle v Harrison* [1997] 4 All ER 705, 734 (CA).

[48] Cf WM Heath, 'The Director's "Fiduciary" Duty of Care and Skill: A Misnomer' (2007) 25 *Companies & Securities Law Journal* 370, 389.

[49] *Equiticorp Industries Group Ltd v R (No 47)* [1998] 2 NZLR 481, 549.

[50] See, eg, *Foley v Hill* (above n 30) 36; *Flitcroft's Case* (above n 38) 534; *Re Lands Allotment Co* (above n 29) 638.

[51] *Lagunas Nitrate Co v Lagunas Syndicate* [1899] 2 Ch 392, 435 (CA). See also *Overend & Gurney Co v Gibb* (1872) LR 5 HL 480, 494–95; *Re Forest of Dean Coal Mining Co* (1878) 10 ChD 450, 451–53 (MR); *Re Faure Electric Accumulator Co* (above n 37) 150–53; *Re City Equitable Fire Insurance Co Ltd* [1925] Ch 407, 426; *Daniels v Anderson* (1995) 37 NSWLR 438, 488–505 and 599–602 (CA); *Re Barings plc (No 5)* [1999] 1 BCLC 433, 488–89 (ChD), approved on appeal: [2000] 1 BCLC 523, 535–36; Heath (above n 48) 391. On trustees' duties of care, see C Stebbings, *The Private Trustee in Victorian England* (Cambridge, Cambridge University Press, 2002) chs 5 and 6.

B. Modern Approach

Words and concepts do not necessarily remain static in their meaning. First, as a basic matter of English language, a single word can have different meanings, both at one point in time and also because the word changes in meaning over a period of time. And just as normal everyday usage of language does not remain static, nor does judicial use of language do so in its description of legal doctrine.[52] Thus, legal concepts and doctrines are able to change over time. The word 'fiduciary' and the legal concept associated with that word are no exceptions.

While the legal institution of the fiduciary relationship has historically performed an important function in exporting the incidents of recognised fiduciary relationships to other analogous relationships, the meaning and importance of the fiduciary concept have recently undergone change. As Austin J said in *Aequitas v AEFC*, 'judicial thinking about the content of fiduciary duties has changed significantly over the last decade.'[53]

i. Genesis and Gestation

The impetus for this change in meaning stretches back to Southin J's complaint in *Girardet v Crease & Co* that the 'word fiduciary is flung around now as if it applied to all breaches of duty by solicitors, directors of companies and so forth.'[54] She objected to the treatment of a breach of a solicitor's duty of care and skill as a breach of fiduciary duty when a breach of the same obligation by an engineer or physician would not be so described. Two years later, in *Lac Minerals Ltd v International Corona Resources Ltd*, La Forest J quoted Southin J's comments with approval,[55] as did Sopinka J.[56] La Forest J stated that 'not every legal claim arising out of a relationship with fiduciary incidents will give rise to a claim for breach of fiduciary duty'[57] and added that 'it is only in relation to breaches of the specific obligations imposed because the relationship is one characterised as fiduciary that a claim for breach of fiduciary duty can be founded.'[58] Five years after that, in *Permanent Building Society v Wheeler*,[59] the Supreme Court of Western Australia approved and adopted this line of Canadian authority. Ipp J, with whom Malcolm CJ and Seaman J agreed,[60] stated:

---

[52] JH Baker, 'Trespass, Case, and the Common Law of Negligence 1500–1700' in EJH Schrage (ed), *Negligence: The Comparative Legal History of the Law of Torts* (Berlin, Duncker and Humblot, 2001) 47, 47. On the relationship between legal and ordinary use of words, see AWB Simpson, 'The Analysis of Legal Concepts' (1964) 80 *Law Quarterly Review* 535.

[53] *Aequitas v AEFC* [2001] NSWSC 14 at [283], (2001) 19 ACLC 1,006. Given the date of Austin J's judgment, the timeframe to which he refers should now be extended to the last *two* decades.

[54] *Girardet v Crease* (above n 28) 362.

[55] *Lac Minerals* (above n 1) 647.

[56] *Ibid*, 597–98.

[57] *Ibid*, 647.

[58] *Ibid*, 647.

[59] *Permanent Building Society v Wheeler* (1994) 11 WAR 187.

[60] *Ibid*, 192.

It is essential to bear in mind that the existence of a fiduciary relationship does not mean that every duty owed by a fiduciary to the beneficiary is a fiduciary duty. In particular, a trustee's duty to exercise reasonable care, though equitable, is not specifically a fiduciary duty.[61]

Two years later, Millett LJ drew on this strain of thought in his judgment in *Bristol & West Building Society v Mothew*. In an analysis of fiduciary doctrine with which Otton LJ agreed[62] and which Staughton LJ expressed himself to be glad to follow,[63] Millett LJ referred to and endorsed the authorities just mentioned. Importantly for present purposes, he said:

> Despite the warning given by Fletcher Moulton LJ in *In re Coomber; Coomber v Coomber*,[64] this branch of the law has been bedevilled by unthinking resort to verbal formulae. It is therefore necessary to begin by defining one's terms. The expression 'fiduciary duty' is properly confined to those duties which are peculiar to fiduciaries and the breach of which attracts legal consequences differing from those consequent upon the breach of other duties. Unless the expression is so limited it is lacking in practical utility. In this sense it is obvious that not every breach of duty by a fiduciary is a breach of fiduciary duty.[65]

Almost contemporaneously, the High Court of Australia decided *Breen v Williams*.[66] All of the judgments in that case contain statements that support the view that a fiduciary's duties are not necessarily all to be treated as fiduciary duties. Brennan CJ, for example, commented that it is 'erroneous to regard the duty owed by a fiduciary to his beneficiary as attaching to every aspect of the fiduciary's conduct'.[67] Similarly, Dawson and Toohey JJ observed that while 'duties of a fiduciary nature may be imposed upon a doctor, they are confined and do not cover the entire doctor–patient relationship',[68] adding that 'what the law exacts in a fiduciary relationship is loyalty, often of an uncompromising kind, but no more than that. The concern of the law in a fiduciary relationship is not negligence or breach of contract'.[69] Gaudron and McHugh JJ recognised that the mere fact that a fiduciary relationship exists between two parties 'does not mean that their relationship would be fiduciary for all purposes'.[70] And Gummow J observed that a trustee's obligations to observe the terms of the trust and to exercise the same care as an ordinary prudent person of business are not fiduciary obligations: 'The trustee is, of course, a fiduciary. But the above obligations arise from a particular characteristic, not of fiduciary obligations

---

[61] *Ibid*, 237.
[62] *Mothew* (above n 17) 24.
[63] *Ibid*, 26.
[64] *Re Coomber* [1911] 1 Ch 723, 728.
[65] *Mothew* (above n 17) 16.
[66] *Breen v Williams* (above n 15).
[67] *Ibid*, 82.
[68] *Ibid*, 92.
[69] *Ibid*, 93.
[70] *Ibid*, 107–8.

generally, but of the trust.'[71] While this does not state the proposition as directly as Millett LJ did in *Mothew*, Gummow J's observation is entirely consistent with the trend shown in the other authorities mentioned above: not all of the duties owed by a fiduciary are necessarily properly described as fiduciary duties.

For ease of reference, this approach to understanding fiduciary doctrine will be referred to by reference to Millett LJ's decision in *Mothew*, although it is obvious from the authorities just discussed that the approach predates that particular judgment and has been applied in jurisdictions outside England.

ii. Justification

It is this more modern approach, which was endorsed in *Mothew*, that provides the framework for the analysis in this book. This view of fiduciary doctrine is something of a break from the traditional approach, which focused more on the question whether the duties applicable to one kind of legal actor (a trustee or other type of fiduciary) ought to be applied to another kind of actor (whether exactly or in a modified form), than on the question whether there is a difference between the various types of duties that the relevant actor might owe. Given that the more modern approach represents a break from the traditional analysis of fiduciary doctrine, its adoption in the context of the present inquiry requires justification. Heydon J, writing extra-curially, has criticised the modern approach on the basis that it 'flies in the face of past common linguistic usage'[72] and has expressed surprise that academic commentators have not been more critical.[73]

One way of defending the approach adopted in *Mothew* would be to argue that it has always been thus. Robert Flannigan, for example, has rejected the view that fiduciary doctrine developed as an extension of trust law principles, arguing instead that 'fiduciary accountability was recognized as an independent general jurisdiction from the beginning of its recorded judicial history.'[74] Seeking to substantiate this view, Flannigan has cited numerous eighteenth-century authorities as support for the proposition that 'fiduciary accountability had formally crystallised in the English jurisprudence by the end of the eighteenth century.'[75]

---

[71] *Ibid*, 137.

[72] JD Heydon, 'Are the Duties of Company Directors to Exercise Care and Skill Fiduciary?' in S Degeling and J Edelman (eds), *Equity in Commercial Law* (Pyrmont, Lawbook Co, 2005) 185, 188.

[73] *Ibid*, 198 (fn 79). One academic commentator, Joshua Getzler, has been particularly critical of the approach endorsed in *Mothew*: see J Getzler, 'Equitable Compensation and the Regulation of Fiduciary Relationships' in PBH Birks and FD Rose (eds), *Restitution and Equity: Resulting Trusts and Equitable Compensation*, vol 1 (London, Mansfield Press, 2000) 235, 254; J Getzler, 'Duty of Care' in PBH Birks and A Pretto (eds), *Breach of Trust* (Oxford, Hart, 2002) 41; J Getzler, 'Am I My Beneficiary's Keeper? Fusion and Loss-Based Fiduciary Remedies' in Degeling and Edelman (eds) (*ibid*) 239.

[74] R Flannigan, 'A Romantic Conception of Fiduciary Obligation' (2005) 84 *Canadian Bar Review* 391, 396. See also R Flannigan, 'The Boundaries of Fiduciary Accountability' (2004) 83 *Canadian Bar Review* 35, 48 (fn 30).

[75] R Flannigan, 'The Adulteration of Fiduciary Doctrine in Corporate Law' (2006) 122 *Law Quarterly Review* 449, 449 (the cases are cited in fn 2).

It will be apparent from what has already been said about the historical use of the fiduciary concept that this argument is open to serious question. The historical evidence cannot be said to be completely compelling one way or the other, but a couple of factors point against Flannigan's analysis. First, it is extremely unusual for a legal doctrine to spring forth in a fully formed state.[76] Fiduciary doctrine was not as fully crystallised by the end of the eighteenth century as Flannigan suggests. Some important aspects of it were not fully crystallised into their modern form until the early nineteenth century, during Lord Eldon's period as Lord Chancellor. As will be seen later, many of Lord Eldon's decisions provide very important statements of principle that continue to be of crucial importance in understanding fiduciary doctrine today.[77] In *Whichcote v Lawrence*, for example, Lord Loughborough LC held that a trustee for sale was not precluded from buying the trust property for himself but rather that 'a trustee to sell *shall not gain any advantage* by being himself the person to buy' (emphasis added).[78] This is not an accurate statement of the modern self-dealing rule, which renders voidable a trustee's (or other fiduciary's) purchase of trust property simply because it is the trustee who buys, irrespective of whether any advantage is thereby obtained.[79] The modern rule was made clear in *Ex parte Lacey*, by Lord Eldon LC, who stated that a trustee is prohibited from purchasing the trust property '*whether he makes advantage, or not*, if the connection does not satisfactorily appear to have been dissolved' (emphasis added).[80] As Grant MR observed in *Attorney-General v Dudley*, 'Lord Rosslyn's [*ie*, Lord Loughborough's] rule mentioned in *Whichcote v Lawrence* has certainly been since corrected by the present Lord Chancellor [*ie*, Lord Eldon].'[81]

This first difficulty in accepting Flannigan's analysis could be overcome with relative ease if his assertion were altered so that it referred to the early nineteenth

---

[76] Joshua Getzler has made an argument that appears similar to Flannigan's but acknowledges this point about the development of legal doctrine and differs from Flannigan's analysis in its conclusion. Rather than fiduciary obligations developing by analogy with trust law, Getzler has argued that the reverse was the case: trust law developed by reference to pre-existing fiduciary notions of accountability. See J Getzler, 'Rumford Market and the Genesis of Fiduciary Obligations' in A Burrows and A Rodger (eds), *Mapping the Law* (Oxford, Oxford University Press, 2006) 577, 590–91. It is unclear, if this is so, why so many nineteenth-century cases draw analogies with trusts, rather than with the pre-existing fiduciary concept that Getzler postulates.

[77] Lord Eldon was responsible for the settling into modern form of many equitable principles: WS Holdsworth, *Some Makers of English Law* (Cambridge, Cambridge University Press, 1938) 198–200.

[78] *Whichcote v Lawrence* (1798) 3 Ves Jun 740, 750 (30 ER 1248).

[79] See, eg, *Tito v Waddell (No 2)* [1977] Ch 106, 225 and 241. The self-dealing rule is discussed below in ch 4, section III-A(i) and ch 5, section IV-A.

[80] *Ex parte Lacey* (1802) 6 Ves 625, 627 (31 ER 1228).

[81] *Attorney-General v Dudley* (1815) G Coop 146, 148 (35 ER 510). Similarly, in *Ex parte James* and *Ex parte Bennett*, Lord Eldon LC made clear, contrary to what Lord Hardwicke LC had apparently earlier suggested in *Whelpdale v Cookson* (1747) 1 Ves Sen 9 (27 ER 856), that the self-dealing rule would prevent a trustee from buying trust property even if he bought it at a public auction: see *Ex parte James* (1803) 8 Ves 337, 349 (32 ER 385) and *Ex parte Bennett* (1805) 10 Ves 381, 393 (32 ER 893).

century rather than the end of the eighteenth century. Even with that alteration, however, a second problem with Flannigan's assertion provides a far greater obstacle to its acceptance as a reason for following the approach endorsed in *Mothew*. As has been mentioned, Flannigan cites several cases from the late eighteenth century to establish that 'fiduciary accountability' had formally crystallised into rules that were concerned only with controlling opportunism in limited access arrangements. The difficulty is that the cases that Flannigan cites do not establish this proposition. The cases are unquestionably consistent with the proposition, in the sense that they do not disprove it, because they are all cases concerned with different forms of opportunism in fiduciary office and, subject to the first difficulty mentioned above, are all largely consistent with the way in which modern fiduciary doctrine would operate. However, not one of those cases indicates that fiduciary doctrine goes no further than the regulation of opportunism. In other words, these cases support the view that fiduciary doctrine's regulation of opportunism was largely settled into its modern form by the end of the eighteenth century and certainly by the beginning of the nineteenth century after Lord Eldon had left his mark on that doctrine. But the cases that Flannigan cites do not provide any evidence that none of the other duties owed by fiduciaries was considered by the courts of the late eighteenth century and early nineteenth century to be fiduciary as well. Most of the earlier cases do not even use the word 'fiduciary', let alone differentiate between fiduciary duties and other kinds of duties owed by a fiduciary. The evidence cannot be described as completely clear one way or the other, but it seems inherently unlikely that courts of that time would have drawn a clear distinction between fiduciary duties on the one hand and duties applicable to fiduciaries but not partaking of a fiduciary character on the other, when even the word 'fiduciary' was used only infrequently. As Len Sealy pointed out:

> The 'trustee' in a strict sense, in whom property is legally vested for the benefit of others, was not separately identified until well into the nineteenth century, when the expression 'fiduciary' was eventually accepted to differentiate true trusts from those other relationships, like that between a director or a promoter and his company, which in some degree resemble them.[82]

Indeed, as late as 1880, when the Court of Appeal decided *Re Hallett's Estate*, Jessel MR used the words 'trustee' and 'fiduciary' interchangeably, 'using the word "trustee" . . . as including all persons in a fiduciary relation'.[83] In the light of these observations and of the historical evidence collected in the first part of this chapter, it seems dangerous to assert that fiduciary doctrine had already taken the stance endorsed in *Mothew* by the end of the eighteenth century or even the

---

[82] Sealy, 'The Director as Trustee' (above n 44) 85–86. See also *Friend v Brooker* [2009] HCA 21 at [72].

[83] *Re Hallett's Estate* (above n 42) 709. Almost identical phraseology appears in EA Swan, *Law Relating to Vendor and Purchaser* (London, Sweet & Maxwell, 1912) 148.

beginning of the nineteenth century. On that basis, some other justification for the approach favoured in *Mothew* needs to be identified before it is followed in this book.

The justification that is offered here for following the approach endorsed in *Mothew* is twofold. First, while that approach seems to involve a change in the way fiduciary doctrine is conceived of, that change appears to have been widely adopted by the courts in the jurisdictions under consideration, such that it represents positive law which deserves serious academic attention. Secondly, there is merit in the change of focus in the sense that it allows for greater clarity of analysis, and hence understanding, of fiduciary doctrine.

As to the first point—whether the approach endorsed in *Mothew* represents positive law—one can point to numerous authorities that indicate extensive judicial approbation in Commonwealth common law systems. In England, for example, the approach seems well entrenched. It has been applied in numerous first instance decisions,[84] and the Court of Appeal has regularly referred to Millett LJ's judgment on this point with approval in reaching decisions subsequent to *Mothew*.[85] Furthermore, in *Hilton v Barker Booth & Eastwood*, Lord Walker commented:

> The relationship between a solicitor and his client is one in which the client reposes trust and confidence in the solicitor. It is a fiduciary relationship. But not every breach of duty by a fiduciary is a breach of fiduciary duty: see the observations of Millett LJ in *Bristol & West Building Society v Mothew*.[86]

---

[84] See, eg, *Bristol & West Building Society v Daniels & Co* [1996] PNLR 323, 326; *Ocular Sciences Ltd v Aspect Vision Care Ltd* [1997] RPC 289, 413; *Bristol & West Building Society v Fancy & Jackson* [1997] 4 All ER 582, 614–15; *Zwebner v The Mortgage Corporation Ltd* [1997] PNLR 504, 514; *Global Container Lines Ltd v Bonyad* [1998] 1 Lloyd's Rep 528, 546–47; *Nationwide Building Society v Balmer Radmore* [1999] Lloyd's Rep PN 241, 259–60; *Mortgage Corp v Alexander Johnson, The Times* (22 Sept 1999) (full judgment available on LexisNexis); *Birmingham Midshires Building Society v Infields* [1999] Lloyd's Rep 874, 880; *Coulthard v Disco Mix Club Ltd* [2000] 1 WLR 707, 728; *Nottingham University v Fishel* [2000] IRLR 471 at [85]; *Regentcrest plc v Cohen* [2001] 2 BCLC 80 at [122]; *Leeds & Holbeck Building Society v Arthur & Cole* [2002] PNLR 78, 84; *Colin Gwyer & Associates Ltd v London Wharf (Limehouse) Ltd* [2002] EWHC 2748 (Ch) at [82], [2003] 2 BCLC 153; *Sphere Drake Insurance Ltd v Euro International Underwriting Ltd* [2003] EWHC 1636 (Comm) at [50], [2003] Lloyd's Rep IR 525; *Sinclair Investment Holdings SA v Versailles Trade Finance Ltd* [2004] EWHC 2169 (Ch) at [23]; *Sinclair Investment Holdings SA v Versailles Trade Finance Ltd* [2007] EWHC 915 (Ch) at [78], [2007] 2 All ER (Comm) 993.
[85] See, eg, *Swindle v Harrison* (above n 47) 719–20 and 731; *Attorney-General v Blake* [1998] Ch 439, 455 (CA); *Portman Building Society v Hamlyn Taylor Neck* [1998] 4 All ER 202, 205; *Michaels v Harley House (Marylebone) Ltd* [2000] Ch 104, 120; *Paragon Finance plc v DB Thakerar & Co* [1999] 1 All ER 400, 406; *Cia de Seguros Imperio v Heath (REBX) Ltd* [2001] 1 WLR 112, 119; *Gwembe Valley Devt Co Ltd v Koshy (No 3)* [2003] EWCA Civ 1048 at [85], [2004] 1 BCLC 131; *Base Metal Trading Ltd v Shamurin* [2004] EWCA Civ 1316 at [19], [2005] 1 All ER (Comm) 17; *Murad v Al-Saraj* [2005] EWCA Civ 959 at [54], [2005] WTLR 1573.
[86] *Hilton v Barker Booth & Eastwood* [2005] UKHL 8 at [29], [2005] 1 WLR 567.

Technically, this comment was an obiter dictum,[87] as *Hilton* concerned a claim for breach of contract rather than a claim for breach of fiduciary duty. Nonetheless, Lord Walker's observation is indicative of the fact that the approach in *Mothew* is being followed judicially on a regular basis and provides the framework for much analysis of fiduciary doctrine in the courts. In the light of that widespread judicial acceptance and of its acceptance at the level of the House of Lords, even if only in an obiter dictum, it is (at the very least) legitimate for it to be treated as representing the law in England at present. Notwithstanding Heydon J's observation that academics 'give themselves a freer hand' than writers of 'conventional textbooks, which naturally tend to accept the law as it is stated in the higher courts',[88] there is surely scope, even for academic commentators, to consider and analyse the law as it is stated in the higher courts and applied by the lower courts: 'the search for principle is a task which judge and jurist share together.'[89] This is not to suggest that there is no place for academic criticism of decisions of the higher courts, but merely to say that there is a place for academic analysis of the doctrine that those decisions create and apply, and of the implications of that doctrine. That is what this book sets out to do.

Nor has acceptance of the approach endorsed in *Mothew* been limited to England. As is already apparent from what has been said about the genesis and gestation of that approach, some Australian courts had explicitly adopted that approach even prior to the decision in *Mothew*,[90] and the approach is entirely consistent with comments made at the highest judicial level in that country.[91] Numerous other decisions across a range of jurisdictions within Australia have applied the approach subsequently, referring both to *Mothew* and to *Wheeler*.[92]

---

[87] J Getzler, 'Inconsistent Fiduciary Duties and Implied Consent' (2006) 122 *Law Quarterly Review* 1, 7.

[88] Heydon (above n 72) 198 (fn 79).

[89] R Goff, 'The Search for Principle' republished in W Swadling and G Jones (eds), *The Search for Principle: Essays in Honour of Lord Goff of Chieveley* (Oxford, Oxford University Press, 1999) 313, 329.

[90] See the authorities mentioned in the text accompanying nn 59–61 above.

[91] See the authorities mentioned in the text accompanying nn 66–71 above. Some doubts have been expressed as to the conclusions to be drawn from following the approach: *Maguire v Makaronis* (1997) 188 CLR 449, 474; *Youyang Pty Ltd v Minter Ellison Morris Fletcher* [2003] HCA 15 at [38]–[40], (2003) 212 CLR 484.

[92] *Macedone v Collins* (1996) 7 Butterworths Prop Rep 15,127, 15,132–34 (NSWCA); *South Australia v Clark* (1996) 66 SASR 199, 223; *South Australia v Peat Marwick Mitchell & Co* (1997) 24 ACSR 231, 266; *Beach Petroleum NL v Abbott Tout Russell Kennedy* (1997) 26 ACSR 114, 263 (NSWSC); *Cade Pty Ltd v Thomson Simmons* [1997] SASC 6603 at [394]; *O'Halloran v RT Thomas & Family Pty Ltd* (1998) 45 NSWLR 262, 274 (NSWCA); *Moage Ltd v Jagelman* (1998) 153 ALR 711, 718–19 (FCA); *Marron v Charham Daunt Pty Ltd* [1998] VSC 110 at [44]; *Beach Petroleum NL v Abbott Tout Russell Kennedy* [1999] NSWCA 408 at [188], (1999) 48 NSWLR 1; *Rogers v Kabriel* [1999] NSWSC 368 at [47]; *Williams v The Minister, Aboriginal Land Rights Act 1983* [1999] NSWSC 843 at [729] and [741]; *Yu v Kwok* [1999] NSWSC 992 at [93]–[95] and [159]; *Espanol Holdings Pty Ltd v Banning* [1999] WASC 49 at [24]; *ASIC v Adler* [2002] NSWSC 171 at [372], (2002) 41 ACSR 72; *Karam v ANZ Banking Group Ltd* [2001] NSWSC 709 at [425]; *Nuthall v Nuthall* [2001] NSWSC 950 at [9]; *Maronis Holdings Ltd v Nippon Credit Australia Ltd* [2001] NSWSC 448 at [407], (2001) 38 ACSR 404; *Tusyn v Tasmania* [2004] TASSC 50 at [11], (2004) 13 TASR 51; *Expectation Pty Ltd v PRD Realty Pty Ltd* [2004] FCAFC 189 at [243] (reported in part at (2004) 209 ALR 568); *Olympic Holdings*

Heydon J has criticised both *Mothew* and *Wheeler* on the basis that they are not historical, or at least that their historical soundness has not been shown.[93] This criticism may well be correct on its own terms,[94] but it is not to the point in the present context: the argument is not that *Mothew* and *Wheeler* were necessarily accurate applications of pre-existing law but rather that they have changed the law. As Jessel MR pointed out in *Hallett's Estate*,

> I intentionally say modern rules, because it must not be forgotten that the rules of Courts of Equity are not, like the rules of the Common Law, supposed to have been established from time immemorial. It is perfectly well known that they have been established from time to time—altered, improved, and refined from time to time. In many cases we know the names of the Chancellors who invented them.[95]

As Lord Goff said in *Kleinwort Benson Ltd v Lincoln City Council*, 'the law is the subject of development by judges—normally, of course, by appellate judges. We describe as leading cases the decisions which mark the principal stages in this development.'[96] As the citations provided above illustrate, courts at all levels in both England and Australia have treated both *Mothew* and *Wheeler* as leading cases, following the lead indicated in those decisions. The fact that the approach in those cases is not completely consonant with the way in which fiduciary doctrine has operated historically does not undermine that fact. That approach has also been followed in New Zealand[97] and, on several occasions, in Canada.[98] This provides sufficient reason for the approach to be treated as positive law in this book.

Pty Ltd v Lochel [2004] WASC 61 at [174]; *Fico v O'Leary* [2004] WASC 215 at [144]; *Bell Group v Westpac (No 9)* (above n 9) [4529]–[4531]. See also *Cubillo v Commonwealth of Australia* [2001] FCA 1213 at [462], (2001) 112 FCR 455, referring to *Breen v Williams* (above n 15).

[93] *Harris v Digital Pulse Pty Ltd* [2003] NSWCA 10 at [434], (2003) 56 NSWLR 298; and Heydon (above n 72) 185.

[94] Although it too has been challenged: see Heath (above n 48).

[95] *Re Hallett's Estate* (above n 42) 710. See also *Allen v Jackson* (1875) 1 ChD 399, 405 (CA); *Cowcher v Cowcher* [1972] 1 All ER 943, 948; *Eves v Eves* [1975] 1 WLR 1338, 1341 (CA); *Mardorf Peach & Co Ltd v Attica Sea Carriers Corp of Liberia* [1977] AC 850, 874; *Re Murphy's Settlements* [1998] 3 All ER 1, 10 (ChD); *Royal Bank of Scotland plc v Etridge (No 2)* [2001] UKHL 44 at [89], [2002] 2 AC 773; R Cross and JW Harris, *Precedent in English Law*, 4th edn (Oxford, Oxford University Press, 1991) 29. Toby Milsom identifies the Chancellors that Jessel MR was referring to as, in particular, Lord Nottingham, Lord Hardwicke and Lord Eldon: SFC Milsom, *Historical Foundations of the Common Law*, 2nd edn (Toronto, Butterworths, 1981) 95. And see Meagher, Heydon and Leeming (above n 1) [1–070].

[96] *Kleinwort Benson Ltd v Lincoln City Council* [1993] AC 349, 377.

[97] *Bank of New Zealand v New Zealand Guardian Trust Co Ltd* [1999] 1 NZLR 213, 245 (HC); *Bank of New Zealand v New Zealand Guardian Trust Co Ltd* [1999] 1 NZLR 664, 680 (CA); *Armitage v Paynter Construction Ltd* [1999] 2 NZLR 534, 543–44 (CA); *Stratford v Shayle-George* [2001] NZCA 299 at [23]; *Tuiara v Frost & Sutcliffe* [2003] 2 NZLR 833 at [47] (HC); *Chirnside v Fay* [2004] 3 NZLR 637 at [51] (CA), [2006] NZSC 68 at [15], [72] and [73], [2007] 1 NZLR 433; *Cornerstone Group Ltd v Edison Ltd* [2006] NZHC 1135 at [46].

[98] See the authorities mentioned in the text accompanying nn 54–58 above, and see *Norberg v Wynrib* [1992] 2 SCR 226, 312; *Granville Savings & Mortgage Corp v Slevin* (1992) 93 DLR (4th) 268, 282 and 300–1 (Man CA); *Hodgkinson v Simms* (above n 1) 405 and 463–64; *Canada Trustco Mortgage Co v Bartlet & Richards* (1996) 28 OR (3d) 768, 774 (Ont CA); *Fasken Campbell Godfrey v Seven-Up*

This point prompts brief mention of the jurisdictions that are treated as the focus of attention in the book, because not all jurisdictions have adopted the approach endorsed in *Mothew* with the same degree of consistency. In particular, while numerous Canadian courts have followed the approach that Southin J recommended in *Girardet* by drawing a distinction between fiduciary and non-fiduciary duties, Cullity J has observed that 'on the present state of the authorities, it is not apparent to me that the principle stated by Sopinka J [in *Lac Minerals*, referring to *Girardet*] has been unequivocally, and finally, accepted by the Supreme Court of Canada.'[99] In *Wewaykum Indian Band v Canada*, for example, speaking for a unanimous Supreme Court, Binnie J stated that 'it is desirable for the Court to affirm the principle . . . that not all obligations existing between the parties to a fiduciary relationship are themselves fiduciary in nature'[100] and then proceeded to restate the relevant fiduciary duties in a way that directly contradicted the approach taken in *Girardet*, *Wheeler* and *Mothew*.[101] In *Norberg v Wynrib*, Sopinka J followed the view that 'not all facets of [a fiduciary's] obligations are fiduciary in nature',[102] but McLachlin J (in dissent) stated that she did 'not think that narrow view of the scope of the fiduciary obligation is correct'.[103] Only four months after it had decided *Norberg v Wynrib*, the Supreme Court followed McLachlin J's approach in deciding *KM v HM*.[104] This lack of consistency at the highest levels led McEachern CJBC to complain in *British Columbia v CA* that 'notwithstanding [Southin J's] clear statement of the law . . . cases in the Supreme Court of Canada before and after *Girardet* have failed to make the law as clear as it should be.'[105]

Thus, while the Supreme Court of Canada has at times emphasised the need to distinguish between fiduciary duties and duties based on other legal concepts, at

---

Canada Inc (1997) 142 DLR (4th) 456, 482–83 (aff'd: (2000) 47 OR (3d) 15 (CA)); *Jostens Canada Ltd v Gibsons Studio Ltd* (1997) 42 BCLR (3d) 149 at [19] (CA); *British Columbia v CA* (1998) 166 DLR (4th) 475 at [78], [85] and [154]–[155] (BCCA); *FSM v Clarke* [1999] 11 WWR 301 at [186] (BCSC); *Hatch v Cooper* [2001] SKQB 491 at [36], [2002] 2 WWR 159; *Wewaykum Indian Band v Canada* [2002] SCC 79 at [81] and [83], [2002] 4 SCR 245; *Cope v Dickson* [2002] BCSC 1406 at [36]–[37]; *KLB v British Columbia* [2003] SCC 51 at [48]–[50], [2003] 2 SCR 403; *Grant v Attorney-General of Canada* (2005) 258 DLR (4th) 725 at [27] (Ont SC); *West Fork Ranch Ltd v Marcotte* [2005] BCSC 898 at [132]; *Van de Geer Estate v Penner* [2006] SKCA 12 at [98], (2006) 275 Sask R 202; *Strother v 3464920 Canada Inc* [2007] SCC 24 at [34], [2007] 2 SCR 177; *Solomon v Alexis Creek Indian Band* [2007] BCSC 459 at [60]; *Sharbern Holding Inc v Vancouver Airport Centre Ltd* [2007] BCSC 1262 at [399]–[401].

[99]   *Grant v Attorney-General* (*ibid*) [28]. See also *Blanco v Canada Trust Co* [2003] MBCA 64 at [31]–[45], [2003] 9 WWR 79.

[100]   *Wewaykum Indian Band v Canada* [2002] SCC 79 at [83], [2002] 4 SCR 245.

[101]   *Ibid* at [86].

[102]   *Norberg v Wynrib* (above n 98) 312.

[103]   *Ibid*, 289.

[104]   *KM v HM* [1992] 3 SCR 6.

[105]   *British Columbia v CA* (above n 98) [79]. See also Huband JA's dissent in *TLB v REC* [2000] MBCA 83 at [103]–[111], [2000] 11 WWR 436.

other times that distinction has been ignored and, influenced by US authority,[106] results have been arrived at which would not be reached in Australia or England.[107] The importance of this is not to suggest, as others have, that these different approaches have been 'achieved by assertion rather than analysis and [without] the development or elucidation of any accepted doctrine'.[108] Rather, 'Canadian equity jurisprudence, perhaps under the influence of United States law, has developed in a quite different way to that of Australia'[109] and England. As Browne-Wilkinson LJ said in *Sidaway v Bethlam Royal Hospital*:

> Although the law of the United States and Canada has the same equitable and common law roots as our own, the present-day law in the different jurisdictions is not necessarily the same. Therefore I am in no way criticising the transatlantic decisions when I say that the reasoning behind those decisions does not accord with the present law of England.[110]

The consequence is that 'Canadian authorities on equity must be treated with considerable caution.'[111]

The case law on fiduciary doctrine in New Zealand needs to be approached with a similar degree of caution, as it has fluctuated over time, leaving it without clear guiding principles. At times, particularly under the leadership of Cooke P, the New Zealand courts aligned their fiduciary jurisprudence with Canadian doctrine.[112] The New Zealand doctrine so developed had, in turn, a reciprocal

---

[106] See, eg, *Emmett v Eastern Dispensary & Casualty Hospital* 396 F 2d 931, 935 (1967) and *Cannell v Medical & Surgical Clinic* 315 NE 2d 278, 280 (1974), both relied upon in *McInerney v MacDonald* [1992] 2 SCR 138, 150. See also *Canterbury v Spence* 464 F 2d 772, 782 (1972).

[107] Compare, eg, (1) *McInerney v MacDonald (ibid)* with *Breen v Williams* (above n 15) and with *Sidaway v Board of Governors of Bethlam Royal Hospital and Maudsley Hospital* [1984] QB 493, 515 and 518–19 (CA), [1985] 1 AC 871, 884; and (2) *KM v HM* (above n 104) and the judgment of McLachlin J (with which L'Heureux-Dubé J agreed) in *Norberg v Wynrib* (above n 98) with *Paramasivam v Flynn* (1998) 90 FCR 489. The right of access to medical records discussed in *R v Mid Glamorgan Family Health Services Authority, ex parte Martin* [1995] 1 WLR 110 (CA) seems to have been based on public law grounds rather than on a fiduciary analysis, the latter basis having been rejected by Popplewell J at first instance: (1993) 16 Butterworths Medico-Legal Rep 81, 94 (QBD).

[108] *Breen v Williams* (above n 15) 95 *per* Dawson and Toohey JJ. See also *Breen v Williams* (1994) 35 NSWLR 522, 570 *per* Meagher JA (CA).

[109] *Harris v Digital Pulse Pty Ltd* [2003] NSWCA 10 at [31], (2003) 56 NSWLR 298 *per* Spigelman CJ. See also *Breen v Williams* (above n 15) 112; *Bodney v Westralia Airports Corp Pty Ltd* [2000] FCA 1609 at [57], (2000) 109 FCR 178; *Pilmer v Duke Group Ltd* [2001] HCA 31 at [121], (2001) 207 CLR 165; *P & V Industries Pty Ltd v Porto* [2006] VSC 131 at [42], (2006) 14 VR 1; AF Mason, 'The Place of Equity and Equitable Remedies in the Contemporary Common Law World' (1994) 110 *Law Quarterly Review* 238, 246–48; RC Nolan, 'A Fiduciary Duty to Disclose?' (1997) 113 *Law Quarterly Review* 220, 225; DWM Waters, 'The Reception of Equity in the Supreme Court of Canada (1875–2000)' (2001) 80 *Canadian Bar Review* 620, 676.

[110] *Sidaway* (CA) (above n 107) 518. This case involved a medical negligence claim, but the comments quoted in the text were concerned with whether North American fiduciary doctrines, which had influenced analysis of medical negligence claims there, ought to be followed in England. See also, in a different context, *B v Auckland District Law Society* [2003] UKPC 38 at [55], [2003] 2 AC 736: 'the common law is no longer monolithic'.

[111] *Harris v Digital Pulse Pty Ltd* [2003] NSWCA 10 at [32], (2003) 56 NSWLR 298.

[112] See, eg, *Day v Mead* [1987] 2 NZLR 443, 451–52 (CA); and Cooke P's dissent in *T v H* [1995] 3 NZLR 37, 42–43 (CA).

influence on Canadian case law, particularly through La Forest J.[113] However, other New Zealand decisions suggest a more restrained approach, relying more on English authority.[114]

As with all legal concepts and doctrines, fiduciary doctrine is not immutable. In other words, the fiduciary concept is a contingent one, dependent on the time when and the jurisdictions within which one examines it. For the reasons just explained, this book offers a detailed analysis of English and Australian decisions on fiduciary doctrine, in an attempt to consider the nature and function of that doctrine in Anglo-Australian law. Reference will be made to decisions in other jurisdictions where these help to highlight a point, whether by agreement or by disagreement, but no attempt is made to provide a full, comparative account of fiduciary doctrine.

The second reason for following the approach endorsed in *Mothew* is that it allows for greater clarity of analysis, and hence understanding, of fiduciary doctrine. While it is true, as Jessel MR recognised in *Hallett's Estate*, that equitable doctrine changes and develops over time,[115] it must also be acknowledged that 'an advance must be justifiable in principle.'[116] This second reason provides the normative justification for the change in meaning of the fiduciary concept that has been wrought by the Anglo-Australian adoption of the approach taken in *Mothew*. The crux of the reason for the change is perhaps best expressed in Millett LJ's observation in *Mothew* that the description 'fiduciary' must be limited to duties that are peculiar to fiduciaries because 'unless the expression is so limited it is lacking in practical utility.'[117]

The utility of the newer approach adopted in *Mothew* can best be understood by comparing it with the utility of continuing to approach fiduciary doctrine in the way it has been addressed earlier in history. The problem with the historical approach to fiduciary duties is that it makes it extremely difficult to identify what generic function might be served by fiduciary duties as a class, which thereby deprives the fiduciary concept of analytical, and therefore predictive, utility.

In order to analyse and understand the function that fiduciary duties serve which marks them out from other kinds of duties, one needs to be able to identify which duties qualify as fiduciary duties. Following the historical approach, fiduciary duties are simply those duties that the courts are prepared to enforce whenever there is a relationship sufficiently analogous to that between a trustee and beneficiary (or other fiduciary and principal) as to justify the imposition of analogous duties. In other words, the fiduciary concept simply meant 'trustee-like'. The problem is that if one seeks to delve beneath that

---

[113] See, eg, *Canson Enterprises Ltd v Boughton & Co* [1991] 3 SCR 534, 577–78 and 583–87; *KM v HM* (above n 104) 61 and 82.

[114] See, eg, *Bank of New Zealand* (CA) (above n 97) 680–82 and 686–88; *Armitage v Paynter Construction* (above n 97) 543–44.

[115] See text accompanying n 95 above.

[116] *Paramasivam v Flynn* (above n 107) 505.

[117] *Mothew* (above n 17) 16.

formulation to identify by what criterion of similarity the courts reach that sort of conclusion, no clear answer emerges because the question is the same as asking when fiduciary duties arise. As has been seen already, no definition of when fiduciary duties arise has attracted widespread judicial endorsement: the fiduciary concept remains a contested one—'a concept in search of a principle'.[118] By contrast, if the description 'fiduciary' is limited to those duties that are peculiar to fiduciaries there is a greater likelihood that a core purpose or function will be able to be identified among those duties. Such an approach allows one to analyse what is special about those peculiar duties, which in turn allows one to describe what function those duties perform which sets them apart from other duties and justifies their differentiation by application of the label 'fiduciary'.

Without a clear conceptual distinction between fiduciary duties and other kinds of duties, it is also more difficult to explain the notoriously stringent remedies that follow breach of fiduciary duty, such as the stripping of the fiduciary's profits or the imposition of a constructive trust over the fiduciary's property.[119] In *Mothew* itself, for example, counsel sought to cast as a breach of fiduciary duty facts that appeared at face value to involve no more than a breach of contract or negligence, in order to gain access to fiduciary doctrine's more extensive remedial regime.[120] If the historical approach to understanding fiduciary duties were followed—if the court took fiduciary duties to mean the duties owed by someone in a trustee-like position—then the difficult question that arises is why that counterintuitive submission should be rejected. Breach of contract or negligence committed by a fiduciary (such as a solicitor) and the same wrong committed by someone who is not a fiduciary should attract the same consequences. To say otherwise would necessarily mean that mere status, rather than conduct, justified the more stringent remedies, which is entirely at variance with a law of wrongs, as opposed to a 'law of status'. The distinctive remedial regime applicable to breach of a fiduciary duty is more readily explained if fiduciary doctrine's remedies are available for breaches of duties that apply only to fiduciaries.

Further, as has already been seen, the exporting of duties to other fiduciaries by analogy with trusteeship has resulted in the imposition of different standards of duties.[121] Thus, for example, while 'trustees are to be kept by courts of equity up to their duty',[122] the standard of care expected of other similarly but not identically situated actors, such as company directors, was lower. This sits uncomfortably alongside the fact that other fiduciary duties were applied in a

---

[118] AF Mason, 'Themes and Prospects' in PD Finn (ed), *Essays in Equity* (Sydney, Law Book Co, 1985) 242, 246.

[119] For a general description of the various remedies for breach of fiduciary duty, see JA McGhee (ed), *Snell's Equity*, 31st edn (London, Sweet & Maxwell, 2005) [7–120]–[7–147]. The remedies for breach of fiduciary duty are considered in more detail below in chs 4 and 6.

[120] *Mothew* (above n 17) 26.

[121] See text accompanying nn 48–51 above.

[122] *Youyang Pty Ltd v Minter Ellison Morris Fletcher* [2003] HCA 15 at [39], (2003) 212 CLR 484.

consistently strict fashion to such actors. Restricting the language of fiduciary duties to those duties that are applied consistently across the spectrum of fiduciary relationships allows both an explanation of that consistency as well as an explanation of the standards that apply differently to different fiduciary relationships.

If fiduciary duties mean those duties that are unique to fiduciaries as a class, it is possible to give a unified explanation for them, of the sort offered in this book. Such an explanation makes the category of 'fiduciary duties' practically useful: it allows lawyers who correctly identify a fiduciary duty to understand and predict the consequences of breaching that duty. It also becomes possible to explain other duties—duties that apply differently to different fiduciaries, or to some kinds of fiduciary but not others, or to fiduciaries and non-fiduciaries alike—by reference to distinct reasons, without clouding or complicating the explanation of fiduciary duties.

The consequence of taking the contrary approach is that the categorisation of duties becomes of little or no normative value because such categories are of little or no significance in the analysis of how courts are likely to react in a given situation. Thus, for example, in the United States the courts are prepared to impose a constructive trust 'not only where the wrongdoer is a fiduciary other than a trustee, but also where he is not in a fiduciary position'.[123] George Palmer considered it a 'great development' for the American courts to 'have freed the remedy [of constructive trust] of any necessary connection with fiduciary relationship.'[124] Similarly in Canada,[125] it has been said that 'the fiduciary requirement is no longer part of the Canadian law of constructive trust',[126] such that 'even in a case in which the only wrong was a common law tort, or even a breach of contract, a constructive trust could be viewed as the appropriate remedy. And in fact there is authority for this possibility for breaches of contract.'[127] Such an approach denudes the fiduciary concept of any analytically valuable meaning.

The approach endorsed in *Mothew* and followed in this book is born of an attempt to avoid analytical nihilism of the sort just described. Its premise is that while legal concepts are not immutable, they are of value in legal analysis by assisting legal actors in predicting accurately what the courts will do when faced with a particular kind of situation and thus allowing those actors to modify their

---

[123]   WA Seavey and AW Scott, 'Restitution' (1938) 54 *Law Quarterly Review* 29, 45.

[124]   GE Palmer, *The Law of Restitution*, Vol 1 (Boston, Little Brown & Co, 1978) 12.

[125]   DWM Waters, 'The Nature of the Remedial Constructive Trust' in PBH Birks (ed), *The Frontiers of Liability*, vol 2 (Oxford, Oxford University Press, 1994) 165, 167–68, 173 and 175.

[126]   GB Klippert, 'The Juridical Nature of Unjust Enrichment' (1980) 30 *University of Toronto Law Journal* 356, 407. See also AJ Oakley, *Constructive Trusts* (London, Sweet & Maxwell, 3rd ed, 1997) 20; DWM Waters, 'The Constructive Trust in Evolution: Substantive *and* Remedial' in SR Goldstein (ed), *Equity and Contemporary Legal Developments* (Jerusalem, Hebrew University, 1992) 457, 465 and 468.

[127]   DWM Waters, MR Gillen and LD Smith, *Waters' Law of Trusts in Canada*, 3rd edn (Toronto, Thomson Carswell, 2005) 506. See also Waters, 'The Nature of the Remedial Constructive Trust' (above n 125) 176.

behaviour accordingly.[128] This is also important when novel questions of law are faced, because an understanding of the nature and function of relevant legal concepts can assist in providing answers (or at least indicating potential answers) to those questions in a way that merely applying pre-existing case law may not. This is not to suggest that an analysis of case law is misplaced. Indeed, quite the contrary. The common law operates by application of a complex reasoning process, whereby general principles are extracted through an inductive process from collections of particular decisions.[129] 'Over time, general principle is derived from judicial decisions upon particular instances, not the other way around.'[130] Those general principles are then used to provide answers to novel questions in further cases as they arise. In turn, through an iterative process, those further particular instances form part of the canon of doctrine from which, again through inductive analysis, general principles are extracted, sometimes in a slightly altered form from that previously extracted.[131] The point is that it is useful, if possible, to extract from the cases a conceptual understanding of the nature and function of fiduciary doctrine, because that understanding can then be used in an attempt to provide more concrete answers to novel questions as they arise in future cases.

So this book is written from a perspective which holds that precision in the nomenclature of legal concepts and categories—or taxonomy—is important to legal analysis. Two points about this claim require brief amplification in order that it not be misunderstood as something it is not. First, this book is written in the belief that 'classification and its relationship with reasoning is . . . an aspect of legal knowledge that ought not to be neglected. . . [I]t helps us *think* about the relationship between words and things.'[132] It is that sort of thought that helps lawyers to focus on the substance of legal concepts, which comprises an integral and fundamental part of the legal reasoning process described above. Thus, the relation between legal categories matters, and taxonomy is important, when these things promote better understanding of legal doctrine.[133] 'The basic aim of legal scholarship is to understand the law better.'[134] What is not being suggested by referring to 'taxonomy' is that the common law operates on the basis of

---

[128] See MDA Freeman, *Lloyd's Introduction to Jurisprudence* (London, Sweet & Maxwell, 8th ed, 2008) 1543–45.

[129] WMC Gummow, *Change and Continuity* (Oxford, Oxford University Press, 1999) xvii–xviii. Legal reasoning may 'not [be] truly inductive, but the direction appears to be from particular to general': EH Levi, 'An Introduction to Legal Reasoning' (1948) 15 *University of Chicago Law Review* 501, 519.

[130] *Roxborough v Rothmans of Pall Mall Australia Ltd* [2001] HCA 68 at [72], (2001) 208 CLR 516. See also *Farah Constructions Pty Ltd v Say-Dee Pty Ltd* [2007] HCA 22 at [154], (2007) 230 CLR 89.

[131] Levi (above n 129) 502–3 and 519; RC Nolan, 'Equitable Property' (2006) 122 *Law Quarterly Review* 232, 234.

[132] G Samuel, 'Can Gaius Really be Compared to Darwin?' (2000) 49 *International & Comparative Law Quarterly* 297, 299–300.

[133] PBH Birks, 'Equity in the Modern Law: An Exercise in Taxonomy' (1996) 26 *University of Western Australia Law Review* 1, 3 and 7.

[134] SA Smith, 'Taking Law Seriously' (2000) 50 *University of Toronto Law Journal* 241, 249.

taxonomically pure and hermetically sealed exclusive categories. That is not so.[135] Thus, the book does not represent an attempt to impose upon the fiduciary concept a rigid and closed definition for the sake of avoiding untidiness or to avoid the supposed chaos that might ensue from overlapping categories.[136] Rather, the analysis offered in the book is provided on the basis that legal concepts have greater value when we have a better understanding of the substance of those concepts and can more fully explain the relationship between that substance and the substance of other concepts. Legal concepts that are understood and can be used in analysis of legal disputes are valuable—more valuable than concepts that lack such analytical traction. It was the pursuit of that form of value that led Millett LJ in *Mothew* to adopt the approach that differentiates fiduciary duties from other duties owed by fiduciaries, and this book adopts the same form of analysis for that reason.

Secondly, the book is not written from the perspective that the word 'fiduciary' means only one thing and that any contrary usage is necessarily wrong or illegitimate. As has already been mentioned, words do not necessarily have a single solitary meaning. As has already been seen, it is possible to describe all of the duties owed by a fiduciary as 'fiduciary duties' in the sense that they are duties owed by fiduciaries. And in some contexts, that remains the way in which the word 'fiduciary' is used. Thus, for example, persons who are not trustees or fiduciaries themselves may nevertheless be held personally liable if they assist in a breach of trust or of fiduciary duty or if they receive property that was transferred to them in breach of trust or of fiduciary duty.[137] In the context of these forms of liability, the fiduciary concept is used to refer to the broader concept of any breach of obligation that is like a trustee's obligations. In other words, it is used to export the incidents of the trustee–beneficiary relationship to other similar relationships. Hence, while breaches of trust are not all breaches of fiduciary duty in the sense of duties that are peculiar to fiduciaries, as Gummow J made clear in *Breen v Williams*,[138] they are all breaches of fiduciary duty in the sense that they are sufficient to give rise to liability in third parties who assist in or receive property as a result of such breaches. Similarly, breaches of duty by company directors are treated as breaches of trust, or 'fiduciary' duty, for the

---

[135] See Gummow (above n 129) 70; Samuel, 'Can Gaius Really be Compared to Darwin?' (above n 132) 298, 311–12, 314 and 316–17; S Waddams, *Dimensions of Private Law* (Cambridge, Cambridge University Press, 2003) 110–11, 227 and 229; G Samuel, 'Can the Common Law be Mapped?' (2005) 55 *University of Toronto Law Journal* 271, 283–84. See also AC Hutchinson, *Evolution and the Common Law* (Cambridge, Cambridge University Press, 2005) ch 2; J Dietrich, 'What is "Lawyering"? The Challenge of Taxonomy' [2006] *Cambridge Law Journal* 549, 575. Cf PBH Birks, 'Equity, Conscience, and Unjust Enrichment' (1999) 23 *Melbourne University Law Review* 1, 9.

[136] Cf PBH Birks, 'Definition and Division: A Meditation on *Institutes* 3.13' in PBH Birks (ed), *The Classification of Obligations* (Oxford, Oxford University Press, 1997) 1, 23; Birks, 'Equity in the Modern Law' (above n 133) 5–6.

[137] A Underhill and DJ Hayton, *Law Relating to Trusts and* Trustees, 17th edn by DJ Hayton, PB Matthews and CCJ Mitchell (London, LexisNexis Butterworths, 2007) [100.1] and [100.17]–[100.86].

[138] See text accompanying n 71 above.

purposes of such liability.[139] The meaning that the word carries depends on the purpose for which it is being used.[140] Thus, the word 'fiduciary' can be used to refer to any breach of duty that is like a breach of trust if the purpose of using the word is to identify breaches of duty that are sufficiently like breaches of trust to justify third-party liability like that which can arise following a breach of trust. When, however, the purpose of using the word 'fiduciary' is to describe duties that are distinctive of fiduciaries, in order to determine what differentiates fiduciary duties from other kinds of duties—and that is what this book seeks to do—then for that purpose it is expedient and proper to confine application of the 'fiduciary' descriptor 'to those duties which are peculiar to fiduciaries'.[141]

---

[139]   See, eg, *Selangor United Rubber Estates (No 3)* (above n 29) 1574–75 and 1577; *Karak Rubber Co Ltd v Burden (No 2)* [1972] 1 WLR 602, 633 (ChD) ; *Belmont Finance (No 2)* (above n 37) 405; *Baden v Société Générale pour Favoriser le Développement du Commerce et de l'Industrie en France SA* [1993] 1 WLR 509n at [242] (ChD); *Rolled Steel Products (Holdings) Ltd v British Steel Corp* [1986] Ch 246, 297–98 (CA); *El Ajou v Dollar Land Holdings plc* [1994] 2 All ER 685, 700 (CA). See also *Re Lands Allotment Co* (above n 29) 631 and 638; *Brown v Bennett* [1999] 1 BCLC 649, 655 (CA). And see A Stafford and S Ritchie, *Fiduciary Duties: Directors and Employees* (Bristol, Jordans, 2008) [7.22].

[140]   See generally Nolan, 'Equitable Property' (above n 131) 255–56; M Conaglen, 'Thinking about Proprietary Remedies for Breach of Confidence' [2008] *Intellectual Property Quarterly* 82, 88–90; RC Nolan, 'Controlling Fiduciary Power' [2009] *Cambridge Law Journal* 293, 295.

[141]   *Mothew* (above n 17) 16.

3

Peculiarly Fiduciary Duties

The ultimate purpose of this book is to identify the nature and function of fiduciary loyalty by analysing the fiduciary duties that comprise that notion of loyalty. As the previous chapter explained and sought to justify, the analysis is a sustained application of the approach endorsed by Millett LJ in *Bristol & West Building Society v Mothew*, proceeding by reference 'to those duties which are peculiar to fiduciaries ... not every breach of duty by a fiduciary is a breach of fiduciary duty'.[1] Therefore, before the analysis can begin in earnest, one must identify which duties are peculiar to fiduciaries, because it is those duties—and not others—that must be analysed.

I. Duty to Perform the Task Undertaken

An obvious place to start is with a trustee's fundamental duty to perform the trusts that he has undertaken: 'The basic right of a beneficiary is to have the trust duly administered in accordance with the provisions of the trust instrument, if any, and the general law.'[2] The trustee's duty to obey the directions of the trust settlement (provided those directions are lawful) is 'the most important of all the rules relating to the duties of trustees'.[3] But it does not follow that the duty is peculiar to fiduciaries. Anyone who has undertaken a legally enforceable duty to act in a particular manner—whether by way of contract, by assumption of a responsibility that is given effect by the law of tort or under a trust—is expected to perform that obligation or to provide recompense in the event that he fails to do so.

Undertaking to perform a task can create a legally enforceable duty to do so, but that legal obligation can arise outside any fiduciary relationship just as well as it can arise within such a relationship. A solicitor's obligation to perform his

---

[1] *Bristol & West Building Society v Mothew* [1998] Ch 1, 16.
[2] *Target Holdings Ltd v Redferns* [1996] AC 421, 434.
[3] A Underhill and DJ Hayton, *Law Relating to Trusts and Trustees*, 17th edn by DJ Hayton, PB Matthews and CCJ Mitchell (London, LexisNexis Butterworths, 2007) [47.2]. See also *Re Brogden* (1888) 38 ChD 546, 571 (CA).

retainer, which has its legal force by virtue of the law of contract, is not different in conceptual terms from the contractual obligation that arises when a horse breeder agrees to sell one of his stock. The terms of those two contracts will undoubtedly differ, but the obligation is fundamentally contractual in nature and is, at root, an obligation to perform the tasks that have been agreed. Similarly, when a trustee agrees to act as such, he agrees to perform the trust as set out in the trust deed. That duty is not fundamentally different from the duty that arises when two parties enter into a contract, as Lord Thurlow observed in *York Buildings v Mackenzie*: 'no man can be trustee for another, but by contract.'[4] This is clearly an overstatement, in that it does not deal with self declarations of trust, and trusts are not necessarily contracts, but it serves to emphasise that a trustee's duty to obey the terms of the trust is not peculiar to fiduciaries in that it is not radically different from the duty that arises when someone has made a legally binding undertaking, whether by contract or otherwise, to perform a particular function. Contractual and tort-based duties are not peculiar to fiduciaries because they can be owed by actors who owe no fiduciary duties. Thus, for example, a contractual duty to account for property received sounds in a claim for damages for breach of contract, rather than as a claim for breach of fiduciary duty—it is simply a claim for breach of an undertaking to act in a particular way.[5]

The conclusion that the duty to perform one's undertaking is not peculiarly fiduciary in nature is also supported by *Breen v Williams*. In particular, as was mentioned in the preceding chapter, Gummow J made it clear that a trustee's duty to obey the terms of the trust is not a fiduciary obligation:

> [T]he trustee is required both to observe the terms of the trust and, in doing so, to exercise the same care as an ordinary, prudent person of business would exercise . . . The trustee is, of course, a fiduciary. But the above obligations arise from a particular characteristic, not of fiduciary obligations generally, but of the trust.[6]

The duty to perform the trust arises not from the fiduciary nature of trusteeship but rather from the fact that the trustee has undertaken that responsibility.

The same point emerges if one considers duties owed by other fiduciaries. For example, fiduciaries will often be obliged to disclose information to their clients in order to provide the assistance that the clients have sought. Thus, for example, solicitors retained to advise a client regarding a specific transaction are obliged to

---

[4] *York Buildings Co v Mackenzie* (1795) 3 Paton 378, 393 (1 Scots RR 717). Lord Nottingham LC also said that "trust is a kind of contract": see DEC Yale, *Lord Nottingham's 'Manual of Chancery' and 'Prolegomena of Chancery and Equity'* (Cambridge, Cambridge University Press, 1965) 238 (*Prolegomena*, ch XII.12). See also *Boson v Sandford* (1690) 1 Show KB 101, 104 (89 ER 477); FW Maitland, *Equity*, 2nd edn rev by J Brunyate (Cambridge, Cambridge University Press, 1936) 54; JH Langbein, 'The Contractarian Basis of the Law of Trusts' (1995) 105 *Yale Law Journal* 625, 650–69; WH Bryson, *Cases Concerning Equity and the Courts of Equity 1550–1660*, vol 1 (London, Selden Society, vol 117, 2001) xxv.

[5] *Paragon Finance plc v DB Thakerar & Co* [1999] 1 All ER 400, 416 (CA); *Coulthard v Disco Mix Club Ltd* [2000] 1 WLR 707, 728 (ChD).

[6] *Breen v Williams* (1996) 186 CLR 71, 137.

disclose information that might affect the client's decision to enter into the transaction.[7] However, the fact that fiduciaries (such as solicitors) can owe such duties does not mean that those duties are fiduciary in nature, given the number of other non-fiduciary persons who owe duties to similar effect. For example, a car mechanic reporting to his customer on the condition of a car prior to its purchase by the customer owes a duty to disclose relevant information and yet would not ordinarily be thought to occupy a fiduciary position vis-à-vis his customer.[8] 'In commercial relationships advice may be given or recommendations made which do not give rise to a fiduciary relationship, eg, banker and customer, petrol company and garage proprietor, landlord and tenant combined with that of employer and employee.'[9]

The particular circumstances of the parties in individual instances of these sorts of relationships can give rise to fiduciary duties, as was the case between a bank and its customer in *Commonwealth Bank of Australia v Smith*,[10] but the fact that they do not do so in all cases indicates that they involve duties that are not peculiar to fiduciaries. In other words, the legal duty to perform an undertaking is not peculiar to fiduciaries. As the Privy Council emphasised in *Goldcorp*, a pleading of fiduciary duty must identify duties that go beyond the mere existence of a contractual obligation to perform an undertaking:

> No doubt the fact that one person is placed in a particular position vis-à-vis another through the medium of a contract does not necessarily mean that he does not also owe fiduciary duties to that other by virtue of being in that position. But the essence of a fiduciary relationship is that it creates obligations of a different character from those deriving from the contract itself. Their Lordships have not heard in argument any submission which went beyond suggesting that by virtue of being a fiduciary the company was obliged honestly and conscientiously to do what it had by contract promised to do.[11]

---

[7]   See, eg, *Spector v Ageda* [1973] Ch 30, 48; *Mortgage Express Ltd v Bowerman & Partners* [1996] 2 All ER 836, 842 (CA).

[8]   PD Finn, *Fiduciary Obligations* (Sydney, Law Book Co, 1977) [397], [399] and [400]; PD Finn, 'The Fiduciary Principle' in TG Youdan (ed), *Equity, Fiduciaries and Trusts* (Toronto, Carswell, 1989) 1, 40; PD Finn, 'Contract and the Fiduciary Principle' (1989) 12 *University of New South Wales Law Journal* 76, 93; RC Nolan, 'The Legal Control of Directors' Conflicts of Interest in the United Kingdom: Non-Executive Directors Following the Higgs Report' (2005) 6 *Theoretical Inquiries in Law* 413, 422. Cf R Flannigan, 'Fiduciary Mechanics' (2008) 14 *Canadian Labour & Employment Law Journal* 25, which is based on a theory as to the incidence of fiduciary duties that is criticised below in ch 9, section I-D.

[9]   *Indata Equipment Supplies Ltd v ACL Ltd* [1998] FSR 248, 254 (CA). See also *Pilmer v Duke Group Ltd* [2001] HCA 31 at [73]–[75], (2001) 207 CLR 165.

[10]   *Commonwealth Bank of Australia v Smith* (1991) 42 FCR 390, 392. See also the examples given in JA McGhee (ed), *Snell's Equity*, 31st edn (London, Sweet & Maxwell, 2005) [7–09]–[7–10].

[11]   *Re Goldcorp Exchange Ltd* [1995] 1 AC 74, 98.

II. Duties of Care and Skill

Duties of care and skill are also not peculiar to fiduciaries, given that many non-fiduciary actors are required to act carefully when performing their duties. As was mentioned in the last chapter, Southin J complained in *Girardet v Crease & Co* that 'to say that simple carelessness in giving advice is . . . a breach [of fiduciary duty] is a perversion of words.'[12] Her reason was that such carelessness, if committed by an engineer or physician, would not be so described. In other words, the law's insistence on careful conduct is not peculiar to fiduciaries. Similarly, in *Permanent Building Society v Wheeler*, Ipp J observed that 'a trustee's duty to exercise reasonable care, though equitable, is not specifically a fiduciary duty.'[13] Gummow J expressed the same conclusion in *Breen v Williams* in the passage quoted in the preceding section of this chapter,[14] as did Millett LJ, almost contemporaneously, in *Mothew*: 'It is similarly inappropriate to apply the expression [fiduciary duty] to the obligation of a trustee or other fiduciary to use proper skill and care in the discharge of his duties.'[15]

Lord Browne-Wilkinson's comments in *Henderson v Merrett* are also consistent with this approach, although somewhat less clearly expressed. The House of Lords unanimously accepted that agents who had managed the insurance business of the plaintiffs could be sued in tort for negligence, but Lord Browne-Wilkinson added that a further claim, which had asserted the agents could be sued for breach of a fiduciary duty to take care in their management of the insurance business, was misconceived. While his speech refers to 'fiduciary duties of care',[16] he explained that the claim for breach of a fiduciary duty of care was misconceived:

> The liability of a fiduciary for the negligent transaction of his duties is not a separate head of liability but the paradigm of the general duty to act with care imposed by law on those who take it upon themselves to act for or advise others . . . [T]he duties which the managing agents have assumed to undertake in managing the insurance business of the Names brings them clearly into the category of those who are liable, *whether fiduciaries or not*, for any lack of care in the conduct of that management (emphasis added).[17]

Undoubtedly, many fiduciaries owe duties of care—as in the case of most trustees, directors and solicitors—but many non-fiduciaries also owe duties of care. The fundamental substance of the obligation does not depend upon whether the duty-bound person is a fiduciary. The duty of care is not peculiar to fiduciaries and so 'is not to be equated with or termed a "fiduciary" duty'.[18]

---

[12]   *Girardet v Crease & Co* (1987) 11 BCLR (2d) 361, 362.
[13]   *Permanent Building Society v Wheeler* (1994) 11 WAR 187, 237.
[14]   See text accompanying n 6 above.
[15]   *Mothew* (above n 1) 16.
[16]   *Henderson v Merrett Syndicates Ltd* [1995] 2 AC 145, 205.
[17]   *Ibid.*
[18]   *Permanent Building Society* (above n 13) 239.

This approach has been applied in subsequent cases.[19] Thus, for example, in *Nationwide Building Society v Vanderpump*, a solicitor was held to have acted in breach of duty when he failed to act as a solicitor of ordinary competence would have acted in the circumstances,[20] but Blackburne J rejected the submission that the solicitor's conduct amounted to a breach of fiduciary duty.[21] Similarly, in *S v Attorney-General* the Court of Appeal of New Zealand observed that 'negligent conduct by a fiduciary will render the fiduciary liable in negligence but is not a breach qua fiduciary, notwithstanding that the fulfilment of the role of a fiduciary is the setting for the negligent act or omission.'[22]

Three further points need to be emphasised in this context. First, it is not being suggested that duties of care are always identical in the degree of care that they require, irrespective of whether the person who owes the duty is a fiduciary or not. That is patently not the case: it is clear that different people can owe different duties of care. As Millett LJ himself recognised in *Mothew*, 'the standard of care is not always the same.'[23] Furthermore, there are subtle differences in the way that equitable and common law duties of care are applied,[24] although these differences are not necessarily great.[25] The different standards of care that are imposed upon different kinds of actors respond to the differences in the circumstances in which those actors are required to perform their undertakings to others. However, those are not differences that depend necessarily on the fact that some actors are fiduciaries while others are not. Directors and trustees—both of which are settled categories of fiduciary relationship—are (or at least have been[26]) held to different standards of care in their conduct.[27] The duty of care reflects differing expectations, based upon the different circumstances within which directors and trustees operate. But the different standards of care are differences of degree rather than kind. Fundamentally, a duty of care is a duty to act carefully in performing the tasks that have been undertaken. That is the case irrespective of whether the person who has undertaken the task is a fiduciary.

---

[19] See, eg, *Ultraframe (UK) Ltd v Fielding* [2005] EWHC 1638 (Ch) at [1300]–[1302]; *Extrasure Travel Insurances Ltd v Scattergood* [2002] EWHC 3093 (Ch) at [87] and [89], [2003] 1 BCLC 598; *Base Metal Trading Ltd v Shamurin* [2004] EWCA Civ 1316 at [19], [2005] 1 All ER (Comm) 17. See also *JD Wetherspoon plc v Van de Berg & Co Ltd* [2009] EWHC 639 (Ch) at [420]–[421].

[20] *Nationwide Building Society v Vanderpump* [1999] Lloyd's Rep PN 422, 434 (ChD).

[21] *Ibid*, 431.

[22] *S v Attorney-General* [2003] 3 NZLR 450 at [77] (CA). See also *A v Roman Catholic Archdiocese of Wellington* [2007] 1 NZLR 536 at [498]–[499] (HC).

[23] *Mothew* (above n 1) 16.

[24] See, eg, *Medforth v Blake* [2000] Ch 86, 98 (CA); *Yorkshire Bank plc v Hall* [1999] 1 WLR 1713, 1728 (CA); *Downsview Nominees Ltd v First City Corp Ltd* [1993] AC 295, 316 (PC).

[25] *Lagunas Nitrate Co v Lagunas Syndicate* [1899] 2 Ch 392, 435 and 437 (CA).

[26] There has been an increase in the standard of care expected of directors in more recent times: BR Cheffins, *Company Law: Theory, Structure and Operation* (Oxford, Oxford University Press, 1997) 539; G Morse, *Charlesworth's Company Law*, 17th edn (London, Sweet & Maxwell, 2005) 311–12; *Dorchester Finance Co Ltd v Stebbing* [1989] BCLC 498, 501–2. This change has now been enshrined in statute in the United Kingdom: Companies Act 2006, s 174; PL Davies, *Gower and Davies' Principles of Modern Company Law*, 8th edn (London, Sweet & Maxwell, 2008) [16–12]–[16–15].

[27] See above ch 2, section II-A.

The second point to be emphasised is that cases decided before the adoption of the modern approach need to be read in the light of the fact that the new approach is a departure from the historical use of the fiduciary concept. It is clear, for example, that courts in the past have used the existence of a fiduciary relationship as a justification for the recognition of duties of care. In *Woods v Martins Bank*,[28] for example, Salmon J held that a fiduciary relationship arose when a bank manager agreed to advise his client, such that the manager owed a duty to act carefully in providing such advice. Similarly, one viable interpretation of *Nocton v Ashburton* is that the fiduciary relationship between Lord Ashburton and his solicitor, Nocton, provided a justification for holding Nocton bound to exercise care in the statements that he made to Ashburton.[29] Against that view, one can argue that *Nocton* is not simply a case of solicitor's liability for negligent misstatement, because Viscount Haldane LC indicated that such a claim would have failed for want of equity.[30] However, on the very next page of his speech, Viscount Haldane also said:

> [T]he facts alleged would none the less, if proved, have afforded ground for an action for mere negligence. . . It was really an action based on the exclusive jurisdiction of a Court of Equity over a defendant in a fiduciary position in respect of matters which at law would also have given a right to damages for negligence.[31]

If that was the true basis of *Nocton v Ashburton*,[32] then like *Woods v Martins Bank*, it can be understood as a situation in which the fiduciary relationship was used as a justification for exporting duties that might be owed by trustees to other similar situations. Trustees clearly owed a duty to exercise care in their conduct, and solicitors could be held to a similar duty on the basis of their fiduciary relationship with their clients at a time when common law duties of care were not as widespread as they are now. As was seen in the last chapter, the fiduciary concept was used historically to export duties from one kind of relationship to another. In that sense one could—and still can—talk about a fiduciary duty of care. With the 'staggering march' of negligence over the twentieth century,[33] that exporting function is no longer as important as it once was. This does not mean that the earlier cases were wrongly decided. But nor does it mean that the more modern insistence that the word 'fiduciary' be reserved for duties that are peculiar to fiduciaries is itself wrong. The word 'fiduciary' has been used in different ways at different times as the law of obligations has developed. Provided that is borne in mind, it is perfectly coherent to accept that

---

[28] *Woods v Martins Bank Ltd* [1959] 1 QB 55, 71–72.

[29] See *Nocton v Ashburton* [1914] AC 932, 947, 948, 957, 958, 964–65, 967, 969, 972 and 977–78.

[30] *Ibid*, 956, referring to *British Mutual Investment Co v Cobbold* (1875) LR 19 Eq 627 (VC).

[31] *Nocton v Ashburton* (above n 29) 957. See also *Chapman v Chapman* (1870) LR 9 Eq 276, 294 (VC).

[32] This issue is considered further below in ch 8, section II-A.

[33] See T Weir, 'The Staggering March of Negligence' in P Cane and J Stapleton (eds), *The Law of Obligations* (Oxford, Oxford University Press, 1998) 97.

'fiduciary' duties of care were recognised in the past, but that such duties of care are now no longer considered fiduciary because they are not peculiar to fiduciaries.

The Court of Appeal's far more recent reference to 'a fiduciary duty of care' in *Silven Properties v Royal Bank of Scotland*[34] is a little more difficult to understand. Ultimately, the case was decided by reference to the equitable principles that control a mortgagee's duty of care and their applicability to receivers. It is well settled that mortgagees do not owe fiduciary duties to their mortgagors with respect to the exercise of their powers.[35] In that light, the similarity between a receiver's duty of care and a mortgagee's duty of care provides no reason to treat either duty of care as fiduciary in nature. 'The fact that the source of the duty is to be found in equity rather than the common law does not make it a fiduciary duty.'[36] Indeed, the fact that mortgagees owe duties of care and yet do not owe fiduciary duties provides further evidence that the duty of care is not peculiar to fiduciaries.

The final point that must be addressed is Peter Birks' discussion of whether the duty of care is properly considered a fiduciary duty.[37] While accepting that 'fiduciary negligence' is an illusory wrong,[38] Birks argued of the trustee's duty of care:

> We must not say that it is not fiduciary. It is. We might say that it is not especially fiduciary, meaning only that its breach is not a wrong distinct from negligence... [I]t is a fiduciary obligation but is not, as such, distinguishable from any contractual or non-contractual duty of care.[39]

With respect, the idea of a duty that is fiduciary but 'not especially fiduciary' is unnecessarily confusing.[40] The source of the confusion is a conflation of the two

---

[34] *Silven Properties Ltd v Royal Bank of Scotland plc* [2003] EWCA Civ 1409 at [29], [2004] 1 WLR 997.

[35] See, eg, *Knight v Marjoribanks* (1849) 2 Mac & G 10, 13–14 (42 ER 4) (LC); *Warner v Jacob* (1882) 20 ChD 220, 224; *Melbourne Banking Corp Ltd v Brougham* (1882) 7 App Cas 307, 315 (PC); *Farrar v Farrars Ltd* (1888) 40 ChD 395, 398 and 410–11 (ChD and CA); *Colson v Williams* (1889) 58 LJ Ch 539, 540; *Kennedy v De Trafford* [1896] 1 Ch 762, 772 (CA); *Cuckmere Brick Co Ltd v Mutual Finance Ltd* [1971] Ch 949, 965–66 (CA); *Bishop v Bonham* [1988] 1 WLR 742, 749–50 (CA); *China and South Sea Bank Ltd v Tan* [1990] 1 AC 536, 545 (PC); *Burgess v Auger* [1998] 2 BCLC 478, 482 (ChD); *Bell v Long* [2008] EWHC 1273 (Ch) at [12]–[17]; WR Fisher and JM Lightwood, *Law of Mortgage*, 12th edn by W Clark (ed) (London, LexisNexis Butterworths, 2006) [30.22]; RE Megarry and HWR Wade, *The Law of Real Property*, 7th edn by C Harpum, S Bridge and MJ Dixon (London, Sweet & Maxwell, 2008) [25–018]; Finn, *Fiduciary Obligations* (above n 8) [17]; McGhee (ed) (above n 10) [38–38].

[36] *Mothew* (above n 1) 16.

[37] This point is returned to below in ch 8, section II-A, when the relationship between fiduciary duties and torts is addressed.

[38] PBH Birks, 'The Content of Fiduciary Obligation' (2000) 34 *Israel Law Review* 3, 35 (republished at (2002) 16 *Trust Law International* 34).

[39] *Ibid*, 36.

[40] A similar confusion underlies Charles Hollander and Simon Salzedo's assertion that 'fiduciary duties are separate, albeit to a large degree co-extensive with the contractual duties' of a professional: C Hollander and S Salzedo, *Conflicts of Interest*, 3rd edn (London, Sweet & Maxwell, 2008) at [2–009].

senses in which the word 'fiduciary' has been used. In the historical sense, whereby the word fiduciary refers to duties that are similar to those owed by trustees, the duty of care has been treated as fiduciary. But in the more modern sense, whereby the word is reserved for duties that are peculiar to fiduciaries, the duty of care is not fiduciary because, as Birks pointed out, it is not distinguishable from duties of care owed in contract and tort. Birks' statement attempts to assert both meanings of the word 'fiduciary' at once. That is possible, provided it is made clear that the word is being used in two distinct senses. In contrast, Birks appears to attempt to treat the word as having a single, unitary meaning, but one that represents both of the senses just described. If one is applying the more modern approach endorsed in *Mothew*, as this book seeks to do, it is more coherent to accept that duties of care are not peculiar to fiduciaries and so do not merit consideration as 'fiduciary' duties.

III. Conflict and Profit Principles

Whereas the two duties that have just been considered are not peculiar to fiduciaries, two further equitable principles clearly are peculiar to fiduciaries: first, the principle that prohibits a fiduciary from acting in a situation in which there is a conflict between the duty that he owes to his principal and his personal interest; and secondly, the principle that prohibits a fiduciary from receiving any unauthorised profit as a result of the fiduciary position. In a classic statement of these two propositions, Lord Herschell said in *Bray v Ford*:

> It is an inflexible rule of a Court of Equity that a person in a fiduciary position . . . is not, unless otherwise expressly provided, entitled to make a profit; he is not allowed to put himself in a position where his interest and duty conflict.[41]

These two principles are widely recognised as being of universal application to fiduciaries,[42] and they are peculiar to fiduciaries in the sense that neither they, nor functionally equivalent alternative doctrines, are applied to actors who are not considered to occupy fiduciary positions. In other words, it is these duties that are particularly associated with the fiduciary concept. For example, in the Court of Appeal in *Breen v Williams*, Meagher JA observed that if one categorises a doctor as a fiduciary, and one asks why that categorisation might matter,

---

[41] *Bray v Ford* [1896] AC 44, 51.
[42] *Aberdeen Railway Co v Blaikie Bros* (1854) 1 Macq 461, 471 (149 RR 32); C Harpum, 'Fiduciary Obligations and Fiduciary Powers: Where are We Going?' in PBH Birks (ed), *Privacy and Loyalty* (Oxford, Oxford University Press, 1997) 145, 146–47; R Cooter and BJ Freedman, 'The Fiduciary Relationship: Its Economic Character and Legal Consequences' (1991) 66 *New York University Law Review* 1045, 1054.

it is generally only to generate the usual fiduciary duties in certain circumstances—not to profit at his patient's expense (beyond his agreed fees) and not to put himself in a position where his interest would conflict with his patient's.[43]

There is an ongoing debate as to whether the profit principle is a wholly contained subset of the conflict principle or instead a separate but related principle. That issue will be addressed later.[44] It does not affect the point that matters at this stage, which is that the conflict and profit principles are peculiar in their application to fiduciaries. As Ernest Weinrib put it, the conflict principle is 'the irreducible core of the fiduciary obligation'.[45] As such, whether they are two separate principles or merely one, the conflict and profit principles clearly merit close consideration in this book.

IV. Good Faith

It is somewhat more difficult to determine whether the duty of good faith is a peculiarly fiduciary duty. Undoubtedly, fiduciaries must act in good faith. Indeed, Millett LJ described the duty of good faith as one of the core facets of a fiduciary's duty of loyalty in his judgment in *Mothew*.[46] Furthermore, the duty to act in good faith forms part of the 'irreducible core of obligations owed by trustees'.[47] However, just as a trustee's duty of care is not a fiduciary duty, the core obligations of trustees are not necessarily all fiduciary. It has already been seen that a trustee's fundamental duty to perform the trust is not a peculiarly fiduciary duty.[48] The fact that two or more duties are applied in common in a given situation does not necessarily entail commonality in the nature of those duties. So, it is suggested that the duty of good faith is not peculiar to fiduciaries.[49]

In particular, a duty of good faith has frequently been recognised in circumstances that are not traditionally considered to be fiduciary relationships and when fiduciary analysis played no part in reaching the court's conclusion. In numerous cases, for example, courts have held that discretionary powers in contracts had to be exercised in good faith. Thus, for example, in *Groom v Crocker*, the Court of Appeal held that an insurer's discretion to exercise control

---

[43] *Breen v Williams* (1994) 35 NSWLR 522, 570 (CA).

[44] See below ch 5, section III-A.

[45] EJ Weinrib, 'The Fiduciary Obligation' (1975) 25 *University of Toronto Law Journal* 1, 16. See also *South Australia v Peat Marwick Mitchell & Co* (1997) 24 ACSR 231, 264 (SASC). And see J Edelman and J Davies, 'Torts and Equitable Wrongs' in A Burrows (ed), *English Private Law*, 2nd edn (Oxford, Oxford University Press, 2007) ch 17 at [17.349], describing this as 'the characteristic fiduciary obligation'.

[46] *Mothew* (above n 1) 18.

[47] *Armitage v Nurse* [1998] Ch 241, 253–54 (CA); DJ Hayton, 'The Irreducible Core Content of Trusteeship' in AJ Oakley (ed), *Trends in Contemporary Trust Law* (Oxford, Oxford University Press, 1996) 47, 57–58.

[48] See above section I.

[49] See also Finn, 'The Fiduciary Principle' (above n 8) 3–4 and 10–26.

over litigation involving the insured was effective 'to give to the insurers the right to decide upon the proper tactics to pursue in the conduct of the action, provided that they do so in what they bona fide consider to be the common interest of themselves and their assured'.[50] In *Price v Bouch*, Millett J held that a committee with power to administer a scheme of development involving mutual restrictive covenants was bound to reach its decisions 'honestly and in good faith and not for some improper purposes'.[51] In *The Product Star*, the Court of Appeal held that a ship-owner's discretion under a charter-party to determine whether foreign ports were too dangerous had to be 'exercised honestly and in good faith [and] having regard to the provisions of the contract by which it is conferred, it must not be exercised arbitrarily, capriciously or unreasonably'.[52] In *Paragon Finance v Nash*, the Court of Appeal held that a mortgagee's contractual power to alter the level of a variable rate of interest was not completely unfettered. Rather, 'there were terms to be implied ... that the rates of interest would not be set dishonestly, for an improper purpose, capriciously or arbitrarily'.[53] And in *Gan Insurance v Tai Ping Insurance*, the Court of Appeal held that a reinsurer's discretion to withhold approval of a settlement entered into by the insurer should be exercised 'in good faith after consideration of and on the basis of the facts giving rise to the particular claim and not with reference to considerations wholly extraneous to the subject matter of the particular reinsurance'.[54] Mance LJ emphasised that this conclusion did not arise from any principles or considerations that were peculiar to insurance law. In other words, the duty was implied as a matter of fact, rather than as a matter of law: the court's conclusion was based on normal contractual construction, taking into account the nature and purpose of the relevant contractual provisions and the factual matrices of the particular cases.[55] Other examples of this process exist.[56] Without turning the analysis into a lengthy list of such instances, it is clear that the courts have often recognised a duty that requires contractual discretions to be exercised in good faith. Importantly in the present

---

[50] *Groom v Crocker* [1939] 1 KB 194, 203.

[51] *Price v Bouch* (1986) 53 P & CR 257, 261 (ChD).

[52] *Abu Dhabi National Tanker Co v Product Star Shipping Line Ltd (The 'Product Star') (No 2)* [1993] 1 Lloyd's Rep 397, 404 (CA).

[53] *Paragon Finance plc v Nash* [2001] EWCA Civ 1466 at [36], [2002] 1 WLR 685; see also at [32].

[54] *Gan Insurance Co Ltd v Tai Ping Insurance Co Ltd (No 2)* [2001] EWCA Civ 1047 at [67], [2001] 2 All ER (Comm) 299 *per* Mance LJ; see also at [76] and [81] *per* Latham LJ, but cf at [91] *per* Sir Christopher Staughton.

[55] *Ibid* at [68]. See also *Price v Bouch* (above n 51) 260; *Lymington Marina Ltd v Macnamara* [2007] EWCA Civ 151 at [34], [2007] 2 All ER (Comm) 825.

[56] See, eg, *Midcon Oil & Gas Ltd v New British Dominion Oil Co Ltd* [1958] SCR 314, 326; *Smith v Morgan* [1971] 1 WLR 803, 808 (ChD); *Cobelfret NV v Cyclades Shipping Co Ltd (The 'Linardos')* [1994] 1 Lloyd's Rep 28, 32 (QBD, Comm Ct); *Phillips Electronique Grand Public SA v British Sky Broadcasting Ltd* [1995] Entertainment & Media Law Rep 472, 484 (CA); *Balfour Beatty Civil Engineering Ltd v Docklands Light Railway* [1996] Commercial Law Cases 1435, 1442 (CA); *Ludgate Insurance Co Ltd v Citibank NA* [1998] Lloyd's Rep IR 221 at [35]; *Burger King Corp v Hungry Jack's Pty Ltd* [2001] NSWCA 187 at [183]–[187], (2001) 69 NSWLR 558; *Redwood Master Fund Ltd v TD Bank Europe Ltd* [2002] EWHC 2703 (Ch) at [105], [2006] 1 BCLC 149; *Lymington Marina Ltd v Macnamara* [2007] EWCA Civ 151 at [42] and [44], [2007] 2 All ER (Comm) 825; *Socimer*

context, these conclusions have been reached on the basis of the normal process of contractual construction, without resorting to fiduciary principles or analysis in any way.

In certain other categories of relationship, duties of good faith have also been implied as a matter of law. Again, these conclusions have been reached without any resort to fiduciary analysis. It is clear, for example, that a mortgagee's powers (such as the power of sale) must be exercised by the mortgagee in good faith.[57] This is so, notwithstanding that mortgagees do not owe fiduciary duties when exercising those powers.[58] Similarly, employers have been held to owe a duty of good faith in dealings with their employees.[59] And in Australia, some decisions suggest that an obligation may be implied by law into all commercial contracts

---

International Bank Ltd v Standard Bank London Ltd [2008] EWCA Civ 116 at [60]–[64] and [66], [2008] 1 Lloyd's Rep 558; *Office of Fair Trading v Abbey National plc* [2008] EWHC 875 (Comm) at [79].

[57] See, eg, *Downsview Nominees* (above n 24) 312, 315 and 317; *Yorkshire Bank plc v Hall* (above n 24) 1728. See also *Kennedy v De Trafford* [1897] AC 180, 185; *Medforth v Blake* (above n 24) 98, 102 and 103.

[58] See above n 35.

[59] See, eg, *Imperial Group Pension Trust Ltd v Imperial Tobacco Ltd* [1991] 1 WLR 589, 597 (ChD); *Malik v Bank of Credit and Commerce International SA* [1997] Industrial Relations Law Rep 462, 465–66 and 468–69 (HL); *National Grid Co plc v Laws* [1997] Occupational Pensions Law Rep 207, 225 (ChD); *Fortex Group Ltd v MacIntosh* [1998] 3 NZLR 171, 180 (CA); *National Grid Co plc v Mayes* [2000] Industrial Cases Rep 174 at [42] (CA); *Johnson v Unisys Ltd* [2001] UKHL 13 at [24], [2003] 1 AC 518; *Hagen v ICI Chemicals and Polymers Ltd* [2002] Industrial Relations Law Rep 31, 30–31 (QBD).
The converse proposition, that employees owe a duty of good faith to their employers, also supports the argument made in the text, in that English courts recognise such a duty while also holding that ordinary employees (as distinct from senior employees) do not necessarily owe fiduciary duties to their employers: see, eg, *Nottingham University v Fishel* [2000] Industrial Relations Law Rep 471, 482–84 (QBD); *Helmet Integrated Systems Ltd v Tunnard* [2006] EWCA Civ 1735 at [26] and [36], [2007] Industrial Relations Law Rep 126; *British Midland Tool Ltd v Midland International Tooling Ltd* [2003] EWHC 466 (Ch) at [94], [2003] 2 BCLC 523; *Hanco ATM Systems Ltd v Cashbox ATM Systems Ltd* [2007] EWHC 1599 (Ch) at [56]–[57] and [63]; *Crowson Fabrics Ltd v Rider* [2007] EWHC 2942 (Ch) at [77]–[87], [2008] Industrial Relations Law Rep 288. See also A Stafford and S Ritchie, *Fiduciary Duties: Directors and Employees* (Bristol, Jordans, 2008) ch 3. And see *RBC Dominion Securities Inc v Merrill Lynch Canada Inc* [2008] SCC 54 at [46]. This point is weakened slightly by the fact that Australian courts appear somewhat more ready to treat *all* employees as a class of fiduciaries: see, eg, *Hospital Products Ltd v United States Surgical Corp* (1984) 156 CLR 41, 96; *Concut Pty Ltd v Worrell* [2000] HCA 64 at [17], (2000) 176 ALR 693; *Harris v Digital Pulse Pty Ltd* [2003] NSWCA 10 at [5], [37], [43], [121] and [396], (2003) 56 NSWLR 298. But the Australian cases are not unanimous in this regard: see, eg, *Francis v South Sydney District Rugby League Football Club Ltd* [2002] FCA 1306 at [267]; *Victoria University of Technology v Wilson* [2004] VSC 33 at [145]; *Woolworths Ltd v Olson* [2004] NSWSC 849 at [212]–[217], (2004) 63 Intellectual Prop Rep 258. Nonetheless, the Australian position does not entail that *all* of an employee's duties are necessarily fiduciary duties.
The English position has been criticised on the basis of an historical doctrinal analysis (R Flannigan, 'The [Fiduciary] Duty of Fidelity' (2008) 124 *Law Quarterly Review* 274) but without reference to the changed nature of the employment relationship over the relevant period, as to which see SF Deakin, 'The Evolution of the Contract of Employment, 1900–1950: The Influence of the Welfare State' in N Whiteside and R Salais (eds), *Governance, Industry and Labour Markets in Britain and France: The Modernising State in the Mid-Twentieth Century* (London, Routledge, 1998) 212; MR Freedland, *The Personal Employment Contract* (Oxford, Oxford University Press, 2003); SF Deakin and GS Morris, *Labour Law*, 4th edn (Oxford, Hart, 2005) [1–16]–[1.19].

requiring both parties to act in good faith,[60] although other decisions suggest that this will not always be the case.[61] The important point is that in these various cases the courts have been careful to make clear that a duty of good faith, when it is recognised, is not a fiduciary duty. One can identify numerous instances of that point being emphasised by courts which have recognised duties of good faith.[62]

A very clear example is found in the cases that discuss an employer's power to withhold consent to proposed amendments to the company's pension scheme. In *Imperial Group Pension Trust v Imperial Tobacco*, which has been described as 'the seminal judgment'[63] in the area, Browne-Wilkinson VC held that, notwithstanding that there was 'no express limitation on the company's right to give or withhold consent',[64] the employer owed an obligation to exercise its discretion in good faith.[65] That obligation arose as an implied term in the contract of employment[66] and also on the basis of an implied limitation on the powers contained in the pension trust deed.[67] Importantly for present purposes, Browne-Wilkinson VC made it explicitly clear that the employer did not owe any fiduciary duties with respect to the exercise of that power.[68] This approach has been followed in subsequent cases.[69] In other words, a duty of good faith was owed,

---

[60] See, eg, *Burger King Corp v Hungry Jack's Pty Ltd* [2001] NSWCA 187 at [163]–[164], (2001) 69 NSWLR 558; *Overlook Management BV v Foxtel Management Pty Ltd* [2002] NSWSC 17 at [59]–[65]; *Commonwealth Development Bank of Australia Pty Ltd v Cassegrain* [2002] NSWSC 965 at [210]; *Vodafone Pacific Ltd v Mobile Innovations Ltd* [2004] NSWCA 15 at [125]; *Pacific Brands Sport & Leisure Pty Ltd v Underworks Pty Ltd* [2005] FCA 288 at [64] (although cf the appeal: [2006] FCAFC 40); *PRP Diagnostic Imaging Pty Ltd v Pittwater Radiology Pty Ltd* [2008] NSWSC 701 at [99]. Other decisions treat the principle as applying to particular classes of contract: see, eg, *Far Horizons Pty Ltd v McDonald's Australia Ltd* [2000] VSC 310 at [120]. See also *GEC Marconi Systems Pty Ltd v BHP Information Technology Pty Ltd* [2003] FCA 50 at [920], (2003) 128 FCR 1.

[61] See, eg, *Vodafone Pacific v Mobile Innovations* (*ibid*) [191]; *Esso Australia Resources Pty Ltd v Southern Pacific Petroleum NL* [2005] VSCA 228 at [25]; *Australian Hotels Association (NSW) v TAB Ltd* [2006] NSWSC 293 at [78]; *Agricultural & Rural Finance Pty Ltd v Atkinson* [2006] NSWSC 202 at [71]; *CGU Workers Compensation (NSW) Ltd v Garcia* [2007] NSWCA 193 at [131]–[134] and [167]–[168], (2007) 69 NSWLR 680; *Reliance Developments (NSW) Pty Ltd v Lumley General Insurance Ltd* [2008] NSWSC 172 at [51]; *Hunter Valley Skydiving Centre Pty Ltd v Central Coast Aero Club Ltd* [2008] NSWSC 539 at [48]; *Insight Oceania Pty Ltd v Philips Electronics Australia Ltd* [2008] NSWSC 710 at [174]–[175].

[62] See, eg, *Midcon Oil & Gas v New British Dominion Oil* (above n 56) 326; *Nottingham University v Fishel* (above n 59) 483–84; *National Grid v Mayes* [2000] (above n 59) [42]; *Johnson v Unisys Ltd* [2001] UKHL 13 at [24], [2003] 1 AC 518; *National Grid Co plc v Mayes* [2001] UKHL 20 at [11], [2001] 1 WLR 864; *Burger King Corp v Hungry Jack's Pty Ltd* [2001] NSWCA 187 at [187], (2001) 69 NSWLR 558; *Overlook Management v Foxtel* (above n 60) [67]; *CGU Workers Compensation (NSW) Ltd v Garcia* [2007] NSWCA 193 at [60], (2007) 69 NSWLR 680; *Ross River Ltd v Cambridge City Football Club Ltd* [2007] EWHC 2115 (Ch) at [232], [2008] 1 All ER 1004.

[63] *Johnson v Unisys Ltd* [2001] UKHL 13 at [24], [2003] 1 AC 518; *National Grid v Laws* (above n 59) 225.

[64] *Imperial Group Pension Trust v Imperial Tobacco* (above n 59) 596.

[65] *Ibid*, 598–99.

[66] *Ibid*, 597.

[67] *Ibid*, 597–98.

[68] *Ibid*, 596. See also *Re Courage Group's Pension Schemes* [1987] 1 WLR 495, 514 (ChD).

[69] *National Grid v Laws* (above n 59) 227; *National Grid v Mayes* [2000] (above n 59) [42]; *Johnson v Unisys Ltd* [2001] UKHL 13 at [24], [2003] 1 AC 518. *Mettoy Pension Trustees Ltd v Evans*

but it was clear that no fiduciary duties were owed. Thus, there is no way in which the duty of good faith could be considered a fiduciary duty in these cases. That provides strong evidence that duties of good faith are not peculiar to fiduciaries and so ought not to be considered as fiduciary duties, at least when analysing the nature and function of duties that are peculiarly fiduciary.

It is perhaps worth emphasising that this is not to say that the duty of good faith cannot be described as a fiduciary duty, if all that is meant by that description is the historical sense by which duties were exported from the paradigm fiduciary office of trusteeship to other similarly situated positions. It is inconceivable that someone who owes duties akin to a trustee's duties would nonetheless be permitted to act in bad faith when performing those duties. But the point that matters here is that the duties of good faith are not peculiar to fiduciaries and so do not require detailed consideration in the context of an analysis of peculiarly fiduciary duties.

V. Proper Purposes Doctrine

The duty to act for proper purposes is also frequently referred to as a fiduciary duty, particularly in the context of company law.[70] However, for reasons related to those that apply to the duty of good faith, it is suggested that the duty to act for proper purposes is not a peculiarly fiduciary duty.

The duty to act for proper purposes is frequently recognised in circumstances in which a duty to act in good faith is also applied. Indeed, in some cases, the duty to act for proper purposes is treated as comprising a part of the duty to act in good faith. In *Imperial Group Pension Trust v Imperial Tobacco*, for example, Browne-Wilkinson VC held that 'the obligation of good faith does require that the company should exercise its rights ... not for the collateral purpose of forcing

---

[1990] 1 WLR 1587 (ChD), which held that an employer's power in such situations is subject to fiduciary limitations, was decided before *Imperial Group v Imperial Tobacco* and so without the benefit of its guidance, and is generally considered to have been wrongly decided on this point: *National Grid v Laws* (above n 59) 227.

[70] See, eg, *Spackman v Evans* (1868) LR 3 HL 171, 189–90; *Mills v Mills* (1938) 60 CLR 150, 185–86; *Re Smith and Fawcett Ltd* [1942] Ch 304, 308 (CA); *Hogg v Cramphorn Ltd* [1967] 1 Ch 254, 269; *Howard Smith Ltd v Ampol Petroleum Ltd* [1974] AC 821, 834 and 837–38 (PC); *Bishopsgate Investment Management Ltd v Maxwell (No 2)* [1994] 1 All ER 261, 265 (CA); *Extrasure Travel Insurances Ltd v Scattergood* [2002] EWHC 3093 (Ch) at [87], [2003] 1 BCLC 598; *Bell Group Ltd v Westpac Banking Corp (No 9)* [2008] WASC 239 at [4574]–[4575] and [4582]; EV Ferran, *Company Law and Corporate Finance* (Oxford, Oxford University Press, 1999) 157–60 and 162–68; RC Nolan, 'The Proper Purpose Doctrine and Company Directors' in BAK Rider (ed), *The Realm of Company Law* (London, Kluwer, 1998) 1, 12; R Teele Langford, 'The Fiduciary Nature of the Bona Fide and Proper Purposes Duties of Company Directors: *Bell Group Ltd (in liq) v Westpac Banking Group (No 9)*' (2009) 31 *Australian Bar Review* 326. See also LD Smith, 'The Motive, Not the Deed' in J Getzler (ed), *Rationalizing Property, Equity and Trusts* (London, LexisNexis, 2003) 53, 68–69.

members to give up their accrued rights in the existing fund.'[71] If the duty to act for proper purposes were merely an application of the duty to act in good faith, one could treat it as not peculiar to fiduciaries simply on the basis that the duty of good faith is not peculiar to fiduciaries: the greater would include the lesser.

However, it is unclear that the duty to act for proper purposes is merely a manifestation of the duty to act in good faith. Undoubtedly, the two duties overlap to a great extent, in that an exercise of a power for purposes foreign to those for which the power was granted will often involve conduct that could be categorised as being in bad faith. On the other hand, it is entirely conceivable that a power be may exercised for purposes beyond those for which it was granted, and yet the person doing so could honestly believe that it was appropriate to do so, thereby acting in good faith.[72] The Court of Appeal pointed out in *Medforth v Blake* that 'the breach of a duty of good faith should, in this area as in all others, require some dishonesty or improper motive, some element of bad faith, to be established.'[73] Such bad faith might be established by showing that the defendant acted 'wilfully and recklessly'[74] but not when the defendant acted entirely honestly. This is well illustrated by *Vodafone Pacific v Mobile Innovations*, in which the New South Wales Court of Appeal rejected an argument that the defendant owed a duty to act in good faith,[75] but Giles JA, with whom the other judges agreed, continued: 'That is not the end, and I come to exercise of a power for an extraneous purpose.'[76] Giles JA made clear that '*apart from* any implied obligations to co-operate and of good faith . . . the law has long provided remedies for the exercise of a power otherwise than for the purpose for which it is conferred'[77] (emphasis added).

It is safer, therefore, to separate the duty to act for proper purposes from the duty to act in good faith, although the two duties can clearly both apply in a given set of circumstances. The question remains, therefore, whether the duty to act for proper purposes is peculiar to fiduciaries. The cases suggest that it is not. As has already been mentioned, the duty to act for proper purposes has often been recognised alongside a duty to act in good faith in cases involving no fiduciary element. Thus, for example, in *Groom v Crocker*, in addition to holding that an insurer must act in good faith when controlling the insured's litigation, Greene MR added:

---

[71] *Imperial Group Pension Trust v Imperial Tobacco* (above n 59) 598–99. See also *National Grid v Laws* (above n 59) 227.

[72] See also RC Nolan, 'Controlling Fiduciary Power' [2009] *Cambridge Law Journal* 293, 298.

[73] *Medforth v Blake* (above n 24) 103. See also *Karger v Paul* [1984] VR 161, 164 (SC).

[74] *Kennedy v De Trafford* [1896] 1 Ch 762, 772 (CA) and [1897] AC 180, 185.

[75] *Vodafone Pacific v Mobile Innovations* (above n 60) [208].

[76] *Ibid* at [209].

[77] *Ibid* at [216].

[T]he insurers are in my opinion clearly not entitled to allow their judgment as to the best tactics to pursue to be influenced by the desire to obtain for themselves some advantage altogether outside the litigation in question with which the assured has no concern.[78]

Statements to the effect that various contractual discretions could not be exercised for an improper or collateral purpose have already been seen in the quotations provided earlier from Browne-Wilkinson VC's judgment in *Imperial Group Pension Trust v Imperial Tobacco*;[79] Millett J's decision in *Price v Bouch*;[80] and the Court of Appeal's decisions in *Paragon Finance v Nash*[81] and *Gan Insurance v Tai Ping Insurance*.[82] Similarly, following Browne-Wilkinson VC's statement in *Imperial Group Pension Trust v Imperial Tobacco*, Robert Walker J held in *National Grid v Laws* that 'the exercise of powers for collateral (and so improper) purposes'[83] was prohibited to the employer company. And the Court of Appeal explained in *Yorkshire Bank v Hall* that a mortgagee owes a 'general duty . . . to use his powers only for proper purposes, and to act in good faith'.[84]

These cases further support the view that the duty to act for proper purposes and the duty to act in good faith ought to be treated as distinct: it is unlikely that so many judges intended to engage in tautology. Secondly, they indicate that the duty to act for proper purposes is not peculiar to fiduciaries. None of the analysis provided in these cases was based on fiduciary considerations. Indeed, in several of the cases the existence of fiduciary duties was explicitly rejected by the courts, and yet those courts were prepared to recognise and enforce duties to act for proper purposes and in good faith.

Before leaving this point, it is worthwhile considering why the company law cases have described the duty to act for proper purposes as a fiduciary duty. The best explanation for this phenomenon is, again, the exporting function that the fiduciary concept performed historically. For example, in *Spackman v Evans*, the House of Lords held invalid an exercise by directors of their power to declare shares in the company forfeit. Lord Cranworth discussed the case on the basis that the directors owed duties 'as trustees'[85] when exercising the power, concluding:

---

[78] *Groom v Crocker* (above n 50) 203.
[79] See text accompanying n 71 above.
[80] See text accompanying n 51 above.
[81] See text accompanying n 53 above.
[82] See text accompanying n 54 above.
[83] *National Grid v Laws* (above n 59) 227.
[84] *Yorkshire Bank plc v Hall* (above n 24) 1728. See also *Downsview Nominees* (above n 24) 312, 315 and 317; *Medforth v Blake* (above n 24) 98, 102 and 103. This means that 'a power of sale is improperly exercised if it is *no* part of the mortgagee's purpose to recover the debt secured by the mortgage': *Meretz Investments NV v ACP Ltd* [2006] EWHC 74 (Ch) at [314], [2007] Ch 197, point not affected on appeal: [2007] EWCA Civ 1303.
[85] *Spackman v Evans* (above n 70) 187.

[I]n thus using the clause of forfeiture, the directors were applying it to a purpose foreign to that to which alone they would be justified in acting on it. . . That which the directors did was, therefore, what is called a fraud on the power, a breach of trust.[86]

This statement is important for two reasons in the present context. First, as was discussed in chapter two, directors are not trustees of a company's property, and Lord Cranworth's reference to trust principles indicates that he was drawing an analogy between trustees and directors for the purpose of identifying the duties owed by the latter. In other words, the fiduciary concept was put to work to export the incidents of trusts to the analogous situation of directors of a company. The fact that it was used in that way does not, however, mean that the duty is peculiar to fiduciaries.

The second important point to emerge from Lord Cranworth's statement arises out of his express treatment of the use of a power for an improper purpose as a 'fraud on the power'. In other words, the duty to act for proper purposes is a manifestation of the doctrine of fraud on a power.[87] This raises for consideration the question whether the doctrine of fraud on a power is a peculiarly fiduciary duty. It is suggested that it is not. It is clear, notwithstanding its name, that the doctrine of fraud on a power 'has little, if anything, to do with fraud'.[88] The Privy Council explained the doctrine in *Vatcher v Paull*:

> The term fraud in connection with frauds on a power does not necessarily denote any conduct on the part of the appointor amounting to fraud in the common law meaning of the term or any conduct which could be properly termed dishonest or immoral. It merely means that the power has been exercised for a purpose, or with an intention, beyond the scope of or not justified by the instrument creating the power.[89]

While the doctrine clearly does apply to powers held by fiduciaries, it applies more broadly than that, also controlling powers held by persons who are not fiduciaries, and so it is not peculiar to fiduciaries: it 'applies to all powers whether fiduciary or non-fiduciary'.[90] When a power is granted to another, the limits of that power are identified in the first instance by construction of the power. But even if the donee of the power acts within the literal terms of the power, the doctrine of fraud on a power prevents the donee from using the power for purposes outside, or 'foreign to',[91] those for which the power was granted. Thus,

---

[86] *Ibid*, 189–90. Similarly, see *Fraser v Whalley* (1864) 2 H & M 10, 28–30 (71 ER 361) (VC).

[87] See also KE Lindgren, 'The Fiduciary Nature of a Company Board's Power to Issue Shares' (1972) 10 *University of Western Australia Law Review* 364, 369; S Worthington, 'Corporate Governance: Remedying and Ratifying Directors' Breaches' (2000) 116 *Law Quarterly Review* 638, 648; R Grantham, 'Company Directors and Compliance with the Company's Constitution' (2003) 20 *New Zealand Universities Law Review* 450, 475; RP Austin, HAJ Ford and IM Ramsay, *Company Directors: Principles of Law and Corporate Governance* (Chatswood, LexisNexis Butterworths, 2005) [7.18].

[88] *Medforth v Blake* (above n 24) 103; *Kain v Hutton* [2008] NZSC 61 at [18], [2008] 3 NZLR 589.

[89] *Vatcher v Paull* [1915] AC 372, 378.

[90] McGhee (ed) (above n 10) [9–02]. See also Underhill and Hayton (above n 3) [1.76].

[91] *Spackman v Evans* (above n 70) 189.

for example, in *Hinchinbrooke v Seymour*,[92] Lord Thurlow LC held that a power of appointment over a trust fund could be exercised for several purposes that would benefit the objects, but its exercise by the objects' father (who held the power) for the purpose of obtaining the fund for himself was bad as it fell outside those permissible purposes. This is an application of the doctrine of fraud on a power,[93] in circumstances in which the power was held by someone who was not a trustee and did not occupy a fiduciary position.[94]

The doctrine of fraud on a power has been said not to be a matter of construction. In *Henty v Wrey*, for example, Lindley LJ commented that the issue of fraud on a power 'is intimately connected with the question of construction [but] there is considerable danger of confusion and error if they are not examined separately'.[95] However, while it is not a matter of pure construction of the letter of the power, the doctrine of fraud on a power is dependent on identifying the substance, or scope,[96] of the power that has been granted, because it is action beyond that scope which constitutes a fraud on the power.[97] Thus, explaining *Hinchinbrooke v Seymour* in *Re Queensberry Leases*, Lord Eldon LC emphasised that the exercise of the power of appointment had been bad, although it 'was according to the letter of the power', because it was '*substantially an appointment*' outside the power[98] (emphasis added). As Lord St Leonards put it in *Keily v Keily*, the appointment was 'not within the intention' of the power, and so there had been a 'fraudulent exercise of this power'.[99] And, in *Kain v Hutton*, Tipping J described fraud on a power as a 'species of excessive execution . . . because it is regular on its face but in reality is undertaken for a purpose not within the donor's mandate'.[100]

Seen in that light, it is clear that the doctrine of fraud on a power applies whenever a power has been granted, irrespective of whether the power has been granted to a fiduciary or to someone who owes no fiduciary duties whatsoever:

---

[92] *Hinchinbrooke v Seymour* (1789) 1 Bro CC 395 (28 ER 1200).
[93] *Henty v Wrey* (1882) 21 ChD 332, 341–43 and 347 (CA); *Keily v Keily* (1843) 2 Connor & Lawson's Ch Rep 334, 342–43; *M'Queen v Farquhar* (1805) 11 Ves 467, 479 (32 ER 1168); *Re Queensberry's Leases* (1819) 1 Bligh 339, 397–98 (4 ER 127). Cf *Wellesley v Mornington* (1855) 2 K & J 143, 153 (69 ER 728) (VC).
[94] See similarly *Wellesley v Mornington* (*ibid*) 162.
[95] *Henty v Wrey* (above n 93) 355; see also pp 353–54. And see *Re Queensberry's Leases* (above n 93) 398; and *Fearon v Desbrisay*, where Romilly MR distinguished between two questions: 'first, was it within the terms of the power, and if so, then, secondly, was it a *bonâ fide* execution within the intent of the settlement?': (1851) 14 Beav 635, 642 (51 ER 428).
[96] See text accompanying n 89 above.
[97] See, eg, *Bishopsgate v Maxwell (No 2)* (above n 70) 265; *Alcatel Australia Ltd v Scarcella* (1998) 44 NSWLR 349, 368 (CA).
[98] *Re Queensberry's Leases* (above n 93) 398.
[99] *Keily v Keily* (above n 93) 343. Connor and Lawson's report of *Keily v Keily* is superior to the alternative report in (1843) 4 Drury & Warren's Rep 38: see *Henty v Wrey* (above n 93) 347.
[100] *Kain v Hutton* [2008] NZSC 61 at [47], [2008] 3 NZLR 589; see also at [46].

The notion of a fraud on a power itself rests on the fundamental juristic principle that *any* form of authority may only be exercised for the purposes conferred, and in accordance with its terms. *The principle is one of general application*[101] (emphasis added).

Thus, it is 'trite law that a power can be exercised only for the purpose for which it is conferred, and not for any extraneous or ulterior purpose'.[102] That proposition is not limited in its application: it is not peculiar to fiduciaries. This explains why so many cases recognise the idea that a power cannot be exercised for improper purposes, irrespective of whether that power is held by a fiduciary.[103] Further examples can be provided. Shareholders, for example, do not normally have any fiduciary relationship with one another,[104] and yet some of the powers that they hold as shareholders, such as powers to alter the articles of association, are limited in the sense that they cannot be used for ulterior or improper purposes: 'like other powers, [they] must be exercised bona fide, and having regard to the purposes for which they are created, and to the rights of persons affected by them.'[105] Similarly, in addition to the cases already mentioned regarding powers of appointment,[106] the doctrine of fraud on a power has also been applied to the exercise of powers of appointment held by beneficiaries (rather than trustees) of trusts of funds.[107] Thus, the doctrine of fraud on a power is not a peculiarly fiduciary doctrine.[108]

---

[101] *Wong v Burt* [2005] 1 NZLR 91 at [27] (CA).

[102] *Re Courage Group's Pension Schemes* (above n 68) 505. See also *Aleyn v Belchier* (1758) 1 Eden 132, 138 (28 ER 634) (LK); *Duke of Portland v Lady Topham* (1864) 11 HLC 32, 54 (11 ER 1242); *Molyneux v Fletcher* [1898] 1 QB 648, 654.

[103] See the cases discussed in the text accompanying nn 71 and 75–84 above.

[104] *Peters' American Delicacy Co Ltd v Heath* (1939) 61 CLR 457, 482 and 504; *North-West Transportation Co Ltd v Beatty* (1887) 12 App Cas 589, 601 (PC); Davies (above n 26) [19–3].

[105] *British Equitable Assurance Co Ltd v Baily* [1906] AC 35, 42. See also *Allen v Gold Reefs of West Africa Ltd* [1900] 1 Ch 656, 671 (CA); *Ngurli Ltd v McCann* (1953) 90 CLR 425, 438–39; *Peters' American Delicacy v Heath* (ibid) 495, 505 and 511–12; *Gambotto v WCP Ltd* (1995) 182 CLR 432, 444–46 and 451–53. And see *Menier v Hooper's Telegraph Works* (1874) LR 9 Ch App 350 (CA); *Alexander v Automatic Telephone Co* [1900] 2 Ch 56, 69 (CA); *Burland v Earle* [1902] AC 83, 93–94 (PC); *Dominion Cotton Mills Co Ltd v Amyot* [1912] AC 546, 552–53 (PC).

[106] See text accompany nn 89–101 above.

[107] See, eg, *Fearon v Desbrisay* (above n 95) 642; *Beere v Hoffmister* (1856) 23 Beav 101, 105–6 (53 ER 40) (MR); *Re Crawshay* [1948] Ch 123, 144 (CA); *Re Dick* [1953] Ch 343, 366 (CA); *Re Brook's Settlement* [1968] 1 WLR 1661, 1669 (ChD). The beneficiaries in these cases were not always life tenants (see, eg, *Beere v Hoffmister*), and even when they were, the point remains undiminished in that life tenants are not fiduciaries vis-à-vis the remaindermen: *Re Biss* [1903] 2 Ch 40, 61 (CA); EB Sugden, *Vendors and Purchasers* (London, Brooke & Clarke and Butterworth, 1805) 301–2. Further, see *Re Radcliffe* [1892] 1 Ch 227 (CA), allowing a life tenant to release his power of appointment. Even when the life tenancy was in settled land, the trusteeship imposed on the life tenant under the Settled Land Acts (see, eg, Settled Land Act 1925, s 107) was not as 'stringent' as that imposed on ordinary trustees: BW Harvey, *Settlements of Land* (London, Sweet & Maxwell, 1973) 96.

[108] See also G Farwell, *Powers*, 3rd edn by CJW Farwell and FK Archer (London, Stevens, 1916) 458–59; HG Hanbury, 'Frauds on a Power: An Opportunity for Stocktaking' (1948) 64 *Law Quarterly Review* 221, 226; Finn, *Fiduciary Obligations* (above n 8) [84]; S Worthington, 'Directors' Duties,

Neither the doctrine of fraud on a power, nor the requirement that powers be exercised only for proper purposes, is peculiar in its application to fiduciaries. These doctrines are not fiduciary in the sense that matters to the analysis offered in this book.

VI. Fiduciary Powers

The next category of doctrine that requires consideration relates to what are commonly referred to as 'fiduciary powers'. This refers not to powers that are in some way inherently fiduciary in nature but rather to powers held in a fiduciary capacity.[109] The question to be addressed is whether the duties that attend the exercise of such powers are peculiar to fiduciaries in the sense that matters to the analysis in this book. In a simplistic sense, the answer would appear to be that the duties are peculiarly fiduciary, because they are applied by reason of the fiduciary capacity of the office holder. However, as has already been seen regarding several other doctrines, the fact that duties are owed by reason of a fiduciary position does not necessarily mean that those duties are peculiar to fiduciaries.

It is easiest to understand the duties attending fiduciary powers by referring first to the duties that arise when other forms of power are held. In particular, it is important to compare fiduciary powers with trust powers (or powers in the nature of a trust) and with mere (or purely personal) powers,[110] because fiduciary powers 'fall midway between'[111] those two kinds of powers.

Mere (or purely personal) powers exist when the donee of a power is able to alter the position of others but is under no duty to exercise the power, so that the court will not exercise the power if the donee refrains from so doing.[112] If the donee chooses to exercise the power, he cannot act beyond the terms of the power and cannot commit a fraud on the power,[113] but 'a donee of a non-fiduciary mere power is under no obligation to do anything at all'[114] and so 'does not have to

---

Creditors' Rights and Shareholder Intervention' (1991) 18 *Melbourne University Law Review* 121, 122; GW Thomas, *Powers* (London, Sweet & Maxwell, 1998) [9–07] and [9–14]; Worthington, 'Corporate Governance' (above n 87) 648.

[109] Finn, *Fiduciary Obligations* (above n 8) [6]. See also Thomas (*ibid*) [1–47].

[110] 'Terminology in this area has not been entirely uniform': *Rawcliffe v Steele* [1993–95] Manx LR 426, 495.

[111] M Cullity, 'Fiduciary Powers' (1976) 54 *Canadian Bar Review* 229, 229.

[112] *Brown v Higgs* (1803) 8 Ves 561, 570 (32 ER 473).

[113] *Re Somes* [1896] 1 Ch 250, 255; *Rawcliffe v Steele* (above n 110) 498; McGhee (ed) (above n 10) [9–02]; DJ Hayton and CCJ Mitchell, *Hayton & Marshall's Commentary and Cases on the Law of Trusts and Equitable Remedies*, 12th edn (London, Sweet & Maxwell, 2005) [3–103].

[114] AJ Oakley, *Parker & Mellows: The Modern Law of Trusts*, 9th edn (London, Sweet & Maxwell, 2008) [3–075].

consider from time to time whether or not to exercise the power and can even release the power so it can never be exercised'.[115]

In contrast, a donee of a trust power has discretion as to *how* the power is exercised but no discretion as to whether to exercise the power.[116] In other words, as Page Wood VC explained in *Lane v Debenham*, 'it is the duty of the trustees to execute the trust,'[117] and the fact that there is a discretion in the performance of the trust does not alter that.[118] 'The trustees would not be allowed by the court to disregard that trust,'[119] and 'if the person, who has that duty imposed upon him, does not discharge it, the Court will, to a certain extent, discharge the duty in his room and place.'[120] In addition to the duty to exercise the power, in reaching their decision as to how to exercise the power, 'a fair consideration of the subject'[121] is expected of the trustees, and 'they must inform themselves, before making a decision, of matters which are relevant to the decision.'[122] As the High Court of Australia put it in *Cock v Smith*, 'the trustees were bound to take all relevant facts into consideration.'[123]

In the case of trust powers, 'the power is merely part of the machinery of the trust.'[124] The duty to give fair consideration to the question how a trust power should be exercised is best understood as an integral part of the trustee's duty to exercise the power, which is itself a part of the trustee's duty to execute the trust: without an adequate consideration of the matter, the trustee is not in a position properly to comply with his duty to distribute the fund as directed by the trust deed.[125] For reasons given already,[126] the trustee's fundamental duty to execute the trust is not a peculiarly fiduciary duty in the sense that matters to the analysis in this book. When the trustee is given a discretion as to how to distribute the trust fund but is nonetheless obliged to make a distribution, the trustee's duty to consider how to exercise that discretion is best considered as part and parcel of the duty to distribute the trust fund. As such, it is not peculiarly fiduciary in the sense that matters here.

---

[115] Hayton and Mitchell (above n 113) [3–103]. See also *Smith v Houblon* (1859) 26 Beav 482 (53 ER 984) (MR); *Re Radcliffe* (above n 107) 233–34; *Re Somes* (above n 113) 254–55; *Re Brown's Settlement* [1939] 1 Ch 944, 954; *Re Gestetner Settlement* [1953] 1 Ch 672, 687; Thomas (above n 108) [6–39].

[116] *Brown v Higgs* (above n 112) 574. Similarly, powers in the nature of a trust are discretionary powers held by non-trustees that *must* be exercised: see Farwell (above n 108) ch 12.

[117] *Lane v Debenham* (1853) 11 Hare 188, 192 (68 ER 1241). See also *McPhail v Doulton* [1971] AC 424, 441, 444 and 445.

[118] *Lane v Debenham* (*ibid*) 194–95. See also *Rawcliffe v Steele* (above n 110) 493–94 and 495.

[119] *Tempest v Lord Camoys* (1882) 21 ChD 571, 578 (CA).

[120] *Brown v Higgs* (above n 112) 571. See also *Re Phene's Trusts* (1868) LR 5 Eq 346, 348 (MR).

[121] *Re Beloved Wilkes's Charity* (1851) 3 Mac & G 440, 448 (42 ER 330) (LC). See also *Tempest v Lord Camoys* (above n 119) 578.

[122] *Scott v National Trust for Places of Historic Interest or Natural Beauty* [1998] 2 All ER 705, 717 (ChD).

[123] *Cock v Smith* (1909) 9 CLR 773, 798.

[124] Farwell (above n 108) 524.

[125] *McPhail v Doulton* (above n 117) 449.

[126] See above section I.

This leaves for consideration the rules that apply to 'fiduciary powers'. Like both mere powers and trust powers, the holder of a fiduciary power must act honestly and cannot 'carry into execution any indirect object' such as would constitute a fraud on the power.[127] Unlike trust powers, the donee of a fiduciary power owes no duty to exercise the power[128] but is nevertheless subject to duties that go beyond the limits placed on the holder of a mere power.[129] Because fiduciary powers occupy this middle ground, partaking of some but not all of the character of trust powers, the courts have considered them by drawing analogies with trust powers.[130] In other words, a fiduciary power holder's 'position is assimilated to that of a trustee'.[131] However, rather than the power holder being under a duty to exercise the power (which would mean the power is actually a trust power), the power holder is 'bound . . . to preserve that power, and to exercise his discretion as circumstances arise from time to time, whether the power should be used or not'.[132] Thus, the donee of a fiduciary power cannot simply ignore the power and is under a duty *to consider* whether to exercise the power,[133] 'calling to their aid all fair attention to the nature of the subject'.[134] The classic modern statement of this duty is found in *Re Hay's Settlement Trusts*:

> [H]e must from time to time consider whether or not to exercise the power, and the court may direct him to do this. . . He must 'make such a survey of the range of objects or possible beneficiaries' as will enable him to carry out his fiduciary duty. He must find out 'the permissible area of selection and then consider responsibly, in individual cases, whether a contemplated beneficiary was within the power and whether, in relation to the possible claimants, a particular grant was appropriate'.[135]

Notwithstanding the reference here to a 'fiduciary duty', the duty to consider properly how to exercise a fiduciary power differs only in degree, rather than in principle,[136] from the duty of consideration that attaches to the exercise of a trust

---

[127]   *Palmer v Locke* (1880) 15 ChD 294, 303 (CA).
[128]   See, eg, *Re Mills* [1930] 1 Ch 654, 659 (CA); *Rawcliffe v Steele* (above n 110) 496.
[129]   *Re Somes* (above n 113) 255; *McPhail v Doulton* (above n 117) 441.
[130]   *McPhail v Doulton* (above n 117) 441. See also *Dickenson v Teasdale* (1862) 1 De G J & S 52, 59–60 (LC) (46 ER 21); *Palmer v Locke* (above n 127) 302–3. This process provides yet another example of the (historical) exporting function of the fiduciary concept.
[131]   *Rawcliffe v Steele* (above n 110) 496; see also 503.
[132]   *Re Eyre* (1883) 49 LT 259, 260 (ChD). See also *Re Bryant* [1894] Ch 324, 331–33; *Re Gestetner Settlement* (above n 115) 688; *Whishaw v Stephens* [1970] AC 508, 518; *Blausten v Inland Revenue Commissioners* [1972] 1 Ch 256, 272 (CA); *Re Manisty's Settlement* [1974] 1 Ch 17, 22 and 25; *Re Beatty* [1990] 1 WLR 1503, 1506 (ChD); *Mettoy Pension Trustees v Evans* (above n 69) 1614; *Kennon v Spry* [2008] HCA 56 at [125], [126] and [137], (2008) 83 ALJR 145.
[133]   *Re Medland* (1889) 41 ChD 476, 481 and 483.
[134]   *Mortlock v Buller* (1804) 10 Ves 292, 308 (32 ER 857); see also pp 311–12.
[135]   *Re Hay's Settlement Trusts* [1982] 1 WLR 202, 209 (ChD), quoting from *McPhail v Doulton* (above n 117) 449 and 457. See also *Blausten v IRC* (above n 132) 273; *Re Hastings-Bass* [1975] 1 Ch 25, 41 (CA); *Rawcliffe v Steele* (above n 110) 496–98.
[136]   *McPhail v Doulton* (above n 117) 449.

power.[137] As such, it is best understood as an adjunct to the trustee's duty to execute the trust by distributing the trust fund.[138] The fiduciary power holder's duty of consideration has been described as fiduciary in the sense that it is analogous to the duty that trustees owe when exercising trust powers,[139] but this does not mean that it is peculiar to fiduciaries.[140] If the trustee's duty to do things required by the trust is not peculiarly fiduciary, then the trustee's duty to consider doing things that are permitted by the trust ought not to be considered peculiarly fiduciary either.

This is not to say that fiduciary power holders owe no fiduciary duties. The holder of a fiduciary power must not 'acquire any benefit for himself'[141] by exercising the power.[142] But this is simply an application of the conflict and profit principles. While those principles undoubtedly are peculiar to fiduciaries, the fact that the combination of limits on the holder of a fiduciary power *includes* peculiarly fiduciary duties does not mean that *all* of the rules and duties that apply to such powers are peculiar to fiduciaries, in just the same way that not every breach of trust committed by a trustee is necessarily a breach of fiduciary duty.

This point assists with understanding why the holders of fiduciary powers are unable to release those powers.[143] This proposition is based on two premises, one peculiarly fiduciary and the other not so. First, the holder of a fiduciary power is bound by fiduciary duties and so cannot release it when doing so would benefit the fiduciary personally.[144] That is an application of the fiduciary principle which prohibits conflicts between duty and interest. The second premise is that such powers are analogous to trust powers in the sense that they are 'evidently intended [to] be retained and freely exercised down to the time when they were called upon to convey the estate'[145] and not simply ignored by the power holder:

---

[137] IJ Hardingham and R Baxt, *Discretionary Trusts*, 2nd edn (Sydney, Butterworths, 1984) at [209].
[138] *Re Bacon* [1907] 1 Ch 475, 479.
[139] Finn, *Fiduciary Obligations* (above n 8) [621].
[140] Paul Finn excluded fiduciary powers from his later discussion of fiduciary doctrine: Finn, 'The Fiduciary Principle' (above n 8) 28.
[141] *Palmer v Locke* (above n 127) 303.
[142] See also *Re Beatty* (above n 132) 1506; *Alexander v Automatic Telephone* (above n 105) 67 and 76; *Kane v Radley-Kane* [1999] Ch 274, 285 and 286–87 (VC). And see *Richardson v Chapman* (1760) 7 Bro PC 318, 324–25 (3 ER 206); *Re National Provincial Marine Insurance Co (Gilbert's Case)* (1870) LR 5 Ch App 559, 565–66 (LJ).
[143] See, eg, *Weller v Ker* (1866) LR 1 Scots App 11, 14–15 and 16; *Re Dunne's Trusts* (1878) LR 1 Ir 516, 523 (MR) and (1880) LR 5 Ir 76, 83; *Re Eyre* (above n 132) 260; *Re Somes* (above n 113) 255; *Re Mills* (above n 128) 661; *Re Gestetner Settlement* (above n 115) 687; *Re Wills' Trust Deeds* [1964] 1 Ch 219, 228–29 and 236–37; *Re Allen-Meyrick's Will Trusts* [1966] 1 WLR 499, 503 (ChD); *Whishaw v Stephens* (above n 132) 518. The ability to release powers, contained in s 155 of the Law of Property Act 1925, does not apply to fiduciary powers: *Re Somes* (above n 113) 255; *Re Mills* (above n 128) 660–61, 665 and 669.
[144] See, eg, *Re Dunne's Trusts* (ibid) 523; *Re Mills* (above n 128) 661; *Re Wills' Trust Deeds* (ibid) 228–29.
[145] *Weller v Ker* (above n 143) 16.

by analogy with the obvious proposition that a trust power cannot be released (because there is a duty to exercise the power),[146] the holder of a fiduciary power can 'no more, by his own voluntary act, destroy a power of that kind than he can voluntarily put an end to or destroy any other trust that may be committed to him'.[147] This second premise is not peculiarly fiduciary.

Like trust powers, fiduciary powers are 'part of the machinery of the trust and . . . intended to be exercised for the purposes of the trust'.[148] Such powers are 'embedded in a trust',[149] and the duty to consider their exercise is best understood as part of the machinery of the trust. As with the duty to give proper consideration to the exercise of trust powers, the duty to consider the exercise of fiduciary powers ought not to be treated as peculiar to fiduciaries.

VII. Duty to Act in Good Faith in the Principal's Best Interests

The final duty to be addressed here is the duty to act in good faith in the principal's best interests. It is frequently asserted, again particularly in the context of company law, that this is a fiduciary duty.[150] But is the duty to act in good faith in the best interests of the principal peculiar to fiduciaries?

The duty to act in the best interests of the principal is not a strict duty.[151] In *Gilbert's Case*, for example, Giffard LJ explained that the defendant director 'ought to have done his best to have had the call made, and that all the other directors ought to have done their best to have a call made'.[152] In other words, the duty is not a duty to act in the best interests of the principal per se but rather a duty to make a reasonable attempt to pursue the best interests of the principal.[153]

---

[146]   *Muir v Inland Revenue Commissioners* [1966] 1 WLR 1269, 1283 (CA).

[147]   *Re Eyre* (above n 132) 260. See also *Re Gestetner Settlement* (above n 115) 688; *Re Allen-Meyrick's Will Trusts* (above n 143) 503.

[148]   *Rawcliffe v Steele* (above n 110) 496.

[149]   *Re Mills* (above n 128) 661.

[150]   See, eg, *Re Cawley & Co* (1889) 42 ChD 209, 233 (CA); *Re Coalport China Co* [1895] 2 Ch 404, 410 (CA); *Knight v Frost* [1999] 1 BCLC 364, 374 (ChD); *Regentcrest plc v Cohen* [2001] 2 BCLC 80 at [120] (ChD); *Item Software (UK) Ltd v Fassihi* [2004] EWCA Civ 1244 at [41], [2005] 2 BCLC 91; *Shepherds Investments Ltd v Walters* [2006] EWHC 836 (Ch) at [85], [2007] 2 BCLC 202; *Bell v Westpac (No 9)* (above n 70) [4574]–[4575] and [4582]; R Grantham, 'The Doctrinal Basis of the Rights of Company Shareholders' [1998] *Cambridge Law Journal* 554, 576–77; A Burrows, 'We Do This at Common Law But That in Equity' (2002) 22 *Oxford Journal of Legal Studies* 1, 8; Davies (above n 26) [16–17]; J Palmer, 'The Availability of Allowances in Equity: Rewarding the Bad Guy' (2004) 21 *New Zealand Universities Law Review* 146, 167 and 171; Morse (above n 26) 299.

[151]   Cheffins (above n 26) 313.

[152]   *Re Gilbert's Case* (above n 142) 566.

[153]   Similarly, for agents, see FMB Reynolds, *Bowstead & Reynolds on Agency*, 18th edn (London, Sweet & Maxwell, 2006) at [6–018].

As such, the duty appears to be another way of stating the duty of care that most fiduciaries owe.

On the other hand, whereas the duty of care is an objective standard of reasonableness, the cases emphasise that the duty to act in the best interests of the principal is fundamentally a subjective duty. As Lord Greene MR said in *Re Smith & Fawcett*, directors 'must exercise their discretion bona fide in what they consider—not what a court may consider—is in the interests of the company'.[154] Explaining this in more detail, Jonathan Parker J said in *Regentcrest v Cohen*:

> The duty imposed on directors to act bona fide in the interests of the company is a subjective one. . . . The question is not whether, viewed objectively by the court, the particular act or omission which is challenged was in fact in the interests of the company; still less is the question whether the court, had it been in the position of the director at the relevant time, might have acted differently. Rather, the question is whether the director honestly believed that his act or omission was in the interests of the company.[155]

In this light, the duty seems to be little more than a restatement of the duty to act in good faith. However, the Privy Council indicated in *Howard Smith v Ampol Petroleum* that mere subjective good faith is insufficient to protect a director, explaining the director's duty to act in the best interests of the company as a duty not to exercise the director's powers for improper purposes.[156]

These various propositions can be reconciled by recognising that the duty to act in good faith in the best interests of the principal has been used in different ways by different courts. The Privy Council's observations in *Howard Smith v Ampol* reflect the idea that directors' powers cannot be exercised for improper purposes, which involves an objective assessment of the purposes for which powers have been exercised and is (as has already been discussed[157]) an application of the doctrine of fraud on a power. In contrast, when the directors' exercise of a power is challenged not on the basis that it was for an improper purpose but rather that, although for a proper purpose, it was not in the best interests of the company, the court's assessment is of the subjective belief of the directors, as *Regentcrest* makes clear, unless the directors can alternatively be shown to have acted negligently. In other words, the concept of acting in good faith in the best interests of the principal indicates to the fiduciary 'to what end he must bend his exertions',[158] but it can be understood as a composite of the duties to act in good

---

[154]   *Re Smith & Fawcett Ltd* [1942] Ch 304, 306 (CA).

[155]   *Regentcrest v Cohen* (above n 150) [120].

[156]   *Howard Smith v Ampol Petroleum* (above n 70) 834–35. See also *Regentcrest v Cohen* (above n 150) [123].

[157]   See above section V.

[158]   Finn, *Fiduciary Obligations* (above n 8) [27]. See also *KLB v British Columbia* [2003] SCC 51 at [46]–[47], [2003] 2 SCR 403.

faith, with the requisite degree of care, and only for proper purposes. As has been argued already, those duties are not peculiarly fiduciary.[159]

It is necessary here to consider Arden LJ's judgment in *Item Software v Fassihi*, which concerned a director's liability for failing to disclose his own misconduct to the company. Arden LJ observed that the defendant was a director and so owed fiduciary duties,[160] and she decided the case on the basis of 'the fundamental duty to which a director is subject, that is the duty to act in what he in good faith considers to be the best interests of the company'.[161] Her description of this as a 'duty of loyalty'[162] and her reference to it as the 'fiduciary principle'[163] suggest that she understood the duty as a fiduciary duty. Nonetheless, this decision does not stand in the way of the argument that has been made here. First, Arden LJ's judgment made no reference to Millett LJ's earlier indication in *Mothew* that the phrase 'fiduciary duty' ought to be limited in its application to duties that are peculiar to fiduciaries.[164] Furthermore, Arden LJ recorded that counsel had been unable to refer the court to any relevant Commonwealth authority,[165] so that no consideration was given to Gummow J's important statement in *Breen v Williams*:

> Fiduciary obligations arise (albeit perhaps not exclusively) in various situations where it may be seen that one person is under an obligation to act in the interests of another. Equitable remedies are available where the fiduciary places interest in conflict with duty or derives an unauthorised profit from abuse of duty. It would be to stand established principle on its head to reason that because equity considers the defendant to be a fiduciary, therefore the defendant has a legal obligation to act in the interests of the plaintiff so that failure to fulfil that positive obligation represents a breach of fiduciary duty.[166]

Austin J summarised the position very crisply in *Aequitas v AEFC*, having considered *Breen v Williams* and the Supreme Court of Canada's contrary decision in *McInerney v MacDonald*:[167] 'Obligations to act in the interests of another, or to act prudently, are not fiduciary obligations.'[168]

The fiduciary status or otherwise of the duty to which Arden LJ referred in *Fassihi* was not crucial to her analysis: what mattered was that directors owe a duty to act in the best interests of their companies. That duty does exist for

[159] See above sections II, IV and V.
[160] *Item Software (UK) Ltd v Fassihi* [2004] EWCA Civ 1244 at [34] and [38], [2005] 2 BCLC 91.
[161] *Ibid* at [41].
[162] *Ibid.*
[163] *Ibid* at [44].
[164] *Mothew* (above n 1) 16.
[165] *Item Software (UK) Ltd v Fassihi* [2004] EWCA Civ 1244 at [30], [2005] 2 BCLC 91.
[166] *Breen v Williams* (above n 6) 137–38. *Fassihi* has been rejected by at least one court in Australia for failing to consider *Breen v Williams*: *P & V Industries Pty Ltd v Porto* [2006] VSC 131 at [43], (2006) 14 VR 1.
[167] *McInerney v MacDonald* [1992] 2 SCR 138.
[168] *Aequitas v AEFC* [2001] NSWSC 14 at [284], (2001) 19 ACLC 1,006.

company directors,[169] and it can be described as the fundamental duty owed by directors, although, as explained above, its content is rather mercurial. But none of that means that the duty must be considered as a fiduciary duty.

Company directors are situated differently from other fiduciaries in the sense that it is extremely difficult to define their fundamental duty other than in terms of acting in the best interests of the company. In contrast, it is far easier to define the fundamental duty that other fiduciaries owe. Thus, for example, while trustees are often said to owe a duty to act in their beneficiaries' best interests,[170] this is actually a contraction of the trustee's duties: trust law's beneficiary principle means that there must be beneficiaries who have an interest in perform-ance of the trust,[171] but the trustee's fundamental duty is to execute the trust as identified in the trust instrument, thereby acting in the beneficiaries' interests but only insofar as the trust deed so provides. Similarly, a solicitor is sometimes said to owe a duty to act in the 'client's best interests and not to do anything likely to damage his client's interests, so far as this is consistent with the solicitor's professional duty',[172] but this is an overstatement, as a solicitor's true duty is to provide the services required by his retainer. Thus, for example, it is common for a solicitor's retainer to be limited in its content (even by implied terms), notwithstanding that it would be in the client's best interests for the solicitor to owe a broader set of enforceable duties.[173] And the fundamental duty of agents is to transact the business in respect of which their assistance was sought.

In contrast, it is very difficult to define in advance the precise duties that a director owes,[174] other than by stipulating that a director must 'promote the success of the company for the benefit of its members as a whole'.[175] In this sense, although the duty to act in the company's best interests is related—principally by way of analogy—to the duties owed by other fiduciaries, it is best understood as a duty that applies because of the particular circumstances of company directors. It is most closely analogous to a trustee's (non-fiduciary) duty to perform the trusts that he has undertaken. It is not fiduciary in the sense that matters to the analysis in this book. Nothing in *Fassihi* necessitates the view that it is.

Thus, while some fiduciaries owe a duty to act in the best interests of their principals, that is not itself a fiduciary duty. Contrary to the approach taken in

---

[169] See, eg, *Benson v Heathorn* (1842) 1 Y & CCC 326, 341 (62 ER 909); *Aberdeen Railway v Blaikie* (above n 42) 471; *Re Cawley & Co* (above n 150) 233; *Bamford v Bamford* [1970] Ch 212, 242 (CA). See now Companies Act 2006 (UK), s 172.

[170] See, eg, *Mortlock v Buller* (above n 134) 309; *Re Hodges* (1878) 7 ChD 754, 762; *Re Medland* (above n 133) 481; *Armitage v Nurse* (above n 47) 253–54.

[171] *Morice v Bishop of Durham* (1804) 9 Ves 399, 404–5 (32 ER 656); Underhill and Hayton (above n 3) [8.144]–[8.147].

[172] *Hilton v Barker Booth & Eastwood* [2005] UKHL 8 at [34], [2005] 1 WLR 567.

[173] See, eg, *Kelly v Cooper* [1993] AC 205 (PC); *Clark Boyce v Mouat* [1994] 1 AC 428 (PC); *Rigg v Sheridan* [2008] NSWCA 79.

[174] *Howard Smith v Ampol Petroleum* (above n 70) 835.

[175] Section 172(1), Companies Act 2006.

some decisions in Canada,[176] Anglo-Australian law contains no 'proper foundations for the imposition upon fiduciaries in general of a quasi-tortious duty to act solely in the best interest of their principals'.[177]

---

[176] See especially *McInerney v MacDonald* (above n 167), although cf *KLB v British Columbia* [2003] SCC 51 at [38]–[50], [2003] 2 SCR 403 and *EDG v Board of School Trustees of School District No 44 (North Vancouver)* [2003] SCC 52 at [23], [2003] 2 SCR 459.

[177] *Breen v Williams* (above n 6) 137; see also 83, 95 and 113. And see *Pilmer v Duke Group Ltd* [2001] HCA 31 at [74], (2001) 207 CLR 165.

4

Fiduciary Loyalty

This chapter turns to the task of identifying what it is that marks peculiarly fiduciary duties out from other kinds of duties. In particular, what do peculiarly fiduciary duties do, and how does that function differ from the function served by other duties?

I. Introduction

It has become common recently to observe that fiduciary duties are proscriptive rather than prescriptive.[1] The foundation for this proposition will be explained later,[2] but it is insufficient in and of itself to identify what sets fiduciary duties apart from other kinds of duties. One can easily identify numerous duties that are proscriptive in nature and yet not peculiar to fiduciaries: examples include the tort law duties not to trespass on another's land, not to defame another and not to conspire to cause injury to another, as well as the contractual duty not to breach a restrictive covenant that one has entered into and the equitable duty not to breach such a covenant concerning land one has acquired subject to the covenant. In other words, the proscriptive nature of fiduciary duties does not alone differentiate them from other kinds of duties.

In *Bristol & West Building Society v Mothew*, Millett LJ said that the 'distinguishing obligation of a fiduciary is the obligation of loyalty',[3] which suggests that one can understand fiduciary duties simply by understanding the concept of

---

[1]   See, eg, *Breen v Williams* (1996) 186 CLR 71, 95 and 113; *Attorney-General v Blake* [1998] Ch 439, 455 (CA), point not discussed on appeal: [2001] 1 AC 268; *Pilmer v Duke Group Ltd* [2001] HCA 31 at [74] and [127], (2001) 207 CLR 165; *Brooker v Friend* [2006] NSWCA 385 at [26]; *P & V Industries Pty Ltd v Porto* [2006] VSC 131 at [23], (2006) 14 VR 1; *Australian Securities and Investments Commission v Citigroup Global Markets Australia Pty Ltd (No 4)* [2007] FCA 963 at [290], (2007) 160 FCR 35; *Bell Group Ltd v Westpac Banking Corp (No 9)* [2008] WASC 239 at [4539]–[4544]; RC Nolan, 'A Fiduciary Duty to Disclose?' (1997) 113 *Law Quarterly Review* 220, 222; PJ Millett, 'Equity's Place in the Law of Commerce' (1998) 114 *Law Quarterly Review* 214, 222–23. See also *Youyang Pty Ltd v Minter Ellison Morris Fletcher* [2003] HCA 15 at [41], (2003) 212 CLR 484; *Friend v Brooker* [2009] HCA 21 at [84].

[2]   See below ch 7, section III.

[3]   *Bristol & West Building Society v Mothew* [1998] Ch 1, 18.

loyalty. In contrast, Peter Birks argued that the concept of altruism is more helpful in understanding fiduciary doctrine, as it is more precise than loyalty.[4] It is difficult to see how that is the case, particularly when it is borne in mind that 'forced selfless behaviour is hardly altruism'.[5] However, even if one rejects Birks' emphasis on altruism and instead follows the case law that emphasises loyalty as the core concept in fiduciary doctrine,[6] the question remains whether the concept of loyalty itself provides any helpful explanation of the function served by fiduciary doctrine. It is suggested that the reverse is the case—that fiduciary duties give meaning and substance to the fiduciary concept of loyalty, such that the latter can only be understood properly by reference to the former.

This point is highlighted if one attempts to consider, in abstract terms without reference to the content of fiduciary doctrine's specific duties, what it might mean to say that a fiduciary must act loyally. According to the *Oxford English Dictionary*, 'loyalty' refers to the quality of faithful adherence to one's promises or obligations.[7] 'Faithful' tends to refer to conscientious or strict adherence to duty,[8] or thorough fulfilment of duty.[9] Of course, legal concepts are best understood by reference to the content of the doctrines that create the concepts rather than by reference to dictionary definitions, but that is the very point being made here: if one follows the words alone, fiduciary doctrine's 'core duty of loyalty' seems merely to require thorough performance of the fiduciary's duty. In other words, from the concept of loyalty alone it is very difficult to see what it is about fiduciary duties that sets them apart from other duties owed by the fiduciary: what do fiduciary duties add if they are merely obligations to perform other duties thoroughly and conscientiously?

Equity traditionally provides a supplement or gloss to the common law,[10] and so it does not normally intervene where common law rules and remedies are adequate.[11] As a creature of equity, one would expect fiduciary doctrine to serve a purpose beyond simply restating duties owed at common law. The Privy Council stressed in *Re Goldcorp Exchange* that 'the essence of a fiduciary relationship is that it creates obligations *of a different character* from those deriving from the contract itself' (emphasis added).[12] Thus, it rejected an argument that a seller of

---

[4] PBH Birks, 'The Content of Fiduciary Obligation' (2000) 34 *Israel Law Review* 3, 11–12 (republished at (2002) 16 *Trust Law International* 34).

[5] AJ Duggan, 'Is Equity Efficient?' (1997) 113 *Law Quarterly Review* 601, 605.

[6] See above ch 1.

[7] J Simpson and E Weiner (eds), *Oxford English Dictionary*, 2nd edn (Oxford, Oxford University Press, 1989) vol 9, 74.

[8] *Ibid*, vol 5, 680 ('faithfully' and 'faithfulness').

[9] *Ibid*, vol 5, 679 ('faithful').

[10] FW Maitland, *Equity*, 2nd edn rev by J Brunyate (Cambridge, Cambridge University Press, 1936) 153; E Coke, *Fourth Part of The Institutes of the Laws of England*, 2nd edn (London, Lee & Pakeman, 1648) 79.

[11] *Barclays Bank plc v Quincecare Ltd* [1992] 4 All ER 363, 375 (QBD); *KLB v British Columbia* [2003] SCC 51 at [48], [2003] 2 SCR 403.

[12] *Re Goldcorp Exchange Ltd* [1995] 1 AC 74, 98. See also *Conway v Ratiu* [2005] EWCA Civ 1302 at [71], [2006] 1 All ER 571n.

gold bullion owed its customers fiduciary duties because the plaintiffs had made no argument 'which went beyond suggesting that by virtue of being a fiduciary the company was obliged honestly and conscientiously to do what it had by contract promised to do',[13] and that was insufficient to amount to a fiduciary duty.

All this underscores the importance of examining the content of the fiduciary obligation of loyalty to determine what distinguishes it from other kinds of obligations. It also indicates that such analysis must proceed by reference to the duties that are peculiarly fiduciary. The position will not be advanced merely by theorising about the nature of loyalty in the abstract. In other words, as one would expect in a system that derives its general principles 'from judicial decisions upon particular instances, not the other way around',[14] the fiduciary concept of loyalty is best explicated by reference to duties that are peculiar to fiduciaries, and which thus comprise the concept of fiduciary loyalty, rather than by reference to some abstract definition of loyalty.

The analysis offered in the preceding chapter suggests that the fiduciary conflict and profit principles are the ones that are most clearly peculiar to fiduciaries. Indeed, in *P & V Industries v Porto*, Hollingworth J described these two principles as encompassing 'the whole content of fiduciary obligations'.[15] The question to be addressed is how best to understand these peculiarly fiduciary principles.

II. Subsidiary Prophylactic Protection

Peculiarly fiduciary duties serve a function that differs from that served by other legal duties. The concept of 'loyalty', when it is used within Anglo-Australian fiduciary doctrine, operates so as to increase the likelihood of the fiduciary's faithful adherence to duty. The key element that separates fiduciary duties from other duties not peculiar to fiduciaries is that fiduciary duties provide this enhanced likelihood of faithful adherence to duty by protecting the fiduciary from influences that are likely to interfere with proper performance of the fiduciary's *non*-fiduciary duties. The presence of such influences carries with it a risk that the fiduciary may be tempted not to perform properly his non-fiduciary duties. Removing the influences therefore increases the likelihood of a fiduciary performing his non-fiduciary duties faithfully. Thus, the concept of fiduciary 'loyalty' encapsulates a subsidiary and prophylactic form of protection for

---

[13] *Goldcorp (ibid)* 98.

[14] *Roxborough v Rothmans of Pall Mall Australia Ltd* [2001] HCA 68 at [72], (2001) 208 CLR 516. See also *Farah Constructions Pty Ltd v Say-Dee Pty Ltd* [2007] HCA 22 at [154], (2007) 230 CLR 89; *Lumbers v W Cook Builders Pty Ltd* [2008] HCA 27 at [77], (2008) 232 CLR 635.

[15] *P & V Industries Pty Ltd v Porto* [2006] VSC 131 at [23], (2006) 14 VR 1.

non-fiduciary duties which is designed to enhance the chance that those non-fiduciary duties will be properly performed.

It is often observed that fiduciary doctrine is applied in a prophylactic manner, although frequently without much clarification of what that means. It is suggested that fiduciary doctrine is prophylactic in more than merely the strictness of its application. The argument advanced here is that fiduciary doctrine is prophylactic *in its very nature*, as it is designed to avert breaches of non-fiduciary duties by seeking to neutralise influences likely to sway the fiduciary away from properly performing those non-fiduciary duties. Fiduciary doctrine is also frequently conceptualised as exhorting more moral behaviour from fiduciaries. Properly understood, the doctrine is far more cynical and instrumentalist in outlook, focusing on lessening the danger that a fiduciary's undertaking will not be properly performed.

This chapter elucidates the idea that fiduciary duties provide a subsidiary and prophylactic form of protection for non-fiduciary duties, showing how the conflict principle provides such protection and the consistency of that view of fiduciary doctrine with the remedies that are available, and defends this view against its critics.

A. Protective Function

Fiduciary duties serve to protect the proper performance of non-fiduciary duties by seeking to prevent fiduciaries from acting in situations in which they face a temptation to breach their non-fiduciary duties. Thus, fiduciary doctrine does not simply replicate or restate non-fiduciary duties and then superimpose more powerful remedies for breach of those duties. Indeed, as will be seen below, fiduciary duties can be breached even though the fiduciary's non-fiduciary duties have been properly performed. Fiduciary doctrine operates in a protective manner. It tries to avoid breach of non-fiduciary duties by seeking to remove incentives that may tempt a fiduciary not to perform his non-fiduciary duties properly. In that way, fiduciary doctrine performs a function quite distinct from the non-fiduciary duties that it protects. The non-fiduciary duties have their own remedial regimes, which are designed to correct situations in which those duties have not been properly performed. Fiduciary duties are designed to lessen both the likelihood of, and the need to remedy, such breaches.

'All Men are liable to Errour; and most Men are in many Points, by Passion or Interest, under Temptation to it.'[16] In the context of fiduciary doctrine operating in a system of positive law, the 'error' to which men are liable is breach of non-fiduciary duty, and fiduciary doctrine is concerned to protect the fiduciary's

---

[16] J Locke, *An Essay Concerning Human Understanding*, ed by PH Nidditch (Oxford, Oxford University Press, 1975) bk 4, ch 20 at [17].

principal from such error by removing the 'temptation to it' that 'interest' can create.[17] This protective function is well illustrated by the fiduciary principle that requires that

> [N]o one having [fiduciary] duties to discharge, shall be allowed to enter into engagements in which he has, or can have, a personal interest conflicting, or which may possibly conflict, with the interests of those whom he is bound to protect.[18]

Thus, for example, in *Aberdeen Railway v Blaikie*, a director of a railway company entered into a contract to purchase iron chairs (sockets used to secure the rails to the sleepers), while also being a principal in the vendor firm. The railway company successfully extricated itself from the contract because there was a conflict between the director's personal interest in the transaction—as a principal in the vendor firm—and the duty that he owed to the railway company 'to make the best bargains he could for the benefit of the Company'.[19] The protective function is seen in Lord Cranworth's explanation:

> [The director's] duty to the Company imposed on him the obligation of obtaining these chairs at the lowest possible price. His personal interest would lead him in an entirely opposite direction, would induce him to fix the price as high as possible. *This is the very evil against which the rule in question is directed* (emphasis added).[20]

A fiduciary is prohibited from acting in a situation in which there is a conflict between the duty that he owes to his principal and his own personal interest because that personal interest is likely to lead the fiduciary away from proper performance of his (non-fiduciary) duty.

This understanding of the function served by fiduciary doctrine is present and consistent throughout the case law. In *Whichcote v Lawrence*, for example, Lord Loughborough LC explained that the concern when a trustee buys trust property for himself is that he 'is not acting with that want of interest, that total absence of temptation'[21] because 'where a trustee has a prospect of advantage to himself, it is a great temptation to him to be negligent.'[22] By requiring the fiduciary to eschew situations that involve temptation not to perform properly his non-fiduciary duties, fiduciary duties make proper performance of those non-fiduciary duties more likely.

---

[17] 'Passion' is less likely to cause concern in fiduciary doctrine than 'interest', although some Canadian authority suggests that it is not completely irrelevant: eg, *Norberg v Wynrib* [1992] 2 SCR 226, 275. However, in Anglo-Australian law, the interests that have been protected by fiduciary doctrine have generally been economic interests: *Paramasivam v Flynn* (1998) 90 FCR 489, 504–8.

[18] *Aberdeen Railway Co v Blaikie Bros* (1854) 1 Macq 461, 471 (149 RR 32).

[19] *Ibid*, 473.

[20] *Ibid*.

[21] *Whichcote v Lawrence* (1798) 3 Ves 740, 750 (30 ER 1248).

[22] *Ibid*, 752.

Similarly, the longstanding rule that trustees are not entitled to take remuneration for their work as trustees[23] (unless the trust deed or statute so permits) exists not because remuneration is somehow repugnant to trusteeship[24] but because 'if [a trustee] be allowed to perform the duties connected with the estate, and to claim compensation for his services, his interest would then be opposed to his duty.'[25] The relevance of that conflict between duty and interest is that it creates a 'danger'[26] that the fiduciary will be tempted by the possibility of personal gain to act in breach of duty towards his principal: as Lord Langdale MR explained in *Stanes v Parker*, 'it is thought unsafe to sanction any such allowance, and thereby *tempt* the solicitor [trustee] to create unnecessary business for his own profit' (emphasis added).[27] The rule is not concerned with identifying particular instances when trustees have succumbed to that temptation but rather to strike at the general risk that such temptation creates.[28] Thus, fiduciary doctrine seeks to have the trustee avoid the temptation altogether, thereby protecting the proper performance of the trustee's non-fiduciary duties from inconsistent influences.

Numerous other cases illustrate this function of fiduciary duties. In *Lonsdale v Church*, for example, Arden MR explained that the defendant, who received harbour duties on behalf of the harbour trustees, had to account for interest that he made on the duties received because 'not being accountable for interest would be a temptation to receivers not to be ready to pay money due from them when demanded.'[29] To allow the defendant to have a personal interest in the performance of his fiduciary office creates a risk that he might place himself in a position where he is unable to perform the duty that he was engaged to perform in the first place.

The link between personal interest and the risk of non-performance of non-fiduciary duty is also apparent in *Boston Deep Sea Fishing & Ice Co v Ansell*, where a director of a fishing company breached his fiduciary duty by placing supply contracts with a company in which he held shares and from which he received bonuses. As Cotton LJ explained, by taking the bonuses, the director 'puts himself in such a position that he has a temptation not faithfully to perform

---

[23]   *Robinson v Pett* (1734) P Wms 249, 251 (24 ER 1049) (LC). See also *How v Godfrey* (1678) Rep t Finch 361, 362 (23 ER 198); *Bonithon v Hockmore* (1685) 1 Vern 316, 316 (23 ER 492); *Scattergood v Harrison* (1729) Mosely 128, 130 (25 ER 310) (LC); *Burden v Burden* (1813) 1 Ves & Bea 170, 172 (35 ER 67) (LC); *Brocksopp v Barnes* (1820) 5 Madd 90, 90 (56 ER 829) (VC); *New v Jones* (1833) 1 H & Tw 632, 634 (47 ER 1562) (LCB) (also reported at 1 Mac & G 685 (41 ER 1429)); *Moore v Frowd* (1837) 3 My & Cr 45, 50 (40 ER 841) (LC); *Stanes v Parker* (1846) 9 Beav 385, 389 (50 ER 392) (MR).

[24]   *Dale v Inland Revenue Commissioners* [1954] AC 11, 27.

[25]   *New v Jones* (above n 23) 634.

[26]   *Moore v Frowd* (above n 23) 50.

[27]   *Stanes v Parker* (above n 23) 389. That temptation is not present where the trustee claims reimbursement for expenses incurred, and so such claims are permitted, provided they were reasonably and honestly incurred: *Scattergood v Harrison* (above n 23) 130; *Burden v Burden* (above n 23) 172; *Re Beddoe* [1893] 1 Ch 547, 558 and 562 (CA).

[28]   *Moore v Frowd* (above n 23) 50.

[29]   *Lonsdale v Church* (1789) 3 Bro CC 41, 45 (29 ER 396).

his duty to his employer'.[30] Fiduciary doctrine seeks to protect proper performance of that non-fiduciary duty by trying to eliminate the inconsistent temptation that the personal interest creates. As Lord Cottenham LC said in *Knight v Marjoribanks*, 'its object is to secure the due execution of the duty which the trustee takes upon himself to perform.'[31]

This protective function of fiduciary doctrine is further underlined by the fact that a breach of fiduciary duty can occur without a breach of non-fiduciary duty. Thus, for example, in *Aberdeen Railway v Blaikie*, the railway company could avoid the contract merely by showing that its director had acted with a conflict between his personal interest and the duty that he owed the company. It was unnecessary to show that the director had actually breached his non-fiduciary duty by failing to get the chairs at the best price possible. Lord Cranworth LC made this explicit, as have numerous other cases,[32] saying:

> [S]o strictly is this [fiduciary conflict] principle adhered to, that *no question is allowed to be raised* as to the fairness or unfairness of a contract so entered into. . . It may sometimes happen that the terms on which a trustee has dealt or attempted to deal with the estate or interests of those for whom he is a trustee, have been as good as could have been obtained from any other person—they may even at the time have been better. But still so inflexible is the rule that *no inquiry on that subject is permitted* (emphasis added).[33]

In other words, the fiduciary conflict principle is unconcerned with whether the fiduciary actually *has acted* in breach of his non-fiduciary duty but rather focuses its attention on circumstances in which there is a *risk* that the non-fiduciary duty might be breached. As Lord Esher MR said of the defendant in *Eden v Ridsdales*, 'it was not that he intended to defraud his principals, but he put himself in a position of temptation to do so.'[34] A fiduciary who acts with a personal interest that conflicts with the non-fiduciary duty he owes his principal has a 'propensity'[35] to breach that non-fiduciary duty. Fiduciary doctrine seeks to protect against that risk of breach by prohibiting the fiduciary from acting in such

---

[30] *Boston Deep Sea Fishing & Ice Co v Ansell* (1888) 39 ChD 339, 357.

[31] *Knight v Marjoribanks* (1849) 2 Mac & G 10, 12 (42 ER 4).

[32] See, eg, *Ex parte James* (1803) 8 Ves 337, 348–49 (32 ER 385) (LC); *Mulvany v Dillon* (1810) 1 Ball & Beatty 409, 418 (LC); *Attorney-General v Dudley* (1815) G Coop 146, 148 (35 ER 510) (MR); *Wormley v Wormley* 21 US (8 Wheat) 421, 463 (1823) (5 L Ed 651); *Gillett v Peppercorne* (1840) 3 Beav 78, 84 (49 ER 31) (MR); *Hamilton v Wright* (1842) 9 Cl & Fin 111, 123 (8 ER 357) (HL); *Murphy v O'Shea* (1845) 8 Ir Eq R 329, 330 and 331 (LC); *Parker v McKenna* (1874) LR 10 Ch App 96, 124–25 (CA); *De Bussche v Alt* (1878) 8 ChD 286, 316 (CA); *Wright v Morgan* [1926] AC 788, 798 (PC); *Re Bulmer* [1937] Ch 499, 508 (CA); *Regal (Hastings) Ltd v Gulliver* [1967] 2 AC 134n, 153; *Boardman v Phipps* [1967] 2 AC 46, 129; *Canadian Aero Service Ltd v O'Malley* [1974] SCR 592, 608–10; *Swain v Law Society* [1982] 1 WLR 17, 29 (CA); *Super 1000 Pty Ltd v Pacific General Securities Ltd* [2008] NSWSC 1222 at [117] and [181], (2008) 221 FLR 427. See also *Coleman Taymar Ltd v Oakes* [2001] 2 BCLC 749 at [66] and [98] (ChD).

[33] *Aberdeen Railway v Blaikie* (above n 18) 471–72.

[34] *Eden v Ridsdales Railway Lamp & Lighting Co Ltd* (1889) 23 QBD 368, 371 (CA).

[35] *Ross River Ltd v Cambridge City Football Club Ltd* [2007] EWHC 2115 (Ch) at [250], [2008] 1 All ER 1004.

situations, which is why it is irrelevant whether the fiduciary can be shown to
have breached his non-fiduciary duty. As Johnson J explained in *Wormley v
Wormley*, the fiduciary conflict principle is one of the 'canons of the court of
equity which have their foundation, not in the actual commission of fraud, but in
that hallowed orison, "lead us not into temptation"'.[36] Fiduciary doctrine seeks to
make it more likely that the non-fiduciary duty will be properly performed and
is, thus, protective of the proper performance of non-fiduciary duties.

Just as it is irrelevant whether the fiduciary has committed a breach of
non-fiduciary duty, similarly, the fiduciary's honesty is not a relevant consideration. A breach of the fiduciary conflict principle 'may be attended with perfect
good faith'.[37] Again, this reflects the protective function served by the fiduciary
conflict principle:

> [T]he honesty of the agent concerned in the particular transaction should not be
> inquired into as a question upon which its validity depends, for by this strictness the
> temptation to embark in what must always be a doubtful transaction is removed.[38]

To understand the protective function served by fiduciary duties, it is important to distinguish carefully the two kinds of duty involved: the *fiduciary* duty
prohibits conflict between duty and interest, but there is also a *non-*fiduciary
duty, the protection of which is the purpose of the fiduciary duty. In *Aberdeen
Railway v Blaikie*, for example, the director owed a non-fiduciary duty to the
company to use his best endeavours to negotiate contracts on behalf of the
company on the terms that would be most beneficial to it. That duty arose
because of his position as a director of the company and the task he was
instructed to perform, but it is not a peculiarly fiduciary duty.[39] Thus, if a
director acts incompetently in negotiating a contract, he acts in breach of a duty
owed to the company, but he does not thereby commit a breach of fiduciary duty.
The fiduciary duty is separate from the non-fiduciary duty. The purpose of the
fiduciary duty is to protect proper performance of the non-fiduciary duty by
prohibiting the fiduciary from acting when he has a personal interest that is
inconsistent with his non-fiduciary duty.

It is imperative that these two duties be kept separate from one another. If they
are not, the fiduciary conflict principle turns in on itself: it would amount to the
proposition that a fiduciary owes a *fiduciary* duty to avoid conflicts between his
fiduciary duty and his personal interest. That formulation is incoherent.[40] It is

[36] *Wormley v Wormley* (above n 32) 463.
[37] *Bray v Ford* [1896] AC 44, 48. See also *Ex parte Lacey* (1802) 6 Ves 625, 630 (31 ER 1228) (LC);
Ex parte James (above n 32) 345 and 348; *Hamilton v Wright* (above n 32) 124; *Aberdeen Railway v
Blaikie* (above n 18) 475 (HL); *Huntington Copper & Sulphur Co (Ltd) v Henderson* (1877) 4 SC (4th
Series) 294, 302 (OH); *Boston Deep Sea Fishing & Ice v Ansell* (above n 30) 369 (CA); *Collinge v Kyd*
[2005] 1 NZLR 847 at [61].
[38] *De Bussche v Alt* (above n 32) 316.
[39] See above ch 3, sections I and VII.
[40] But it is not unknown: see, eg, C Hollander and S Salzedo, *Conflicts of Interest*, 3rd edn
(London, Sweet & Maxwell, 2008) [3–001]; DJ Hayton and CCJ Mitchell, *Hayton & Marshall's*

also entirely unnecessary, because the fiduciary conflict principle makes perfect sense if it is understood as the proposition that a fiduciary owes a *fiduciary* duty to avoid conflicts between his *non*-fiduciary duty and his personal interest. In other words, the fiduciary duty that comprises the conflict principle and the non-fiduciary duty that it protects 'must be different duties'.[41]

Thus, cases that contain apparently contradictory statements to the effect that a fiduciary's 'liability does not really depend upon breach of duty'[42] but that there 'was a breach of his obligations'[43] in acting with a conflict between duty and interest can be explained if the first duty referred to is the non-fiduciary duty. That need not be breached for fiduciary liability to arise; but it must exist and must be in conflict with the fiduciary's personal interest. The second duty is the fiduciary duty, which is breached by the fiduciary acting in such a situation of conflict. Clarity of thought and analysis militates in favour of differentiating these duties rather than conflating them.

Birks described the fiduciary duty as 'parasitic'[44] to explain that the two duties are not both fiduciary duties and to describe the relationship between the two kinds of duty. He was correct to point out that one needs to refer to both a fiduciary and a non-fiduciary duty in order to make sense of the conflict principle. But it is suggested that the relationship between those two duties is better understood if the fiduciary duty is seen as *protective* of non-fiduciary duties, rather than parasitic upon them, as that better describes the function that fiduciary duties serve vis-à-vis non-fiduciary duties.

B. Prophylaxis

The protection that fiduciary doctrine provides to non-fiduciary duties is pro-phylactic in nature. It is commonly observed that fiduciary duties are prophylac-tic,[45] but there is more to the prophylactic aspect of fiduciary doctrine than is

---

Commentary and Cases on the Law of Trusts and Equitable Remedies, 12th edn (London, Sweet & Maxwell, 2005) [9–234]; A Underhill and DJ Hayton, *Law Relating to Trusts and Trustees*, 17th edn by DJ Hayton, PB Matthews and CCJ Mitchell (London, LexisNexis Butterworths, 2007) [46.1]; *Chan v Zacharia* (1984) 154 CLR 178, 198; *Armitage v Paynter Construction Ltd* [1999] 2 NZLR 534, 545 (CA); *Youyang Pty Ltd v Minter Ellison Morris Fletcher* [2003] HCA 15 at [18], (2003) 212 CLR 484; *Marks & Spencer plc v Freshfields Bruckhaus Deringer* [2004] EWHC 1337 (Ch) at [12], [2004] 1 WLR 2331.

[41] LD Smith, 'The Motive, Not the Deed' in J Getzler (ed), *Rationalizing Property, Equity and Trusts* (London, LexisNexis, 2003) 53, 56.

[42] *G E Smith Ltd v Smith* [1952] NZLR 470, 476. See also *Regal (Hastings) v Gulliver* (above n 32) 153 and 159.

[43] *G E Smith v Smith* (*ibid*) 476.

[44] Birks, 'The Content of Fiduciary Obligation' (above n 4) 29, 31 and 33.

[45] See, eg, Hayton and Mitchell, 12th edn (above n 40) [6–24]; *Pilmer v Duke Group Ltd* [2001] HCA 31 at [153], (2001) 207 CLR 165; *Maguire v Makaronis* (1997) 188 CLR 449, 492; V Brudney, 'Contract and Fiduciary Duty in Corporate Law' (1997) 38 *Boston College Law Review* 595, 603; J Berryman, 'Equitable Compensation for Breach by Fact-Based Fiduciaries: Tentative Thoughts on Clarifying Remedial Goals' (1999) 37 *Alberta Law Review* 95, 98 and 107.

ordinarily meant by such observations. They generally refer to equity having set the boundaries of liability for fiduciaries more widely than might strictly be necessary to meet the normative justifications for that liability.[46] That prophylactic methodology does distinguish fiduciary doctrine from other legal doctrines, but fiduciary duties are marked out from other kinds of duties in a more fundamental way, in that prophylaxis forms *the very reason* for their existence rather than merely a description of the over-inclusive breadth of their operation.

The ordinary description of fiduciary duties as prophylactic treats those duties as 'over-inclusive': they capture situations in which no true wrong has been committed—or at least in which it is not clear that any such wrong has been committed—in order to be sure that they also capture situations in which wrongs have occurred. Thus, in *Keech v Sandford*, Lord King LC ruled that a trustee who had renewed a trust lease in his own name, rather than as trustee, would nonetheless hold the renewed lease on constructive trust.[47] The prophylactic element in Lord King's holding is laid bare by the fact that the landlord was unwilling to renew the lease for the benefit of the trust beneficiary (an infant), and yet the trustee still could not renew the lease for himself. Lord King reasoned:

> I very well see, if a trustee, on the refusal to renew, might have a lease to himself, few trust-estates would be renewed to *cestui que* use. . . This may seem hard, that the trustee is the only person of all mankind who might not have the lease: but it is very proper that rule should be strictly pursued, and not in the least relaxed; for it is very obvious what would be the consequence of letting trustees have the lease, on refusal to renew to *cestui que* use.[48]

It is inherent in this reasoning that trustees of property such as a lease are obliged to attempt to renew the lease for the benefit of their beneficiaries: 'the trustee had a conflict between his interest in obtaining a lease for himself and his duty to obtain a renewal for the trust.'[49] One could craft a rule of liability for the trustee's failure to renew on behalf of the trust which attempted to achieve that goal more accurately than the approach adopted by Lord King by, for example, imposing liability only when the trustee could not show that to obtain a renewal was impossible. However, Lord King instead took a prophylactic approach in the case, effectively preventing trustees from taking any renewals of leases for their own personal benefit, irrespective of whether they could possibly have been obtained for the benefit of the trust.

---

[46]   See, eg, Brudney (*ibid*) 604 (fn 20).
[47]   *Keech v Sandford* (1726) Sel Cas t King 61 (25 ER 223).
[48]   *Ibid*, 62.
[49]   *Blythe v Northwood* [2005] NSWCA 221 at [192], (2005) 63 NSWLR 531.

It is the harshness or strictness of the rule that traditionally attracts the prophylactic epithet,[50] in that the rule treats the trustee as having acted inappropriately even if there was nothing further that he could have done to try to obtain the lease for the trust beneficiary. Thus, 'the foundation of the governing [fiduciary] principle is prophylactic [in the sense that its] object [is] not merely to afford remedies when a breach can be proved.'[51] The rationale for this strict prophylactic approach lies in the difficulty of proving whether the fiduciary actually has done everything he ought to have done:

> To relax standards for situations where the defendant allegedly acted 'properly' cannot be allowed because most of the relevant evidence will be peculiarly within the defendant's knowledge and control, so making it very difficult for the disadvantaged plaintiff beneficiaries to know whether or not they have a case for saying the defendant acted 'improperly'.[52]

Thus, in *Ex parte Bennett*, Lord Eldon LC explained *Keech v Sandford* on the basis that

> the trustee then took [the lease], and rightly in point of moral honesty, for his own benefit: but this Court said, it has so little power of obtaining a complete discovery in all cases, that the property should be thrown back to the lessor, rather than the trustee should have it.[53]

Difficulties of proof also influenced the decisions in other cases in which fiduciaries had acted in situations involving a conflict between duty and interest. For example, Lord Eldon LC explained in *Ex parte James* that the fiduciary rule that prohibits trustees from purchasing trust property 'stands much more upon general principle than upon the circumstances of any individual case . . . as no Court is equal to the examination and ascertainment of the truth in much the greater number of cases',[54] as he had also explained the year before in *Ex parte Lacey*.[55] Or, as Johnson J put it in *Wormley v Wormley*, 'human ingenuity, will enable it generally to baffle the utmost subtlety of legal investigation. Hence the fairness or unfairness of the transaction, or the comparison of price and value, is not suffered to enter into the consideration of the court.'[56] In other words, difficulties of proof justify the imposition of a rule that captures all transactions involving a conflict between duty and interest, irrespective of the fairness of the particular transaction at stake, because it can be difficult to determine whether the transaction actually is fair to the principal.

---

[50] SM Beck, 'The Saga of Peso Silver Mines: Corporate Opportunity Reconsidered' (1971) 49 *Canadian Bar Review* 80, 86; RP Austin, 'Fiduciary Accountability for Business Opportunities' in PD Finn (ed), *Equity and Commercial Relationships* (Sydney, Law Book Co, 1987) 141, 177–78.

[51] *Ebner v Official Trustee in Bankruptcy* [2000] HCA 63 at [159], (2000) 205 CLR 337.

[52] Hayton and Mitchell, 12th edn (above n 40) [6–24].

[53] *Ex parte Bennett* (1805) 10 Ves 381, 395 (32 ER 893).

[54] *Ex parte James* (above n 32) 345.

[55] *Ex parte Lacey* (above n 37) 627.

[56] *Wormley v Wormley* (above n 32) 463.

This form of prophylaxis in fiduciary doctrine is essentially a matter of methodology. It concerns difficulties of proof and the way fiduciary doctrine is applied.[57] However, there is a further aspect of prophylaxis in fiduciary doctrine that is not quite reached by the sorts of observations that have just been mentioned. The very nature of fiduciary doctrine, as opposed merely to its methodology, is itself prophylactic, in the sense that its very object is to try to remove or neutralise incentives that might tempt or otherwise motivate a fiduciary not to perform properly his non-fiduciary duties.

Birks observed that when designing legal rules with the aim of preventing certain mischief:

> instead of waiting for the mischief to supervene, you can take steps beforehand to guard against its coming about. One prophylactic technique is to impose a duty not to bring about a situation in which the mischief in question *might* happen.[58]

But Birks did not advert to the form of prophylaxis more commonly identified in discussions of fiduciary doctrine, nor did he discuss the relationship between the two forms of prophylaxis.

When the traditionally recognised form of prophylaxis is employed, a rule is crafted so as to capture a particular form of 'wrong', and it is that wrong which provides the normative justification for regulation. However, the prophylactic rule is drawn more widely than the wrong itself, recognising that it will capture other conduct that does not involve any element of the 'wrong'. The rationale for drawing the rule in that way is that the benefit of ensuring the capture of all instances of 'wrong' is thought to outweigh the detriment of also capturing some instances of 'non-wrong'. In other words, the traditionally recognised form of prophylaxis is intended to try to capture *all* of the situations that are considered 'wrong', recognising that in order to do so confidently, it is necessary to draw the rules in such a way that some 'non-wrongs' will also be caught. Procedural and evidential difficulties mean a more narrowly crafted cause of action might fail to meet the concerns that underlie the rule.

In contrast, the less commonly recognised form of prophylaxis, which is central to the argument developed in this book, simply operates to make a wrong *less likely*, by requiring that actors subject to the rule avoid situations in which that wrong is more likely to occur. Here, prophylaxis forms the very reason for the existence of a cause of action, rather than merely the reason for the over-inclusive breadth of the cause of action.

The difference between this form of prophylaxis and the traditional form of prophylaxis is highlighted by the fact that rules created in accordance with the

---

[57] See, eg, JH Langbein, 'The Contractarian Basis of the Law of Trusts' (1995) 105 *Yale Law Journal* 625, 655–56; J Palmer, 'The Availability of Allowances in Equity: Rewarding the Bad Guy' (2004) 21 *New Zealand Universities Law Review* 146, 169.

[58] PBH Birks, *An Introduction to the Law of Restitution*, rev edn (Oxford, Oxford University Press, 1989) 332.

traditional form will by definition encompass all cases of the wrong that they seek to regulate, whereas rules created in accordance with the other form will not necessarily do so: they attempt to prevent the wrong from coming about, but they may not actually succeed. This point is well illustrated by fiduciary doctrine. Fiduciary doctrine's purpose is to seek to make breach of non-fiduciary duty less likely by insulating the fiduciary from situations in which such breaches might be encouraged. However, that approach cannot guarantee that there will be no breach of non-fiduciary duty. A perfectly loyal fiduciary, for example, who has shunned completely all inconsistent personal interests, might nonetheless be incompetent in the appointed task and thus fail to meet the standard of conduct required by his duty of care or act in breach of contract. 'A servant who loyally does his incompetent best for his master is not unfaithful and is not guilty of a breach of fiduciary duty',[59] but he is liable for breach of the duty of care. There has been a breach of non-fiduciary duty, notwithstanding that there has been no breach of fiduciary duty.

Hence, while fiduciary doctrine certainly captures situations in which there has been no breach of non-fiduciary duty,[60] it is not simply an over-broad capturing of all of the 'wrongs' that constitute breach of non-fiduciary duty. Rather, its purpose is to provide prophylactic protection designed to make such wrongs less likely to occur. Its failure to capture all situations that involve a breach of non-fiduciary duty does not detract from it as a prophylactic form of protection for non-fiduciary duties: it is designed in an attempt to avoid or prevent a wrong (breach of non-fiduciary duty) from being perpetrated by seeking to ensure that the surrounding circumstances are such that the wrong is less likely to occur. Indeed, this form of prophylaxis perhaps even more aptly deserves the description than does the traditional usage in the sense that something is prophylactic when it is a precautionary measure that 'defends from or tends to prevent disease',[61] rather than being something that cures a disease by excising it along with other non-diseased material.

Thus, the cases refer to the 'dangerous consequence'[62] of allowing trustees and other fiduciaries to enter into transactions when the fiduciary's personal interest conflicts with the duties he owes his principal. There is danger in allowing such transactions because it is difficult to determine whether the fiduciary has fully performed the duty that he owes to his principal but *also*, and more fundamentally, because there is a heightened risk in such situations that the fiduciary will

---

[59] *Mothew* (above n 3) 18 (CA).

[60] A fiduciary can act in breach of fiduciary duty even though he has acted palpably in the best interests of his principal: see above nn 32–33.

[61] Simpson and Weiner (eds), *Oxford English Dictionary* (above n 7) vol 12, 644 ('prophylactic'). See also *Harris v Digital Pulse Pty Ltd* [2003] NSWCA 10 at [409], (2003) 56 NSWLR 298.

[62] *Whelpdale v Cookson* (1747) 1 Ves Sen 9, 9 (27 ER 856) (LC). See also *Keech v Sandford* (above n 47) 62 (LC); *Ex parte Bennett* (above n 53) 394 and 396 (LC); *Thompson v Havelock* (1808) 1 Camp 527, 528–29 (170 ER 1045); *Re Bloye's Trusts* (1849) 1 Mac & G 488, 495 (41 ER 1354) (LC).

be tempted to breach his non-fiduciary duty. Thus, for example, a trustee selling trust property must sell as advantageously as possible. Hence, fiduciary doctrine requires that he

> shall not buy for himself. Why? The reason is, that it would not be safe, with reference to the administration of justice in the general affairs of trust, that a trustee should be permitted to purchase; for human infirmity will in very few instances permit a man to exert against himself that providence, which a vendor ought to exert, in order to sell to the best advantage.[63]

Lord Herschell's famous dictum in *Bray v Ford* also highlights this prophylactic protective function of fiduciary doctrine:

> It is an inflexible rule of a Court of Equity that a person in a fiduciary position . . . is not allowed to put himself in a position where his interest and duty conflict. . . [H]uman nature being what it is, there is danger, in such circumstances, of the person holding a fiduciary position being swayed by interest rather than by duty, and thus prejudicing those whom he is bound to protect.[64]

This lays bare the fundamentally prophylactic nature of the fiduciary conflict principle, as the normative justification for its existence is to avoid situations that involve a risk of breach of non-fiduciary duties: the concern is that the fiduciary might be swayed by interest away from proper performance of his non-fiduciary duties. 'The rule is a rule to protect directors, trustees and others against the fallibility of human nature.'[65]

This protective form of prophylaxis is manifest in Lord Ellenborough's observation in *Thompson v Havelock* that 'no man should be allowed to have an interest against his duty. . . [T]here would be no security in any department of life or of business.'[66] The lack of 'security' arises because the potentially corrupting influence of the fiduciary's personal interest may subvert the function that the fiduciary undertook to serve and that his non-fiduciary duties require that he does serve. Lord Cottenham LC's decision in *Re Bloye's Trusts* also exposes the point:

> The reason why a trustee is not permitted to purchase is because the Court will not permit a man to have an interest adverse and inconsistent with the duty which he owes to another; and as a trustee for sale is bound to get the best price for property to be sold he can, the Court will not permit him to have an interest of his own adverse to the discharge of his duty to his principal. If he is the purchaser he is interested in getting the property at the lowest price he can; but if he is acting *bonâ fide* for the owner of the property his duty is to sell at the best price he can obtain; and the Court will not permit a party to place himself in a situation in which his interest conflicts with his duty; for,

---

[63] *Ex parte Bennett* (above n 53) 394.
[64] *Bray v Ford* (above n 37) 51.
[65] *Costa Rica Railway Co Ltd v Forwood* [1901] 1 Ch 746, 761 (CA).
[66] *Thompson v Havelock* (above n 62) 528–29.

taking mankind at large, it is not very safe to allow a man to put his private interest in conflict with the duty which he owes to another.[67]

The principle exists 'to protect the purity of transactions between trustee and *Cestui que Trust*.[68] Thus, it is the *possibility* that the fiduciary might not perform his non-fiduciary duties properly that is the concern of the conflict principle, so that 'it is sufficient if [the fiduciary] was in a position in which his judgment and his conduct ... *might* be influenced' (emphasis added).[69] 'The law, so far as it can, protects principals against the danger of having their interests so sacrificed.'[70] As Lord Brougham put it in *Hamilton v Wright*:

> There cannot be a greater mistake than to suppose ... that a trustee is only prevented from doing things which bring an actual loss upon the estate under his administration. It is quite enough that the thing which he does has a tendency to injure the trust; *a tendency to interfere with his duty* (emphasis added).[71]

When a fiduciary has a personal interest conflicting with his duty, equity's fundamental concern is the risk that the personal interest generates that the fiduciary will not perform properly the duty that he owes his principal. That risk is 'the very evil against which the rule in question is directed'.[72] The fundamental basis of the fiduciary conflict principle is a prophylactic desire to insulate the fiduciary from such temptations, so as better to ensure that the fiduciary will comply with his non-fiduciary duties.

The prophylactic element in the fiduciary conflict principle is also evident in the fact that a breach of fiduciary duty can occur irrespective of whether the fiduciary breached his non-fiduciary duty:[73] the very purpose of the fiduciary duty is to avoid breaches of non-fiduciary duty so that it would be perverse to require a breach of non-fiduciary duty to be shown before a breach of fiduciary duty could be identified. And, applying the form of prophylactic methodology traditionally associated with fiduciary doctrine, a breach of fiduciary duty is made out if the fiduciary acted with a conflict between duty and interest even if the fiduciary has complied with his non-fiduciary duty.[74]

---

[67] *Re Bloye's Trusts* (above n 62) 495, upheld on appeal: *Lewis v Hillman* (1852) 3 HLC 607, 630 (10 ER 239).

[68] *Ex parte Bennett* (above n 53) 395.

[69] *Re Hill* [1934] 1 Ch 623, 631 (CA).

[70] *Huntington Copper & Sulphur v Henderson* (above n 37) 301.

[71] *Hamilton v Wright* (above n 32) 123.

[72] *Aberdeen Railway v Blaikie* (above n 18) 473.

[73] See above nn 32–33.

[74] See, eg, *Ex parte Lacey* (above n 37) 627; *Ex parte James* (above n 32) 347 and 348; *Randall v Errington* (1805) 10 Ves 423, 428 (32 ER 909) (MR); *Brookman v Rothschild* (1829) 3 Sim 153, 214 (57 ER 957) (VC); *Lewis v Hillman* (above n 67) 629; *Aberdeen Railway v Blaikie* (above n 18) 471–72; *Wentworth v Lloyd* (1863) 32 Beav 467, 472 (55 ER 183) (MR); *De Bussche v Alt* (above n 32) 316; *Boardman v Phipps* (above n 32); *Swain v Law Society* (above n 32) 29; *Re Thompson's Settlement* [1986] 1 Ch 99, 118; *Coleman Taymar v Oakes* (above n 32) [98].

As the purpose of fiduciary doctrine is to encourage fiduciaries to avoid such situations altogether, that purpose would be undermined if a fiduciary were permitted to argue, as a defence to a claim for breach of fiduciary duty, that he ought to be exonerated because he had in fact not acted in breach of any non-fiduciary duty. As Robert Flannigan observes, 'even given monitoring and market controls, fiduciaries invariably are in a position to manipulate the appearance of relations and transactions.'[75] Allowing fiduciaries to argue that they duly performed their non-fiduciary duties as a defence to claims for breach of fiduciary duty opens up the possibility of fiduciaries acting in a way that will conceal breaches of non-fiduciary duty, in order to avoid fiduciary liability, which is directly opposed to the purpose that fiduciary doctrine is designed to achieve. As James LJ put it in *Parker v McKenna*:

> this Court . . . is not entitled, in my judgment, to receive evidence, or suggestion, or argument as to whether the principal did or did not suffer any injury in fact by reason of the dealing of the agent; for the safety of mankind requires that no agent shall be able to put his principal to the danger of such an inquiry as that.[76]

This prophylactic methodology is an implementation of the prophylactic purpose that fiduciary doctrine serves. Fiduciary doctrine strikes at the *risk* of breach of non-fiduciary duty that is inherent in situations involving conflicts between duty and interest, and thus it applies irrespective of whether the risk actually matures into an eventuality in any given case. The question is 'not what was done, but what might be done'.[77]

Hence, fiduciary doctrine is prophylactic *both* in its strict mode of application *and*, importantly, in its fundamental purpose. Fiduciary doctrine's prophylactic methodology is best understood and explained by reference to the fundamentally prophylactic nature of fiduciary doctrine. Identifying that it is difficult to prove certain matters does not establish that proof of, or failure to prove, those matters should cause any concern. On the other hand, a prophylactic approach to issues of proof and enforcement is far more easily understood if the very reason for the existence of the relevant rule is to provide prophylactic protection for other legal duties:

> [Fiduciary rules] are prophylactic in the sense that they tend to prevent the disease of temptation in the fiduciary—they preserve or protect the fiduciary from that disease. . . The prevention of or protection from the relevant disease is assisted by the strictness of the standard imposed and the absence of defences justifying departure from it.[78]

---

[75]   R Flannigan, 'The Strict Character of Fiduciary Liability' [2006] *New Zealand Law Review* 209, 210. See also text accompanying n 56 above. And see Lord Eldon LC's comment in *Ex parte Lacey* (above n 37) 627: 'the probability is, that a trustee, who has once conceived such a purpose, will never disclose it.'

[76]   *Parker v McKenna* (above n 32) 124–25.

[77]   *Wright v Morgan* (above n 32) 798. See also *Ex parte James* (above n 32) 345; cf JC Shepherd, *The Law of Fiduciaries* (Toronto, Carswell, 1981) 148–50.

[78]   *Harris v Digital Pulse Pty Ltd* [2003] NSWCA 10 at [414]–[415], (2003) 56 NSWLR 298.

As has already been observed, this sort of protection is not a perfect means of preventing all breaches of non-fiduciary duties because removing temptations to breach non-fiduciary duties does not guarantee that those non-fiduciary duties will always be performed properly.[79] Nonetheless, the fiduciary conflict principle seeks to make breaches of non-fiduciary duty *less likely* than they would be if temptation were allowed to remain.

Fiduciary doctrine therefore involves rules of a kind quite different from non-fiduciary duties. The fundamental objective is to make 'faithful' performance of those non-fiduciary duties more likely, but the means by which that objective is sought to be achieved involves a prophylactic form of protection for the non-fiduciary duties: the fiduciary conflict principle seeks to remove temptations that have a tendency to cause a fiduciary not to perform properly his non-fiduciary duties. Thus, the requisite elements of a breach of fiduciary duty are quite distinct from and independent of the elements that must be proven to make out breach of a non-fiduciary duty.

C. Subsidiarity

The significance of referring to fiduciary doctrine as 'subsidiary' in nature is that it helps to capture the distinct natures of fiduciary and non-fiduciary duties, as well as the nature of the relationship between them. As has just been seen, fiduciary duties are distinct from non-fiduciary duties, and proof of breach of a fiduciary duty is not dependent upon proof of breach of a non-fiduciary duty. Hence, fiduciary doctrine does not achieve its protective function merely by increasing or superseding the remedies made available for breach of non-fiduciary duties. Fiduciary doctrine seeks to *avoid* breaches of non-fiduciary duty, not to stigmatise them as a more egregious kind of breach.

Fiduciary duties are thus subsidiary duties, in the sense that they protect non-fiduciary duties. The concept of subsidiarity does not here denote second-ariness. Secondary duties arise upon breach of primary duties, such as the secondary duty to pay damages that arises when primary contractual duties have been breached.[80] Fiduciary duties do not serve that sort of function. Rather, fiduciary duties subsist concurrently alongside non-fiduciary duties with a view to making proper performance of those non-fiduciary duties more likely. As John Finnis has explained in a different context, '"subsidiarity" . . . signifies not secondariness or subordination, but assistance: the Latin for help or assistance is *subsidium*.'[81] Fiduciary duties assist with securing the proper performance of

---

[79] See text accompanying n 59 above.

[80] See, eg, *Photo Production Ltd v Securicor Transport Ltd* [1980] AC 827, 848–49. See also *Moschi v Lep Air Services Ltd* [1973] AC 331, 350; J Austin, *Lectures on Jurisprudence*, 5th edn by R Campbell (London, John Murray, 1885) 43 and 761–68, esp at pp 763–64 (Lecture XLV).

[81] JM Finnis, *Natural Law and Natural Rights* (Oxford, Oxford University Press, 1980) 146.

non-fiduciary duties by seeking to insulate fiduciaries against situations in which they might be swayed away from providing such proper performance.

III. Remedies

An analysis of the remedies that are made available for breach of fiduciary duties, and of what must be proven in order to claim those remedies, shows that these remedies are also consistent with, and thereby further support, the view that fiduciary doctrine serves a protective function vis-à-vis non-fiduciary duties. As has been seen, fiduciary doctrine seeks to avoid situations in which a fiduciary's personal interest conflicts with his non-fiduciary duty because there is in such situations an inherent temptation not to perform the non-fiduciary duty properly. The remedies for breach of fiduciary duties attempt to deter fiduciaries from acting in such situations, predominantly by removing any benefits that a fiduciary might obtain by acting in contravention of the fiduciary conflict principle. In other words, the remedies are the means by which fiduciary doctrine gives practical effect to its subsidiary and prophylactic protective function.

A. Rescission and Profit-Stripping

When a fiduciary generates a profit from a transaction in which his personal interest conflicted with his duty, those profits can generally be stripped: (a) by rescinding the transaction; (b) more directly, by way of an account of the profits; or (c) through a proprietary constructive trust over the property representing the profits and anything for which they have been substituted, less an allowance for expenses that the fiduciary incurred in acquiring (or sometimes improving) the property.

i. Rescission

Thus, for example, if a trustee purchases the trust property for himself, he acts with a clear conflict between his personal interest and the duty that he owes the beneficiaries. Such a purchase is prohibited by the 'self-dealing' rule, which holds that 'if a trustee sells the trust property to himself, the sale is voidable by any beneficiary *ex debito justitiae*, however fair the transaction.'[82] The principal may rescind the transaction even if it has been executed[83] and even when the property

---

[82] *Tito v Waddell (No 2)* [1977] Ch 106, 241. See also *Ex parte Bennett* (above n 53) 400 (LC); *McPherson v Watt* (1877) 3 App Cas 254, 264, 266, 269 and 271–72 (HL); *McKenzie v McDonald* [1927] VLR 134, 146 (SC); *Re Sherman* [1954] Ch 653, 656 and 657; PD Finn, *Fiduciary Obligations* (Sydney, Law Book Co, 1977) [517].

[83] *York Buildings Co v Mackenzie* (1795) 3 Paton 378 (1 Scots RR 717) (HL); *Armstrong v Jackson* [1917] 2 KB 822, 826.

has changed in value.[84] Rescission will result in the property being returned to the trust corpus and the trustee being reimbursed the amount he paid for the property.[85] Similarly, if a trustee or other fiduciary sells his own property to the trust, the transaction may be avoided, at the option of the beneficiaries, regardless of whether the sale price was fair.[86]

The position is slightly more complicated when the transaction involves a third party. Thus, for example, a principal can rescind a transaction entered into with a third party when the principal's agent received a bribe or secret commission from the third party in connection with the transaction,[87] provided the third party was aware of the fiduciary's interest.[88] The fiduciary has acted with a clear conflict between duty and interest,[89] which justifies rescission of the transaction. However, the third party's involvement in the transaction means that rescission is only permitted when the third party is privy to the breach of fiduciary duty. Thus, the party seeking to rescind 'must establish that they were deprived of the disinterested advice of their agent by or at least to the knowledge of' the counterparty against whom rescission is sought.[90]

Dominic O'Sullivan, Steven Elliott and Rafal Zakrzewski have argued recently that breach of the self-dealing rule renders the transaction void, rather than

---

[84] *Armstrong v Jackson* (*ibid*) 828–29.

[85] *Re Sherman* (above n 82) 657; *Re Lord Ranelagh's Will* (1884) 26 ChD 590, 596; *Great Luxembourg Railway Co v Magnay (No 2)* (1858) 25 Beav 586, 593–94 and 595–96 (53 ER 761) (MR); *York Buildings v Mackenzie* (above n 83) 402. There must be *restitutio in integrum*: *Erlanger v New Sombrero Phosphate Co* (1878) 3 App Cas 1218, 1278; *Transvaal Lands Co v New Belgium (Transvaal) Land & Development Co* [1914] 2 Ch 488, 505 (CA); *Armstrong v Jackson* (above n 83) 828; *Hely-Hutchinson v Brayhead Ltd* [1968] 1 QB 549, 586 (CA); *Maguire v Makaronis* (above n 45) 467.

[86] *Re Cape Breton Co* (1885) 29 ChD 795, 803 (CA); *Burland v Earle* [1902] AC 83, 99 (PC); *Transvaal Lands v New Belgium (Transvaal) Land & Development* (*ibid*) 505; *Cook v Deeks* [1916] AC 554, 563–64 (PC); *Jacobus Marler Estates Ltd v Marler* (1913) 114 LT 640n, 640 (HL); *Armstrong v Jackson* (above n 83) 824; *Hely-Hutchinson v Brayhead* (*ibid*) 585, 589–90 and 594; *Maguire v Makaronis* (above n 45) 467 and 475; Underhill and Hayton (above n 40) [1.58]; Finn, *Fiduciary Obligations* (above n 82) [518].

[87] *Panama & South Pacific Telegraph Co v India Rubber, Gutta Percha, & Telegraph Works Co* (1875) LR 10 Ch App 515, 526 (Div Ct); *Grant v Gold Exploration & Development Syndicate Ltd* [1900] 1 QB 233, 248–49 (CA); *Re a Debtor* [1927] 2 Ch 367, 374 (CA); *Taylor v Walker* [1958] 1 Lloyd's Rep 490, 513 (QBD); *Armagas Ltd v Mundogas SA* [1986] AC 717, 742–43; *Hurstanger Ltd v Wilson* [2007] EWCA Civ 299 at [38], [2007] 4 All ER 1118.

[88] *Logicrose Ltd v Southend United Football Club Ltd* [1988] 1 WLR 1256, 1261 (ChD).

[89] *Shipway v Broadwood* [1899] 1 QB 369, 373 (CA); *Tesco Stores Ltd v Pook* [2003] EWHC 823 (Ch) at [41] and [44], [2004] Industrial Relations Law Rep 618; *Daraydan Holdings Ltd v Solland International Ltd* [2004] EWHC 622 (Ch) at [52], [2005] Ch 119.

[90] *Logicrose v Southend United Football Club* (above n 88) 1261. See also *Hambro v Burnand* [1904] 2 KB 10, 25 (CA); *Bartrum & Sons v Lloyd* (1904) 90 LT 357, 359 (CA); *Lloyds Bank Ltd v Chartered Bank of India, Australia and China* [1929] 1 KB 40, 56 (CA); *Richard Brady Franks Ltd v Price* (1937) 58 CLR 112, 142. Relying on *Logicrose*, Briggs J has recently concluded that rescission is only available against someone who 'actually knows … or is wilfully blind to the question whether the agent has concealed the payment from his principal': *Ross River Ltd v Cambridge City Football Club Ltd* [2007] EWHC 2115 (Ch) at [205], [2008] 1 All ER 1004. See also *Hurstanger Ltd v Wilson* [2007] EWCA Civ 299 at [47]–[51], [2007] 1 WLR 2351.

voidable.[91] The cases, on the other hand, make it quite clear that the rule renders a transaction voidable, not void, if it infringes the rule.[92] A few obiter dicta appear to suggest that such a transaction is void,[93] but these are based on a conflation and consequent confusion of three distinct rules: the 'two party' rule, the 'genuine transaction' rule and the 'self-dealing' rule.

The 'two party' rule requires that any contract or conveyance involve more than one party: 'there is no contract at all which can be sued upon at law when one of the contracting parties covenants with himself and others jointly. It is obvious, of course, there can be none between a man and himself alone.'[94] At one stage, the two party rule prevented a person from occupying a position on either side of a contract or conveyance, but that disability has been very largely removed by statute.[95] The two party rule does not represent the true basis of the 'self-dealing' rule.[96]

The 'genuine transaction' rule operates to limit certain powers. In particular, a power of sale can only be validly exercised if there are two independent minds involved, one purchasing and the other buying. Thus, if there are two separate legal persons transacting, the two party rule is satisfied, but if there are not two independent minds in the transaction, then the power of sale has not been validly exercised.[97] Thus, where a *sole* trustee purports to sell trust property to himself:

> The sale is bad because it purports to be that which it is not, viz an arm's length sale of the trust property to an independent third party. A trustee's power of sale does not authorise the trustee to sell the trust property except to someone with whom he can deal at arm's length. A sale to his nominee, being unauthorised, is incapable of overreaching the interests of the beneficiaries.[98]

---

[91]   D O'Sullivan, S Elliott and R Zakrzewski, *The Law of Rescission* (Oxford, Oxford University Press, 2008) at [1.65]–[1.69].

[92]   *Campbell v Walker* (1800) 5 Ves 678, 680 (31 ER 801) (MR); *Dover v Buck* (1865) 5 Giff 57, 63 (144 RR 344) (VC); *Kaye v Croydon Tramways Co* [1898] 1 Ch 358, 368 (CA); *Re Sherman* (above n 82) 656; *Hely-Hutchinson v Brayhead* (above n 85) 585, 589–90 and 594; *Guinness plc v Saunders* [1990] 2 AC 663, 697; *Ingram v Inland Revenue Commissioners* [1997] 4 All ER 395, 424–25 (CA), affirmed on appeal: [2000] 1 AC 293, 305 and 310; *Clay v Clay* [2001] HCA 9 at [51], (2001) 202 CLR 410. See also *York Buildings Co v Mackenzie* (above n 83) 397 and 399; *Great Luxembourg Railway v Magnay (No 2)* (above n 85) 595 (MR); *Cape Breton* (above n 86) 803; *Burland v Earle* (above n 86) 99; *Re Drexel Burnham Lambert UK Pension Plan* [1995] 1 WLR 32, 41 (ChD).

[93]   *Morse v Royal* (1806) 12 Ves 355, 372 (33 ER 134) (LC); *Denton v Donner* (1856) 23 Beav 285, 290 (53 ER 112) (MR); *Franks v Bollans* (1868) LR 3 Ch App 717, 719 (LJJ); *Williams v Scott* [1900] AC 499, 508 (PC).

[94]   *Boyce v Edbrooke* [1903] 1 Ch 836, 842. See also *Henderson v Astwood* [1894] AC 150, 158 (PC); *Rye v Rye* [1962] AC 496, 513.

[95]   Law of Property Act 1925, ss 72 and 82.

[96]   See, eg, *Whichcote v Lawrence* (above n 21) 750 (LC); *Robertson v Robertson* [1924] NZLR 552, 553 (SC). See further below ch 5, section IV-A.

[97]   *Farrar v Farrars Ltd* (1888) 40 ChD 395, 409 (CA). See also *Australia & New Zealand Banking Group Ltd v Bangadilly Pastoral Co Pty Ltd* (1978) 139 CLR 195, 227.

[98]   *Ingram v IRC* (above n 92) 425.

This principle is distinct from the 'self-dealing' rule.[99] Thus, when two trustees (*X* and *Y*) sell trust property to one of them alone (*Y*), *X* provides an independent mind as to sale and *Y* as to purchase, so that there is a genuine transaction and hence an exercise of the power of sale. Nonetheless, such a transaction breaches the 'self-dealing' rule, because *Y* is on both sides of the transaction. The transaction is not void, because there has been no breach of the 'two party' rule, and the transaction is a genuine sale involving independent minds on both sides; but it is voidable under the self-dealing rule. Thus, as Millett LJ said in *Ingram v Inland Revenue Commissioners*, when a trustee purchases trust property,

> the purchase is not a nullity, though it is voidable at the instance of any beneficiary however honest and fair the transaction may be and even if it is at a price higher than that which could be obtained on the open market. . . The vice of the transaction is not that it is unfair or that it is not the product of negotiations between independent parties dealing with each other at arm's length, but that it infringes the principle that a man may not put himself in a situation where his interest conflicts with his duty.[100]

A transaction entered into in breach of the self-dealing rule is not, by that fact,[101] void but rather voidable.[102]

ii. Accounts of Profits and Constructive Trusts

When a fiduciary enters into a transaction for his own benefit, and in which his personal interest conflicts with the duty that he owes his principal, the principal can generally capture the benefit that the fiduciary has acquired either by way of an account of profits or by a constructive trust over property that represents the traceable proceeds of those profits. Thus, for example, when an agent has entered into a contract on behalf of his principal but has taken a bribe from the

[99] That there is a difference between the 'genuine transaction' rule and the fiduciary 'self-dealing' rule can also be seen from the fact that the genuine transaction rule applies to the exercise of a mortgagee's power of sale whereas a mortgagee is not a fiduciary and so is not bound by the self-dealing rule: see, eg, *Farrar v Farrars* (above n 97) 404–5 (ChD) and 409–10 (CA); *Tse Kwong Lam v Wong Chit Sen* [1983] 1 WLR 1349, 1355 (PC). The transactions that these two cases discuss could be rescinded if entered into by a fiduciary as they would infringe the self-dealing rule: see, eg, *Cape Breton* (above n 86) 803 and 811; *Cavendish-Bentinck v Fenn* (1887) 12 App Cas 652, 658; *Burland v Earle* (above n 86) 99.
[100] *Ingram v IRC* (above n 92) 424–25.
[101] Circumstances in which there has been a breach of the self-dealing rule might also involve facts that constitute a breach of the 'two party' rule or the 'genuine transaction' rule, with the effect that the transaction can be argued to be void on that other ground. There is no conceptual difficulty in a claimant having a choice between two alternative arguments as to the status of a transaction: *A v A* [2007] EWHC 99 (Fam) at [16], [2007] 2 FLR 467; RC Nolan, 'Controlling Fiduciary Power' [2009] *Cambridge Law Journal* 293, 322–23.
[102] This conclusion is reinforced by the Law of Property Act 1925, section 72(4): 'Two or more persons (whether or not being trustees or personal representatives) may convey, and shall be deemed always to have been capable of conveying, any property vested in them to any one or more of themselves in like manner as they could have conveyed such property to a third party; provided that if the persons in whose favour the conveyance is made are, by reason of any fiduciary relationship or otherwise, precluded from validly carrying out the transaction, the conveyance shall be *liable to be set aside*' (emphasis added).

contractual counterparty, the bribe creates a clear conflict between the agent's duty and his personal interest.[103] Without needing to rescind the contract, the principal can force the agent to disgorge the bribe as an unauthorised profit, and can do so either by way of the personal remedy of an account of profits[104] or by way of a proprietary constructive trust over the bribe and anything into which the bribe can be traced.[105] Similarly, in *Bhullar v Bhullar*,[106] the Court of Appeal confirmed that directors held property on constructive trust for their company when they bought it for themselves in circumstances involving a conflict between their duty to the company and their personal interest.

iii. Connection with Fiduciary Protection

The importance of these various profit-stripping remedies is that they remove from the fiduciary any benefit that he received from a transaction entered into while he had a conflict between duty and interest. The purpose of these profit-stripping awards is to deter fiduciaries from entering into such transactions in the first place, by seeking to remove any attraction that the transaction might hold for the fiduciary. Removing the fruits of temptation is an effective means of reducing the temptation itself. It seeks to nullify the temptation by rendering it pointless: 'the remedy of account of profits to capture unlawful gains . . . can have a deterrent effect, because it tends to make the unlawful conduct in question futile.'[107]

Some commentators have criticised this understanding of the remedies that follow a breach of fiduciary duty. Lionel Smith, for example, has criticised it as inadequate and 'implausible'.[108] He argues that 'a rule that only takes away the defendant's gain is not much of a deterrent'[109] and that 'an explanation based on deterrence is inconsistent with the internal rationality of private law.'[110] Neither point is convincing.

---

[103] See above n 89.

[104] *East India Co v Henchman* (1791) 1 Ves Jun 287, 289 (30 ER 347) (LC); *Boston Deep Sea Fishing & Ice v Ansell* (above n 30) 355 and 367 (CA); *Lister & Co v Stubbs* (1890) 45 ChD 1, 12 and 15 (CA); *Daraydan Holdings Ltd v Solland International Ltd* [2004] EWHC 622 (Ch) at [51], [2005] Ch 119. See also *Powell & Thomas v Evan Jones & Co* [1905] 1 KB 11, 19–20 (CA).

[105] *Attorney-General for Hong Kong v Reid* [1994] 1 AC 324, 336 (PC); *Zobory v Federal Commissioner of Taxation* (1995) 64 FCR 86; *Daraydan Holdings Ltd v Solland International Ltd* [2004] EWHC 622 (Ch) at [86], [2005] Ch 119; *Ultraframe (UK) Ltd v Fielding* [2005] EWHC 1638 (Ch) at [1490]; *Primlake Ltd v Matthews Associates* [2006] EWHC 1227 (Ch) at [334], [2007] 1 BCLC 666; *Pakistan v Zardari* [2006] EWHC 2411 (Comm) at [164]; *Sinclair Investment Holdings SA v Versailles Trade Finance Ltd* [2007] EWHC 915 (Ch) at [105], [2007] 2 All ER (Comm) 993.

[106] *Bhullar v Bhullar* [2003] EWCA Civ 424, [2003] 2 BCLC 241.

[107] *Harris v Digital Pulse Pty Ltd* [2003] NSWCA 10 at [408], (2003) 56 NSWLR 298; see also at [161] and [169]–[170] *per* Mason P. And see *Benson v Heathorn* (1842) 1 Y & CCC 326, 342–43 (62 ER 909); *Guth v Loft Inc* 5 A 2d 503, 510 (1939); *Strother v 3464920 Canada Inc* [2007] SCC 24 at [77], [2007] 2 SCR 177.

[108] Smith (above n 41) 61 (fn 37).

[109] *Ibid*, 60.

[110] *Ibid*, 61.

Smith's first point is an application of a standard economic analysis of profit-stripping, which argues that merely stripping the profit itself does not deter the conduct that generates the profit: unless there is universal enforcement, there is no deterrence in the absence of a penalty.[111] There are two answers to this point. First, it ignores the fact that a fiduciary can often be left worse off after profit-stripping remedies have been applied than he was before. Several examples illustrate this point, in a variety of situations. First, fiduciary doctrine's profit-stripping remedies generally operate so as to remove the fruits of the fiduciary's conduct without compensating the fiduciary for his effort in generating those profits. Allowances for skill and effort can be made[112] when 'it would be inequitable now for the beneficiaries to step in and take the profit without paying for the skill and labour which has produced it'.[113] However, such allowances are made only rarely[114] and are 'restricted to those cases where [they] cannot have the effect of encouraging trustees in any way to put themselves in a position where their interests conflict with their duties as trustees'.[115] Thus, a fiduciary whose profit is stripped is ordinarily worse off than before to the extent of his uncompensated labour costs in producing the profit.[116] Secondly, any negative reputational effect that the successful claim for breach of fiduciary duty has is not recouped in the accounting process.[117] Thirdly, an account of profits can place the defendant in a position worse than that he would have occupied had he acted properly in that the entire profit is stripped irrespective of whether the principal would have been prepared to authorise the fiduciary to take part of the profit (for example, in a profit-sharing arrangement) had the fiduciary made full disclosure and sought the principal's fully informed consent.[118]

---

[111] Others have made the same argument: Shepherd (above n 77) 82 (fn 122); R Cooter and BJ Freedman, 'The Fiduciary Relationship: Its Economic Character and Legal Consequences' (1991) 66 *New York University Law Review* 1045, 1053. See also G Williams, 'The Aims of the Law of Tort' [1951] *Current Legal Problems* 137, 147.

[112] See, eg, *Brown v Litton* (1711) 1 P Wms 140, 142 (24 ER 329) (LK); *Brown v de Tastet* (1821) Jac 284, 294, 298 and 299 (37 ER 858) (LC); *Cook v Collingridge* (1823) Jac 607, 623 (37 ER 979) (LC); *Lord Provost, Magistrates & Town Council of Edinburgh v Lord Advocate* (1879) 4 App Cas 823, 839; *Re Macadam* [1946] Ch 73, 82–83; *Boardman v Phipps* (above n 32) 104 and 112; *O'Sullivan v Management Agency & Music Ltd* [1985] 1 QB 428, 459, 468 and 472 (CA); *Fraser Edmiston Pty Ltd v AGT (Qld) Pty Ltd* [1988] 2 Qd R 1, 12; *Warman International Ltd v Dwyer* (1995) 182 CLR 544, 568; *Badfinger Music v Evans* [2001] WTLR 1 (ChD); *Lindsley v Woodfull* [2004] EWCA Civ 720 at [6] and [8], [2004] 2 BCLC 131.

[113] *Phipps v Boardman* [1964] 1 WLR 993, 1018 (ChD).

[114] Allowances are not 'ordinarily made': cf *Mid-City Skin Cancer & Laser Centre v Zahedi-Anarak* [2006] NSWSC 844 at [273], (2006) 67 NSWLR 569.

[115] *Guinness v Saunders* (above n 92) 701.

[116] See *Benson v Heathorn* (above n 107) 343.

[117] Such effects are felt as real by fiduciaries: see, eg, *Bray v Ford* (above n 37).

[118] See, eg, *Gray v New Augarita Porcupine Mines Ltd* [1952] 3 DLR 1, 15 (PC); *Murad v Al-Saraj* [2005] EWCA Civ 959 at [67], [71] and [111]–[112], [2005] WTLR 1573. The fiduciary is not here worse off than he would have been had he done nothing (if one leaves aside the two previous points made in the text), which is a permissible course of conduct, but he is worse off than he would be had he acted properly in seeking fully informed consent from his principal.

McLachlin CJ has suggested, obiter, in her dissent in *Strother v 3464920 Canada Inc* [2007] SCC 24 at

The second problem with the first point raised by Smith is that while perfect disgorgement may not provide the same degree of deterrence as could be achieved by a penalty, Anglo-Australian equitable doctrine has traditionally set its face against punitive action.[119] The policy underlying the fiduciary conflict principle is to discourage fiduciaries from acting in situations that carry a heightened risk of breach of non-fiduciary duties. Fiduciary doctrine's profit-stripping remedies give effect to that deterrent, perhaps imperfectly but as fully as possible while remaining within the constraints of traditional equitable doctrine.

Smith's second point is that a deterrent purpose involves seeking to influence the conduct of others in the future, which he says is inconsistent with the internal or 'immanent'[120] rationality of private law, as it is not concerned with issues of corrective justice between two parties.[121] The short answer to this criticism is that 'that is not the way in which a system based on case law develops.'[122] The fact that this aspect of fiduciary doctrine does not match a theoretical model of the common law advanced by commentators does not make the deterrent purpose that fiduciary doctrine pursues any less a part of private law. The common law, including equity in this regard, 'is a pragmatic, working, authority-based system. It is not a school of philosophy.'[123] For example, exemplary damages can be criticised on the basis that their deterrent function is inconsistent with corrective

---

[152]–[158], [2007] 2 SCR 177, that perhaps a fiduciary ought not to have to account for profits where the profit did not arise out of property held for the principal and where the breach of fiduciary duty caused no loss to the principal. Her argument is inconsistent with, and ignores, *Gray v New Augarita* and *Murad v Al-Saraj*, as well as the High Court of Australia's ruling in *Warman v Dwyer* that an account of profits is available virtually as of right: see *Warman International v Dwyer* (above n 112) 560. McLachlin CJ instead sought to rely on an article by David Hayton which discusses the question whether a *proprietary* remedy ought to be available in such circumstances, as opposed to a merely *personal* remedy: DJ Hayton, 'Unique Rules for the Unique Institution, the Trust' in S Degeling and J Edelman (eds), *Equity in Commercial Law* (Pyrmont, Lawbook Co, 2005) 279, 284, cited by McLachlin CJ at [155]. That issue is irrelevant to the entirely different question whether the orthodox *profit-stripping* remedy of an account should be unavailable where no *loss* has been caused by the breach of fiduciary duty. Longstanding authority holds that the profit can be stripped, even where no loss has been caused, and McLachlin CJ's suggestions provide no reason to depart from that position.

[119] See, eg, *Attorney-General v Alford* (1855) 4 De GM & G 843, 851 (43 ER 737, 741) (LC); *Burdick v Garrick* (1870) LR 5 Ch App 233, 241 (Div Ct); *Vyse v Foster* (1872) LR 8 Ch App 309, 333, affirmed on appeal: (1874) LR 7 HL 318, 336; *Westdeutsche Landesbank Girozentrale v Islington London Borough Council* [1996] AC 669, 692–93 and 723; *Harris v Digital Pulse Pty Ltd* [2003] NSWCA 10 at [336]–[337], [408], [415] and [420], (2003) 56 NSWLR 298. Punitive awards for breach of fiduciary duty have been allowed in New Zealand: see, eg, *Aquaculture Corp v New Zealand Green Mussel Co Ltd* [1990] 3 NZLR 299, 301–2 (CA); *Cook v Evatt (No 2)* [1992] 1 NZLR 676, 705.

[120] EJ Weinrib, *The Idea of Private Law* (Cambridge, Harvard University Press, 1995) 206–8.

[121] See EJ Weinrib, 'Legal Formalism: On the Immanent Rationality of Law' (1988) 97 *Yale Law Journal* 949; EJ Weinrib, 'Corrective Justice in a Nutshell' (2002) 52 *University of Toronto Law Journal* 349.

[122] *Roxborough v Rothmans of Pall Mall Australia Ltd* [2001] HCA 68 at [72], (2001) 208 CLR 516. See also *Farah Constructions Pty Ltd v Say-Dee Pty Ltd* [2007] HCA 22 at [154], (2007) 230 CLR 89.

[123] J Hackney, 'More than a Trace of the Old Philosophy' in PBH Birks (ed), *The Classification of Obligations* (Oxford, Oxford University Press, 1997) 123, 155.

justice,[124] and yet they exist nonetheless.[125] Indeed, 'tort law is a mosaic in which principles of corrective justice and distributive justice are interwoven',[126] and yet it is a fundamental part of private law. In the fiduciary context, the cases make it emphatically clear that deterrence is an important function of the profit-stripping remedies. As Lord Brougham LC said in *Docker v Somes*, the situation is 'discouraged by intercepting its gains, and thus frustrating the intentions that caused it'.[127] Similar sentiments are found littered throughout the case law. In *Harris v Digital Pulse*, Mason P referred to

[the] well-established proposition that some equitable remedies awarded against defaulting fiduciaries have undoubted deterrent purpose. These include the personal remedy of account of profits and proprietary remedies such as constructive trust. . . There are many statements attesting to the deterrent function of these remedies directed at recalcitrant fiduciaries.[128]

Similarly, Arden LJ referred to the deterrent purpose in *Lindsley v Woodfull*,[129] and in *Murad v Al-Saraj* she stated:

it [is] clear that equity imposes stringent liability on a fiduciary as a deterrent—*pour encourager les autres*. . . [I]n the interests of efficiency and to provide an incentive to fiduciaries to resist the temptation to misconduct themselves, the law imposes exacting standards on fiduciaries and an extensive liability to account.[130]

Fiduciary doctrine prohibits a fiduciary from acting when his personal interest conflicts with his non-fiduciary duty in order to make it more likely that the fiduciary will perform his non-fiduciary duty properly. In order to deter the fiduciary from acting, unauthorised profits that flow to him from such a transaction can be stripped, thereby reinforcing the protection of the non-fiduciary duty. Consistently with the substance of the duty-interest principle, secret profits are stripped irrespective of whether the fiduciary acted in breach of

---

[124] See, eg, *Cassell & Co Ltd v Broome* [1972] AC 1027, 1086–87; *Kuddus v Chief Constable of Leicestershire Constabulary* [2001] UKHL 29 at [95] and [110], [2002] 2 AC 122; *Aggravated, Exemplary and Restitutionary Damages* (Law Com No 247, 1997) at [5.20]–[5.21] and [5.28]; A Beever, 'The Structure of Aggravated and Exemplary Damages' (2003) 23 *Oxford Journal of Legal Studies* 87, 105–10.

[125] See, eg, *Cassell & Co v Broome* (*ibid*) 1114; *Kuddus v Chief Constable of Leicestershire Constabulary* [2001] UKHL 29 at [4] and [68], [2002] 2 AC 122; *A v Bottrill* [2002] UKPC 44 at [3] and [20], [2003] 1 AC 449; *Taylor v Beere* [1982] 1 NZLR 81, 89–91 (CA); *Daniels v Thompson* [1998] 3 NZLR 22, 28–29 and 68–69 (CA); *Aggravated, Exemplary and Restitutionary Damages* (Law Com No 247, 1997) at [5.22]–[5.27] and [5.29]–[5.39]; J Edelman, *Gain-Based Damages: Contract, Tort, Equity & Intellectual Property* (Oxford, Hart, 2002) 9–21.

[126] *McFarlane v Tayside Health Board* [2000] 2 AC 59, 83. See also Williams (above n 111) 172; *Smith New Court Securities Ltd v Citibank NA* [1997] AC 254, 279–80; *Brodie v Singleton Shire Council* [2001] HCA 29 at [319], (2001) 206 CLR 512.

[127] *Docker v Somes* (1834) 2 My & K 655, 665 (39 ER 1095).

[128] *Harris v Digital Pulse Pty Ltd* [2003] NSWCA 10 at [161], (2003) 56 NSWLR 298. See also text accompanying n 107 above; *Warman International v Dwyer* (above n 112) 557–58.

[129] *Lindsley v Woodfull* [2004] EWCA Civ 165 at [30], [2004] 2 BCLC 131.

[130] *Murad v Al-Saraj* [2005] EWCA Civ 959 at [74], [2005] WTLR 1573.

non-fiduciary duty[131] and irrespective of whether any loss was caused to the principal.[132] It need not be shown that the secret profit influenced the fiduciary's conduct,[133] as he ought not to have acted with a conflict between duty and interest: it is a transaction 'in which he ought never to have embarked'.[134] The fiduciary's failure to heed that stricture is remedied by forcing him to disgorge his profits in an attempt to deter both him and others from acting when they ought not.

The profit-stripping remedies are thus consistent with the thesis that the fiduciary conflict principle is concerned to provide a subsidiary and prophylactic form of protection for non-fiduciary duties. They do not, however, prove that thesis directly, given that profit-stripping remedies are also made available in a variety of circumstances at common law,[135] most of which are concerned with punishing and deterring wrongdoing[136] rather than protecting against breach of other duties. Thus, for example, some breaches of contract[137] and some torts[138] can be remedied by an account of profits.

Profit-stripping remedies are generally made available for breaches of contract or torts in 'circumstances of cynical and wilful wrongdoing'.[139] In contrast, fiduciary doctrine is concerned to deter *all* breaches of fiduciary duty, to which end the profit-stripping remedies are made available virtually as a matter of right[140] and regardless of whether the fiduciary acted honestly.[141] Profit-stripping remedies are made available in fiduciary cases because the very purpose of the doctrine is to seek to prevent breaches of non-fiduciary duty by deterring fiduciaries from acting in situations in which there is a conflict between duty and interest. Stripping such profits is thus a direct response to the risk of breach of non-fiduciary duty that the possibility of profit creates. As such, fiduciary doctrine's profit-stripping remedies are consistent with it serving a subsidiary and prophylactic function in protecting non-fiduciary duties.

---

[131] See, eg, *De Bussche v Alt* (above n 32) 315–16.
[132] *Gray v New Augarita Porcupine Mines* (above n 118) 15; *Murad v Al-Saraj* (above n 130) [67], [71] and [111]–[112].
[133] *Shipway v Broadwood* (above n 89) 373; *Hovenden & Sons v Millhoff* (1900) 83 LT 41, 43 (CA); *Parker v McKenna* (above n 32) 124–25; *Re a Debtor* (above n 87) 373.
[134] *Benson v Heathorn* (above n 107) 342.
[135] See generally Edelman, *Gain-Based Damages* (above n 125).
[136] *Rookes v Barnard* [1964] AC 1129, 1228; *A v Bottrill* [2002] UKPC 44 at [20]–[21] and [29], [2003] 1 AC 449; Edelman, *Gain-Based Damages* (above n 125) 83; DM Fox, 'Restitutionary Damages to Deter Breach of Contract' [2001] *Cambridge Law Journal* 33, 33 and 35.
[137] *Attorney-General v Blake* [2001] 1 AC 268, 284–85; *Experience Hendrix LLC v PPX Enterprises Inc* [2003] EWCA Civ 323 at [17]–[30] and [58], [2003] 1 All ER (Comm) 830.
[138] See Edelman, *Gain-Based Damages* (above n 125) 136–48.
[139] *Ibid*, 216.
[140] *Warman International v Dwyer* (above n 112) 560.
[141] See, eg, *Boston Deep Sea Fishing & Ice v Ansell* (above n 30) 369 (CA).

B. Compensation for Loss

The question whether equitable compensation for loss can be awarded for breach of fiduciary duty is more complicated. This renders the relationship between a compensatory remedy and the subsidiary and prophylactic function of fiduciary doctrine somewhat less clear.

i. Availability

There are two sources of doubt as to the availability of equitable compensation as a potential remedy for breach of fiduciary duties. First, several commentators argue that equitable compensation for loss is conceptually inconsistent with fiduciary doctrine, and so unavailable. Secondly, some authority suggests that equitable compensation is unavailable in certain contexts involving specific kinds of breach of fiduciary duty.

Sarah Worthington has argued:

> [P]rofit disgorgement is the limit of the remedy for breach of fiduciary obligation. . . [I]f the director's disloyal behaviour is not profitable to the director, then the company cannot obtain a remedy *for breach of the duty of loyalty* . . . although the facts might support alternative claims to achieve these ends. The duty of loyalty is not designed to remedy losses; other duties fulfil that role.[142]

The reason for this limitation is not made clear. Worthington recognises that the danger in allowing conflicts between duty and interest is that the fiduciary will be swayed by interest in an anticipated profit,[143] and so the idea may be that the prospect of causing loss does not create any such danger. Birks offered a fuller justification for compensatory remedies being unavailable for breaches of fiduciary duty, arguing that the sanction for a prophylactic rule 'cannot ever be compensatory damages, since, *ex hypothesi*, you are not waiting for the loss to supervene'.[144] Lord Millett has offered a different justification for this position:

> Equity, in the exercise of its exclusive jurisdiction over trustees and fiduciaries . . . does not award compensation for loss. Trustees are stewards of other persons' property. Their primary obligation is to account for their stewardship. The primary remedy of a beneficiary is to have the account taken, to surcharge or falsify the account, and to make the trustee make good any deficiency which appears. . . If a trustee or fiduciary has committed a breach of trust or fiduciary duty, Equity makes him account as if he had not done so. . . This is a radically different approach [to the common law]; indeed it is

---

[142] S Worthington, 'Corporate Governance: Remedying and Ratifying Directors' Breaches' (2000) 116 *Law Quarterly Review* 638, 664–65. See also JD McCamus, 'Prometheus Unbound: Fiduciary Obligation in the Supreme Court of Canada' (1997) 28 *Canadian Business Law Journal* 107, 133–34; S Worthington, 'Fiduciaries: When is Self-Denial Obligatory?' [1999] *Cambridge Law Journal* 500, 507.

[143] See Worthington, 'Corporate Governance' (*ibid*) 663.

[144] Birks, *An Introduction to the Law of Restitution* (above n 58) 332.

the converse approach. It does not treat the defendant as a wrongdoer; it disregards his wrongdoing, makes him account as if he has acted properly throughout, and does not permit him to deny that he has done so.[145]

Two comments are appropriate. First, it is not clear that Lord Millett's distinction between calculation of loss at common law and the process of taking an account in equity identifies a fundamental difference between the purposes of the two forms of calculation. There are differences, particularly with regard to issues such as causation and remoteness,[146] but both are fundamentally designed to determine where the claimant would have stood had there been no breach of duty.[147] In other words, notwithstanding differences in the rules that are applied, 'the principles underlying both systems are the same':[148] at root, both seek to determine in what position the claimant would have stood had the defendant acted lawfully.

Second, Lord Millett treats trustees and fiduciaries identically in the first sentence but then discusses only trustees (and their obligation to account for their stewardship) in the second, third and fourth sentences, before expanding the ambit of his comments in the fifth sentence so as to include (again) all fiduciaries. The relevance of this is that 'whilst the trustee is the archetype of the fiduciary, the trust has distinct characteristics,'[149] prime amongst which is the trustee's obligation to account for the trust property.[150] Not all fiduciaries are stewards of property. As Joshua Getzler has observed, 'the equitable account action cannot easily be applied to remedy losses outside a narrow band of fiduciary relationships, namely continuous and custodial trusteeship.'[151] When there is no stewardship, so that there are no accounts to be taken, but nonetheless a breach of fiduciary duty has caused a loss, the question is whether there should be compensation for that loss.

---

[145] PJ Millett, 'Proprietary Restitution' in Degeling and Edelman (eds) (above n 118) 309, 310.

[146] *Re Dawson (dec'd)* [1966] 2 NSWR 211, 214–15; *Target Holdings Ltd v Redferns* [1996] 1 AC 421, 432.

[147] *Dornford v Dornford* (1806) 12 Ves 127, 129 (33 ER 49) (MR); *Grayburn v Clarkson* (1868) LR 3 Ch App 605, 607 and 609 (CA); R Chambers, 'Liability' in PBH Birks and A Pretto (eds), *Breach of Trust* (Oxford, Hart, 2002) 1, 12–13. When an account is surcharged, the court determines what the trustee ought to have done with the trust assets, to determine in what shape the account should stand: see, eg, *Nestle v National Westminster Bank plc* [1993] 1 WLR 1260, 1269 and 1283–84 (CA); *Re Mulligan (dec'd)* [1998] 1 NZLR 481, 501 and 507 (HC). If the account is falsified, the court ensures that the account reads as it would have had the trustee acted lawfully. There is no need to plead or prove a breach of trust in order to falsify, but the trustee will be unable to justify the account as it stands unless he has acted lawfully: *Angullia v Estate & Trust Agencies (1927) Ltd* [1938] AC 624, 636–37 (PC); *Byrchall v Bradford* (1822) 6 Madd 235, 240–41 (56 ER 1081) (VC).

[148] *Target Holdings v Redferns* (above n 146) 432. See also *Re HIH Insurance Ltd* [2002] NSWSC 171 at [748], (2001) 41 ACSR 72; *Premium Real Estate Ltd v Stevens* [2009] NZSC 15 at [37], [2009] 2 NZLR 384.

[149] *Maguire v Makaronis* (above n 45) 473.

[150] Underhill and Hayton (above n 40) [60.1].

[151] J Getzler, 'Equitable Compensation and the Regulation of Fiduciary Relationships' in PBH Birks and FD Rose (eds), *Restitution and Equity: Resulting Trusts and Equitable Compensation*, vol 1 (London, Mansfield Press, 2000) 235, 250.

One answer to that question, apparently favoured by Worthington, is to say that the remedies available for breach of *non*-fiduciary duties, insofar as any may have been committed, are all that can be provided. However, there is no conceptual inconsistency between the protective function that fiduciary doctrine serves and the availability of compensation for loss when fiduciary doctrine's protective rules have been infringed. Furthermore, while equitable compensation previously 'languished apparently unnoticed and unwanted',[152] it is now widely recognised in the cases as a potential remedy for breach of fiduciary duty.[153]

The second source of doubt as to the availability of equitable compensation arises from cases concerning breach of the fiduciary dealing rules. When a fiduciary has sold property to his principal which he first obtained while not in any fiduciary relationship with the principal, an account of profits will not be ordered.[154] If the principal is unable to rescind the transaction (for example, because it subsequently sold the property so that it cannot now be returned to the fiduciary[155]), it may be possible for a court to make a monetary award, which has the *effect* of rescission without actually rescinding the transaction;[156] but the

---

[152] PD Finn, 'Fiduciary Law and the Modern Commercial World' in E McKendrick (ed), *Commercial Aspects of Trusts and Fiduciary Obligations* (Oxford, Oxford University Press, 1992) 7, 40. See also CEF Rickett, 'Equitable Compensation: The Giant Stirs' (1996) 112 *Law Quarterly Review* 27, 29.

[153] See, eg, *Catt v Marac Australia Ltd* (1986) 9 NSWLR 639, 659; *Commonwealth Bank of Australia v Smith* (1991) 42 FCR 390, 394; *Gemstone Corp of Australia Ltd v Grasso* (1994) 13 ACSR 695 (SASC); *Warman International v Dwyer* (above n 112) 559; *Breen v Williams* (above n 1) 113 and 135–36; *Rama v Millar* [1996] 1 NZLR 257 (PC); *Greater Pacific Investments Pty Ltd v Australian National Industries Ltd* (1996) 39 NSWLR 143, 153–54 (CA); *Swindle v Harrison* [1997] 4 All ER 705 (CA); *Bristol & West Building Society v Daniels & Co* [1997] PNLR 323, 326–27 and 328 (ChD); *Mothew* (above n 3) 17 (CA); *Schipp v Cameron* [1998] NSWSC 997 at [741]; *Nationwide Building Society v Balmer Radmore* [1999] Lloyd's Rep PN 241, 262 (ChD); *Platt v Platt* [1999] 2 BCLC 745 at [31]–[32] (ChD); *JJ Harrison (Properties) Ltd v Harrison* [2001] 1 BCLC 158, 173, not questioned on appeal: [2001] EWCA Civ 1467 at [21], [2002] 1 BCLC 162; *CMS Dolphin Ltd v Simonet* [2001] 2 BCLC 704 at [140] (ChD); *Aequitas v AEFC* [2001] NSWSC 14 at [428] and [442], (2001) 19 ACLC 1,006; *LC Services Ltd v Brown* [2003] EWHC 3024 at [95]; *Re MDA Investment Management Ltd* [2003] EWHC 227 (Ch) at [70]; *Cassis v Kalfus (No 2)* [2004] NSWCA 315 at [99]; *GM & AM Pearce & Co Pty Ltd v Australian Tallow Producers* [2005] VSCA 113 at [51]; *Také Ltd v BSM Marketing Ltd* [2006] EWHC 1085 (QB) at [206]; *Wilson v Hurstanger Ltd* [2007] EWCA Civ 299 at [34]–[35] and [49]; *Také Ltd v BSM Marketing Ltd* [2007] EWHC 2031 (QB); *PNC Telecom plc v Thomas* [2007] EWHC 2157 (Ch) at [89], [2008] 2 BCLC 95; *Super 1000 Pty Ltd v Pacific General Securities Ltd* [2008] NSWSC 1222 at [122], (2008) 221 FLR 427; *Multi Installations Ltd v Varsani* [2008] EWHC 657 (Ch) at [38]–[41]; *Sandhu v Sidhu* [2009] EWHC 983 (Ch) at [122]. See also IE Davidson, 'The Equitable Remedy of Compensation' (1982) 13 *Melbourne University Law Review* 349, 350 and 372–91; WMC Gummow, 'Compensation for Breach of Fiduciary Duty' in TG Youdan (ed), *Equity, Fiduciaries and Trusts* (Toronto, Carswell, 1989) 57, 61–62; RP Meagher, JD Heydon and MJ Leeming, *Meagher, Gummow & Lehane's Equity: Doctrines and Remedies*, 4th edn (Chatswood, Butterworths LexisNexis, 2002) [5]–[260]; MDJ Conaglen, 'Equitable Compensation for Breach of Fiduciary Dealing Rules' (2003) 119 *Law Quarterly Review* 246; Underhill and Hayton (above n 40) [59.1].

[154] *Cape Breton* (above n 86) 805; *Ladywell Mining Co v Brookes* (1887) 35 ChD 400, 412–13 (CA); *Jacobus Marler* (above n 86) 641; *Burland v Earle* (above n 86) 99.

[155] See, eg, *Ladywell Mining v Brookes* (*ibid*) 408 and 414; *Re Lady Forrest (Murchison) Gold Mine Ltd* [1901] 1 Ch 582, 590.

[156] See, eg, *McKenzie v McDonald* (above n 82); *Mahoney v Purnell* [1996] 3 All ER 61 (QBD); Nolan, 'A Fiduciary Duty to Disclose?' (above n 1) 222; PBH Birks, 'Unjust Factors and Wrongs:

'orthodox view'[157] is that an award of equitable compensation for loss is unavailable.[158] That view is based largely on *Re Cape Breton Co*[159] and *Jacobus Marler Estates Ltd v Marler.*[160] However, when considered closely,[161] those cases do not provide strong support for the view that equitable compensation is unavailable, whereas several others substantiate the contrary view.

In *Cape Breton,* a director of a company was one of a group that sold property to the company. The company could not recover from the director the difference between what he had initially paid for the property (when he owed no fiduciary duties to the company) and the price the company paid him for it, because an account of the director's profits in that form would rewrite the bargain between the company and the director.[162] However, in reaching that conclusion, Cotton LJ expressly stated that he was not deciding whether a fiduciary could be made to compensate his principal for the difference between the price the principal paid to the fiduciary for the property and the market value of the property at the time of that sale.[163]

Similarly, in *Jacobus Marler,* Lord Moulton said that if directors sell to a company property that they did not acquire as fiduciary agents of the company, they 'cannot be made accountable for the profits that they make upon the transaction. If the Company holds them to the bargain so made it must take the bargain as it is; the Court will not frame a new bargain to which the parties have never consented.'[164] However, he did not address what happens if the company has no choice but to accept the transaction because rescission has been rendered impossible without the company's fully informed consent. Indeed, the unreported transcript of the Lords' speeches makes it clear that the case was ultimately argued on the basis of liability in negligence, rather than as a claim for equitable compensation for breach of fiduciary duty.[165] The case is therefore of little assistance in determining whether the latter jurisdiction exists.

Pecuniary Rescission for Undue Influence' [1997] *Restitution Law Review* 72, 73; RC Nolan, 'Conflicts of Interest, Unjust Enrichment, and Wrongdoing' in WR Cornish, RC Nolan, J O'Sullivan and GJ Virgo (eds), *Restitution: Past, Present and Future* (Oxford, Hart, 1998) 87, 114–15.

[157]　Underhill and Hayton (above n 40) [1.58].

[158]　See, eg, LS Sealy, 'Some Principles of Fiduciary Obligations' [1963] *Cambridge Law Journal* 119 124, 135 and 136–37; Meagher, Heydon and Leeming, 4th edn (above n 153) [5–170]; LS Sealy, 'Fiduciary Obligations, Forty Years On' (1995) 9 *Journal of Contract Law* 37, 51–52; Worthington, 'Corporate Governance' (above n 142) 664–65; LS Sealy, 'Directors' Duties Revisited' (2001) 22 *Company Lawyer* 79, 80–81.

[159]　*Re Cape Breton Co* (above n 86).

[160]　*Jacobus Marler Estates Ltd v Marler* (above n 86).

[161]　For detailed examination of this issue, see Conaglen, 'Equitable Compensation for Breach of Fiduciary Dealing Rules' (above n 153).

[162]　*Cape Breton* (above n 86) 805.

[163]　*Ibid.*

[164]　*Jacobus Marler Estates Ltd v Marler* (Transcript, HL, 14 April 1913) 40.

[165]　*Ibid*, 20 and 34.

In contrast, the House of Lords decision on appeal from *Cape Breton* suggests that such a jurisdiction does exist.[166] The fact that *restitutio in integrum* had become impossible was held not to preclude the possibility of a pecuniary award,[167] nor was such an award ruled out by the company's inability to claim an account of profits. Lord Herschell noted that there would be liability to pay compensation when deceit is proven,[168] but he appeared also to recognise a distinct[169] compensatory liability when a fiduciary breaches his duty by omitting to make full disclosure of his personal interest in the transaction.[170] Lord Macnaghten recognised a liability to compensate the company for loss if the director committed 'a misfeasance in the nature of a breach of trust',[171] and Lord FitzGerald said the director 'was guilty of a breach of duty if he did not disclose the fact that he himself had a large pecuniary interest in the purchase by the Cape Breton Company'.[172]

On the facts, non-disclosure was not actually established, and the plaintiff had not shown that it paid more than 'a fair and reasonable price',[173] so it could establish no loss. The important point, however, is the recognition of a jurisdiction to compensate for loss that flows from a breach of the fiduciary dealing rules. Furthermore, given the director was not a fiduciary agent when he first acquired the property, any liability for loss must arise on the basis of his fiduciary role as a director at the time the company bought the property.

Other cases provide further support for the view that this jurisdiction exists.[174] In *Hardwicke v Vernon*, for example, an agent bought, via a fictitious purchaser, part of an estate that he had been employed to sell; he was required to pay the difference between the contract price and the actual value of the property bought.[175] Similarly, in *Leeds & Hanley Theatres of Varieties*, a company promoter had to pay compensation for loss[176] when he sold two music halls to a company, which he had promoted after buying the music halls, without disclosing his profit

---

[166] *Cavendish-Bentinck v Fenn* (above n 99). See also Nolan, 'Conflicts of Interest, Unjust Enrichment, and Wrongdoing' (above n 156) 103–4. This decision is curiously ignored by proponents of the orthodox view when they rely on *Cape Breton*: see, eg, Meagher, Heydon and Leeming, 4th edn (above n 153), which does not even mention this decision.

[167] *Cavendish-Bentinck v Fenn* (above n 99) 665. See also *Hichens v Congreve* (1831) 4 Sim 420, 428 (58 ER 157) (VC); *Re Olympia Ltd* [1898] 2 Ch 153, 178–79 (CA); *Gluckstein v Barnes* [1900] AC 240, 249 and 252–54.

[168] *Cavendish-Bentinck v Fenn* (above n 99) 662; see also p 666 *per* Lord Watson.

[169] *Ibid*, 662 and 663.

[170] *Ibid*, 661.

[171] *Ibid*, 669.

[172] *Ibid*, 667.

[173] *Ibid*, 668.

[174] See also Nolan, 'Conflicts of Interest, Unjust Enrichment, and Wrongdoing' (above n 156) 103–4.

[175] *Hardwicke v Vernon* (1798) 4 Ves 411, 416 (31 ER 209).

[176] Poor evidence forced the court to estimate the plaintiff's loss by reference to the defendant's gain (*Re Leeds & Hanley Theatres of Varieties Ltd* [1902] 2 Ch 809, 826–27), but the court's concern was clearly with the plaintiff's loss (see p 825).

on the sale or that he was the vendor.[177] In *Swindle v Harrison*, the Court of
Appeal unanimously accepted that equitable compensation could be awarded for
a breach of fiduciary duty when a solicitor acted with a personal interest in a
transaction with his client,[178] although ultimately the claimant's loss had not
been caused by the breach of fiduciary duty. And in *JJ Harrison (Properties) Ltd v
Harrison*, compensation was a potential remedy when a director had bought
property from his company without properly disclosing his interest in the
property,[179] notwithstanding that rescission was no longer possible.[180]

ii. Causation and Loss

The compensatory remedy is most important when the principal's loss exceeds
any profit that the fiduciary has made,[181] which is rare. It is not, however,
unknown. In *Také v BSM Marketing*,[182] for example, the defendant was an agent
acting for a furniture importer. In breach of fiduciary duty, the agent created
importing arrangements directly between the manufacturer and retailer, elimi-
nating his principal from the transactions. The profit made by the agent (in the
form of commission) appears to have been less than the business profits lost by
his principal. The principal sued, successfully, for compensation for its losses,
rather than for an account of the agent's profits. Similarly, in *Swindle v Harrison*,[183] the plaintiff sought compensation when she lost her home in a disastrous
business transaction in which her solicitor had made a small personal profit.
Here, however, the claimant failed to recover her loss because she had not shown
that it was caused by the solicitor's breach of fiduciary duty.

This emphasises the practical importance of understanding how causation is
approached in claims for breach of fiduciary duty. The causal question is
addressed here, before considering the way in which the compensatory remedy
coheres with the function that fiduciary doctrine serves.

'The detailed rules of equity as to causation and the quantification of loss
differ, at least ostensibly, from those applicable at common law.'[184] Indeed,
claimants have openly pleaded breach of fiduciary duty in order to argue that
compensation for loss can be awarded following such a breach without needing

[177] *Ibid*, 823 and 831–32 (CA).
[178] *Swindle v Harrison* (above n 153) 718, 726 and 733.
[179] *JJ Harrison (Properties) Ltd v Harrison* (above n 153) [54].
[180] The possibility of a compensatory remedy was also mentioned without criticism by the Court of Appeal: *JJ Harrison (Properties) Ltd v Harrison* [2001] EWCA Civ 1467 at [21], [2002] 1 BCLC 162.
[181] When a breach of fiduciary duty generates both a profit for the fiduciary and a loss suffered by the principal, the principal can elect (at judgment) whether to strip the profit or to recover its losses: *Warman International v Dwyer* (above n 112) 559; *Island Records Ltd v Tring International plc* [1996] 1 WLR 1256, 1258–59 (ChD); *Tang Man Sit v Capacious Investments Ltd* [1996] 1 AC 514, 520–21 (PC). See also *Neilson v Betts* (1871) LR 5 HL 1, 22; *De Vitre v Betts* (1873) LR 6 HL 319, 321.
[182] *Také Ltd v BSM Marketing Ltd* [2006] EWHC 1085 (QB) and [2007] EWHC 2031 (QB), affirmed on appeal: [2009] EWCA Civ 45.
[183] *Swindle v Harrison* (above n 153).
[184] *Target Holdings v Redferns* (above n 146) 432.

to address the issue of causation.[185] That argument is misguided. The argument is generally founded on Street J's comment in *Re Dawson* that when equitable compensation is sought, 'considerations of causation, foreseeability and remoteness do not readily enter into the matter'[186] and on Lord Thankerton's statement in *Brickenden v London Loan & Savings Co*:

> When a party, holding a fiduciary relationship, commits a breach of fiduciary duty by non-disclosure of material facts, which his constituent is entitled to know in connection with the transaction, he cannot be heard to maintain that disclosure would not have altered the decision to proceed with the transaction. . . Once the Court has determined that the non-disclosed facts were material, speculation as to what course the constituent, on disclosure, would have taken, is not relevant.[187]

Mr Brickenden was a solicitor who acted for both lender and borrower in a loan transaction without disclosing a personal interest in the transaction.[188] The Supreme Court of Canada, affirmed on appeal by the Privy Council, held that the lender was entitled to 'damages' such as would leave it 'placed as nearly as possible in the position in which [it] would have been had there been no breach of duty on the part of Brickenden'.[189] Lord Thankerton's dictum is therefore confusing. As Dyson Heydon pointed out, it seems to rely on a notion akin to estoppel in the first sentence ('he cannot be heard'), apparently preventing the calling of evidence as to what the claimant would have done but for the breach, but then states that 'speculation' as to what the claimant would have done will not be permitted, which is the very thing that evidence would help to avoid.[190]

Courts have grappled with the precise meaning of Lord Thankerton's dictum. Notwithstanding its precedent status in Canada, the dictum has been reinterpreted there so that the fiduciary now bears the burden of proving that the claimant would have acted in the same way had there been proper disclosure. Mere speculation is insufficient proof of this, but a court can draw inferences from the evidence if they are clear. If the fiduciary fails to prove that the claimant would have acted in the same way, the claimant is entitled to compensation for the loss that arose from the transaction.[191] The same approach has been adopted

---

[185] Eg, *Swindle v Harrison* (above n 153) 722; *Bristol & West Building Society v Daniels & Co* (above n 153) 325.

[186] *Re Dawson* (above n 146) 215.

[187] *Brickenden v London Loan & Savings Co* [1934] 3 DLR 465, 469 (PC).

[188] *Biggs v London Loan & Savings Co* (1930) 39 OWN 126, 128 (Ont SC); *London Loan & Savings Co v Brickenden* [1933] SCR 257, 263; *Brickenden v London Loan & Savings* (*ibid*) 468.

[189] *London Loan & Savings v Brickenden* (*ibid*) 258.

[190] JD Heydon, 'Causal Relationships between a Fiduciary's Default and the Principal's Loss' (1994) 110 *Law Quarterly Review* 328, 332.

[191] See, eg, *Commerce Capital Trust Co v Berk* (1989) 68 OR (2d) 257, 261 and 263 (CA); *Hodgkinson v Simms* [1994] 3 SCR 377, 441; Berryman (above n 45) 108.

in New Zealand[192] and has been recognised as a 'subtle but important shift from the earlier understanding of the *Brickenden* approach'.[193]

In Australia, the courts have also gradually moved away from *Brickenden*.[194] In *Stewart v Layton*, for example, Foster J held that *Brickenden* relieves the court of the 'tedious and painstaking task' of 'unravelling and exposing the strands of causation connecting breach with damage',[195] but it 'does not mean, however, that the court must be otherwise blind to the reality of the situation'.[196] The trend of the more recent authority is to favour the view that 'a claim for equitable compensation for breach of a fiduciary duty requires a causal link between the breach and the loss.'[197] As the New South Wales Court of Appeal has said, '*Brickenden* is not, in our opinion, authority for the general proposition that, in no case involving breach of fiduciary duty, may the court consider what would have happened if the duty had been performed.'[198] Thus, in *Short v Crawley* White J held that 'the plaintiff must establish that, but for the breach of fiduciary duty, the losses would not have been incurred.'[199]

In England, the issue of what *Brickenden* means in fiduciary claims was addressed most directly in *Swindle v Harrison*.[200] Unfortunately, however, all three judges in the Court of Appeal expressed differing and rather opaque views on the matter. Evans LJ considered that *Brickenden* created a 'stringent rule of causation' to be applied when the 'equitable equivalent of fraud' is proven,[201] but he did not explain that concept. It cannot mean the same thing as 'equitable fraud'[202] because, whatever its outer boundaries, the concept of 'equitable fraud'

---

[192]   *Everist v McEvedy* [1996] 3 NZLR 348, 355 (HC); *Gilbert v Shanahan* [1998] 3 NZLR 528, 535 (CA); *Bank of New Zealand v New Zealand Guardian Trust Co Ltd* [1999] 1 NZLR 664, 687 (CA); *Taylor v Schofield Peterson* [1999] 3 NZLR 434, 445–46 (HC); *Amaltal Corp Ltd v Maruha Corp* [2007] NZSC 40 at [30], [2007] 3 NZLR 192; *Premium Real Estate v Stevens* (above n 148) [85].

[193]   *Everist v McEvedy* (*ibid*) 353. See also *Premium Real Estate v Stevens* (above n 148) [85].

[194]   *White v Illawarra Mutual Building Society Ltd* [2004] NSWCA 164 at [137].

[195]   *Stewart v Layton* (1992) 111 ALR 687, 713. See also *Commonwealth Bank of Australia v Smith* (above n 153) 395–96.

[196]   *Stewart v Layton* (*ibid*) 713–14.

[197]   *O'Halloran v RT Thomas & Family Pty Ltd* (1998) 45 NSWLR 262, 274 (CA). See also *Greater Pacific Investments v Australian National Industries* (above n 153) 154; *Beach Petroleum NL v Abbott Tout Russell Kennedy* [1999] NSWCA 408 at [429], (1999) 48 NSWLR 1; *Short v Crawley (No 30)* [2007] NSWSC 1322 at [419].

[198]   *Beach Petroleum NL v Abbott Tout Russell Kennedy* [1999] NSWCA 408 at [444], (1999) 48 NSWLR 1. See also *Cassis v Kalfus (No 2)* (above n 153) [94]; *Rigg v Sheridan* [2008] NSWCA 79 at [56].

[199]   *Short v Crawley (No 30)* (above n 197) [428]; see also at [429] and [436]. And see *Rigg v Sheridan* (*ibid*) [52] and [57]; *Super 1000 Pty Ltd v Pacific General Securities Ltd* [2008] NSWSC 1222 at [122], (2008) 221 FLR 427.

[200]   *Swindle v Harrison* (above n 153).

[201]   *Ibid*, 716–17.

[202]   Cf M Broderick, 'Equitable Compensation: Its Place in the Remedial Sphere' (2005) 33 *Australian Business Law Review* 369, 383.

is generally taken to encompass all breaches of fiduciary duty,[203] whereas Evans
LJ clearly did not intend his phrase to include *all* breaches of fiduciary duty: he
thought there was a breach of fiduciary duty in *Swindle* but that it was not the
equitable equivalent of fraud, and so the stringent rule of causation did not
apply.[204] He seems to have meant his phrase to comprehend particularly egregious breaches of fiduciary duty, such as dishonest or intentional breaches.[205]

In his judgment in *Swindle*, Hobhouse LJ considered that *Brickenden* related
solely to rescission and not to damages.[206] That is manifestly wrong: the remedy
sought and awarded in *Brickenden* was compensation for loss.[207] Mummery LJ
thought that *Brickenden* meant that a fiduciary entering a transaction with his
principal acts in breach of fiduciary duty if he fails to disclose relevant information, even if that information would not alter how the principal acts.[208] This is
correct,[209] but it does not explain the *Brickenden* dictum, which came *after* the
Privy Council had decided that Brickenden had breached his duty *and after* it said
that 'it remains to consider . . . whether any damage has been proved.'[210]

Leaving to one side the difficulties with each individual judgment, the court's
overall decision in *Swindle v Harrison* was that, although there had been a breach
of fiduciary duty, in determining what loss that breach might have caused, the
court considers what the claimant would have done 'but for' the breach.[211] In

---

[203] *Armitage v Nurse* [1998] Ch 241, 252–53 (CA). See also *Nocton v Lord Ashburton* [1914] AC
932, 954; *SZFDE v Minister for Immigration & Citizenship* [2007] HCA 35 at [10], (2007) 232 CLR
189.
[204] *Swindle v Harrison* (above n 153) 718.
[205] *Nationwide Building Society v Balmer Radmore* (above n 153) 278. Richard Nolan has argued
that Lord Thankerton's advice in *Brickenden* itself indicates that Brickenden 'had been charged with
criminal fraud and conspiracy in connection with the loan': Nolan, 'Conflicts of Interest, Unjust
Enrichment, and Wrongdoing' (above n 156) 113 (fn 134). It is not clear, however, that that is so: it
appears that the Privy Council used the word 'charged' to mean 'pleaded' as opposed to 'charged with
a crime', as it had been at the level below: see *London Loan & Savings v Brickenden* (above n 188) 259.
See also the House of Lords' usage to the same effect in *Overend & Gurney Co v Gibb* (1872) LR 5 HL
480, 486, 490, 493, 495, 499 and 500 and *Regal (Hastings) v Gulliver* (above n 32) 154, as well as that of
the Privy Council in *Gray v New Augarita Porcupine Mines* (above n 118) 12.
[206] *Swindle v Harrison* (above n 153) 726.
[207] *Brickenden v London Loan & Savings* (above n 187) 466. See also, *Maguire v Makaronis* (above
n 45) 471–72, where the High Court of Australia considered *Brickenden* irrelevant to their delibera-
tions, as the case they had to decide concerned rescission rather than a claim to compensation.
[208] *Swindle v Harrison* (above n 153) 733. See also *Johnson v EBS Pensioner Trustees Ltd* [2002]
EWCA Civ 164 at [72], [2002] Lloyd's Rep PN 309.
[209] *Demerara Bauxite Co Ltd v Hubbard* [1923] AC 673, 681 (PC); *Moody v Cox & Hatt* [1917] 2
Ch 71, 80 (CA); *Gray v New Augarita Porcupine Mines* (above n 118) 14–15; *Commerce Capital Trust v
Berk* (above n 191) 262; *Johnson v EBS Pensioner Trustees Ltd* [2002] EWCA Civ 164 at [55], [70]–[72]
and [83] (although cf at [54]), [2002] Lloyd's Rep PN 309. See also G Spencer Bower, *Actionable
Non-Disclosure*, 2nd edn by AK Turner and RJ Sutton (London, Butterworths, 1990) [3.07]–[3.09].
The contrary view, that information is only material, and so only needs to be disclosed, where it
would affect the principal's decision was adopted by Kirby J in *Maguire v Makaronis* (above n 45)
492–94, but this renders the *Brickenden* dictum nonsensical: *Commerce Capital Trust v Berk* (above n
191) 262; *Short v Crawley (No 30)* (above n 197) [426].
[210] *Brickenden v London Loan & Savings* (above n 187) 469.
[211] See also *Edmonds v Donovan* [2005] VSCA 27 at [78]; *Satnam Investments Ltd v Dunlop
Heywood & Co Ltd* [1999] 3 All ER 652, 668 (CA); *Rama v Millar* (above n 153) 261.

Swindle v Harrison, the claimant lost because 'she would have accepted the loan and completed the purchase, even if full disclosure had been made to her.'[212] Thus, 'liability is not unlimited. There is no equitable by-pass of the need to establish causation.'[213]

Indeed, the context of Street J's oft cited statement that 'considerations of causation, foreseeability and remoteness do not readily enter into'[214] analyses of equitable compensation makes it clear that he was concerned to exclude only *common law* notions of causation, foreseeability and remoteness,[215] rather than *all* causal analysis. He explicitly accepted that when equitable compensation is claimed, a causal analysis is required: 'the inquiry in each instance would appear to be whether the loss would have happened if there had been no breach.'[216]

Thus, the position in England appears to be similar to that in Australia. A claimant who can establish that a breach of fiduciary duty has been committed is able to seek an award of equitable compensation for loss, but the claimant must be able to show that the loss was caused by the breach of fiduciary duty, at least in the sense that the loss would not have been suffered but for the breach. In *Nationwide Building Society v Balmer Radmore*, for example, Blackburne J held that the principal, as claimant, bears the primary onus of proving that 'but for the breach, [he] would not have acted in the way which has caused his loss',[217] but if that onus is met the court may draw inferences (but cannot merely speculate) as to what would have happened if the fiduciary had performed his duty properly. And in the absence of evidence to justify such inferences, the beneficiary is entitled to be placed in the position he was in before the breach occurred, unless the fiduciary is able to show what the principal would have done if there had been no breach of fiduciary duty.[218]

The question that remains to be considered is how the availability of equitable compensation as a remedy for breach of the fiduciary conflict principle relates to the protective function served by fiduciary doctrine.

iii. Connection with Fiduciary Protection

The compensatory jurisdiction supports fiduciary doctrine's protective function by providing some degree of deterrence and by providing a compensatory

---

[212] *Swindle v Harrison* (above n 153) 718; see also pp 728 and 735. And see *Rawleigh v Tait* [2008] NZCA 525 at [35], upheld on appeal: [2009] NZSC 11.

[213] *Swindle v Harrison* (above n 153) 733; see also pp 718 and 726. And see *Collins v Brebner* [2000] Lloyd's Rep PN 587 at [64] (CA); *Youyang Pty Ltd v Minter Ellison Morris Fletcher* [2003] HCA 15 at [44], (2003) 212 CLR 484; *Blythe v Northwood* [2005] NSWCA 221 at [78], (2005) 63 NSWLR 531; *Premium Real Estate v Stevens* (above n 148) [36].

[214] *Re Dawson* (above n 146) 215.

[215] See *ibid*, 214–15.

[216] *Ibid*, 215.

[217] *Nationwide Building Society v Balmer Radmore* (above n 153) 278.

[218] *Ibid*, 278–79. See also *Super 1000 Pty Ltd v Pacific General Securities Ltd* [2008] NSWSC 1222 at [125], (2008) 221 FLR 427.

remedy when fiduciary doctrine's main deterrence has failed to achieve its purpose. Each of these two points merits amplification.

First, compensatory remedies can serve a deterrent function, in that they make breach of duty financially unattractive. As the Supreme Court of Canada observed, expressing reservations regarding the need for an award of exemplary damages in *Royal Bank of Canada v Got*, 'deterrence, may not, taken alone, justify exemplary damages. As a rule, deterrence can be achieved through the award of compensatory damages and refusal to grant exemplary damages is not condonation of the violation of the rule of law.'[219] The primary purpose of compensatory awards is to repair harm done as a result of a breach of duty, rather than to punish or deter conduct that will cause that harm,[220] but it is not possible to segregate completely the functions of compensatory awards from awards that serve a deterrent function: a single award of damages can serve multiple purposes.[221] When a fiduciary's profit is small (or nonexistent) compared with the principal's loss, liability to compensate for the (larger) loss can provide more of a deterrent than simply stripping the (smaller) profit that might be generated for the fiduciary by breaching his fiduciary duties.[222] Birks' argument that compensatory awards are inappropriate in the context of prophylactic rules because the purpose of such rules is to prevent the loss as opposed to waiting for it to happen[223] misses the point that compensatory awards are a legitimate part of a scheme of remedies employed by fiduciary doctrine in order to deter breaches of fiduciary duty.

The deterrent function of compensatory awards, whether in fiduciary situations or elsewhere, should not be overstated. Certainly, any deterrence they provide in the fiduciary context is of secondary importance when compared with the deterrence that the profit-stripping remedies supply.[224] The disgorgement required by the profit-stripping remedies 'is designed, as far as remedies can be, to ensure that the imposed obligation is *not* breached, not that a breach does no harm'.[225] Equitable compensation does perform something of a deterrent function, but its primary purpose is to manage the consequences when that deterrence has failed to achieve its purpose.

---

[219] *Royal Bank of Canada v W Got Associates & Electric Ltd* [1999] 3 SCR 408 at [28]. See also *Rookes v Barnard* (above n 136) 1221; *Cassell & Co v Broome* (above n 124) 1114; *Uren v John Fairfax & Sons Pty Ltd* (1966) 117 CLR 118, 150–51, upheld on appeal: *Australian Consolidated Press Ltd v Uren* [1969] 1 AC 590, 644 (PC); *Taylor v Beere* (above n 125) 95; Edelman, *Gain-Based Damages* (above n 125) 246.

[220] *Rookes v Barnard* (above n 136) 1221; *Taylor v Beere* (above n 125) 87–88; *Donselaar v Donselaar* [1982] 1 NZLR 97, 109 (CA).

[221] *Smith New Court Securities v Citibank* (above n 126) 279–80.

[222] See also M McInnes, 'Account of Profits for Common Law Wrongs' in Degeling and Edelman (eds) (above n 118) 405, 428.

[223] See text accompanying n 144 above.

[224] As to which, see above section III-A(iii).

[225] S Worthington, 'Reconsidering Disgorgement for Wrongs' (1999) 62 *Modern Law Review* 218, 237.

But this does not mean that the compensatory jurisdiction is inconsistent with the protective function served by fiduciary doctrine. As has been emphasised in this chapter, the fiduciary conflict principle exists because 'there is a danger . . . of the person holding a fiduciary position being swayed by interest rather than by duty, and *thus prejudicing those whom he was bound to protect*' (emphasis added).[226] Fiduciary doctrine seeks to insulate the principal from that prejudice by requiring the fiduciary to avoid situations that carry this danger. To that end, it makes available profit-stripping remedies, with the overt aim of deterring fiduciaries from acting in situations in which a conflict between duty and interest exists, because such situations carry a heightened risk of breach of non-fiduciary duty and thus prejudice to the principal. But if in a given case a fiduciary has breached the rules that seek to provide that insulation, the compensatory jurisdiction exists to ensure that any prejudice that is caused to the principal by reason of that breach is compensated. That, after all, is what the conflict principle was designed to avoid in the first place.

Often, such harm will be caused by breach of a non-fiduciary duty and so will be recoverable as such under the non-fiduciary remedial regime. But fiduciary duties can be breached without there necessarily being any breach of a non-fiduciary duty. In addition to providing part of the deterrence against breach of fiduciary duty, the compensatory jurisdiction serves an important function in ensuring that loss is recoverable when it has been brought about by a breach of fiduciary duty. Profit-stripping deters fiduciaries from acting in certain situations by removing the fruits of those situations, but if such deterrence has failed, the objective in providing a compensatory remedy as an alternative to a profit-stripping remedy is to ensure that any prejudice suffered by the principal is capable of full redress. Such prejudice may well lie in a loss, and loss-based remedies are therefore appropriately available: 'once deterrence and control have failed, and disloyalty has caused harm, there should be compensation for that harm.'[227]

This is not to suggest that compensation is the central weapon in fiduciary doctrine's remedial armoury. It is of secondary importance, in terms of both the function that it serves and the frequency with which it arises, behind the pre-eminent profit-stripping remedies. Nevertheless, the compensatory jurisdiction exists, and it is not inconsistent with the protective function of fiduciary doctrine. The protective function served by fiduciary doctrine is given effect through the duty-interest conflict principle, which in turn explains the availability of profit-stripping remedies for its breach. The availability of compensation for breach of that principle, when such breaches can be shown to have caused loss, reinforces that protective function rather than detracts from it, by filling a lacuna left by the profit-stripping remedies.

---

[226] *Bray v Ford* (above n 37) 51.
[227] RC Nolan and DD Prentice, 'The Issue of Shares: Compensating the Company for Loss' (2002) 118 *Law Quarterly Review* 180, 185.

IV. Critics

It has been argued that what marks peculiarly fiduciary duties out from other kinds of legal duties is the subsidiary and prophylactic form of protection for non-fiduciary duties that they provide, which enhances the likelihood of the fiduciary's faithful adherence to his non-fiduciary duties. As is perhaps only natural, other commentators have disagreed. This section of the chapter responds to their criticisms.

Perhaps most vociferous amongst the critics has been Rebecca Lee, who has argued that this analysis[228] 'is conceptually superfluous and doctrinally unsound'[229] and 'a travesty of the fiduciary doctrine [that] must be discarded.'[230] Perhaps surprisingly in such circumstances, Lee does not herself offer any contrary conceptualisation of fiduciary doctrine: she concludes that 'one can only await further analyses of how fiduciary obligations fit into the map of private law obligations since none that have appeared so far are convincing.'[231] Lee's criticisms are essentially threefold: (*i*) that the case law does not support the analysis proposed here; (*ii*) that the remedies for breach of fiduciary duty are not peculiar to fiduciary doctrine and so cannot provide any support for that analysis; and (*iii*) that the proposed analysis is predicated on the need to show a breach of non-fiduciary duty, which is inconsistent with fiduciary doctrine.

Lee's first criticism is that the cases do not support the proposed analysis of fiduciary doctrine. In particular, she focuses attention on Lord Cranworth LC's speech in *Aberdeen Railway v Blaikie*.[232] She points out that Lord Cranworth did not address the question whether a director's duty to act in the best interests of the company is a non-fiduciary duty, and she argues that it 'is not authority for the view that fiduciary duties operate to protect non-fiduciary duties. Such protection is at best incidental.'[233] The first point is obvious. Given the case was decided long before the courts began to differentiate peculiarly fiduciary duties from other duties owed by fiduciaries, it is hardly surprising that Lord Cranworth did not address that particular question. But that does not detract from the proposition that the duty to which he referred can be understood, in modern terms, as a non-fiduciary duty, as has been explained in chapter three. Lee's more significant point is that *Aberdeen Railway v Blaikie* 'did not address the issue

---

[228] Clearly, neither Lee nor any of the other critics discussed here could have been replying directly to the arguments presented in this book. Unless otherwise indicated, their criticisms relate to an article published in 2005 that outlined the analysis which is presented more fully in this book: M Conaglen, 'The Nature and Function of Fiduciary Loyalty' (2005) 121 *Law Quarterly Review* 452.

[229] R Lee, 'In Search of the Nature and Function of Fiduciary Loyalty: Some Observations on Conaglen's Analysis' (2007) 27 *Oxford Journal of Legal Studies* 327, 328.

[230] *Ibid*, 338.

[231] *Ibid*.

[232] *Aberdeen Railway v Blaikie* (above n 18) 471.

[233] Lee (above n 229) 329.

whether . . . fiduciary duties served the subsidiary function of protecting non-fiduciary duties'.[234] In seeking to substantiate this, Lee quotes Lord Cranworth's statement of the director's duty to act in the best interests of the company, which Lord Cranworth himself explained 'imposed on [the director] the obligation of obtaining these chairs at the lowest possible price'.[235] But Lee does not refer to the fact that immediately after stating that the director had a duty to get the chairs at the lowest possible price, Lord Cranworth explained that having a personal interest in such a transaction 'would lead [a director] in an entirely opposite direction, would induce him to fix the price as high as possible. This is the very evil against which the rule in question is directed.'[236] Obtaining the chairs at as high a price as possible, as opposed to as low a price as possible, would be a clear breach of the director's duty to the company. Lord Cranworth considered this 'the very evil' against which the fiduciary conflict principle is directed. To describe fiduciary doctrine's attempt to avoid that result as 'at best incidental' is, to say the least, odd.

Lee further argues that all of the other cases that have been cited as the basis for the protective function of fiduciary doctrine 'likewise merely show that the mischief behind the fiduciary rule is the pursuit of inconsistent self-interest'.[237] Ironically, this statement actually supports rather than detracts from the analysis offered here, because the question that naturally follows from Lee's observation is, with what is the self-interest inconsistent, and why should that be of concern to the law? As has been explained earlier in this chapter, the answer to that question is clear from the cases: the fiduciary's self-interest is inconsistent with his non-fiduciary duty, and the reason fiduciary doctrine prohibits that is because it creates 'a temptation not faithfully to perform his duty'.[238]

Lee's second criticism is that fiduciary doctrine's remedial regime does not support the argument that fiduciary duties offer a subsidiary and prophylactic form of protection for non-fiduciary duties. In particular, she rejects the argument that rescission is available in the context of a breach of fiduciary duty because the transaction ought never to have taken place: in her words, 'regrettably, this represents only a very rudimentary understanding of the remedy of rescission.'[239] The essence of her argument is that rescission is not peculiar to breaches of fiduciary duty and so cannot tell us anything about fiduciary doctrine. This argument misunderstands the relevance of remedies to the analysis presented here. *None* of the remedies for breach of fiduciary duty is peculiar to fiduciary doctrine. Rescission, for example, is available following a successful allegation of undue influence, as Lee points out. Compensatory remedies are

---

[234] *Ibid.*

[235] *Aberdeen Railway v Blaikie* (above n 18) 473.

[236] *Ibid.* Lord Cranworth's words were quoted in the article that Lee set out to criticise: Conaglen, 'The Nature and Function of Fiduciary Loyalty' (above n 228) 461.

[237] Lee (above n 229) 329.

[238] *Boston Deep Sea Fishing & Ice v Ansell* (above n 30) 357 (CA).

[239] Lee (above n 229) 330.

clearly available for torts and breaches of contract, and profit-stripping remedies, such as accounts of profits, are also available for other legal wrongs, such as breaches of confidence[240] and of contract.[241] Indeed, even proprietary constructive trusts can be awarded in contexts other than when there has been a breach of fiduciary duty, such as when a proprietary estoppel claim succeeds.[242]

It is the duties that are peculiar to fiduciary doctrine, rather than the remedies. The argument is that the purpose of fiduciary duties—protecting against breach of non-fiduciary duties—is *consistent* with the various remedies that fiduciary doctrine employs. In particular, the preeminent profit-stripping remedies (rescission and accounts) are designed to deter breaches of fiduciary duty and to undo the consequences of such breaches if that deterrence is ineffective. That proposition is not undermined by the fact that the same remedies might be used elsewhere in the law, potentially for a different purpose. A single remedy can be awarded for more than one reason,[243] and use of that remedy in different contexts does not mean that it is always being used for the same reason. And even if it is, that does not undermine the proposition that the duties are performing a distinct function: all that is then happening is that the distinct function of the duties is being remedied in similar ways because the law has a limited range of remedies from which to choose to implement the different purposes that it serves through distinct doctrines. The focus of the analysis offered here is on the duties, as those are what distinguish fiduciary doctrine. The point about remedies is that they are consistent with the analysis that has been offered of those duties. That consistency supports the argument in two respects: first, the argument would be untenable if the remedies were inconsistent with it, but they are not; and secondly, understanding the function served by the remedies that apply when there has been a breach of fiduciary duty helps with understanding the purpose of the duties themselves.

Lee's third criticism is perhaps the most substantively important. But it is ill-founded. She argues that 'if the function of fiduciary loyalty is to protect performance of non-fiduciary duties, then, as a corollary, performance of those non-fiduciary duties shall absolve a fiduciary from liability for breach of fiduciary duty.'[244] In criticising this position, Lee points out that failure to act in breach of non-fiduciary duty is no defence to a claim for breach of fiduciary duty and concludes that 'securing enhanced performance of non-fiduciary duties is at

---

[240] See, eg, *Peter Pan Manufacturing Corp v Corsets Silhouette Ltd* [1964] 1 WLR 96, 106 (ChD); *Ansell Rubber Co Pty Ltd v Allied Rubber Industries Pty Ltd* [1967] VR 37, 52; *AB Consolidated Ltd v Europe Strength Food Co Pty Ltd* [1978] 2 NZLR 515, 526–27; *Attorney-General v Observer Ltd* [1990] 1 AC 109, 255–56, 262 and 288; *Brandeis (Brokers) Ltd v Black* [2001] 2 All ER (Comm) 980 at [51] (QBD); *OBG Ltd v Allan* [2007] UKHL 21 at [276], [2008] 1 AC 1.

[241] See, eg, *Attorney-General v Blake* [2001] 1 AC 268.

[242] See, eg, *Yaxley v Gotts* [2000] Ch 162 (CA).

[243] *Smith New Court Securities v Citibank* (above n 126) 279–80.

[244] Lee (above n 229) 334.

most of peripheral relevance to fiduciary loyalty.'[245] This criticism misunderstands the argument at which it is directed. Lee suggests, for example, that the
argument implies that the director in *Aberdeen Railway v Blaikie* would be
exonerated in a claim for breach of fiduciary duty if he showed that he had used
'his best endeavours to negotiate for the company . . . even if he failed to obtain
the most beneficial bargain'.[246] But whether the director acted in breach of his
non-fiduciary duties is entirely irrelevant to the question whether he acted in
breach of fiduciary duty. It is not in any way a corollary of the analysis advanced
here that a breach of fiduciary duty is avoided by complying with non-fiduciary
duties—in fact, quite the opposite. The point of fiduciary duties is that they seek
to enhance the likelihood that non-fiduciary duties will be properly performed
by requiring fiduciaries to eschew situations in which that eventuality is put at
greater risk by the presence of conflicting interests. But there is always a risk of
breach of non-fiduciary duty, and fiduciary doctrine cannot entirely eliminate
that risk. What fiduciary doctrine does do is to try to reduce the risk, thus making
such breaches less likely, by trying to eliminate one particular cause of such risk:
inconsistent self-interest. In so doing, fiduciary duties are subsidiary to non-
fiduciary duties, but they are also prophylactic: they seek to prevent breaches of
non-fiduciary duties. And the risk of breach of non-fiduciary duty that self-
interest creates is considered sufficiently serious that it is irrelevant whether or
not a breach of non-fiduciary duty eventuates. Far from being 'of peripheral
relevance', as Lee suggests, enhancing the chance of proper performance of
non-fiduciary duties is the core function served by the fiduciary conflict principle.

Deborah DeMott has raised a different criticism of the analysis advanced here,
although one which is related in concept to the last-mentioned of Rebecca Lee's
criticisms. DeMott summarised the argument advanced here as 'a possible
generalization . . . that duties of loyalty play an exclusively subsidiary function'[247]
and commented:

> Although this generalization helps explain much about the consequences that follow
> breaches of duties of loyalty, its explanatory force has limits. . . [I]f duties of loyalty have
> purely subsidiary functions, it's odd that the common law consistently denies the agent
> an affirmative defense of establishing due performance of the agent's duties of perform-
> ance.[248]

While the concern is a relevant one, the difficulty with it is that it focuses
attention only on the subsidiary nature of the conflict principle without reference
to the prophylactic function that the doctrine serves. Furthermore, DeMott's
criticism is aimed at the prophylactic *methodology* by which fiduciary doctrine is

[245] *Ibid*, 336.
[246] *Ibid*, 334.
[247] DA DeMott, 'Disloyal Agents' (2007) 58 *Alabama Law Review* 1049, 1057.
[248] *Ibid*, 1058.

implemented, in that it is no defence for a fiduciary to show that non-fiduciary duties were not breached, but the fact that such a methodology has been adopted does not demonstrate that the *function* that fiduciary doctrine sets out to serve is not subsidiary and prophylactic.

More importantly, perhaps, fiduciary doctrine's protection for non-fiduciary duties is not 'purely' or 'exclusively' subsidiary, as DeMott's criticism suggests. As well as being subsidiary, fiduciary doctrine also provides prophylactic protection for non-fiduciary duties. That fact is vitally important in meeting DeMott's criticism. Fiduciary doctrine is subsidiary and prophylactic in that it seeks to reduce the risk of breach of non-fiduciary duties. In seeking to achieve that objective it employs a prophylactic methodology in that it applies irrespective of whether the risk became a reality, because the concern is to avoid the risk altogether. The doctrine need not necessarily have been created in this way, in that a defence of the sort envisaged by DeMott could have been recognised. But, as has already been argued, the problem with allowing fiduciaries to plead and prove an affirmative defence of that sort is that it creates an incentive structure for fiduciaries that is opposed to the purpose of the fiduciary principle.[249] Such a defence would severely limit the deterrence that fiduciary doctrine holds for fiduciaries, thereby reducing the subsidiary prophylaxis that the doctrine provides vis-à-vis non-fiduciary duties. Refusing to recognise a defence of that sort was a perfectly rational position for the courts to adopt in the light of the prophylactic function that fiduciary doctrine is designed to perform.

Getzler has offered a different criticism of the analysis proposed here:

> The obvious counter-argument is that heightened prophylactic pressure is appropriate in order to enforce the fiduciary's duties of competence and diligence just as for any other core fiduciary duties... [T]he contexts and traditions of the various duties of care in law and equity are too varied to be combined into a monotonic duty.[250]

This is not an 'obvious counter-argument' to the present analysis of fiduciary duties. First, the argument that has been advanced here is not dependent on the existence of a 'monotonic' duty of care: the equitable and statutory duties of care owed by trustees may well differ in content from the equitable, common law and statutory duties of care owed by other fiduciaries, such as directors, and again from the common law and equitable duties of care owed by non-fiduciaries. Duties of care do not need to be identical amongst all such actors for them to be grouped together and described as duties of care. The point is that if one follows the approach endorsed in *Mothew*, fiduciary duties are to be understood by reference to the duties that are peculiar to fiduciaries. If that approach is followed, duties of care are neither peculiar to fiduciaries nor '*core* fiduciary

---

[249] See text accompanying nn 73–77 above. See also I Samet, 'Guarding the Fiduciary's Conscience: A Justification of a Stringent Profit-Stripping Rule' (2008) 28 *Oxford Journal of Legal Studies* 763.

[250] J Getzler, 'Am I My Beneficiary's Keeper? Fusion and Loss-Based Fiduciary Remedies' in Degeling and Edelman (eds) (above n 118) 239, 267 (fn 112).

duties'.[251] The ultimate source of the difference between this analysis and that offered by Getzler is that he believes *Mothew* was wrongly decided and is a committed opponent of that approach.[252] Obviously, anyone who adheres to his view will not accept an analysis that is based on the approach adopted in *Mothew*. The problem with that is that *Mothew* is now very well accepted.[253]

Secondly, Getzler's response to the proposed analysis refers to the prophylactic aspect of fiduciary duties, but he does so to the exclusion of the subsidiarity of such duties. The argument that has been advanced is not that fiduciary duties are merely protective, and so prophylactic, but that they are protective of other duties and thus are subsidiary to those other (non-fiduciary) duties. Duties of care do not offer a prophylactic and subsidiary form of protection for non-fiduciary duties in the way that fiduciary duties do. While duties of care can be conceived of as protective of the persons to whom the duties are owed, in the sense that they protect those persons against unreasonable suffering of harm, they are not protective of the proper performance of other duties owed to those persons. They are most commonly relevant in the context of a fiduciary's exercise of adminis-trative powers,[254] as opposed to duties. Thus, for example, when a trustee exercises a power to invest the trust fund he owes a duty of care regarding the investment. But the duty is the duty of care—the power of investment is not a duty but provides an equitable immunity against suit allowing the trustee lawfully to deviate from what otherwise would be his fundamental duty to retain the trust property in specie.[255] The duty of care qualifies that equitable immunity, such that it will not protect the trustee if he has failed to exercise the necessary care and skill. In so doing, the duty of care thereby protects the beneficiary against unjustifiable harm when the trustee exercises the power, but it does not protect the proper performance of the trustee's other duties. Indeed, even when the duty of care is applied in the context of the performance of duties owed by the trustee, such as when a trustee is obliged to exercise care and skill in considering the standard investment criteria and advice about how to exercise his power to invest,[256] the duty of care is not *protective* of proper performance of those duties but rather *defines* what constitutes proper performance of those

---

[251] Even when duties of care are owed by fiduciaries, they can be abrogated by exclusion clauses: see, eg, *Armitage v Nurse* (above n 203) 250–56; Trustee Act 2000, s 2 and Sch 1 para 7. This makes it difficult to conceive of them as *core* duties owed by fiduciaries, irrespective of whether they are peculiar to fiduciaries.

[252] See, eg, Getzler, 'Equitable Compensation and the Regulation of Fiduciary Relationships' (above n 151) 254–57; J Getzler, 'Duty of Care' in Birks and Pretto (eds) (above n 147) 41, 71–72; Getzler, 'Am I My Beneficiary's Keeper?' (above n 250) 263. Similarly, see JD Heydon, 'Are the Duties of Company Directors to Exercise Care and Skill Fiduciary?' in Degeling and Edelman (eds) (above n 118) 185.

[253] See above ch 2, section II-B(ii).

[254] See, eg, the application of the duty of care to the exercise of numerous trustees' powers in Trustee Act 2000, Sch 1, paras 1–6.

[255] RC Nolan, 'Understanding the Limits of Equitable Property' (2006) 1 *Journal of Equity* 18, 20–24.

[256] Trustee Act 2000, ss 4–5 and Sch 1, para 1(b).

duties. In other words, the thesis advanced in this book is not merely that fiduciary duties are protective duties—many legal duties can be cast as protective of individuals or their interests—but rather that they offer a particular kind of protection, which is subsidiary and prophylactic protection for non-fiduciary duties. Getzler's counter-argument does not destabilise that argument in the context of the framework for analysis that has been adopted in this book.

Finally, Lionel Smith has argued that 'the essence of the fiduciary obligation ... lies in the justiciability of motive.'[257] Smith's argument is not a criticism aimed directly at the analysis proposed here,[258] but it is inconsistent with that analysis and so it is as well to address it here. He rejects an analysis of fiduciary duties as based on deterrence as implausible.[259] For reasons discussed earlier,[260] that rejection is unconvincing. In place of a deterrent theory, Smith argues:

> [T]he attempt to understand the duty of loyalty in terms of results will always fail, because the duty is not directed to any result, not even a negative one. Rather, it is a required *manner* of doing what one does, or not doing what one does not do. . . It is a duty to act (or not) with the right motive.[261]

Smith's focus on ensuring that fiduciaries act for the right motive leads him to conclude that, because fiduciary doctrine is concerned with motive, the conflict and profit principles are not themselves fiduciary duties. Rather, those rules are prophylactic rules designed to protect against violation of the fiduciary obligation to act with the right motive.[262]

Smith's analysis is premised on the view that the requirement that holders of powers exercise them for a proper purpose is a fiduciary doctrine.[263] That doctrine is concerned not with the result of a decision reached by a power holder but with the reasons for that decision,[264] which leads to Smith's view that it imposes 'a required *manner* of doing what one does'.[265] This understanding of the fraud on a power doctrine is itself questionable,[266] but the important point for

---

[257] Smith (above n 41) 53; see also pp 64 and 68–69.
[258] Smith's chapter predated the article that the other commentators have criticised.
[259] See text accompanying nn 108–10 above.
[260] See text accompanying nn 111–30 above.
[261] Smith (above n 41) 65.
[262] *Ibid*, 73.
[263] *Ibid*, 67–71.
[264] See, eg, *Henty v Wrey* (1882) 21 ChD 332, 354 (CA); *Vatcher v Paull* [1915] AC 372, 379–80 (PC); *Re Burton's Settlement* [1955] 1 Ch 82, 100; *Re Brook's Settlement* [1968] 1 WLR 1661, 1666 (ChD).
[265] See text accompanying n 261 above.
[266] Technically, the fraud on a power doctrine is concerned with purpose rather than with motive—ie, that which is objectively sought to be achieved (purpose) rather than the subjective reasons for seeking to achieve that result (motive): see, eg, *Vane v Lord Dungannon* (1804) 2 Sch & Lef 118, 130–31 (9 RR 63) (LC(I)); *Topham v Duke of Portland* (1863) 1 De GJ & S 517, 570–71 (46 ER 205) (LJJ); *Topham v Duke of Portland* (1869) LR 5 Ch App 40, 57 (CA); G Farwell, *Powers*, 3rd edn by CJW Farwell and FK Archer (London, Stevens, 1916) 484–85; HG Hanbury, 'Frauds on Power: An Opportunity for Stocktaking' (1948) 64 *Law Quarterly Review* 221, 227. As such, 'the proper purpose doctrine is not about reviewing the manner in which power is exercised, but about controlling the

present purposes is that Smith constructs his theory about the nature of fiduciary duties on the foundation of his understanding of the fraud on a power doctrine. As was discussed in detail above in chapter three, the doctrine of fraud on a power is not peculiar in its application to fiduciaries.[267] As such, it provides an unstable foundation on which to construct a theory as to the nature of peculiarly fiduciary duties.[268]

Smith's analysis is consistent with and seeks to support the North American view that the core fiduciary duty is the 'duty to act in what [the fiduciary] perceives to be the best interests of the beneficiary'.[269] He explains that he agrees 'with Burrows that the prophylaxis is not itself the fiduciary duty. . . Burrows' approach is more convincing in finding the heart of the duty of loyalty, not in the prophylactic rules but, in a duty to advance another's interests.'[270] As has been explained above in chapter three,[271] the view that there is a *fiduciary* duty to act in the best interests of the fiduciary's principal is problematic, particularly in the light of *Breen v Williams*.[272] In Anglo-Australian law, a fiduciary's duty to act in the interests of his principal is given legal force through non-fiduciary duties derived from various sources. Those non-fiduciary duties are in turn given subsidiary and prophylactic protection by fiduciary duties. Smith's analysis sits uncomfortably with the fundamental precepts found in the Anglo-Australian case law on fiduciary doctrine.

At one level, of course, fiduciary doctrine can be said to be concerned with motive: removing the fruits of temptation is designed to avoid fiduciaries being motivated by those temptations. Smith is also correct to point out that fiduciary doctrine is not generally 'judged by result'.[273] But this does not mean that motives take the place of results as the normative concern underpinning fiduciary doctrine. Smith argues that 'the prophylactic rules entitle the beneficiary *not to have to wonder about the fiduciary's motive*.'[274] But prophylaxis is not merely an evidential or methodological aspect of fiduciary doctrine—it is a fundamental

ends for which it is exercised': RC Nolan, 'The Proper Purpose Doctrine and Company Directors' in BAK Rider (ed), *The Realm of Company Law* (London, Kluwer, 1998) 1, 21. See also Nolan, 'Controlling Fiduciary Power' (above n 101) 298 (fn 36).
[267] See above ch 3, section V.
[268] Insofar as Smith's analysis does not adhere to the 'peculiarity' criterion, it is not made clear why he privileges one doctrine that applies to fiduciary power holders (the doctrine of fraud on a power) over the rest of the suite of doctrines that also apply (whether peculiarly or not) to such power holders in his search for 'the heart of the fiduciary obligation': Smith (above n 41) 64. For an overview of the entire suite of doctrines that apply to the holders of such powers, see Nolan, 'Controlling Fiduciary Power' (above n 101).
[269] Smith (above n 41) 76. See also, eg, *Norberg v Wynrib* (above n 17) 272; *Canson Enterprises Ltd v Boughton & Co* [1991] 3 SCR 534, 543; *BCE Inc v 1976 Debentureholders* [2008] SCC 69 at [37]; Palmer (above n 57) 167.
[270] Smith (above n 41) 63.
[271] See above ch 3, section VII.
[272] *Breen v Williams* (above n 1) 137–38.
[273] Smith (above n 41) 73.
[274] *Ibid*, 75.

part of its purpose. That purpose is prophylactic in the sense that it is concerned to reduce the likelihood of a fiduciary acting in breach of non-fiduciary duty. As Lord Herschell emphasised in *Bray v Ford*, it is 'based on the consideration that, human nature being what it is, there is danger, in such circumstances, of the person holding a fiduciary position being swayed by interest rather than by duty, and thus prejudicing those whom he is bound to protect'.[275] Motives do not cause harm in and of themselves and are not the focus of fiduciary doctrine's concern. The harm caused by breach of non-fiduciary duty is the mischief at which fiduciary doctrine strikes, and it does so by providing subsidiary and prophylactic protection for the proper performance of non-fiduciary duties.

---

[275] *Bray v Ford* (above n 37) 51.

5

Fiduciary Doctrine and Morality

This book expounds a fundamentally instrumentalist understanding of fiduciary doctrine: that it exists to provide a subsidiary and prophylactic form of protection for non-fiduciary duties, thereby increasing the likelihood of the proper performance of those non-fiduciary duties. This runs counter to an alternative view of fiduciary doctrine, which holds that it is concerned with exacting from fiduciaries more moral conduct than that required of other legal actors. In *Meinhard v Salmon*, for example, Cardozo CJ said:

> Many forms of conduct permissible in a workaday world for those acting at arm's length, are forbidden to those bound by fiduciary ties. A trustee is held to something stricter than the morals of the market place. Not honesty alone, but the punctilio of an honor the most sensitive, is then the standard of behavior. As to this there has developed a tradition that is unbending and inveterate. . . Only thus has the level of conduct for fiduciaries been kept at a level higher than that trodden by the crowd.[1]

Were such a view of fiduciary doctrine correct, it would clearly undermine the instrumentalist analysis of fiduciary doctrine advanced in this book, as it suggests that fiduciary doctrine is concerned with eliciting more moral conduct on the part of a fiduciary or more than proper performance of the non-fiduciary duties he owes. However, properly understood, fiduciary doctrine's purpose is not to single out fiduciaries from the rest of the 'crowd' in order to make them more honourable and morally better people. Rather, it seeks to increase the likelihood of proper performance of non-fiduciary duties by insulating the fiduciary from situations that involve a heightened risk of breach of those duties.

This chapter assesses various bases on which it might be thought that a moralistic view of fiduciary doctrine is appropriate, demonstrating the flaws in such analyses.

---

[1] *Meinhard v Salmon* 164 NE 545, 546 (1928).

I. General Observations

It must be acknowledged that the view that fiduciary doctrine is designed to exhort more moral conduct of fiduciaries is not limited to American dicta like that contained in *Meinhard v Salmon*. For example, in *Parker v McKenna*, Lord Cairns LC referred to the duty–interest conflict principle as 'a rule founded upon the highest and truest principles of morality',[2] a view he repeated in *Aberdeen Town Council v Aberdeen University*.[3] Rigby LJ made a similar comment in the *Lagunas Nitrate* case,[4] and in *Armstrong v Jackson*, McCardie J observed that the 'rule is not one merely of law but of obvious morality'.[5] During argument in *O'Sullivan v Management Agency*, Fox LJ even raised the possibility of it being considered morally worse to obtain an advantage by breaching a fiduciary duty than to obtain the same advantage by fraud.[6] In Canada too, in *Girardet v Crease*, Southin J commented that 'an allegation of breach of fiduciary duty carries with it the stench of dishonesty—if not of deceit, then of constructive fraud.'[7] In Australia, the High Court has quoted favourably from Cardozo CJ's dictum in *Meinhard v Salmon*.[8] And in New Zealand, in *BNZ v Guardian Trust*, Tipping J said that 'the greater moral turpitude of the wrongdoer'[9] in cases concerning breach of fiduciary duty warrants a different approach from that applied in cases involving breach of a duty of care.

On the other hand, a moralistic view of fiduciary doctrine rings somewhat hollow when it is recalled that trustees—the paradigm category of fiduciaries— 'may even have to act dishonourably (though not illegally) if the interests of their beneficiaries require it'.[10] This does not directly refute the moralistic view of fiduciary doctrine, but its recognition that a fiduciary may be legally obliged to act in a dishonourable manner strongly suggests that the moralistic view, at the very least, needs a more nuanced notion of morality than that which emanates from the cases mentioned in the preceding paragraph.

Furthermore, the House of Lords' decision in *Bray v Ford*[11] is direct authority against the moralistic view of fiduciary doctrine. Mr Ford was vice-chairman of, and had acted as solicitor for, the Yorkshire College. Mr Bray, one of the governors of the college, wrote to Ford alleging that he had acted in breach of

---

[2]　*Parker v McKenna* (1874) LR 10 Ch App 96, 118.
[3]　*Aberdeen Town Council v Aberdeen University* (1877) 2 App Cas 544, 549.
[4]　*Lagunas Nitrate Co v Lugunas Syndicate* [1899] 2 Ch 392, 442 (CA).
[5]　*Armstrong v Jackson* [1917] 2 KB 822, 824.
[6]　*O'Sullivan v Management Agency & Music Ltd* [1985] 1 QB 428, 455 (CA).
[7]　*Girardet v Crease & Co* (1987) 11 BCLR (2d) 361, 362.
[8]　*Warman International Ltd v Dwyer* (1995) 182 CLR 544, 557.
[9]　*Bank of New Zealand v New Zealand Guardian Trust Co Ltd* [1999] 1 NZLR 664, 688 (CA). See also *Cavell Leitch Pringle & Boyle v Thornton Estates Ltd* [2008] NZCA 191 at [50].
[10]　*Cowan v Scargill* [1985] Ch 270, 288 (VC). See also *Buttle v Saunders* [1950] 2 All ER 193, 195 (ChD); A Underhill and DJ Hayton, *Law Relating to Trusts and Trustees*, 17th edn by DJ Hayton, PB Matthews and CCJ Mitchell (London, LexisNexis Butterworths, 2007) [52.25].
[11]　*Bray v Ford* [1896] AC 44.

fiduciary duty by taking fees for acting as solicitor to the college and circulated the letter to 300 other governors. Ford sued for libel, making the relationship between the allegation of breach of fiduciary duty and any moral impropriety on Ford's part of central importance. Lord Watson observed:

> Your Lordships can entertain no doubt that the respondent was neither entitled to charge profit costs in respect of these services, nor to retain them when received by him. Such a breach of the law may be attended with perfect good faith, and it is, in my opinion, insufficient to justify a charge of moral obliquity, unless it is shewn to have been committed knowingly or with an improper motive.[12]

Thus, an allegation of breach of fiduciary duty does not, on its own, necessarily carry moral obloquy—something more must be shown before such a breach carries with it any form of moral disgrace. Lord Herschell expressed the same opinion:

> It does not appear to me that this rule is, as has been said, founded upon principles of morality. I regard it rather as based on the consideration that, human nature being what it is, there is danger, in such circumstances, of the person holding a fiduciary position being swayed by interest rather than by duty, and thus prejudicing those whom he was bound to protect. It has, therefore, been deemed expedient to lay down this positive rule. But I am satisfied that it might be departed from in many cases, without any breach of morality, without any wrong being inflicted, and without any consciousness of wrong-doing.[13]

In other words, a breach of fiduciary duty may be committed without the fiduciary necessarily acting immorally. Rather than being moralistic in its outlook, fiduciary doctrine is cynical, 'derived from a profound knowledge of human characteristics and motives'.[14]

This amoral view of fiduciary doctrine is also borne out by numerous other cases in which fiduciaries were held liable for breach of fiduciary duty despite having acted without any moral improbity. For example, in *Ex parte Bennett*, Lord Eldon LC applied the fiduciary conflict principle to the transaction in question notwithstanding that 'in point of moral honesty'[15] the fiduciary had done nothing wrong. And in *Ex parte Lacey*, he emphasised that the principle applied even though the fiduciary had 'acted honestly, meaning to act for the benefit of the creditors and fairly'.[16] Lord Brougham's statement in *Hamilton v Wright* that 'the conduct of the trustee not being blameable in the purchase, is nothing to the purpose'[17] reflects the same idea. Fiduciary doctrine applies no matter how honestly or morally the fiduciary may have acted. As the Court of

---

[12] *Ibid*, 48.
[13] *Ibid*, 51–52.
[14] *Guth v Loft Inc* 5 A 2d 503, 510 (1939).
[15] *Ex parte Bennett* (1805) 10 Ves 381, 395 (32 ER 893). See also *Ex parte James* (1803) 8 Ves 337, 345 (32 ER 385).
[16] *Ex parte Lacey* (1802) 6 Ves 625, 630 (31 ER 1228).
[17] *Hamilton v Wright* (1842) 9 Cl & Fin 111, 124 (8 ER 357) (HL).

Appeal put it in *De Bussche v Alt*, 'the honesty of the agent concerned in the particular transaction should not be inquired into.'[18] Similarly, courts refuse to consider whether the fiduciary's conduct was for the benefit of the principal when addressing an allegation of breach of fiduciary duty.[19] Fiduciary analysis does not depend upon such matters, as the doctrine's fundamental concern is not with raising the standard of performance expected of fiduciaries. Imprecise references to morality, ungrounded in the fiduciary principles applied in the case law, do not accurately reflect the basis of fiduciary doctrine. Fiduciary doctrine is concerned with removing temptations that might cause a fiduciary to act in breach of his non-fiduciary duties, rather than with attempting to ensure fiduciaries meet an ill-defined standard of morality in their conduct.

Increasing the likelihood of proper performance of non-fiduciary duties can of course be described as a moral outcome, in the sense that it is for the benefit of the principal. If all that were meant when fiduciary doctrine is described as based on principles of morality is that it is moral to make proper performance of someone's duties more likely, then the proposition is unobjectionable, although relatively uninformative. But that is not what is normally meant by the high-handed moral rhetoric that frequently encrusts discussion of fiduciary doctrine. 'Pulpit-thumping rhetoric about the sanctity of fiduciary obligations'[20] should be discarded as it misguides inquiry into the true nature and function of fiduciary doctrine.

II. The Argument from History

Leonard Rotman has argued for a far more moralist view of fiduciary doctrine. His argument is difficult to encapsulate in a few sentences, but the following two statements reflect its tenor: first, he argues that '"fiduciary" is one of the means by which law transmits its ethical resolve to the spectrum of human interaction';[21] and secondly, 'the fiduciary concept imposes law's highest ethical standards on a potentially infinite number of actors involved in a variety of circumstances.'[22]

---

[18] *De Bussche v Alt* (1878) 8 ChD 286, 316.

[19] See, eg, *Aberdeen Railway Co v Blaikie Bros* (1854) 1 Macq 461, 472 (149 RR 32); *Wright v Morgan* [1926] AC 788, 798.

[20] JH Langbein, 'The Contractarian Basis of the Law of Trusts' (1995) 105 *Yale Law Journal* 625, 629.

[21] LI Rotman, *Fiduciary Law* (Toronto, Thomson Carswell, 2005) 2; see also p 153. Similarly, see R Cotterell, 'Trusting in Law: Legal and Moral Concepts of Trust' [1993] *Current Legal Problems* 75, 76–77 and 85–86; S FitzGibbon, 'Fiduciary Relationships Are Not Contracts' (1999) 82 *Marquette Law Review* 303, 338.

[22] Rotman (*ibid*) 244.

This analysis is problematic.[23] Rotman's assessment of fiduciary doctrine is premised on his analysis of the nature of equitable jurisdiction, particularly by reference to its historical derivation.[24] Thus, he argues:

> The philosophical and jurisprudential underpinnings of the fiduciary concept are premised upon broad notions of fairness, conscience, reason, and flexibility which are entirely reflective of fundamental tenets of Equity generally and of English Equity more particularly. . . [T]o understand the fiduciary concept, one must appreciate the purpose and function of Equity generally and English Equity specifically.[25]

In developing this analysis, Rotman refers to the well-known Aristotelian view of equity as a corrective for injustices that can arise because 'all law is universal but about some things it is not possible to make a universal statement which shall be correct'[26] and to the concept of equity as concerned with conscience, reflected in Lord Ellesmere's statement in the *Earl of Oxford's Case*: 'The Office of the Chancellor is to correct Mens Consciences for Frauds, Breach of Trusts, Wrongs and Oppressions, of what Nature soever they be, and to soften and mollify the Extremity of the Law.'[27] Rotman argues that 'Equity is perceived to be of a higher moral order than the common law [and] a tool to further or facilitate the pursuit of justice'[28] and that contemporary understandings of equity, and of fiduciary doctrine in particular, 'mark a return to its historical and doctrinal ancestry'.[29] Thus, his reference to the transmission of an 'ethical resolve to the spectrum of human interaction' appears to be based on his view of the historical nature of conscience in equity as a form of morality: he argues that 'the fiduciary concept may fairly be said to be the most doctrinally pure expression of Equity.'[30]

It is not clear that this foray into the history of equity provides a sound basis on which to build a contemporary theory of fiduciary doctrine. First, it is not clear that the Aristotelian view of equity is an accurate reflection of the way law and equity developed in England. As Toby Milsom has said, 'in England, and perhaps generally, the true newcomer was not equity but positive law.'[31] Furthermore, while conscience has clearly been important to the development of the equitable jurisdiction, it has meant different things at different periods in the development of that jurisdiction.[32] At times, the concept of conscience was far

---

[23] For further criticisms of Rotman's analysis, see R Flannigan, 'A Romantic Conception of Fiduciary Obligation' (2005) 84 *Canadian Bar Review* 391.

[24] Rotman (above n 21) ch 4.

[25] *Ibid*, 154–55.

[26] Aristotle, *Ethica Nicomachea*, trans by WD Ross (London, Oxford University Press, 1925) Book V.10. See also *Earl of Oxford's Case* (1615) 1 Chan Rep 1, 6 (21 ER 485); *Dudley v Dudley* (1705) Prec Ch 241, 244 (24 ER 118).

[27] *Earl of Oxford's Case* (*ibid*) 7.

[28] Rotman (above n 21) 159.

[29] *Ibid*, 160.

[30] *Ibid*, 154.

[31] SFC Milsom, *Historical Foundations of the Common Law*, 2nd edn (London, Butterworths, 1981) 88.

[32] M Macnair, 'Equity and Conscience' (2007) *Oxford Journal of Legal Studies* 659, 670–71.

more procedural than substantive,[33] referring to equity's ability to act on a defendant's conscience to obtain evidence that could not be obtained at law.[34] Later, this distinction fell away:[35]

[T]he sixteenth-century distinction between compellable conscience and the conscience of the party became Lord Nottingham's distinction between his natural and his civil conscience. What mattered now was the civil conscience of the court, which was nothing other than a new system of law; and the conscience of the party slowly passed out of consideration. The dialogue between certainty and justice, law and morals, had been acted out in real life; and the end of it was two systems of certainty, two systems of law.[36]

Contemporary equity is not simply a form of individualised justice.[37] As Jessel MR observed of the Chancery Division, 'this Court is not, as I have often said, a Court of conscience, but a Court of law.'[38] In other words, 'undefined notions of "justice" and what was "fair" had given way in the law of equity to the rule of ordered principle which is of the essence of any coherent system of rational law.'[39] 'It is not enough for a party to cry "equity" and expect to be compensated. One must identify the relevant principle of equity on which a claim can be properly founded.'[40] The need to treat like cases alike is 'a basic principle of the administration of justice'.[41] As Neil MacCormick has said, 'I cannot for the life of me understand how there can be such a thing as a good reason for deciding any single case which is not a good generic reason for deciding cases of the particular type in question.'[42] Thus, 'equity is as much a matter of what is universalisable as is justice.'[43] Over time, the equitable jurisdiction developed into 'a well-defined

[33]   DEC Yale, *Lord Nottingham's Chancery Cases*, vol 1 (London, Selden Society, vol 73, 1957) xxxviii; Milsom (above n 31) 82–86.
[34]   Macnair (above n 32) 672–77.
[35]   *Ibid*, 679.
[36]   Milsom (above n 31) 95. See also WS Holdsworth, *Some Makers of English Law* (Cambridge, Cambridge University Press, 1938) 148–50.
[37]   *Baylis v Bishop of London* [1913] 1 Ch 127, 140 (CA); *Holt v Markham* [1923] 1 KB 504, 513–14 (CA).
[38]   *Re National Funds Assurance Co* (1878) 10 ChD 118, 128.
[39]   *Muschinski v Dodds* (1985) 160 CLR 583, 616. See also *Cook v Fountain* (1676) 3 Swans 585, 591–92 and 600 (36 ER 984) per Lord Finch LC (later Lord Nottingham); *Gee v Pritchard* (1818) 2 Swans 402, 414 per Lord Eldon LC; *Campbell Discount Co Ltd v Bridge* [1961] 1 QB 445, 458–59 (CA); *Bridge v Campbell Discount Co Ltd* [1962] AC 600, 626; *Carly v Farrelly* [1975] NZLR 365, 367; *Tito v Waddell (No 2)* [1977] Ch 106, 209–10 (VC); *Cobbe v Yeoman's Row Management Ltd* [2008] UKHL 55 at [17] and [46], [2008] 1 WLR 1752.
[40]   *Attorney-General v Equiticorp Industries Group Ltd* [1996] 1 NZLR 528, 537 (CA). See also *Re Diplock* [1948] Ch 465, 481–82 (CA).
[41]   R Cross and JW Harris, *Precedent in English Law*, 4th edn (Oxford, Oxford University Press, 1991) 3.
[42]   DN MacCormick, 'Formal Justice and the Form of Legal Arguments' in C Perelman (ed), *Études de Logique Juridique*, vol 6 (Bruxelles, Établissements Emile Bruylant, 1976) 103, 111.
[43]   *Ibid*, 113. See also RA Wasserstrom, *The Judicial Decision* (Stanford, Stanford University Press, 1961) 96–97 and 108–9.

system of jurisprudence—being under the control of fixed maxims and prior authorities, as much as judges of the courts of common law'.[44]

It is therefore unsafe to treat the concept of conscience as synonymous in this context with morality or ethical resolve. As John Baker has said:

> [M]any of the rules applied to uses by the Chancery had no moral content; the trustee was bound by them in conscience merely because they were positive law. A case of 1522 showed that a trustee was not to follow his own conscience, but was to obey his beneficiary; his conscience, like the chancellor's, was ordered by law.[45]

Thus, the history of equity does not provide a sound basis for Rotman's assertion that 'equity is perceived to be of a higher moral order than the common law'[46] or that fiduciary doctrine 'transmits [an] ethical resolve'.[47]

The second problem with Rotman's analysis lies in its reliance on the history of the equitable jurisdiction *in general*. Rotman seeks to identify 'the historical origins of the fiduciary concept through examinations of broader notions of Equity . . . to reveal the conceptual rationale underlying the fiduciary concept'.[48] Even if his analysis accurately reflected how the concept of conscience was employed in equity, an analysis of the nature of the chancery jurisdiction in general cannot identify the 'conceptual rationale underlying the fiduciary concept' as the fiduciary concept is only one part of the equitable jurisdiction. Rotman's assertion about the ethical nature of fiduciary doctrine can be supported only by detailed reference to and analysis of the case law concerning fiduciary duties, as opposed to other equitable doctrines. Rotman does seek to provide such an analysis. However, general references to equitable notions of conscience cannot avoid the effect of judicial remarks like Lord Herschell's statement in *Bray v Ford* that the fiduciary conflict principle is 'not . . . founded upon principles of morality'.[49] Rotman discusses this dictum as follows:

> Curiously, this frequently-cited statement is often taken out of context. . . [J]ust as Lord Herschell's comments clearly indicate the potential dangers of fiduciaries' conflicts of interest, they equally demonstrate that it may be possible to excuse fiduciaries from liability for such conflicts.[50]

Ironically, Rotman himself misconstrues what Lord Herschell meant.[51] Seeking to justify his proposition, Rotman emphasises Lord Herschell's observation that

---

[44] J Campbell, *Lives of the Lord Chancellors*, 5th edn, vol 1 (London, John Murray, 1868) 11. See also Yale (above n 33) xli, xlv–xlvi, lvi–lviii, xci and cxxxi–cxxxii; WH Bryson, *Cases Concerning Equity and the Courts of Equity 1550–1660*, vol 1 (London, Selden Society, vol 117, 2001) xlviii–xlix.

[45] JH Baker, *An Introduction to English Legal History*, 4th edn (London, Butterworths LexisNexis, 2002) 110.

[46] Rotman (above n 21) 159.

[47] *Ibid*, 2.

[48] *Ibid*, 155.

[49] *Bray v Ford* (above n 11) 51.

[50] Rotman (above n 21) 345–46.

[51] Others have also misunderstood Lord Herschell's speech: see, eg, *Badfinger Music v Evans* [2002] Entertainment & Media Law Rep 35, 48–49 *per* Lord Goldsmith QC (ChD); GH Jones, 'Unjust

the fiduciary conflict principle 'might be departed from in many cases'.[52] But what Lord Herschell meant by that remark, as Lord Watson meant in his statement that 'a breach of the [conflict principle] may be attended with perfect good faith',[53] was that the fiduciary principle can be *breached* without acting immorally, not that it can be breached *with impunity* when the breach is not immoral: 'Lord Herschell was not authorising departure from the rule but was saying . . . that there was nothing necessarily immoral in the solicitor-plaintiff having retained fees despite being a trustee'.[54] In other words, fiduciary doctrine operates *irrespective* of whether a fiduciary acts in a morally reprehensible manner. As Rigby LJ said in *Costa Rica Railway v Forwood*,

> [I]t does not depend upon fraud, and in the present case no imputation is made of anything approaching to fraudulent conduct on the part of [the defendant director]; but it does not in the least follow that, with perfect honesty of purpose, he may not have done something which, without his being aware of it, was contrary to principle and for which he must be made liable.[55]

The defendant in that case argued that the court ought not to hold him accountable, despite his breach of the self-dealing rule, because it would not be fair to do so. Vaughan Williams LJ rejected that argument outright: 'without going at length into authorities . . . there is no ground for any such contention'.[56]

Notwithstanding Rotman's argument, neither the history of equity generally nor the history of fiduciary doctrine in particular supports the view that fiduciary doctrine is best understood 'as a vehicle through which law imposes its standard of ethics'.[57]

III. The Profit Principle

In *Chan v Zacharia*, Deane J observed that 'what is conveniently regarded as the one "fundamental rule" [of fiduciary liability] embodies two themes'.[58] The first theme is the fiduciary conflict principle, the objective of which 'is to preclude the fiduciary from being swayed by considerations of personal interest'.[59] The second theme—which can usefully be referred to as the profit principle in order to differentiate it from the conflict principle—Deane J described as requiring

Enrichment and the Fiduciary's Duty of Loyalty' (1968) 84 *Law Quarterly Review* 472, 472–73; J Palmer, 'The Availability of Allowances in Equity: Rewarding the Bad Guy' (2004) 21 *New Zealand Universities Law Review* 146, 170.

52 *Bray v Ford* (above n 11) 52.
53 *Ibid*, 48.
54 *Re Drexel Burnham Lambert UK Pension Plan* [1995] 1 WLR 32, 37 (ChD).
55 *Costa Rica Railway Co Ltd v Forwood* [1901] 1 Ch 746, 753 (CA). See also *Ex parte Lacey* (above n 16) 628.
56 *Costa Rica Railway v Forwood* (*ibid*) 760.
57 Rotman (above n 21) 2.
58 *Chan v Zacharia* (1984) 154 CLR 178, 198.
59 *Ibid*, 198.

the fiduciary to account for any benefit or gain obtained or received by reason of or by use of his fiduciary position or of opportunity or knowledge resulting from it: the objective is to preclude the fiduciary from actually misusing his position for his personal advantage.[60]

He added that 'the two themes, while overlapping, are distinct. Neither theme fully comprehends the other and a formulation of the principle by reference to one only of them will be incomplete.'[61] The distinction drawn between these two themes, particularly the differently stated objectives of each theme, raises the question whether the profit principle is consistent with what has been said in the previous chapter about the conflict principle. In particular, Deane J's reference to the profit principle's objective as being 'to preclude the fiduciary from *actually misusing* his position' might suggest a concern with rooting out immoral conduct on the part of the fiduciary.

In order to examine this issue thoroughly, two points must be addressed. First, Deane J considered the two themes to be distinct, whereas other authorities suggest that the profit principle is simply a subset or application of the conflict principle. If the latter view is correct, the profit principle does not require detailed analysis in the present context, as it ought not to reveal anything inconsistent with what has already been seen above in chapter four. On the other hand, if Deane J's view of the profit principle as a separate (although overlapping) principle is correct, the second question that arises concerns the relationship between the separate profit principle and the protective function that has been identified as the basis of the conflict principle. These two points will therefore be taken in turn.

A. Existence of the Profit Principle

Numerous authorities treat the profit principle as a mere application of the conflict principle. For example, Lord Upjohn said in *Boardman v Phipps*:

> The relevant rule for the decision of this case is the fundamental rule of equity that a person in a fiduciary capacity must not make a profit out of his trust which is part of the wider rule that a trustee must not place himself in a position where his duty and his interest may conflict.[62]

Similarly, Lord Herschell's comment in *Bray v Ford* that a fiduciary 'is not, unless otherwise expressly provided, entitled to make a profit; he is not allowed to put himself in a position where his interest and duty conflict'[63] seems to treat these two propositions as alternative statements of a single principle, as does the Privy

---

[60] *Ibid*, 198–99.
[61] *Ibid*, 199.
[62] *Boardman v Phipps* [1967] 2 AC 46, 123.
[63] *Bray v Ford* (above n 11) 51.

Council's statement in *New Zealand Netherlands Society v Kuys* that 'the obligation not to profit from a position of trust, or, as it is sometimes relevant to put it, not to allow a conflict to arise between duty and interest, is one of strictness.'[64] Similarly, in *Conway v Ratiu*, Auld LJ referred to a fiduciary making an unauthorised profit as 'a common instance of such conflict'.[65]

On the other hand, it is not difficult to point to authorities that adopt Deane J's separation thesis. For example, in *Queensland Mines Ltd v Hudson*, the Privy Council approved Wootten J's statement at first instance of the defendant director's fiduciary obligation as 'twofold':

[H]e should not make a profit or take a benefit through his position as fiduciary without the informed consent of his principal, and . . . he should not act in a way in which there was a possible conflict between his own interest and that of his principal.[66]

This approach has been followed in more recent Australian authorities.[67] Similarly, recent English case law has treated the two principles as distinct. In *Don King Productions v Warren*, Morritt LJ observed that 'it is appropriate to consider separately each of the strands',[68] which would be superfluous if analysis of one necessarily captured whatever results the other might reveal. Brooke LJ's statement and explanation of the two principles in *In Plus Group Ltd v Pyke*[69] also supports that view, and in *Ultraframe (UK) Ltd v Fielding*, Lewison J said that 'these two strands ... must be considered separately.'[70]

Deciding between these two views is difficult because the facts of any given case can generally be explained either on the basis that the fiduciary made a profit out of his position or on the basis that, in so doing, his personal interest in making the profit conflicted with the duties that he owed to his principal.[71] The possibility of analysing most cases on either, or both, of these bases makes it difficult to isolate cases that prove clearly the existence of separate principles. Thus, for example, in *De Bussche v Alt*, the Court of Appeal explained the law 'under which an agent is prevented from making a profit out of his employment'[72] by reference to the conflict between the agent's personal interest and the

---

[64] *New Zealand Netherlands Society 'Oranje' Inc v Kuys* [1973] 1 WLR 1126, 1129.

[65] *Conway v Ratiu* [2005] EWCA Civ 1302 at [59], [2006] WTLR 101 (also partially reported at [2006] 1 All ER 571n).

[66] *Queensland Mines Ltd v Hudson* (1978) 52 ALJR 399, 401.

[67] See, eg, *Oceanic Life Ltd v HIH Casualty & General Insurance Ltd* [1999] NSWSC 292 at [42], (1999) 10 ANZ Ins Cases 74,968; *Gibson Motorsport Merchandise Pty Ltd v Forbes* [2006] FCAFC 44 at [12], (2006) 149 FCR 569; *Australian Securities & Investments Commission v Citigroup Global Markets Australia Pty Ltd (No 4)* [2007] FCA 963 at [291], (2007) 160 FCR 35.

[68] *Don King Productions Inc v Warren* [2000] Ch 291 at [42].

[69] *In Plus Group Ltd v Pyke* [2002] EWCA Civ 370 at [71], [2002] 2 BCLC 201. See also *Quarter Master UK Ltd v Pyke* [2004] EWHC 1815 (Ch) at [53]–[55], [2005] 1 BCLC 245.

[70] *Ultraframe (UK) Ltd v Fielding* [2005] EWHC 1638 (Ch) at [1306]. See also *O'Donnell v Shanahan* [2009] EWCA Civ 751 at [52]–[76].

[71] *Wilkinson v West Coast Capital* [2005] EWHC 3009 (Ch) at [254], [2007] BCC 717.

[72] *De Bussche v Alt* (above n 18) 316.

non-fiduciary duty owed to his principal.[73] And in *Boston Deep Sea Fishing v Ansell*, Cotton LJ made clear that a director could not keep 'a profit arising from a contract which he, on the part of the company, entered into'[74] but also explained that by receiving such a benefit the director 'puts himself in such a position that he has a temptation not faithfully to perform his duty to his employer'.[75] Examples could easily be multiplied of how difficult it is to determine whether cases were decided on the basis of contravention of the conflict principle or of a separate profit principle.

However, the House of Lords did seem to apply a separate profit principle in *Brown v Inland Revenue Commissioners*,[76] in *Regal (Hastings) Ltd v Gulliver*[77] and in *Boardman v Phipps*.[78] In *Brown*, a solicitor had to account to his clients for interest earned on money held for them in his client account. Lord Reid and Lord Upjohn both justified this conclusion on what appears to be an independent profit principle,[79] without any reference to the conflict principle, although they did so without analysing the relationship between the two principles.

Eilís Ferran has described *Regal (Hastings) v Gulliver* as 'the apotheosis of a strict no-profit rule which is not dependent on a conflict requirement'.[80] Directors took investment opportunities that came to them by virtue of their positions as directors because the company could not raise sufficient finance to subscribe for all of the shares in a subsidiary it had created. The directors later sold the shares they had bought at a profit, and the House of Lords unanimously held them accountable to their principal company for that profit. Numerous statements in the speeches suggest that this liability to account arose merely because a profit had been made out of the fiduciary position. For example, Lord Russell said:

> The rule of equity which insists on those, who by use of a fiduciary position make a profit, being liable to account for that profit, in no way depends on fraud, or absence of bona fides; or upon such questions or considerations as whether the profit would or

---

[73]   *Ibid*.
[74]   *Boston Deep Sea Fishing & Ice Co v Ansell* (1888) 39 ChD 339, 355.
[75]   *Ibid*, 357.
[76]   *Brown v Inland Revenue Commissioners* [1965] AC 244.
[77]   *Regal (Hastings) Ltd v Gulliver* [1967] 2 AC 134n (also reported at [1942] 1 All ER 378).
[78]   *Boardman v Phipps* (above n 62).
[79]   *Brown v Inland Revenue Commissioners* [1965] AC 244, 256 *per* Lord Reid and 265 *per* Lord Upjohn. See also *Re Lewis* (1910) 103 LT 495, 496 (ChD); AJ McClean, 'The Theoretical Basis of the Trustee's Duty of Loyalty' (1969) 7 *Alberta Law Review* 218, 223–24.
[80]   EV Ferran, *Company Law and Corporate Finance* (Oxford, Oxford University Press, 1999) 190. This position has been altered for company directors in the United Kingdom by s 176(4) of the Companies Act 2006, which provides that a director does not act in breach of duty by accepting a benefit from a third party by reason of his being a director 'if the acceptance of the benefit cannot reasonably be regarded as likely to give rise to a conflict of interest'. This statutory provision is seen as a rejection of the previous law (PL Davies, *Gower and Davies' Principles of Modern Company Law*, 8th edn (London, Sweet & Maxwell, 2008) [16–65]), which emphasises the distinct profit principle applied in *Regal (Hastings) v Gulliver*. Section 176(4) does not alter fiduciary doctrine for fiduciaries other than directors.

should otherwise have gone to the plaintiff, or whether the profiteer was under a duty to obtain the source of the profit for the plaintiff. . . The liability arises from the mere fact of a profit having, in the stated circumstances, been made.[81]

Lord Macmillan and Lord Porter also focused on the fact that the directors entered 'into a transaction in which they utilised the position and knowledge possessed by them in virtue of their office as directors, and that the transaction resulted in a profit to themselves'.[82] Viscount Sankey's speech did likewise,[83] although he also referred to the conflict principle.[84] Lord Wright referred to the liability to account being based on the presence of a profit, although his analysis suggests his true concern was with conflict between duty and interest rather than mere profit-making:

> [I]f a person in a fiduciary relationship makes a secret profit out of the relationship, the court will not inquire whether the other person is damnified or has lost a profit which otherwise he would have got. The fact is in itself a fundamental breach of the fiduciary relationship. Nor can the court adequately investigate the matter in most cases. The facts are generally difficult to ascertain or are solely in the knowledge of the person who is being charged. They are matters of surmise; they are hypothetical because the inquiry is as to what would have been the position if that party had not acted as he did, or what he might have done if there had not been the temptation to seek his own advantage, if, in short, interest had not conflicted with duty.[85]

In *Boardman v Phipps*, the solicitor for a trust bought shares in a company in which the trustees held shares. He did so having used his position as solicitor to the trust to obtain information about the company that he could not otherwise have obtained. Through considerable hard work, he reversed the fortunes of the previously ailing target company, thereby benefitting himself but also the beneficiaries of the trust through its shareholding. By a majority, the House of Lords held the solicitor liable to account to the trustees for his profits because he had acted in breach of fiduciary duty.

The two dissentients, Viscount Dilhorne and Lord Upjohn, accepted that the solicitor would have had to account for his profit if he had bought the shares in circumstances in which he 'had or could have had a personal interest conflicting with the interests of those [he was] bound to protect'.[86] But neither considered that there was any relevant conflict, as two of the three trustees had no interest in purchasing further shares in the target company, and so they considered the solicitor had not acted in breach of fiduciary duty.[87]

[81] *Regal (Hastings) v Gulliver* (above n 77) 144–45.
[82] *Ibid*, 153 *per* Lord Macmillan and 159 *per* Lord Porter.
[83] *Ibid*, 139.
[84] *Ibid*, 137.
[85] *Ibid*, 154.
[86] *Boardman v Phipps* (above n 62) 88 *per* Viscount Dilhorne and 123–24 *per* Lord Upjohn.
[87] *Ibid*, 88, 92, 130–31 and 133.

In the majority, Lord Cohen and Lord Hodson considered that there was a possibility of conflict between duty and interest. Lord Cohen said that a conflict arose because the solicitor 'would not have been able to give unprejudiced advice if he had been consulted by the trustees and was at the same time negotiating for the purchase of the shares on behalf of himself'.[88] The use of the word 'if' in this explanation indicates the completely hypothetical nature of the conflict,[89] as does Lord Hodson's acceptance that the conflict 'was but a remote possibility'.[90] In his dissent, Lord Upjohn identified that a more plausible conflict could have been found in the form of a potential conflict between the solicitor's duty to advise the trustees as to whether the shares were worth purchasing and his personal interest in purchasing the shares for himself, but this had not been pleaded or argued.[91]

While it is not productive to quibble with the majority's conclusion that the solicitor's conflict was sufficient, given that is an issue on which 'different minds may reach different conclusions',[92] the point that matters for present purposes is that the analysis based on conflict between duty and interest was not considered compelling, even by those in the majority, which suggests that the foundation for the majority's decision rests more soundly on their application of the profit principle. Lord Cohen, Lord Hodson and Lord Guest all considered that the fact that a profit had been made out of the defendant's fiduciary position justified an account of his profits, following *Regal (Hastings) v Gulliver*.[93] For example, Lord Cohen explained that the solicitor had obtained information about the shares through his fiduciary position and that the opportunity to purchase the shares had come to him through the trust.[94] He added that this conclusion was sufficient to dispose of the case but went on to say that there would also be liability to account for the profit on the basis of a conflict between duty and interest,[95] suggesting that he saw the two principles as separate and alternative bases justifying the result.

One cannot be categorical, one way or the other, regarding the existence of a separate profit principle, as the courts may simply have used the profit principle as a convenient ellipsis for a full explanation of the conflict involved in these cases: one can conceive of conflicts that could have been relied upon to justify the

---

[88] *Ibid*, 103–4.

[89] See also PD Finn, *Fiduciary Obligations* (Sydney, Law Book Co, 1977) [567]. And see the Privy Council's earlier rejection of an argument that the defendant was disqualified from purchasing property because he might later become trustee of the property: *Clark v Clark* (1884) 9 App Cas 733, 737. Thus, Matthew Harding goes too far in arguing that 'a possible conflict of interest and duty may arise where . . . there is a possibility that the interest will, *at some moment in the future*, come into conflict with a non-fiduciary obligation that the fiduciary does not presently but may at the future moment owe to the principal': M Harding, 'Two Fiduciary Fallacies' (2007) 2 *Journal of Equity* 1, 16.

[90] *Boardman v Phipps* (above n 62) 111.

[91] *Ibid*, 131–32.

[92] *Pilmer v Duke Group Ltd* [2001] HCA 31 at [79], (2001) 207 CLR 165. See also *Boardman v Phipps* (above n 62) 125; *Maguire v Makaronis* (1997) 188 CLR 449, 468.

[93] *Boardman v Phipps* (above n 62) 100–1, 103, 105 and 118.

[94] *Ibid*, 101 and 103.

[95] *Ibid*, 103.

result in most of these kinds of cases. In *Regal (Hastings) v Gulliver*, for example, the directors might have been held liable to account for their profits on the basis of a conflict between their personal interest in acquiring the shares and their duty to the parent company to consider whether it ought to try to borrow money so as to be able to subscribe for those shares itself. However, such rationalisations can become rather strained, as with Lord Cohen's attempt to identify a conflict in *Boardman v Phipps*.[96] As Lord Upjohn explained in *Boardman v Phipps*, for the conflict principle to apply there must be 'a real sensible possibility of conflict: not that you could imagine some situation arising which might, in some conceivable possibility in events not contemplated as real sensible possibilities by any reasonable person, result in conflict'.[97]

Bearing that in mind, the analysis in these cases based on the existence of a separate profit principle appears to be the more compelling justification for their results. The apparent separateness of the profit principle, as well as the lack of complete clarity as to that point, is noticeable in the High Court of Australia's observation:

> [I]t may still be arguable in this Court that, notwithstanding general statements and perhaps even decisions to the contrary in cases such as *Regal (Hastings) Ltd v Gulliver* and *Phipps v Boardman*, the liability to account for a personal benefit or gain obtained or received by use or by reason of fiduciary position, opportunity or knowledge will not arise in circumstances where it would be unconscientious to assert it or in which, for example, there is no possible conflict between personal interest and fiduciary duty.[98]

Even without a clear resolution of this argument in Australia, such dicta further support the view that the profit principle has been recognised as a distinct principle of fiduciary doctrine, at least in England.[99] As such, the profit principle

---

[96] See text accompanying nn 88–90 above.

[97] *Boardman v Phipps* (above n 62) 124. Lord Upjohn was in dissent in *Boardman v Phipps* 'on the facts but not on the law': *Queensland Mines Ltd v Hudson* (above n 66) 400 (PC). His statement was based on what Lord Cranworth LC had said in *Aberdeen Railway v Blaikie* (above n 19) 471 and is generally regarded as an accurate statement of the doctrine: see, eg, *Industrial Development Consultants Ltd v Cooley* [1972] 1 WLR 442, 450–51; *Swain v Law Society* [1982] 1 WLR 17, 31 (CA); *Framlington Group plc v Anderson* [1995] 1 BCLC 475, 495 (ChD); *Beach Petroleum NL v Abbott Tout Russell Kennedy* [1999] NSWCA 408 at [425], (1999) 48 NSWLR 1; *Bhullar v Bhullar* [2003] EWCA Civ 424 at [30] and [42], [2003] 2 BCLC 241; *Quarter Master UK Ltd v Pyke* [2004] EWHC 1815 (Ch) at [55], [2005] 1 BCLC 245; *Conway v Ratiu* [2005] EWCA Civ 1302 at [59], [2006] WTLR 101 (also partially reported at [2006] 1 All ER 571n); *Foster Bryant Surveying Ltd v Bryant* [2007] EWCA Civ 200 at [52], [2007] 2 BCLC 239; *Commonwealth Oil & Gas Co Ltd v Baxter* [2007] CSOH 198 at [169]; *Rigg v Sheridan* [2008] NSWCA 79 at [39]–[41]; *Bell Group Ltd v Westpac Banking Corp (No 9)* [2008] WASC 239 at [4506]–[4507]; RP Meagher, JD Heydon and MJ Leeming, *Meagher, Gummow & Lehane's Equity: Doctrines and Remedies*, 4th edn (Chatswood, Butterworths LexisNexis, 2002) [5–065]; PH Pettit, *Equity and the Law of Trusts*, 11th edn (Oxford, Oxford University Press, 2009) 441.

[98] *Chan v Zacharia* (above n 58) 204–5, quoted with approval in *Warman International v Dwyer* (above n 8) 559.

[99] See also McClean (above n 79) 227; J Mowbray, L Tucker, N Le Poidevin, E Simpson and J Brightwell, *Lewin on Trusts*, 18th edn (London, Sweet & Maxwell, 2008) [20–27]; cf R Lee, "Rethinking the Content of the Fiduciary Obligation" [2009] *Conveyancer* 236, 240 and 242.

merits analysis in the context of this book's investigation into the nature and function of the doctrines that are peculiar in their application to fiduciaries. Certainly, that is the safer path to take in circumstances in which the separateness of the principle is not completely clear: if the profit principle is a wholly contained subset of the conflict principle, one loses nothing except time by considering it separately; whereas, if it is not, one runs the risk of reaching faulty conclusions if one ignores it and considers only the more clearly established conflict principle.

B. Relationship to the Conflict Principle

Therefore, the question that arises is whether, as Deane J's comments in *Chan v Zacharia* suggest,[100] the profit principle is based on some sort of moral concern to prevent abuse of the fiduciary's position. As has been explained in the previous chapter, the recoverability of a profit made by a fiduciary in a situation in which there was a conflict between duty and interest is simply explained: the fiduciary breaches the conflict principle by acting in that situation without consent, and any profit that flows to the fiduciary as a consequence can be stripped by the principal. This is simply the remedial aspect of the protective function served by the conflict principle. The question that must be addressed here is why a fiduciary must account for a profit he has made in circumstances in which no conflict of interest has been identified.

The best way to understand the profit principle is as an outgrowth from the conflict principle. In other words, the current juridical justification for the profit principle is fundamentally drawn from the justification for the conflict principle, applied in related but slightly different circumstances. In that way, the profit principle can be understood, as Lord Upjohn suggested in *Boardman v Phipps*,[101] as part of the wider conflict principle, but it is a 'part' in the sense that it is related to and draws its justification from the conflict principle, rather than being a wholly contained subset of the conflict principle. The reason for the profit principle having been developed as a separate doctrinal principle seems to be that courts recognised that when a fiduciary has made an unauthorised profit out of his fiduciary position there will *commonly* or *ordinarily* be a conflict between duty and interest. In other words, in virtually all cases in which a profit is made out of a fiduciary position, the fiduciary will have acted in a way that involves a conflict between his non-fiduciary duty and his personal interest. That explains the difficulty in separating the two rules from one another, while also explaining the reason for the existence of the profit rule: it is simply a pragmatic response to the likelihood of a conflict being present in such settings. Thus, the profit principle is a prophylactic application of the conflict principle: the likelihood of

---

[100] See text accompanying nn 58–61 above.
[101] *Boardman v Phipps* (above n 62) 123.

there being a conflict in such circumstances is treated as sufficient justification for equity to prohibit all unauthorised profits, without requiring strict proof in every case that there was a conflict. It is noteworthy in that regard that the profit rule applies only when a fiduciary makes a profit 'by use of a fiduciary position'[102] or 'by reason and in virtue of their fiduciary office'.[103] Profits that are made without any such connection to the fiduciary role do not give rise to a risk of conflict between duty and interest.

This view of the relationship between the profit principle and the conflict principle has support in the case law and, to some degree, in the historical development of the two principles. The historical position is not absolutely clear, in large part because the history of fiduciary doctrine has not yet been fully investigated. Albert McClean opined that the development of two separate principles occurred 'perhaps more by default rather than by conscious decision'[104] but considered that 'the original basis for judicial intervention in England was the possibility of a conflict of duty and interest.'[105] Similarly, Stanley Beck concluded that 'the conflict rule is the broader rule of general application out of which the profit rule grew.'[106] More recently, however, Joshua Getzler has argued that a fiduciary principle existed before the development of the modern trust and that the function of the trust 'is to export the incidents of the fiduciary obligation to new situations'.[107] Getzler places the profit principle at the centre of this analysis, focusing on the decision in *Keech v Sandford*[108] as 'the *fons et origo* of this doctrine. . . The rule does not seem to have been followed before Lord King enunciated it in 1726.'[109] Yet in *Holt v Holt*, decided in 1670, Bridgeman LK and Twisden, Wyld, Rainsford and Windham JJ all agreed that 'in the Case of an Executorship in Trust, the Renewal of such a Lease shall go to the Benefit of the *Cestuy que* Trust.'[110] However, as Getzler points out,[111] the profit principle was not applied at all consistently through the seventeenth and eighteenth centuries: in some cases a version of the profit principle was applied,[112] whereas in other

---

[102] *Regal (Hastings) v Gulliver* (above n 77) 144.

[103] *Ibid*, 153; see also pp 149, 154 and 159. And see *Williams v Barton* [1927] 2 Ch 9, 13; *Re Macadam* [1946] 1 Ch 73, 82; *Attorney-General for Hong Kong v Reid* [1994] 1 AC 324, 338 (PC); *Warman International v Dwyer* (above n 8) 557; *O'Donnell v Shanahan* (above n 70) [60]; P Koh, 'Once a Director, Always a Fiduciary?' [2003] *Cambridge Law Journal* 403, 406.

[104] McClean (above n 79) 236.

[105] *Ibid*, 219.

[106] SM Beck, 'The Saga of Peso Silver Mines: Corporate Opportunity Reconisdered' (1971) 49 *Canadian Bar Review* 80, 90.

[107] J Getzler, 'Rumford Market and the Genesis of Fiduciary Obligations' in A Burrows and A Rodger (eds), *Mapping the Law* (Oxford, Oxford University Press, 2006) 577, 578.

[108] *Keech v Sandford* (1726) Sel Cas t King 61 (25 ER 223) (LC).

[109] Getzler (above n 107) 586.

[110] *Holt v Holt* (1670) 1 Chan Cas 189, 191 (22 ER 756). See also *Walley v Walley* (1687) 1 Vern 484 (23 ER 609) (LK).

[111] Getzler (above n 107) 582.

[112] See, eg, *Rushworth's Case* (1676) 2 Freeman 13, 13 (fn 1) (22 ER 1026); *Rakestraw v Brewer* (1728) 2 P Wms 511, 513 (24 ER 839) (MR). These cases often applied the principle as a property principle (a 'graft upon his stock': *Rushworth's Case* (1676) 2 Freeman 13, 13; see also *Owen v Williams*

cases it was not.[113] 'It was not until [*Keech v Sandford*] that it became rigid and fixed.'[114] As was seen in chapter four, Lord King LC's explanation for his decision in *Keech v Sandford* was short and cryptic but can easily be understood as an application of fiduciary conflict reasoning. After *Keech*, the conflict principle developed into a clear principle of fiduciary doctrine, particularly during Lord Eldon's period as Lord Chancellor in the early nineteenth century. The profit principle appeared to become rather lost behind the shadow of the clearly enunciated and explained conflict principle. Insofar as vestiges of a pure profit principle remained, they contended for position with the now more fundamental conflict principle.

The cases decided during and since the nineteenth century also contain statements that indicate this form of relationship between the two principles. In *Huntington Copper & Sulphur Co v Henderson*, Lord Young observed:

> It is the simple and familiar rule of trust law that a trustee (using the term in its largest sense), shall not without the knowledge and consent of his constituent make profit out of his office, or take any personal benefit from his execution of it. It is not a different rule, but *merely a development and instance* of the same rule, that a trustee shall not be permitted to do anything which involves or may involve a conflict between his personal interest and his trust duty (emphasis added).[115]

In *Costa Rica Railway v Forwood*, Rigby LJ explained that 'to those who have had experience in such matters, [the profit principle] is found to be a principle of necessary application in order to make sure that people will do their duty when they are acting under circumstances of unusual difficulty.'[116] In other words, the profit principle takes its modern justification from the avoidance of conflict between duty and interest. Thus, for example, in *Attorney-General v Edmunds*, a clerk of patents was entitled to make a profit by buying stamps from the Inland Revenue with his own money and retailing them at a higher price because

> it certainly was *no part of the duty* of [the clerk] or any one in the Patents Office, to have stamps ready, or to buy stamps, or to supply stamps. Therefore, as far as any profit was made by the application of [his] own money to the purchase of stamps . . . he is not liable. *It was not part of the duty which he had to perform*; it was something apart from it, and he had a perfect right to make that profit (emphasis added).[117]

(1773) Amb 734, 736 (27 ER 474)), rather than as a general principle of fiduciary doctrine. See, however, *Mansel v Mansel* (1732) 2 Barn KB 187, 188 (94 ER 438).

[113] See, eg, *Lesley's Case* (1680) 2 Freeman 52, 52 (22 ER 1053).

[114] S Cretney, 'The Rationale of *Keech v Sandford*' (1969) 33 *Conveyancer* 161, 178 (fn 16).

[115] *Huntington Copper & Sulphur Co Ltd v Henderson* (1877) 4 SC (4th Series) 294, 299. Lord Young's decision was approved by the Inner House as having 'been very accurately, ably, and exhaustively treated': p 305 *per* Lord Deas.

[116] *Costa Rica Railway v Forwood* (above n 55) 753. See also *Boston Deep Sea Fishing & Ice Co v Ansell* (above n 74) 363 (CA); *Consul Development Pty Ltd v DPC Estates Pty Ltd* (1975) 132 CLR 373, 397.

[117] *Attorney-General v Edmunds* (1868) LR 6 Eq 381, 393 (VC). (The clerk had to account for profits made on stamps he had bought with public moneys. Such profits do generate a conflict between the clerk's personal interest and his duty to safeguard the public money.)

In contrast, in *Williams v Barton*, a trustee of an estate convinced the estate to employ his firm to value the testator's securities, for which he received a commission from his firm. Russell J held that the trust could recover that commission. He said that 'a trustee may not make a profit out of his trust,'[118] but the explanation he gave for that proposition treats conflict between duty and interest as the mischief at which the profit principle strikes: 'it seems to me evident that the case falls within the mischief which is sought to be prevented by the rule. The case is clearly one where his duty as trustee and his interest in an increased remuneration are in direct conflict.'[119] Similarly, in *Furs Ltd v Tomkies*, Rich, Dixon and Evatt JJ observed of a director:

> If, when it is his duty to safeguard and further the interests of the company, he uses the occasion as a means of profit to himself, he raises an opposition between the duty he has undertaken and his own self interest, beyond which it is neither wise nor practicable for the law to look for a criterion of liability.[120]

Lord Nicholls' speech in *Attorney-General v Blake* also treats the profit principle as a deliberately over-inclusive, prophylactic application of the rationale underlying the conflict principle:

> Equity reinforces the duty of fidelity owed by a trustee or fiduciary by requiring him to account for any profits he derives from his office or position. This ensures that trustees and fiduciaries are financially disinterested in carrying out their duties. They may not put themselves in a position where their duty and interest conflict. To this end they must not make any unauthorised profit.[121]

Thus, there is support in the cases for the view that the profit principle, at least in its modern form, is based on fiduciary doctrine's 'large and important principle'[122] concerning conflicts between a fiduciary's personal interest and proper performance of his duty. Cases in which the profit principle applies but the conflict principle does not are very few in number and are difficult to identify. But that phenomenon is easily understood if the modern profit principle operates merely as an outgrowth from the core conflict principle which operates in the penumbra of that principle. In most cases in which a profit has been made by reason of the fiduciary position, there will have been a conflict between duty and interest.

The importance of this is that the profit principle ought not to be understood as involving any moral condemnation of the fiduciary taking the profit[123] but rather as a prophylactic application of the protective concerns that underpin the

---

[118] *Williams v Barton* (above n 103) 11.
[119] *Ibid*, 12.
[120] *Furs Ltd v Tomkies* (1936) 54 CLR 583, 592; see also p 598.
[121] *Attorney-General v Blake* [2001] 1 AC 268, 280.
[122] *Huntington Copper & Sulphur v Henderson* (above n 115) 299 (OH).
[123] *Halton International Inc (Holding) SARL v Guernroy Ltd* [2005] EWHC 1968 (Ch) at [141], [2006] 1 BCLC 78.

fiduciary conflict principle. This is supported by the fact that the profit principle applies even if the defendant fiduciary acted bona fide and was in fact acting in the best interests of his principal,[124] which renders difficult any alignment of the profit principle with a prohibition of immoral conduct. Certainly, if the profit principle is to be understood as somehow instantiating equity's condemnation of immoral conduct, the immorality at which it strikes requires far greater clarification and explanation than one can glean from the cases. Alternatively, and consistently with the case law, one can understand the 'misuse' that a fiduciary makes as a result of taking an unauthorised profit as based on the conflict between duty and interest that such profit-taking normally involves: 'the objectives which the [profit] rule seeks to achieve are to preclude the fiduciary from being swayed by considerations of personal interest and from accordingly misusing the fiduciary position for personal advantage.'[125]

The view of the profit principle advanced here is further supported by the courts' refusal to relieve a fiduciary from liability to account when it is argued that the profit could not have been obtained for the principal,[126] and particularly by the justification given for that refusal, perhaps the clearest instance of which is found in *Irving Trust Co v Deutsch*:

> The defendants' argument . . . that the equitable rule that fiduciaries should not be permitted to assume a position in which their individual interests might be in conflict with those of the corporation can have no application where the corporation is unable to undertake the venture, is not convincing. If directors are permitted to justify their conduct on such a theory, there will be a temptation to refrain from exerting their strongest efforts on behalf of the corporation since, if it does not meet the obligations, an opportunity of profit will be open to them personally.[127]

In other words, notwithstanding that the principal might not have been able to acquire the profit for itself, the fiduciary cannot be permitted to take it himself (absent proper authorisation) because to allow that would undermine the objectives of the conflict principle: it would foster in the fiduciary a temptation to underperform his non-fiduciary duties in the hope of being able to take a profit personally. Similarly, Peter Millett wrote:

> There are two fundamental rules of equity: (1) a fiduciary must not place himself in a position where his interest may conflict with his duty; and (2) a fiduciary must not

---

[124] See, eg, *Regal (Hastings) v Gulliver* (above n 77) 137, 143–45 and 153; *Boardman v Phipps* (above n 62) 104, 105 and 123.

[125] *Warman International v Dwyer* (above n 8) 557–58.

[126] See, eg, *Keech v Sandford* (above n 108) 62; *Regal (Hastings) v Gulliver* (above n 77) 144–45, 149–50 and 155; *Boardman v Phipps* (above n 62) 102–3, 109 and 117.

[127] *Irving Trust Co v Deutsch* 73 F 2d 121, 124 (1934). See also Beck, 'The Saga of Peso Silver Mines' (above n 106) 102–3; DD Prentice, 'Directors' Fiduciary Duties: The Corporate Opportunity Doctrine' (1972) 50 *Canadian Bar Review* 623, 630; DD Prentice, 'The Corporate Opportunity Doctrine' (1974) 37 *Modern Law Review* 464, 467; S Scott, 'The Corporate Opportunity Doctrine and Impossibility Arguments' (2003) 66 *Modern Law Review* 852, 861 and 867.

make a personal profit out of his position without his principal's knowledge and consent . . . [T]he second rule invites the question 'why not?'; the first supplies the answer.[128]

The central focus of fiduciary doctrine is thus to protect the proper performance of non-fiduciary duties as far as possible from the fallibility of human nature. As Stephenson LJ said in *Swain v Law Society,*

> With certain exceptions, neither directly nor indirectly may a trustee make a profit from his trust. This rule is part of the wider principle that in order to protect a trustee against the fallibility of human nature he may not put himself in a position where his duty and his interest may conflict.[129]

In other words, rather than being concerned with immoral abuse of the fiduciary position, the profit principle is based fundamentally on the same concern as the conflict principle: it too focuses on situations that carry an increased *risk* of the fiduciary abandoning his non-fiduciary duty in favour of his personal interest. The protection provided to non-fiduciary duties by the profit principle is perhaps less obvious than the protection afforded by the conflict principle. It is nonetheless fundamentally concerned with subsidiary and prophylactic protection of non-fiduciary duties.

Thus, the profit principle does not justify the view that fiduciary doctrine is concerned with preventing fiduciaries from acting immorally or otherwise 'misusing' or 'taking advantage' of their positions. Fiduciary doctrine has not developed a sophisticated understanding of what it means to 'misuse' or 'take advantage' of a fiduciary position, as one would expect it to have done over several hundred years of evolution if that were its central concern. Rather, it has been vigilant in its scrutiny of transactions entered into by fiduciaries in order to determine whether there was conflicting interest that put proper performance by the fiduciaries of their non-fiduciary duties in jeopardy. That vigilance has extended in a relatively small number of cases to the stripping of profits where a conflict has not been carefully identified, but the prophylactic extension of the core conflict principle in this way does not detract from the central importance and guiding influence of that core principle. Insofar as it is a separate doctrine, the profit principle should be treated in modern times as an outgrowth from the more well established conflict principle, rather than as a separate *kind* of doctrine.

IV. The Fair-Dealing Rule

The 'fair-dealing' rule appears prima facie to involve some form of judicial assessment of the fairness of the fiduciary's conduct, thus calling into question

---

[128] PJ Millett, 'Bribes and Secret Commissions' [1993] *Restitution Law Review* 7, 10.
[129] *Swain v Law Society* (above n 97) 29, endorsed on appeal: [1983] AC 598, 620.

the amoral, instrumentalist view of fiduciary doctrine that is advanced here. However, notwithstanding its name, it would be a mistake to view the fair-dealing rule as an implementation of some form of moral evaluation of fiduciary transactions. Understood in context, it is better thought of as an application of the fiduciary conflict principle, which has already been seen to be based on instrumentalist concerns to protect non-fiduciary duties rather than on moral principles. To make this clear, it is helpful first to consider the 'self-dealing' rule, as a clear understanding of that rule makes it easier to see the true basis of the fair-dealing rule.

A. The Self-Dealing Rule

The self-dealing rule, which dates from at least the time of Lord King LC,[130] renders voidable a trustee's purchase of trust property: 'any trustee purchasing the trust property is liable to have the purchase set aside, if in any reasonable time the *Cestuy que trust* chooses to say, he is not satisfied with it.'[131] The rule applies broadly, whenever a fiduciary[132] enters a transaction and is on both sides of the transaction.[133] The self-dealing rule is one of substance rather than form,[134] which goes beyond contract law's 'two party' rule.[135] As Salmond J said in *Robertson v Robertson*,

[130]   See, eg, *Whitackre v Whitackre* (1725) Sel Cas t King 13, 13 (25 ER 195); *Fox v Mackreth* (1788) 2 Cox 320, 327 (30 ER 148) (LC), affirmed on appeal: (1791) 2 Cox 320, 339 (30 ER 148) (HL); *Wilkinson v Stafford* (1789) 1 Ves Jun 32, 42 (30 ER 216) (LC); *Whichcote v Lawrence* (1798) 3 Ves 740, 750 (30 ER 1248) (LC); *Ex parte Lacey* (above n 16) 626 (LC); *Ex parte James* (above n 15) 345 (LC); *Parkes v White* (1805) 11 Ves 209, 226 (32 ER 1068) (LC); *Randall v Errington* (1805) 10 Ves 423, 426 (32 ER 909) (MR); *Cane v Allen* (1814) 2 Dow 289, 300 (3 ER 869) (HL); *Downes v Grazebrook* (1817) 3 Mer 200, 207 (36 ER 77) (LC); *Baker v Carter* (1835) 1 Y & C Ex 250, 254 (160 ER 102) (LCB); *Re Bloye's Trusts* (1849) 1 Mac & G 488, 495 (41 ER 1354) (LC), affirmed on appeal: *Lewis v Hillman* (1852) 3 HLC 607, 629 (10 ER 239); *Williams v Scott* [1900] AC 499, 503 (PC); *Robertson v Robertson* [1924] NZLR 552, 553 (SC); *Tito v Waddell (No 2)* (above n 39) 225 and 241.

[131]   *Campbell v Walker* (1800) 5 Ves 678, 680 (31 ER 801) (MR). See also *Dover v Buck* (1865) 5 Giff 57, 63 (66 ER 921) (VC).

[132]   The rule applies to fiduciaries generally: see, eg, *Hall v Hallet* (1784) 1 Cox 134, 139 (29 ER 1096) (LC); *York Buildings Co v Mackenzie* (1795) 3 Paton 378, 393 (1 Scots RR 717; also reported at 8 Bro PC 42 (3 ER 432)) (HL); *Ex parte James* (above n 15) 348 (LC); *Mulvany v Dillon* (1810) 1 Ball & Beatty 409, 418 (LC(I)); *Lees v Nuttall* (1829) 1 Russ & M 53, 54 (39 ER 21) (MR), affirmed on appeal: (1834) 2 My & K 819 (39 ER 1157) (LC); *Brookman v Rothschild* (1829) 3 Sim 153, 214 (57 ER 957) (VC), affirmed on appeal: (1831) 2 Dow & Cl 188 (6 ER 699) (HL); *Gillett v Peppercorne* (1840) 3 Beav 78, 83–84 (49 ER 31) (MR); *Alven v Bond* (1841) Fl & K 196, 211 (MR); *Wentworth v Lloyd* (1863) 32 Beav 467, 471 (55 ER 183) (MR), affirmed by the House of Lords: (1863) 32 Beav 467, 474; *Kimber v Barber* (1872) LR 8 Ch App 56, 59 (LC); *Nugent v Nugent* [1908] 1 Ch 546, 548–49, 550 and 551 (CA).

[133]   *Re Thompson's Settlement* [1986] 1 Ch 99, 115; *Jones v Firkin-Flood* [2008] EWHC 2417 (Ch) at [221].

[134]   For the relevance of substance or intention over form in equity, see JA McGhee (gen ed), *Snell's Equity*, 31st edn (London, Sweet & Maxwell, 2005) [5–24]; Meagher, Heydon and Leeming, 4th edn (above n 97) [3–160]–[3–200].

[135]   Thus, for example, the self-dealing rule applies when the fiduciary seeks to transact via an agent, nominee or trustee: see, eg, *Whitackre v Whitackre* (above n 130) 13; *Sanderson v Walker* (1807)

It is well established that a trustee for sale cannot purchase the trust property for himself . . . [S]uch a purchase is voidable ex debito justitiae at the suit of the beneficiary even though full value was given by the trustee. . . The rule is not based on any technical considerations relative to any difficulty, real or supposed, in the way of a person transferring property to himself. It is based on considerations of public policy, with intent to protect beneficiaries of a trust by precluding the trustee from placing himself in a position where his interests conflict with his duty.[136]

Similar statements throughout the case law indicate that it is the fiduciary conflict principle that animates the self-dealing rule: it is 'an application of the wider principle that a man must not put himself in a position where duty and interest conflict'.[137] As Parker CJ put it in *Farnam v Brooks*, 'because of the temptations trustees are under and the opportunities they have to serve their own interests to the prejudice of the cestui que trust [they] cannot be themselves purchasers of trust property.'[138]

Understanding that the self-dealing rule is an application of the fiduciary conflict principle explains why the substantive fairness of a transaction that falls within the self-dealing rule is generally considered irrelevant when determining whether that transaction can be maintained. As has been seen already, a fiduciary cannot act with a conflict between his duty and interest even though his conduct may be palpably to the benefit of his principal—the fairness of the transaction is irrelevant.[139] Applied to the self-dealing rule, this explains why it is not to the point for a fiduciary to argue that he acted with all due care in setting the price at which he bought property in a self-dealing transaction. The mere fact of the conflict between his duty to obtain the best price possible for the property[140] and his personal interest in the transaction is sufficient grounds for avoiding the transaction: 'it is perfectly immaterial whether the Transaction be fair or not.'[141]

---

13 Ves 601, 602–3 (33 ER 419) (LC); *Downes v Grazebrook* (above n 130) 207–8; *Whitcomb v Minchin* (1820) 5 Madd 91, 91 (56 ER 830) (VC); *Alven v Bond* (above n 132) 225; *Re Bloye's Trusts* (above n 130) 495–96; *Popham v Exham* (1860) 10 Ir Ch Rep 440, 457 (MR); *Guest v Smythe* (1870) LR 5 Ch App 551, 556 (LJ); *Silkstone & Haigh Moor Coal Co v Edey* [1900] 1 Ch 167, 167 and 171; *Tataurangi Tairuakena v Mua Carr* [1927] NZLR 688, 696 (CA). On the other hand, the two party rule would not apply to such transactions: *Ingram v Inland Revenue Commissioners* [1997] 4 All ER 395, 420–26 (CA), affirmed on appeal: [2000] 1 AC 293, 305, 308 and 310. See also the discussion above in ch 4, section III-A(i).

[136] *Robertson v Robertson* (above n 130) 553.

[137] *Re Thompson's Settlement* (above n 133) 115. See also *Wright v Morgan* (above n 19) 796–97 (PC). And see eg, *Hall v Hallet* (above n 132) 139–40; *Whichcote v Lawrence* (above n 130) 750; *Campbell v Walker* (above n 131) 681; *Lewis v Hillman* (above n 130) 629–30; *Ingram v IRC* (above n 135) 425 and 426 (CA); *Newgate Stud Co v Penfold* [2004] EWHC 2993 (Ch) at [230], [2008] 1 BCLC 46.

[138] *Farnam v Brooks* 26 Mass 212, 227 (1830).

[139] See above ch 4, section II-B.

[140] See, eg, *Re Bloye's Trusts* (above n 130) 495; *Aberdeen Railway v Blaikie* (above n 19) 473; *Beningfield v Baxter* (1886) 12 App Cas 167, 178 (PC); *Newgate Stud Co v Penfold* [2004] EWHC 2993 (Ch) at [227], [2008] 1 BCLC 46.

[141] *Mulvany v Dillon* (above n 132) 418 (LC). See also *Ex parte Lacey* (above n 16) 627 (LC); *Ex parte James* (above n 15) 347 (LC); *Randall v Errington* (above n 130) 428; *Attorney-General v Dudley*

It is also important, in order to understand the fair-dealing rule properly, to recognise that the self-dealing rule is not an absolute rule: a fiduciary can avoid its effect, but only in a few situations. For example, as Arden MR said in *Campbell v Walker*, the rule is avoided if a trustee 'should apply to this Court by motion to let him be the purchaser'[142] or when the fiduciary obtains his principal's fully informed consent.[143] As Lord Eldon LC explained in *Sanderson v Walker*,

> a trustee for sale may be the purchaser, in this sense; that he may contract with his *Cestui que trust*, that with reference to the contract of purchase they shall no longer stand in the relative situation of trustee and *Cestui que trust*; and the trustee, having through the medium of that sort of bargain evidently, distinctly, and honestly, proved, that he had removed himself from the character of trustee, his purchase may be sustained.[144]

However, such consent must be 'freely given, after full information'.[145] If he wishes to uphold a self-dealing transaction, the fiduciary is 'bound to show, by clear evidence, that the [principal] knew at the time the real nature of these transactions, and with full knowledge of their nature assented to them'.[146]

B. The Fair-Dealing Rule

Whereas the self-dealing rule deals with situations in which a fiduciary is involved on both sides of a transaction, the fair-dealing is concerned with situations in which a fiduciary deals with his principal.[147] The fair-dealing rule allows the principal to avoid such transactions, although they are not automatically avoided at the principal's behest.[148] In *Clarke v Swaile*, for example, a beneficiary under a trust for sale agreed to convey the trust property to the

---

(1815) G Coop 146, 148 (35 ER 510) (MR); *Brookman v Rothschild* (above n 132) 214; *Gillett v Peppercorne* (above n 132) 84; *Murphy v O'Shea* (1845) 8 Ir Eq R 329, 331 (LC); *Lewis v Hillman* (above n 130) 629; *Wright v Morgan* (above n 19) 798 (PC); *Re Bulmer* [1937] Ch 499, 508 (CA); *Re Thompson's Settlement* (above n 133) 118. A self-dealing transaction conducted at an undervalue can provide evidence of fraud, but one conducted at full value is still a breach of the self-dealing rule: *Wentworth v Lloyd* (above n 132) 472–73.

[142]   *Campbell v Walker* (above n 131) 681. See also *Farmer v Dean* (1863) 32 Beav 327, 328 (55 ER 128) (MR); *Coaks v Boswell* (1886) 11 App Cas 232, 237 and 242. 'The making of such an order ought to be rare and exceptional': *Coaks v Boswell* (above) 245.

[143]   *Ex parte Lacey* (above n 16) 626 (LC); *Downes v Grazebrook* (above n 130) 208.

[144]   *Sanderson v Walker* (above n 135) 601; see also p 602.

[145]   *Ex parte James* (above n 15) 353; see also p 348.

[146]   *Rothschild v Brookman* (1831) 2 Dow & Cl 188, 197 (6 ER 699) (HL). See also *Segrave v Kirwan* (1828) Beatty 157, 166 (LC(I)); *Chambers v Waters* (1833) Coop t Brough 91, 92–93 (47 ER 33) (LC), affirmed on appeal: *Waters v Groom* (1844) 11 Cl & Fin 684 (8 ER 1262) (HL); *Re Bloye's Trusts* (above n 130) 497; *Imperial Mercantile Credit Association v Coleman* (1873) LR 6 HL 189, 200 and 205; *Dunne v English* (1874) LR 18 Eq 544, 533–35 (MR); *Gray v New Augarita Porcupine Mines Ltd* [1952] 3 DLR 1, 14 (PC); *Boardman v Phipps* (above n 62) 109; *Oranje* (above n 64) 1132 (PC).

[147]   Again, the fair-dealing rule applies to fiduciaries generally: see, eg, *Gibson v Jeyes* (1801) 6 Ves 266, 277 (31 ER 1044) (LC); *Johnson v EBS Pensioner Trustees Ltd* [2002] EWCA Civ 164 at [48], [50] and [67], [2002] Lloyd's Rep PN 309; Meagher, Heydon and Leeming, 4th edn (above n 97) [5–175].

[148]   *Tito v Waddell (No 2)* (above n 39) 241.

trustee, and yet subsequent attempts to have the transaction set aside failed. Lord Henley LC said that he 'did not like the circumstance of a trustee dealing with his cestuy que trust . . . [H]owever . . . upon the whole, he did not see any principle upon which he could set the transaction aside.'[149] As Megarry VC put it in *Tito v Waddell*, a fair-dealing transaction can be maintained if the fiduciary can show that he took 'no advantage of his position and that the beneficiary was fully informed and received full value'.[150]

The primary difference between the fair-dealing rule and the self-dealing rule therefore appears to be the relevance of substantive fairness to the validity of a transaction that is caught by the fair-dealing rule, whereas such considerations appear to be irrelevant with transactions caught by the self-dealing rule. It is this apparent difference that requires careful consideration here, as it seems to involve the court in a moral evaluation of the transaction when determining whether it will be upheld. Upon closer investigation, however, this difference proves to be more apparent than real. The true concern of the fair-dealing rule is not the substantive fairness of the transaction but (like the self-dealing rule) the conflict between duty and interest that the fiduciary faces when entering the transaction. The substantive fairness of the transaction provides evidence as to whether the principal's consent to the transaction was fully informed.

i. References to 'Fairness'

Many dicta in the cases undoubtedly suggest that the fair-dealing rule is concerned with whether the transaction was fair to the principal or whether the fiduciary took advantage of his position. In *Coles v Trecothick*, for example, Lord Eldon LC, who championed the view that advantage-taking is irrelevant in a self-dealing transaction,[151] said:

> [A] trustee may buy from his *cestui que trust*, provided there is a distinct and clear contract, ascertained to be such after a jealous and scrupulous examination of all the circumstances, proving, that the *cestui que trust* intended, the trustee should buy; and there is no fraud, no concealment, no advantage taken, by the trustee of information, acquired by him in the character of trustee.[152]

The point that matters for present purposes is the apparent requirement that the fiduciary affirmatively prove that the transaction was substantively fair to the principal. In *Morse v Royal*, Lord Erskine LC said, in the context of a transaction between trustee and beneficiary, that he needed 'to see, that the transaction was fair; that no advantage was taken; that there was no concealment'.[153] Similarly, in

---

[149] *Clarke v Swaile* (1762) 2 Eden 134, 135–36 (28 ER 847).

[150] *Tito v Waddell (No 2)* (above n 39) 225.

[151] See *Ex parte Lacey* (above n 16) 627 (LC); *Ex parte James* (above n 15) 347.

[152] *Coles v Trecothick* (1804) 9 Ves 234, 246–47 (32 ER 592). See also *Gibson v Jeyes* (above n 147) 271; *Harris v Tremenheere* (1808) 15 Ves 34, 42 (33 ER 668) (LC).

[153] *Morse v Royal* (1806) 12 Ves 355, 377 (33 ER 134).

Marquis of Clanricarde v Henning, Romilly MR, discussing a solicitor purchasing from his client, noted that 'the Court . . . requires the solicitor to prove that he gave his client the full value.'[154] Lord Cairns LC made a similar observation, regarding a trustee purchasing from his beneficiary, in *Thomson v Eastwood*:

> [A] Court of Equity will examine into it, will ascertain the value that was paid by the trustee, and will throw upon the trustee the *onus* of proving that he gave full value, and that all information was laid before the *cestui que trust* when it was sold.[155]

Notwithstanding such statements, however, careful analysis of the case law shows that 'fairness' does not play such a central role in evaluating the validity of fair-dealing transactions as these dicta suggest, and the role that it does play is not to determine whether the fiduciary acted in a morally acceptable manner.

ii. Non-Critical Relevance of 'Fairness'

First, other dicta describe the court's inquiries into fair-dealing transactions without any reference to the substantive fairness of the transaction. In *Woodhouse v Meredith*, for example, Plumer MR said that 'if he meant . . . to become the purchaser, it was his duty to have done it openly . . . An agent or trustee may buy, if his principal or *cestui que* trust, being fully informed of it, is willing.'[156] And in *Williams v Scott*, the Privy Council said:

> The burthen of proof that the transaction was a righteous one rests upon the trustee, who must produce clear affirmative proof that the parties were at arm's length; that the cestui que trusts had the fullest information upon all material facts; and that, having this information, they agreed to and adopted what was done.[157]

Of course, the mere recitation of examples where the courts have not referred to substantive fairness cannot prove that it is unimportant in fair-dealing cases without explaining why other cases, some of which have just been seen, do refer to 'fairness' as a relevant consideration. Nonetheless, the dicta in cases like *Woodhouse v Meredith* and *Williams v Scott* do suggest that fairness is not the critical criterion in deciding whether a fair-dealing transaction will be upheld, in that if it were critical, one would not expect Plumer MR and the Privy Council to have failed to mention it altogether.

Far more important, however, are the cases that explain what the courts *are* fundamentally concerned to find when determining whether to uphold transactions that fall within the fair-dealing rule. The crucial criterion for upholding

---

[154] *Marquis of Clanricarde v Henning* (1861) 30 Beav 174, 185 (54 ER 855). See also *Edwards v Meyrick* (1842) 2 Hare 60, 68 (67 ER 25) (VC); *Spencer v Topham* (1856) 22 Beav 573, 577 (52 ER 1229) (MR); *Pisani v Attorney-General for Gibraltar* (1874) LR 5 PC 516, 538; *Ward v Sharp* (1884) 53 LJ Ch 313, 322; *Wright v Carter* [1903] 1 Ch 27, 60 and 61 (CA). Similarly, when an executor bought from a legatee, see *Gray v Warner* (1873) 42 LJ (NS) Ch 556, 557 (VC).

[155] *Thomson v Eastwood* (1877) 2 App Cas 215, 236.

[156] *Woodhouse v Meredith* (1820) 1 Jac & W 204, 222 (37 ER 353).

[157] *Williams v Scott* (above n 130) 508.

such a transaction is the fully informed consent of the fiduciary's principal. Even when the fairness of the transaction is referred to, the courts also require the fiduciary to show he 'has made full disclosure to the beneficiary'.[158]

That this element—disclosure and consent—is the critical criterion of assessment is shown by two related strands of reasoning within the case law. First, several cases indicate that a fair-dealing transaction will *not* be upheld if the fiduciary cannot prove that the principal gave fully informed consent, *even if* the fiduciary can establish that the transaction was substantively fair. Secondly, other cases show that a fair-dealing transaction *will* be upheld, *notwithstanding* that the court considers the transaction involved an unfair or unequal exchange of value, *provided* the principal gave fully informed consent to the transaction in that form.

The first line of cases is well illustrated by *McPherson v Watt*. Trustees, who had sought advice from a solicitor regarding the sale of four trust houses, agreed to sell the houses to the solicitor's brother. However, the trustees were not told that the solicitor was himself going to buy two of the houses from his brother once his brother had bought the four houses from the trustees. In effect, therefore, although unknown to the clients, the transaction was between themselves on the one hand and their solicitor and his brother on the other. The non-disclosure of the solicitor's interest in the transaction was fatal to it, given the fiduciary relationship between the solicitor and the trustees.[159] Lord Cairns LC said:

> Assume, if you please, that in every respect, as to price, and as to all other things connected with the sale, this was a sale which might have been supported had the [trustees] been told that [the solicitor] was the purchaser, in my opinion it cannot be supported from the circumstance that that fact was not disclosed to them.[160]

Lord O'Hagan observed that although 'there has been the fullest information, the most disinterested counsel and the fairest price, if the purchase be made covertly in the name of another, without communication of the fact to the vendor, the law condemns and invalidates it utterly.'[161] Similarly, Lord Blackburn commented that if the solicitor had disclosed the fact that he was interested in the transaction as a purchaser, it would have been unassailable.[162] He added:

> The mere fact ... that he does not disclose that he is a purchaser ... gives the client a right [to rescind, and] in such cases we do not inquire whether it was a good bargain or a bad bargain, before we set it aside.[163]

---

[158] *Tito v Waddell (No 2)* (above n 39) 241. See also text accompanying nn 152–53 and 155 above.
[159] *McPherson v Watt* (1877) 3 App Cas 254, 263. See also, eg, *Hardwicke v Vernon* (1798) 4 Ves 411, 416 (31 ER 209) (LC); *Lewis v Hillman* (above n 130) 629–30; *Ingle v Richards (No 1)* (1860) 28 Beav 361, 365 (54 ER 405) (MR); *Imeson v Lister* (1920) 149 LT Jo 446 (ChD).
[160] *McPherson v Watt* (*ibid*) 264.
[161] *Ibid*, 266.
[162] *Ibid*, 271.
[163] *Ibid*, 272.

Numerous other cases show that the courts' true concern is with ensuring that the principal's consent to the transaction was fully informed, rather than with determining whether the transaction was substantively fair. In *Jones v Thomas*, Alderson B observed that 'even a fair transaction of this nature, between an attorney and his client, in a matter entrusted to the attorney in his character of attorney, may be set aside',[164] as did Sugden LC in *Murphy v O'Shea*.[165] In *Randall v Errington*, Grant MR observed that a beneficiary could not be taken to have consented to a trustee's purchase from him 'until it is previously ascertained, that the *Cestui que trust* knew, his trustee had become the purchaser',[166] even when there was 'evidence, that [the beneficiary] was not then dissatisfied with the price'.[167]

In *Barker v Harrison*, a selling-agent bought the property himself, substantially below value. Knight Bruce VC was 'not sure, however, that upon this record the mere fact of substantial undervalue can be regarded as sufficient to entitle the Plaintiff to relief'.[168] What did convince him to grant relief to the plaintiff was the fact that the defendant had failed to inform his principal that other potential purchasers were willing to pay a higher and fair price.[169] In *Smedley v Varley*, a testamentary trustee could not purchase undivided shares in the residue from the beneficiaries, but the value of the transaction was irrelevant: 'this is wholly immaterial . . . for it is clear that the [beneficiaries] knew nothing about the value.'[170] Thus, as Lord Chelmsford LC observed in *Tate v Williamson*, a transaction between a fiduciary and his principal is liable to be set aside

> once it is established that there was a concealment of a material fact, which the [fiduciary] was bound to disclose. Nor, after this, is it of any importance to ascertain the real value of the property. Even if the [fiduciary] could have shewn that the price which he gave was a fair one, this would not alter the case against him.[171]

If any material facts have not been disclosed, the principal's consent is inadequate and the transaction can be avoided at the principal's behest, irrespective of whether the transaction was conducted at a fair value. 'It is not enough for an agent to tell the principal that he is going to have an interest in the purchase, or to have a part in the purchase. He must tell him all the material facts. He must make a full disclosure.'[172]

---

[164] *Jones v Thomas* (1837) 2 Y & C Ex 498, 520 (160 ER 493).
[165] *Murphy v O'Shea* (above n 141) 333–34; see also pp 330 and 331.
[166] *Randall v Errington* (above n 130) 427.
[167] *Ibid*, 428.
[168] *Barker v Harrison* (1846) 2 Coll 546, 553 (63 ER 854).
[169] *Ibid*, 553–54.
[170] *Smedley v Varley* (1857) 23 Beav 358, 359 (53 ER 141) (MR).
[171] *Tate v Williamson* (1866) LR 2 Ch App 55, 65–66.
[172] *Dunne v English* (above n 146) 533. See also *Imperial Mercantile Credit Association v Coleman* (above n 146) 200 and 205; *Gray v New Augarita Porcupine Mines* (above n 146) 14; *Wrexham Association Football Club Ltd v Crucialmove Ltd* [2006] EWCA Civ 237 at [39], [2008] 1 BCLC 508. There is no need to disclose facts that are equally known to both parties: *Farnam v Brooks* (above n

The second strand of reasoning in the cases establishes the opposite side of the coin, in that a transaction which falls within the fair-dealing rule can be upheld, notwithstanding that the courts might consider it substantively unfair to the principal, provided the principal has given fully informed consent. Thus, for example, in *Selsey v Rhoades*, Leach VC explained:

> [W]here the transaction is mixed with motives of bounty, there *the steward is bound to make out that the employer was fully informed* of every circumstance respecting the property which either was within the knowledge of the steward, or ought to have been within his knowledge, which could tend to demonstrate the value of the property and the precise measure and extent of the bounty of the employer... The employer may, if he pleases, treat with his steward preferably to any other person; and this preference is a bounty. But the steward cannot take advantage of this preference, unless he fully imparts to his employer all the circumstances of existing competition (emphasis added).[173]

In other words, if the principal knowingly consents to a transaction with his fiduciary at an undervalue, the transaction will not fail simply by reason of that undervalue.[174] Thus, Lord Selsey's lease of property to his steward and rent-collector at a rent lower than that offered by a third party was not voidable, as Lord Selsey was well aware of the other offer when he confirmed the agreement with the steward.[175] Leach VC also rejected an argument that the lease was unusually long as he considered this 'was obviously intended to be an indulgence and kindness to the Defendant'.[176]

Similarly, in *Hatch v Hatch*, Lord Eldon LC observed:

> There may not be a more moral act, one, that would do more credit to a young man beginning the world, or afford a better omen for the future, than if, a trustee having done his duty, the *cestuy que trust*, taking it into his fair, serious, and well-informed, consideration, were to do an act of bounty like this. But the Court cannot permit it; except quite satisfied, that the act is of that nature.[177]

Again, in *Hunter v Atkins*, Lord Brougham LC pointed out:

---

138) 232. When the fiduciary was retained to advise the principal regarding the transaction, the principal will only have given fully informed consent if the fiduciary has provided that advice as if the transaction were between the principal and a stranger (eg, *Dunbar v Tredennick* (1813) 2 Ball & Beatty 304, 315; *Cane v Allen* (above n 130) 294 and 299; *Ward v Sharp* (above n 154) 319–20) or arranged for another adviser who had all the material facts available to do so (eg, *Scott v Dunbar* (1828) 1 Molloy 442, 457), in order that he can be said to have explained fully his interest in the transaction, and obtained a truly informed consent thereto from his principal: *Andrews v Mowbray* (1807) Wils Ex 71, 104 (159 ER 835); *Segrave v Kirwan* (above n 146) 166.

[173] *Selsey v Rhoades* (1824) 2 Sim & St 41, 50 (57 ER 260), affirmed on appeal: (1827) 1 Bligh NS 1 (4 ER 774) (LC).

[174] See also *Rudd v Sewell* (1840) 4 Jur 882, 882 (LC).

[175] *Selsey v Rhoades* (above n 173) 51.

[176] *Ibid*, 55.

[177] *Hatch v Hatch* (1804) 9 Ves 292, 297 (32 ER 615). See also *Coles v Trecothick* (above n 152) 248.

A client . . . may naturally entertain a kindly feeling towards an attorney or solicitor by whose assistance he has long benefited; and . . . he may wish to give him the advantage of a sale or a lease. No law that is tolerable among civilised men—men who have the benefits of civility without the evils of excessive refinement and overdone subtlety—can ever forbid such a transaction, provided the client be of mature age and of sound mind, and there be nothing to shew that deception was practised, or that the attorney or solicitor availed himself of his situation to withhold any knowledge.[178]

In *Jones v Linton*, a solicitor arranged with his client that the solicitor would repay six mortgagees to whom the client owed funds, and the solicitor would then take over the debts, secured by a single mortgage granted by the client. Bacon VC commented that this 'was a hard bargain, no doubt, but hard as it is I cannot interfere with it. . . The evidence before me is that the terms of the deed were fully explained to the [client], and that he assented to them.'[179]

Taken together, these two strands of case law make it clear that the fundamental concern of the fair-dealing rule is to ensure that the principal gave fully informed consent when entering into a transaction with his fiduciary. Such consent is required because of the conflict that arises when a fiduciary enters into a transaction with his client where the subject-matter of the transaction is the subject of the fiduciary relationship: the fiduciary owes duties to his principal in respect of the subject-matter of the transaction, and those duties will generally, at least potentially, be in conflict with the fiduciary's personal interest in the transaction. In other words, again, the essential concern of the fair-dealing rule is the fundamental fiduciary conflict principle. As Lord Manners LC explained in *Bellew v Russell*,

this Court will not permit an Attorney to make a Purchase from his Client, while the Relation subsists. . . [I]n such Cases, the Interests, of the Attorney purchasing, clash with those of his Client, in a Manner not to be endured by the Court, while the Relation between them subsists.[180]

Understanding the fair-dealing rule as an application of the fundamental fiduciary conflict principle explains the frequent statements in the case law which require that the fiduciary must make full disclosure of all material facts and obtain the principal's consent in order to maintain such a transaction.[181] As Hart

---

[178] *Hunter v Atkins* (1834) 3 My & K 113, 135–36 (40 ER 43); see also p 134.
[179] *Jones v Linton* (1881) 44 LT 601, 602.
[180] *Bellew v Russell* (1809) 1 Ball & Beatty 96, 104. See also *Tennant v Trenchard* (1869) 38 LJ (NS) Ch 661, 663 (LC).
[181] See, eg, *Cane v Allen* (above n 130) 294; *Woodhouse v Meredith* (above n 156) 222 (MR); *Segrave v Kirwan* (above n 146) 166; *Farnam v Brooks* (above n 138) 227–28, 234–35 and 237; *Edwards v Meyrick* (above n 154) 69; *Molony v Kernan* (1842) 2 Drury & Warren 31, 38–39; *Savery v King* (1856) 5 HLC 627, 666 (10 ER 1046); *Thomas v Lloyd* (1857) 3 Jur NS 288, 289 (108 RR 925) (VC); *Spring v Pride* (1864) 4 De GJ & S 395, 405 (46 ER 971) (LJJ); *McPherson v Watt* (above n 159) 272; *Williams v Scott* (above n 130) 508; *Law v Law* [1905] 1 Ch 140, 157 (CA). See also *Rudd v Sewell* (above n 174) 882 (LC); *Mason's Hall Tavern Co v Nokes* (1870) 22 LT (NS) 503, 505 (MR), where full knowledge was clearly established.

LC explained in *Scott v Dunbar*, an agent is 'not disqualified from dealing with his principal, but if he dealt with him, the onus lay upon him to show that in that transaction he put his principal in possession of all the facts, and set him at arms' length with all the knowledge he had acquired'.[182]

This explains the dicta seen earlier that describe the fair-dealing rule without referring to the substantive fairness of the relevant transaction:[183] if there is fully informed consent then the fairness or otherwise of the transaction is not to the point. And if the principal's consent is not fully informed, again the fairness or otherwise of the transaction is irrelevant.

iii. Fairness as Evidence of Full Disclosure

The question that remains outstanding is why there are dicta which suggest that the substantive fairness of a fair-dealing transaction is a relevant consideration in determining its validity? Those dicta are best understood on the basis that the fairness of a transaction can provide *evidence* as to whether the fiduciary made full disclosure of all material facts. The fairness or otherwise of a transaction assists courts in determining whether the principal's consent to the transaction was fully informed, because the substantive content of the transaction can support inferences about whether the fiduciary disclosed all material information to the principal.

It can be difficult to determine whether a fiduciary had any special information about the subject-matter of the transaction and whether that information was properly shared with the principal:

> The principle is, that as the trustee is bound by his duty to acquire all the knowledge possible, to enable him to sell to the utmost advantage for the *cestui que trust*, the question, what knowledge he has obtained, and whether he has fairly given the benefit of that knowledge, to the *cestui que trust*, which he always acquires at the expence of the *cestui que trust*, no Court can discuss with competent sufficiency or safety to the parties.[184]

Knowing whether a transaction between fiduciary and principal was at full market value provides relevant evidence in this regard: if the transaction was not at full market value, the courts may infer that the fiduciary had information regarding the transaction that was not disclosed.[185]

In *Re Worssam*,[186] for example, the plaintiff was one of five children who had an interest in her father's estate. She sought to avoid the effect of a deed she entered into in 1871 by which she released her interest in the estate to two of her

---

[182] *Scott v Dunbar* (above n 172) 457. See also *Woodhouse v Meredith* (above n 156) 222; *Driscoll v Bromley* (1837) 1 Jur 238, 238; *Dougan v Macpherson* [1902] AC 197, 205 and 206;

[183] See text accompanying nn 156–57 above.

[184] *Ex parte James* (above n 15) 348–49; see also p 345.

[185] See also T Frankel, 'Fiduciary Duties as Default Rules' (1995) 74 *Oregon Law Review* 1209, 1239.

[186] *Re Worssam* (1882) 46 LT 584 (ChD).

brothers, who were administering the estate. Fry J considered the plaintiff had understood the general nature of the transaction, had been free from undue influence and had received independent advice. However, he appears to have been of the view that there had been inadequate disclosure to her regarding the true value of her share in the estate:

> [T]his is a bargain by a *cestui que trust* with her trustees that the latter shall no longer act as such; and the question is, whether this bargain has been entered into under circumstances which show that the *cestui que trust* was at the time of the bargain so completely at arm's length with the trustees, and so free from influence, and whether such complete disclosure had been made by the trustees, that I am not in a position to say that the bargain can stand. *In order to decide that, I must have reference to the precise terms of the bargain of 1871* (emphasis added).[187]

A schedule to the 1871 deed revealed an 1869 valuation of the plaintiff's interest, but Fry J noted:

> [V]arious changes had happened [between 1869 and 1871] and I think that further inquiry into these matters is necessary, and that [the plaintiff's] brothers have not shown all necessary disclosure to have been made, or that [the plaintiff] was placed at arm's length in the way which is essential before a trustee can buy from a *cestui que trust*.[188]

The content of a transaction can thus support inferences about what a fiduciary disclosed to his principal when entering into the transaction. The point is also illustrated by *Luff v Lord*. A trustee bought his beneficiary's legacy, which was worth £2000, paying only £450. Upholding the transaction, despite the apparently gross inadequacy of consideration, Romilly MR considered it important that the beneficiary 'perfectly well knew his position'[189] as he had been attending to legal proceedings concerning the validity of the legacy for many years with the assistance of a solicitor. Furthermore, the sale had originally been the beneficiary's idea and was only reluctantly acceded to by the trustee.[190] Romilly MR concluded:

> [I]t is difficult to say that it can be set aside, unless there was some concealment, some knowledge possessed by Mr Lord which was not possessed by the vendor, which made the amount of the purchase-money inadequate. *Now upon that, it is important once more to consider what was the nature of the interest that was bought by Mr Lord* (emphasis added).[191]

The litigation as to the validity of the legacy, which was still outstanding at the time of the transaction, made it unclear whether the legacy would ever be paid. The subsequent conclusion of the litigation revealed the legacy to be worth

---

[187]   *Ibid*, 591.
[188]   *Ibid*.
[189]   *Luff v Lord* (1864) 34 Beav 220, 228 (55 ER 619).
[190]   *Ibid*, 229.
[191]   *Ibid*, 230.

considerably more than had been paid for it, but the uncertainty surrounding the litigation meant that the amount paid represented the value of the legacy at the time the trustee bought it. Thus, there was nothing to suggest that the trustee had concealed or failed to disclose any material facts known to him at the time of the transaction.[192]

A similar idea is implied in Lord Erskine LC's observation in *Morse v Royal*:

> If the Court can discover, that some advantage has been taken, some information acquired, which the other did not possess, though it is not to be precisely discovered, inadequacy, without going to the length of requiring it to be such as shocks the conscience, will go a vast way to constitute fraud.[193]

Thus, the 'advantage taken' rests not in the imbalance of consideration itself but in the fiduciary's failure to disclose all relevant 'information acquired' to his principal, and inadequacy of consideration assists the court in reaching the conclusion that there has been some such non-disclosure. As Parker CJ explained in *Farnam v Brooks*,

> trustees . . . are still further obliged in their bargains relating to the trust fund, not only not to misrepresent, and not to conceal, but also to disclose every thing known to them which in the mind of a prudent man would be likely to affect the bargain. And if this is not done, although there may be no design to cheat, it is a constructive fraud. . . The exhibit of a balance considerably larger than the sum offered for it is of itself one pretty strong ground for inquiry, and an intimation of contingencies which may affect the bargain.[194]

Thus, the substantive fairness of a transaction between fiduciary and principal does have a role in whether transactions between a fiduciary and his principal will be upheld, but its role is evidential, as the foundation for a possible inference, rather than substantive.[195] Even a court of equity 'suffers no man to overreach another [but] it helps no man who hath overreached himself without any practice or contrivance of his adversary. . . Chancery mends no man's bargain.'[196] Inadequacy of consideration is not generally grounds on its own for setting aside any transaction,[197] but such inadequacy can provide the basis from which to infer

---

[192] Lord Westbury LC affirmed Romilly MR's decision as the beneficiary was 'thoroughly well informed of the circumstances': *Luff v Lord* (1865) 11 LT 695, 697.

[193] *Morse v Royal* (above n 153) 373. The reference to 'fraud' here is to 'constructive fraud': *Plowright v Lambert* (1885) 52 LT 646, 654 (ChD).

[194] *Farnam v Brooks* (above n 138) 236–37. See also *Andrews v Mowbray* (above n 172) 103–4 (LC).

[195] Cf V Brudney, 'Contract and Fiduciary Duty in Corporate Law' (1997) 38 *Boston College Law Review* 595, 598 and 605.

[196] *Maynard v Moseley* (1676) 3 Swans 653, 654–55 (36 ER 1010) (LC). See also *Willis v Jernegan* (1741) 2 Atk 251, 251–52 (26 ER 555) (LC); Yale (above n 33) xcii–xciv.

[197] See, eg, *Kingsland v Barnewall* (1706) 4 Bro PC 154, 155 (2 ER 105); *Fox v Mackreth* (above n 130) 688; *Fox v Mackreth* (1788) 2 Bro CC 400, 420 (29 ER 224) (LC); *Low v Barchard* (1803) 8 Ves 133, 137 (32 ER 303) (LC); *Lowther v Lowther* (1806) 13 Ves 95, 103 (33 ER 230) (LC); *Farnam v Brooks* (above n 138) 235; *Cockell v Taylor* (1852) 15 Beav 103, 115 (51 ER 475) (MR).

that there was some wrongdoing in the way the transaction was brought about.[198] As it is only an inference, it can be rebutted by other evidence that there was full disclosure and hence fully informed consent from the principal.

iv. Relationship to the Self-Dealing Rule and Conflict Principle

In *Tito v Waddell*, Megarry VC accepted that 'both rules, or both limbs, have a common origin' but nonetheless considered the fair-dealing and self-dealing rules to be distinct: 'I see no merit in attempting a forced union which has to be expressed in terms of disunity. I shall accordingly treat the rules as being in essence two distinct though allied rules.'[199] However, while the two rules are distinct in their fields of application, they are not conceptually distinct: each is an application of the fundamental fiduciary conflict principle, and there is no 'forced union' or 'disunity' involved in understanding them as such.[200]

In a self-dealing transaction, the conflict is clear: for example, a trustee who sells trust property has a duty to seek to obtain the highest price possible, but he has a conflicting personal interest if he buys the property for himself, in seeking to purchase at the lowest price possible. This is also the case in a fair-dealing situation: for example, a solicitor whose professional advice and assistance has been sought regarding the sale of his client's property owes a duty that conflicts with his personal interest if he buys the property. The apparent difference between the self-dealing rule and the fair-dealing rule is simply a function of the slightly different facts that are relevant in each type of transaction in determining whether the principal consented to the conflict and whether that consent was sufficiently well informed. In situations that fall within the fair-dealing rule, the principal normally knows that he is entering into a transaction with his fiduciary[201] and therefore agrees to the fiduciary's involvement in the transaction. In situations that fall within the self-dealing rule, the principal is not normally involved, and so he cannot be said to have consented simply by virtue of the transaction having been made. A separate enquiry has to be made in such cases as to whether the principal gave fully informed consent. When the fair-dealing rule is at issue, however, the principal is a party to the transaction and so can be taken to have consented to it to some degree. The question that arises in such cases is whether that consent was sufficiently well informed to protect the fiduciary from liability. The fairness of the transaction is then relevant, in that it provides

[198] See, eg, *Floyer v Sherard* (1743) Amb 18, 18 (fn 1) (27 ER 10); *Gartside v Isherwood* (1778) 1 Bro CC 558, 564 (28 ER 1297); *Crowe v Ballard* (1790) 1 Ves Jun 215, 219 (30 ER 308) (LC); *Low v Barchard* (ibid) 137; *Coles v Trecothick* (above n 152) 246; *Lowther v Lowther* (ibid) 103; *Whalley v Whalley* (1816) 1 Mer 436, 446 (35 ER 734) (MR); *Cockell v Taylor* (ibid) 115; *Tennent v Tennents* (1870) LR 2 Sc & Div 6, 9.
[199] *Tito v Waddell (No 2)* (above n 39) 241.
[200] This argument is advanced in more detail in M Conaglen, 'A Re-Appraisal of the Fiduciary Self-Dealing and Fair-Dealing Rules' [2006] *Cambridge Law Journal* 366, 390–96.
[201] Although not always: see, eg, *McPherson v Watt* (above n 159) 263–64, 266 and 271; *Randall v Errington* (above n 130) 428.

evidence from which the court can determine whether the fiduciary made full disclosure so that the principal's consent was fully informed.

In general, Anglo-Australian courts do not sit in moral judgment on the substantive propriety or otherwise of transactions entered into between autonomous legal persons.[202] Properly understood, fiduciary doctrine's fair-dealing rule is not an exception to this general proposition. A court's assessment of the substantive fairness of fair-dealing transactions is not the critical determinant when considering whether such transactions will stand. The existence and quality of the principal's consent is the crucial criterion by which that decision is reached. Attention is paid to the substantive content of a fair-dealing transaction only insofar as it founds an *evidential* inference of some irregularity in the procedural elements of the transaction. The courts do not simply reach a conclusion that they will not uphold transactions that they consider to be substantively unfair. The fair-dealing rule and the self-dealing rule appear different only because they are practical applications of one principle to differing factual situations: both are applications of the fundamental fiduciary principle regarding conflicts between duty and interest.[203] As such, the fair-dealing rule does not provide any support for a moralistic view of fiduciary doctrine beyond anything provided by the conflict principle itself. The fiduciary conflict principle is not moralistic but rather serves an instrumentalist function in protecting the proper performance of non-fiduciary duties. The fair-dealing rule does not detract from that proposition.

V. The Corporate Opportunity Doctrine

Some commentators have identified 'a separate corporate opportunity doctrine' that is said to involve a 'new approach to conflicts of interest [which] is very different to the inflexible and somewhat draconian fiduciary duty'.[204] The reason for considering this doctrine here is that some have treated it as a vehicle for

---

[202] See generally R Bigwood, 'Conscience and the Liberal Conception of Contract: Observing Basic Distinctions' (2000) 6 *New Zealand Business Law Quarterly* 3, 20–21.

[203] The fiduciary conflict principle is of *general* application when a fiduciary finds himself in such a conflict, irrespective of whether any established rule or previous authority deals precisely with the situation at hand: see, eg, *Dent v Bennett* (1835) 7 Sim 539, 546 (58 ER 944) (VC); *Reed v Norris* (1837) 2 My & Cr 361, 374 (40 ER 678) (LC); *Hamilton v Wright* (above n 17) 122 and 124–25; *Huntington Copper & Sulphur v Henderson* (above n 115) 299 (OH); *Industrial Development Consultants v Cooley* (above n 97) 453–54. Hart J was wrong to suggest otherwise in *Public Trustee v Cooper* [2001] WTLR 901, 933 and 934 (ChD).

[204] R Teele, 'The Necessary Reformulation of the Classic Fiduciary Duty to Avoid a Conflict of Interest or Duties' (1994) 22 *Australian Business Law Review* 99, 100.

exacting a commercially appropriate level of morality from company directors.[205] In *Canadian Aero Service v O'Malley*, for example, the Supreme Court of Canada considered that the case law

> shows the pervasiveness of a strict ethic in this area of law [that] disqualifies a director or senior officer from usurping for himself or diverting to another person or company with whom or with which he is associated a maturing business opportunity which his company is actively pursuing.[206]

This moralistic view of the doctrine may have been influenced by US law in this area,[207] wherein what has emerged 'is an imprecise ethical standard "which prohibits an 'executive' . . . from appropriating to himself a business opportunity which in fairness should belong to the corporation"'.[208]

However, there is no need to understand the Anglo-Australian doctrine as implementing a moral or ethical standard of behaviour in the business context. On the contrary, the doctrine is better described as 'no more than a straight forward application of equity's "inflexible rule" that a person standing in a fiduciary position cannot benefit from his position without, at least, full disclosure having been made to and approval being obtained from his principals'.[209] In other words, the corporate opportunity doctrine is merely another specific application of fiduciary doctrine's conflict and profit principles.[210] As Dan Prentice observed, 'it would be supererogatory to develop a doctrine of corporate opportunity to embrace the situations in these cases as they fall squarely within the ambit of the principle proscribing the making of profits by a fiduciary from his position.'[211]

Prentice went on, however, to argue that a corporate opportunity doctrine is needed when a director exploits an opportunity based on information received in a capacity other than as a director,[212] citing as an example *Industrial Development Consultants v Cooley*.[213] However, *Cooley* can be explained, and indeed was decided, on the basis of a straightforward application of the fiduciary conflict principle. Cooley, who had been managing director of IDC, obtained a contract for himself which IDC had sought to acquire. The contractual counterparty, EGB, had rebuffed approaches made by Cooley on behalf of IDC but later approached Cooley in his personal capacity. Roskill J held that the facts 'disclosed

---

[205] See, eg, DD Prentice, '*Regal (Hastings) Ltd v Gulliver*: The Canadian Experience' (1967) 30 *Modern Law Review* 450, 450.

[206] *Canadian Aero Service Ltd v O'Malley* [1974] SCR 592, 607.

[207] SM Beck, 'The Quickening of Fiduciary Obligation: *Canadian Aero Services v O'Malley*' (1975) 53 *Canadian Bar Review* 771, 793.

[208] *Canadian Aero Service v O'Malley* (above n 206) 612, quoting from Note, 'Corporate Opportunity' (1961) 74 *Harvard Law Review* 765, 765.

[209] Prentice, 'Directors' Fiduciary Duties' (above n 127) 625.

[210] *Kingsley IT Consulting Ltd v McIntosh* [2006] EWHC 1288 (Ch) at [51]–[52].

[211] Prentice, 'The Corporate Opportunity Doctrine' (above n 127) 465.

[212] *Ibid*.

[213] *Industrial Development Consultants v Cooley* (above n 97) (Birmingham Assize).

the plainest conflict of interest'[214] between Cooley's duty to inform IDC that he had been approached by EGB[215] and his personal interest in taking the contract for himself. Even when a director learns of an opportunity by chance from an advertisement, so that his company was not actively considering it, nonetheless there can be a real sensible possibility of conflict between the director's duties to the company and his personal interest:

> Whether the Company could or would have taken that opportunity, had it been made aware of it, is not to the point: the existence of the opportunity was information which it was relevant for the Company to know, and it follows that the [defendant directors] were under a duty to communicate it to the Company. . . 'reasonable men looking at the facts would think there was a real sensible possibility of conflict'.[216]

A director acts in breach of fiduciary duty in these cases because he acts with a conflict between his personal interest and the (non-fiduciary) duty that he owes to the company.[217] As such, the corporate opportunity doctrine provides no basis on which to construct a theory that fiduciary doctrine seeks to measure the conduct of fiduciaries by moral or ethical standards. Rather than being moralistic in its nature and function, fiduciary doctrine is fundamentally concerned to provide prophylactic and subsidiary protection for the proper performance of non-fiduciary duties. Like the fair-dealing rule, the corporate opportunity doctrine is no more than a specific application of the general protective function served by fiduciary doctrine.

---

[214] *Ibid*, 447; see also p 451.

[215] *Ibid*, 451.

[216] *Bhullar v Bhullar* [2003] EWCA Civ 424 at [41]–[42], [2003] 2 BCLC 241; see also at [27]–[28]. And see *Commonwealth Oil & Gas v Baxter* (above n 97) [185].

[217] The (non-fiduciary) duty recognised in *IDC v Cooley* has been described as 'mildly revolutionary': see Finn (above n 89) [568] (fn 35); see also at [556]. And see Prentice, 'Directors' Fiduciary Duties' (above n 127). Roskill J's analysis can be rationalised on the basis of a conflict between Cooley's interest and a different duty—his duty to try to secure the EGB contract for IDC: see *CMS Dolphin Ltd v Simonet* [2001] 2 BCLC 704 at [90] (ChD). But it is not a long stretch from saying that Cooley had a duty to try to secure the contract for IDC to saying that he ought to have disclosed to IDC that EGB had approached him, at least when he could not reasonably conclude that it was not in the interests of IDC to know that: see, eg, *Item Software (UK) Ltd v Fassihi* [2004] EWCA Civ 1244 at [44], [2005] 2 BCLC 91. Whether any such non-fiduciary duty is owed will, however, 'depend upon how the particular company's business is organised and the part which the director could reasonably have been expected to play': *Bishopsgate Investment Management Ltd v Maxwell (No 2)* [1994] 1 All ER 261, 264 (CA). See also *Framlington Group v Anderson* (above n 97) 497; *Foster Bryant Surveying Ltd v Bryant* [2007] EWCA Civ 200 at [64]–[65], [2007] 2 BCLC 239; A Stafford and S Ritchie, *Fiduciary Duties: Directors and Employees* (Bristol, Jordans, 2008) [2.156].

6

Conflicts between Inconsistent Duties

The previous two chapters have argued that fiduciary doctrine is best understood as performing a fundamentally instrumental, rather than moralistic, task. It seeks to enhance the likelihood of due performance of the non-fiduciary duties that a fiduciary has undertaken by requiring him to eschew situations involving temptations inconsistent with due performance. This chapter considers whether a subsidiary and prophylactic form of protection for non-fiduciary duties also applies when a fiduciary owes duties to more than one principal and the performance of those duties is or may be in some way inconsistent.

Several relatively recent cases confirm the proposition that it 'automatically constitutes a breach of fiduciary duty'[1] for a fiduciary to act for two principals when the duties that he owes to each are inconsistent, unless the fiduciary has fully informed consent from both principals to his action.[2] It has also become clear that this is so irrespective of whether the fiduciary has any personal interest in the transaction:

> Not only must the fiduciary avoid, without informed consent, placing himself in a position of conflict between duty and personal interest, but he must eschew conflicting engagements ... [I]t is not to the point that the fiduciary himself may not stand to

---

[1] *Bristol & West Building Society v Mothew* [1998] Ch 1, 19 (CA).

[2] See, eg, *Marks & Spencer plc v Freshfields Bruckhaus Deringer* [2004] EWHC 1337 (Ch) at [12], [2004] 1 WLR 2331; *Ultraframe (UK) Ltd v Fielding* [2005] EWHC 1638 (Ch) at [1315]–[1317]. See also *Callaghan v Thompson* [2000] Lloyd's Rep IR 125, 132 (QBD); *Breen v Williams* (1996) 186 CLR 71, 135; *Haira v Burbery Mortgage Finance & Savings Ltd* [1995] 3 NZLR 396, 405–7 (CA); *North & South Trust Co v Berkeley* [1971] 1 WLR 470, 484–85 (QBD); *Anglo-African Merchants Ltd v Bayley* [1970] 1 QB 311, 323–24; *Fullwood v Hurley* [1928] 1 KB 498, 501 (CA). And see *Hesse v Briant* (1856) 6 De GM & G 623, 629 (43 ER 1375).

In *Cholmondeley v Clinton* (1815) 19 Ves 261, 276 (34 ER 515) Lord Eldon LC held that a solicitor could not, without his client's consent, cease to act for one party to litigation and proceed to act for the other, but that decision appears to have been based on principles concerned with the confidentiality of information, rather than conflict between duties. As Lord Eldon explained, the solicitor 'ought not, *if he knows any thing, that may be prejudicial to the former client,* to accept the new brief' (emphasis added): (1815) 19 Ves 261, 275. See also *Bricheno v Thorp* (1821) Jac 300, 303 (34 ER 864); *Johnson v Marriott* (1833) 2 C & M 183, 187 and 188–89 (149 ER 725) (Exch).

profit from the transaction he brings about between the parties. The prohibition is not against the making of a profit . . . but of the avoidance of conflict of duties.[3]

I. Origins

Notwithstanding this relatively clear modern position, the origins of this doctrine are rather murky.[4] It is worth considering those origins briefly as they show that the doctrine regarding conflict between duties developed over time by analogy with the doctrine regarding conflict between duty and interest.

In earlier cases in which there was conflict between the duties that a fiduciary owed to multiple principals, courts often focused on conflicts between duty and interest that were also present on the facts. Thus, for example, in *Salomons v Pender*, a land agent arranged for his client's land to be bought by a company of which the agent was a shareholder and director. Notwithstanding the conflict between the duty the agent owed to his client and the duty he owed to the company as a director, the Court of Exchequer proceeded on the basis of a conflict between the agent's personal interest as a shareholder and his contractual duty to the client.[5] Such cases did, however, sometimes contain comment on the conflict between duties. In *Ex parte Lacey*, for example, Lord Eldon LC noted:

> [T]here is no case, in which it is useful upon general principles, that the same Solicitor should be employed on all sides: in many cases it is a great saving of expence certainly: but, where property is brought to sale, to pay creditors &c, great mischief is occasioned by it.[6]

But such comments were obiter,[7] and it is not clear to what degree they were thought to represent actual doctrine.[8] When there was a conflict between a fiduciary's duty and his interest, because the fiduciary was personally and beneficially interested in the impugned transaction, the duty-interest conflict rule

---

[3] *Commonwealth Bank of Australia v Smith* (1991) 42 FCR 390, 392. This passage has been cited with approval in England: *Bristol & West Building Society v May May & Merrimans* [1996] 2 All ER 801, 815–16 (ChD).

[4] For more detail, see M Conaglen, 'Fiduciary Regulation of Conflicts between Duties' (2009) 125 *Law Quarterly Review* 111, 112–22.

[5] *Salomons v Pender* (1865) 3 H & C 639, 641–44 (159 ER 682). Similarly, see *Hardwicke v Vernon* (1798) 4 Ves 411, 416 (31 ER 209) (LC); *McPherson v Watt* (1877) 3 App Cas 254, 263.

[6] *Ex parte Lacey* (1802) 6 Ves 625, 631 (31 ER 1228).

[7] *Lacey* itself involved a clear application of the duty-interest principle.

[8] Lord Eldon's observation in *Lacey* was a comment on Lord Thurlow's decision in *York Buildings v Mackenzie* (1795) 3 Paton 378 (1 Scots RR 717) (also reported at 8 Bro PC 42 (3 ER 432)). At the time of both cases, it seems to have been common for the same counsel and agents to be employed on both sides in purchases and in mortgage transactions: see, eg, *Brotherton v Hatt* (1706) 2 Vern 574, 574–75 (23 ER 973) (LK); *Warrick v Warrick* (1745) 3 Atk 291, 293 and 294 (26 ER 970) (LC); *Le Neve v Le Neve* (1747) Amb 436, 439 (27 ER 291) (LC) (also reported at 1 Ves Sen 64, 65 (27 ER 893) and 3 Atk 646, 648 (26 ER 1172)); *Doe d Willis v Martin* (1790) 4 TR 39, 66 (100 ER 882) (LCJ); *Toulmin v Steele* (1817) 3 Mer 210, 222 (36 ER 81) (MR); *Mountford v Scott* (1818) 3 Madd 34 (56 ER 422); *Kennedy v Green* (1834) 3 My & K 699, 717 (40 ER 266) (LC); *Dryden v Frost* (1838) 3 My & Cr 670, 673 (40 ER 1084) (LC); *Colyer v Finch* (1856) 5 HLC 905, 924–25 (10 ER 1159).

sufficed to condemn the transaction without the court needing to consider whether a conflict between inconsistent duties might also have done so.

In other cases, when the fiduciary had no personal beneficial interest but was involved in a transaction as an agent or other intermediary, the courts again tended to reach their decisions by reference to the venerable duty-interest principle, even if this meant using the concept of 'interest' in a rather loose manner. Thus, for example, in *Ex parte Bennett*, a bankruptcy commissioner was held unable to purchase the bankrupt's property even though he was buying on behalf of another person. As Lord Eldon LC explained, just as trustees cannot purchase from themselves, nor can bankruptcy commissioners purchase the bankrupt's estate, as their duties in respect of the bankruptcy are inconsistent with their personal interest.[9] Although there was a conflict between the duties that the commissioner owed *qua* commissioner and those that he owed to the principal for whom he bought as agent, the decision in *Bennett* to overthrow his purchase rested not on the commissioner's conflicting duties but on the fact that he was also a party to the transaction, even if only as an agent, and so had an interest in it that conflicted with his duty.[10] The conflict between duties appears to have been treated as providing insufficient reason not to apply the duty-interest principle, rather than as providing a separate ground for setting the transaction aside.[11]

Similarly, in *Transvaal Lands Co v New Belgium (Transvaal) Land & Development Co*, the duty-interest principle was again applied to a situation involving conflicting duties. The plaintiff bought shares in a company from the defendant without being told that one of the plaintiff's directors who had voted for the transaction, Harvey, held shares in the defendant. Harvey held the shares on trust, but that did not save the transaction from rescission. Astbury J explained:

> I cannot see on principle why, if a man is interested as a trustee to do the best he can for his cestui que trust instead of doing the best he can for himself if he were interested personally, that ought to make any difference in principle as to that duty being in conflict with the duty which he owes to the company of which he is a director in such a transaction as the present.[12]

As Paterson J said recently in *Collinge v Kyd*, in *Transvaal Lands Co* 'it was immaterial whether the conflicting interest belonged to [the fiduciary] beneficially or as trustee for others.'[13]

Cases like *Bennett* and *Transvaal Lands Co* occupy a middle-ground between, on the one hand, situations like *Lacey* in which the fiduciary is beneficially

---

[9] *Ex parte Bennett* (1805) 10 Ves 381, 396–98 (32 ER 893). See also *Lacey* (above n 6) 628.

[10] This is how Malins VC understood *Ex parte Bennett* in *Delves v Delves* (1875) LR 20 Eq 77, 83.

[11] See also *Coles v Trecothick* (1804) 9 Ves 234, 248 (32 ER 592) (LC); *Moody v Cox & Hatt* [1917] 2 Ch 71, 81–82, 85 and 91 (CA).

[12] *Transvaal Lands Co v New Belgium (Transvaal) Land & Development Co* [1914] 2 Ch 488, 497, affirmed on appeal: [1914] 2 Ch 500.

[13] *Collinge v Kyd* [2005] 1 NZLR 847 at [65]; see also at [58].

interested in a transaction, and on the other hand, situations in which the fiduciary is not a party to the transaction but was involved in bringing it about. The latter class of case provides the true test for a separate doctrine regarding conflict between inconsistent duties, but the intermediate cases provided an important stepping stone in the development of that separate principle: when the fiduciary was a party to the transaction, albeit not one with a personal *beneficial* interest therein, the fiduciary's involvement in the transaction meant the courts did not have to make the leap necessary for the recognition of a separate principle, as they could say that the fiduciary had an 'interest' in the transaction, thereby allowing them to apply the principle regarding conflicts between duty and interest.

Thus, for example, in the Court of Appeal's decision in *Transvaal Lands Co*, one can identify the beginnings of a fiduciary doctrine that captures conflicts between duties as well as conflicts between duty and interest, although without yet divorcing that completely from the fiduciary's 'interest' in the transaction:

> Where a director of a company has an interest as shareholder in another company or is in a fiduciary position towards and owes a duty to another company which is proposing to enter into engagements with the company of which he is a director, he is in our opinion within this rule. He has a personal interest within this rule or owes a duty which conflicts with his duty to the company of which he is a director. It is immaterial whether this conflicting interest belongs to him beneficially or as trustee for others. He is bound to do as well for his cestuis que trust as he would do for himself.[14]

In other words, 'similar reasoning applies where the alleged conflict is between competing duties, for example, where a solicitor acts on both sides of a transaction',[15] as applies where the conflict is between duty and interest. In somewhat loose terms, a conflicting duty can be described as such an 'interest',[16] but the important point is that it came to be seen that it could operate as a temptation or motivation not to perform properly one's other duties. Thus, for example, in *Harrods Ltd v Lemon*, Harrods acted in breach of duty when one of its departments acted as estate agent to find a purchaser for a property, while another department provided the prospective purchaser with a surveyor's report on the property. Avory J identified Harrods' breach as 'putting themselves in such a position that they had a temptation not faithfully to perform their duty to their employers'.[17] In other words, the principle regarding conflict between duties is motivated by the same concern as that underpinning the principle regarding conflict between duty and interest. The temptation for the fiduciary not to perform properly his non-fiduciary duties may be less when it arises because of a conflicting duty than when the temptation is created by the fiduciary's personal

---

[14] *Transvaal Lands Co* (above n 12) 503; see also p 501.

[15] *Pilmer v Duke Group Ltd* [2001] HCA 31 at [78], (2001) 207 CLR 165.

[16] See, eg, *Boardman v Phipps* [1967] 2 AC 46, 126; *Movitex Ltd v Bulfield* [1988] BCLC 104, 112 (ChD); *Bolkiah v KPMG* [1999] 2 AC 222, 237; Companies Act 2006 (UK), s 175(7).

[17] *Harrods Ltd v Lemon* [1931] 2 KB 157, 162, affirmed on appeal: [1931] 2 KB 163.

interest in a transaction, but it does still create a risk that the fiduciary will not perform his duties properly. Though perhaps less than in a duty-interest context, the risk is thought sufficient to warrant the intervention of fiduciary doctrine, as Lord Eldon noted in *Bennett*:

> [I]f the principle be, that the Solicitor cannot buy for his own benefit, I agree, where he buys for another, the temptation to act wrong is less: yet, if he could not use the information he has for his own benefit, it is too delicate to hold, that the temptation to misuse that information for another person is so much weaker, that he should be at liberty to bid for another . . . That distinction is too thin to form a safe rule of justice.[18]

Or, as the New South Wales Court of Appeal put it more recently in *Beach Petroleum v Abbott Tout*:

> This case involves an alleged conflict of duty and duty, rather than a conflict of interest and duty. However, in both categories what is involved is a breach of the same overriding duty of undivided loyalty. . . 'Duty and self-interest, like God and mammon, make inconsistent calls on the faithful.' Conflicts of duty and duty also make such inconsistent calls. . . In the case of a duty and duty conflict, there is no aspect of 'human nature' which tends to bias choice in a particular direction. Rather: '. . . the fiduciary . . . may be unable to discharge adequately the one obligation without conflicting with the requirement for observance of the other obligation.' Expressed in this way, there is no substantive difference between a duty and interest conflict and a duty and duty conflict.[19]

Thus, based on analogical development from the principle regarding conflicts between duty and interest, a cognate fiduciary principle has evolved that regulates situations in which a fiduciary owes inconsistent duties, despite there being no necessary conflict between those duties and the fiduciary's personal interest.

II. Content and Function

Given that it developed by analogy with the principle regarding conflicts between duty and interest, it is not surprising that fiduciary doctrine's duty-duty conflict principle exhibits a function similar to that served by the duty-interest principle. There may be less temptation to act in breach of duty when the incentive is proper performance of another duty than when the incentive is the fiduciary's own personal interest in a transaction, but there is still a risk that the fiduciary's performance of one set of his non-fiduciary duties may lead him not to perform properly the other set of non-fiduciary duties. As the Federal Court of Australia explained in *Commonwealth Bank of Australia v Smith*, a fiduciary 'must eschew

---

[18] *Bennett* (above n 9) 399. Further, the difficulties of proof that exist when dealing with conflicts between duty and interest are no less when the conflict is between multiple duties: see pp 396–98.
[19] *Beach Petroleum NL v Abbott Tout Russell Kennedy* [1999] NSWCA 408 at [196]–[202], (1999) 48 NSWLR 1.

conflicting engagements. The reason is that, by reason of the multiple engagements, the fiduciary may be unable to discharge adequately the one without conflicting with his obligation in the other.'[20] Fiduciary doctrine seeks to reduce that risk.

However, in order to defend the proposition that fiduciary doctrine's regulation of duty-duty conflict situations is designed to enhance the likelihood of proper performance of the fiduciary's non-fiduciary duties, it is necessary to analyse the various constituent parts of the duty-duty principle. These were identified in detail by Millett LJ in *Mothew*,[21] where he held that a fiduciary would act in breach of fiduciary duty if he acted in a situation in which his duties to two principals were potentially in conflict, or when the conflict was actual, and also when he intentionally or consciously favoured one principal over another. It is important to examine each of these propositions in turn, in order to assess their compatibility with the argument that the fiduciary duty-duty doctrine is designed to protect non-fiduciary duties.

A. Potential Conflicts

The protective function served by fiduciary doctrine's duty-duty principle is perhaps clearest when a fiduciary owes non-fiduciary duties to more than one principal, the performance of which is potentially inconsistent. A clear statement of the rule regarding potentially conflicting duties is found in Millett LJ's judgment in *Mothew*:

> A fiduciary who acts for two principals with potentially conflicting interests without the informed consent of both is in breach of the obligation of undivided loyalty; he puts himself in a position where his duty to one principal *may* conflict with his duty to the other... This is sometimes described as 'the double employment rule'. Breach of the rule automatically constitutes a breach of fiduciary duty.[22]

The parallel between this and fiduciary doctrine's prohibition of conflict between duty and interest is unmistakable, particularly when one bears in mind Lord Cranworth LC's description of the latter doctrine in *Aberdeen Railway Co v Blaikie*:

> [N]o one having [fiduciary] duties to discharge, shall be allowed to enter into engagements in which he has, or can have, a personal interest conflicting, or which may possibly conflict, with the interests of those whom he is bound to protect.[23]

Thus, fiduciary doctrine's duty-duty principle prohibits a fiduciary from acting not only when there is an actual conflict between the duties owed by the fiduciary

---

[20] *Commonwealth Bank of Australia v Smith* (above n 3) 392 (cited with approval in England: *Bristol & West v May May & Merrimans* (above n 3) 815).

[21] *Mothew* (above n 1) 18–19.

[22] *Ibid.* See also *Waxman v Waxman* (2004) 7 ITELR 162 at [646] (Ont CA).

[23] *Aberdeen Railway Co v Blaikie Bros* (1854) 1 Macq 461, 471 (149 RR 32).

but also when he acts with multiple sets of duties that potentially conflict: 'It is quite clear that the rule exists to prevent potential conflicts of interest and the prohibition is upon acting without informed consent where there is a potential conflict, not only where there is an actual conflict.'[24] For example, in *Bristol & West Building Society v Fancy & Jackson*,[25] a solicitor committed a breach of fiduciary duty when, while acting for a mortgagee, he failed to inform the mortgagee that he was also acting for the mortgagor and for an intermediate vendor in a sub-sale transaction.[26]

The potential conflict rule is concerned 'to preclude the fiduciary from putting himself in a position "where he may be required to choose between conflicting duties, or be led to an attempt to reconcile conflicting interests".'[27] If a fiduciary has undertaken duties and there is a 'real sensible possibility'[28] that the perform-ance of those duties may potentially conflict with his performance of other duties, the fact that both sets of duties are owed by, and so must be performed by, the same person creates a risk that one set of duties will not be performed properly. It is that risk—the concern about what might happen—that fiduciary doctrine seeks to avoid by requiring that a fiduciary not act when he owes duties that might conflict. As with the duty-interest principle, the rule regarding potential conflicts between duties is designed to improve the chances that the fiduciary will properly perform his non-fiduciary duties, by imposing a duty that requires the fiduciary to avoid situations in which there is a heightened risk of breach of those non-fiduciary duties.

Thus, the potential conflict rule exhibits a subsidiary and prophylactic protec-tive function vis-à-vis non-fiduciary duties. It imitates the subsidiary and pro-phylactic protection of non-fiduciary duties provided by fiduciary doctrine's fundamental duty-interest conflict principle, as one would expect given that it developed by analogy from that principle. The protection is subsidiary in that the fiduciary duty is designed to assist with the performance of other (non-fiduciary) duties. And it is prophylactic in the sense that the object is to avoid situations in which proper performance of the non-fiduciary duties is jeopardised: the likeli-hood of a fiduciary acting in breach of one or other (or both) of multiple sets of duties that he owes to different principals is reduced if he is prohibited from acting in such situations. Again, as with the duty-interest principle, to insist that a fiduciary eschew such situations does not guarantee that the fiduciary will properly perform his non-fiduciary duties. Such duties can be breached for a

---

[24] *Bristol & West Building Society v Daniels & Co* [1997] PNLR 323, 326 (ChD).
[25] *Bristol & West Building Society v Fancy & Jackson* [1997] 4 All ER 582, 614 (ChD).
[26] Similarly, see *Bristol & West v Daniels* (above n 24) 326.
[27] PD Finn, 'Fiduciary Law and the Modern Commercial World' in E McKendrick (ed), *Commercial Aspects of Trusts and Fiduciary Obligations* (Oxford, Oxford University Press, 1992) 7, 24.
[28] *Beach Petroleum NL v Abbott Tout Russell Kennedy* [1999] NSWCA 408 at [425], (1999) 48 NSWLR 1. See also *Re Baron Investments (Holdings) Ltd* [2000] 1 BCLC 272, 282 (ChD); *Marks & Spencer plc v Freshfields Bruckhaus Deringer* [2004] EWHC 1337 (Ch) at [15], [2004] 1 WLR 2331; *Rigg v Sheridan* [2008] NSWCA 79 at [37]–[42].

variety of reasons that have nothing to do with the existence of any conflicting duties. For example, a fiduciary may still act incompetently. But the principle that requires a fiduciary to avoid acting when he owes duties the performance of which may potentially conflict with one another does nevertheless reduce the likelihood that there will be a breach of non-fiduciary duty, by removing at least one possible cause of such breaches.

B. Actual Conflicts

In *Mothew*, Millett LJ also explained:

> [T]he fiduciary must take care not to find himself in a position where there is an *actual* conflict of duty so that he cannot fulfil his obligations to one principal without failing in his obligations to the other. . . If he does, he may have no alternative but to cease to act for at least one and preferably both.[29]

Self-evidently, when a fiduciary owes duties that are actually in conflict with each other, the risk is high that at least one set of those duties will be breached: if two sets of duties cannot both be performed consistently, performance of one set necessarily entails breach of the other. Again, the actual conflict rule requires fiduciaries to avoid acting in situations in which duties conflict in that way. In so doing, the rule reduces the risk that the non-fiduciary duties will be breached.

In *Stewart v Layton*,[30] for example, a solicitor acted for both vendor and purchaser, where each of them knew this. Over time, 'a clear conflict'[31] developed between the duties he owed to each client, as it was in the purchaser's interest for the transaction to proceed, whereas the vendor should have withdrawn. By continuing to act for both parties thereafter, the solicitor committed a breach of the actual conflict rule. As Foster J's judgment shows, that rule is designed to avoid situations in which breach of non-fiduciary duties is virtually inevitable:

> Despite the fact that the [solicitor] acted at all stages with the best of intentions towards the [vendor] he, nevertheless, committed a breach of his fiduciary duty towards her as her solicitor, which breach was rooted in the fact that he continued to act for both parties in a conveyancing transaction after a conflict of duties arose. In his strenuous endeavour to fulfil both duties, he failed properly to fulfil his duty to the [vendor].[32]

The fiduciary rule regarding actual conflicts between non-fiduciary duties is aimed at enhancing the likelihood of proper performance of non-fiduciary duties

---

[29]   *Mothew* (above n 1) 19. See also *Neushul v Mellish & Harkavy* (1967) 111 Sol Jo 399 (CA); *Goody v Baring* [1956] 1 WLR 448, 450 (ChD); *Moody v Cox & Hatt* (above n 11) 81; *Commonwealth Bank of Australia v Smith* (above n 3) 393; *Armitage v Paynter Construction Ltd* [1999] 2 NZLR 534, 544 (CA); *Ball v Druces & Attlee (No 2)* [2004] EWHC 1402 (QB) at [340], [2004] PNLR 745; *3464920 Canada Inc v Strother* [2005] BCCA 35 at [25], (2005) 7 ITELR 748.
[30]   *Stewart v Layton* (1992) 111 ALR 687 (FCA).
[31]   *Ibid*, 708.
[32]   *Ibid*, 711.

by prohibiting the fiduciary from acting when the existence of multiple sets of non-fiduciary duties means that at least one set of non-fiduciary duties will be breached. One cannot easily predict which set of duties will be breached as, unlike the situation in which a fiduciary has a personal interest, it is harder to predict which way the fiduciary might be swayed. Hence, it is preferable that the fiduciary ceases to act for both principals,[33] but he must cease to act for at least one in order to remove the risk that he will breach the duties owed to the other. This again reflects the subsidiary, prophylactic form of protection of non-fiduciary duties that underlies the duty-interest conflict principle as well as the potential conflicts rule. The protection is again subsidiary in that the fiduciary duty is designed to assist with ensuring proper performance of non-fiduciary duties. And it is prophylactic in the sense that the object is to avoid situations in which proper performance of the non-fiduciary duties is placed in jeopardy. If the fiduciary ceases to act when there is an actual conflict of duties, the two principals (or, if the fiduciary continues to act for one, the other principal) can engage independent fiduciaries, each of whom will be capable of performing his duties properly.

C. Inhibition

In *Mothew*, Millett LJ made clear, perhaps for the first time, that fiduciary doctrine's regulation of conflicts between multiple duties is not confined to the potential and actual conflict rules: a further rule applies, which Millett LJ described as the 'inhibition principle'. It is far harder to identify the nature and function served by this rule than is the case with the actual and potential conflict rules. It is useful, therefore, to quote in full the lengthy passage from Millett LJ's judgment in *Mothew* concerning 'inhibition' before analysing the content of the principle:

> Even if a fiduciary is properly acting for two principals with potentially conflicting interests he must act in good faith in the interests of each and must not act with the intention of furthering the interests of one principal to the prejudice of those of the other. . . I shall call this 'the duty of good faith'. But it goes further than this. He must not allow the performance of his obligations to one principal to be influenced by his relationship with the other. He must serve each as faithfully and loyally as if he were his only principal.
>
> Conduct which is in breach of this duty need not be dishonest but it must be intentional. An unconscious omission which happens to benefit one principal at the expense of the other does not constitute a breach of fiduciary duty, though it may

---

[33] See text accompanying n 29 above. See also *Moody v Cox & Hatt* (above n 11) 81; *Goody v Baring* (above n 29) 450; *Neushul v Mellish & Harkavy* (above n 29); *Spector v Ageda* [1973] Ch 30, 47; *Fox v Everingham* (1983) 50 ALR 337, 345 (FCA); *Farrington v Rowe McBride & Partners* [1985] 1 NZLR 83, 90–91 and 96–97 (CA); *Commonwealth Bank of Australia v Smith* (above n 3) 393; *Armitage v Paynter Construction* (above n 29) 544.

constitute a breach of the duty of skill and care. This is because the principle which is in play is that the fiduciary must not be inhibited by the existence of his other employment from serving the interests of his principal as faithfully and effectively as if he were the only employer. I shall call this 'the no inhibition principle'. Unless the fiduciary is inhibited or believes (whether rightly or wrongly) that he is inhibited in the performance of his duties to one principal by reason of his employment by the other his failure to act is not attributable to the double employment.[34]

The question is whether this aspect of fiduciary doctrine can also be understood as providing protection for non-fiduciary duties or whether it has some other basis. The element of intention, in particular, seems foreign to fiduciary doctrine. However, Millett LJ clearly did identify intention—or at least consciousness—as a necessary element before a breach of the inhibition principle is made out. The questions that arise are why that should be the case, and what it shows about the inhibition principle as a part of fiduciary doctrine's regulation of conflicts between multiple duties.

It is difficult to answer those questions, partly because it is not entirely clear from Millett LJ's description of the inhibition principle what constitutes its true basis. One possibility is that it is simply an application of the doctrine of good faith. As has been seen earlier, fiduciaries do owe a duty to act in good faith, but duties of good faith are not peculiar to fiduciaries.[35] If the inhibition principle is simply an application of the duty of good faith, then it is a duty that fiduciaries owe, but as it is not peculiar to fiduciaries, it need not be considered in an analysis of the peculiarly fiduciary duties that apply when there is a conflict between inconsistent duties.

On the other hand, having stated the good faith principle in *Mothew*, Millett LJ immediately added 'But it goes further than this'[36] and then explained the inhibition principle. And his explanation of that principle reflects the same concerns as the actual and potential conflict rules: as he said, 'the principle which is in play is that the fiduciary must not be inhibited by the existence of his other employment from serving the interests of his principal as faithfully and effectively as if he were the only employer.'[37] This suggests that he considered the inhibition principle to be distinct from the duty of good faith, as did Waller LJ in *Seguros Imperio v Heath*.[38] When this is coupled with the fact that there is no evidence of the inhibition principle being applied to legal actors other than fiduciaries, there is a legitimate basis for thinking that the inhibition principle is a duty that is distinct from the duty of good faith and is peculiar to fiduciaries. As such, its place within the array of fiduciary obligations merits exploration. In order to do that, it is helpful first to identify the pattern of facts that constitute

---

[34] *Mothew* (above n 1) 19.
[35] See above ch 3, section IV.
[36] *Mothew* (above n 1) 19.
[37] *Ibid.*
[38] *Cia de Seguros Imperio v Heath (REBX) Ltd* [2001] 1 WLR 112, 119 (CA).

breach of the principle, before considering the relationship between that pattern and the protective function served by fiduciary doctrine in general.

i. Pattern of Liability

The inhibition principle operates most importantly in situations in which it is possible for both sets of duties to be performed properly. If there is an *actual* conflict between duties owed to two principals, the inhibition principle is less important because the fiduciary acts in breach of fiduciary duty by continuing to act, without the claimant needing to prove any intentional favouring of one client over the other. And, if there is a *potential* conflict between the duties owed to those two principals, but the informed consent of each has not been obtained, the fiduciary is acting in breach of fiduciary duty without more, and so a claimant need not show a breach of the inhibition principle. Hence, the inhibition principle applies when 'a fiduciary is *properly* acting for two principals with potentially conflicting interests' (emphasis added),[39] which will be the case only if he has obtained the informed consent of each principal.

Thus, a breach of non-fiduciary duty is not inevitable in situations in which the inhibition principle applies: both sets of non-fiduciary duties could be performed properly. The inhibition principle is breached not simply by acting when there is a conflict between non-fiduciary duties but rather by the fiduciary breaching one set of non-fiduciary duties with the intention of preferring his other principal.[40] The need to show both a breach of non-fiduciary duty and the requisite mental element is apparent in cases that have applied the inhibition principle since *Mothew*. In *Leeds & Holbeck Building Society v Arthur & Cole*, for example, a solicitor acted for both lender and borrower in a mortgage transaction. Morland J said that he had 'to decide [the solicitor's] state of mind at the time he failed to discharge his contractual duties to the claimant'.[41] The pattern of liability here is a twofold combination of (*i*) breach of a non-fiduciary duty (the duty to disclose information), coupled with (*ii*) the mental element of intentional and conscious breach of that duty: 'the claimant must prove that [the solicitor] did not disclose matters which he admittedly ought to have done to the claimant, intentionally and consciously, knowing at the time that he should disclose them to the claimant.'[42]

---

[39] *Mothew* (above n 1) 19.

[40] He need not act dishonestly: *Mothew* (above n 1) 19; cf *Zwebner v Mortgage Corp Ltd* [1997] PNLR 504, 514 (ChD); *Bristol & West v Fancy & Jackson* (above n 25) 614. However, it may be hard to distinguish conscious preference of one client over another from dishonesty, especially when the preferred client was himself acting dishonestly: see, eg, *Birmingham Midshires Building Society v Infields* [1999] Lloyd's Rep PN 874, 880 (TCC).

[41] *Leeds & Holbeck Building Society v Arthur & Cole* [2002] PNLR 78 at [16]. See also *Bristol & West v Fancy & Jackson* (above n 25) 613; *Nationwide Building Society v Goodwin Harte* [1999] Lloyd's Rep PN 338, 345 (ChD).

[42] *Leeds & Holbeck v Arthur & Cole* (ibid) [12] (QBD); see also at [14]. *Wilkinson v Feldworth Financial Services Pty Ltd* (1998) 29 ACSR 642, 727 and 738 involved a similar approach, albeit

A breach of the inhibition principle occurs when there is a breach of non-fiduciary duty and the reason for that breach was an intentional or conscious choice to prefer the interests of one client over those of the other. Thus, in *Mortgage Corp v Alexander Johnson*,[43] a claim for breach of fiduciary duty was struck out when there was no pleading of an intention to prefer: the pleading was of a failure to inform, coupled with knowledge of the facts that were not disclosed, but this was insufficient as a pleading for breach of *fiduciary* duty because mere knowledge on the defendant's part is consistent with an inadvertent and unintentional breach of duty in failing to disclose, and 'an inadvertent failure which owes nothing to the double employment'[44] is not a breach of fiduciary duty.

ii. Function

Therefore, the inhibition principle is designed to deal with situations in which a breach of non-fiduciary duty is not inevitable but occurs because of the existence of conflicting duties. It is concerned with the reasons for a breach of non-fiduciary duty.

The requirement that there be a breach of non-fiduciary duty *and* that the breach be intentional or conscious is an unusual pattern of liability in the context of fiduciary duties. Fiduciary liability does not normally require a breach of non-fiduciary duty: a breach of fiduciary duty can occur irrespective of whether non-fiduciary duties have been breached.[45] Equally, a fiduciary's mental state is generally irrelevant. In the context of conflicts between duty and interest, the normative basis for fiduciary doctrine's intervention is the risk of a fiduciary 'being swayed by interest rather than by duty',[46] but it is clear that fiduciary liability under that rule does not rest on any assessment of the fiduciary's state of mind. The presence or lack of consciousness of wrongdoing is irrelevant[47] and is not inquired into.[48] In other words, it is not necessary to show that the fiduciary was as a matter of fact 'swayed by interest rather than by duty' in order to make

---

without explicit adoption of the inhibition principle and on the basis that the defendant's conduct amounted to a breach of trust. This point was not challenged on appeal: *Alexander v Perpetual Trustees WA Ltd* [2004] HCA 7 at [18], (2004) 216 CLR 109.

[43]   *Mortgage Corp v Alexander Johnson, The Times* (22 Sept 1999) (full judgment available on LexisNexis).

[44]   *Mothew* (above n 1) 21.

[45]   See, eg, *Regal (Hastings) Ltd v Gulliver* [1967] 2 AC 134n, 153 and 159; *Boardman v Phipps* (above n 16); *Ex parte James* (1803) 8 Ves 337, 349 (32 ER 385) (LC); *Hamilton v Wright* (1842) 9 Cl & Fin 111, 123–24 (8 ER 357) (HL); *Aberdeen Railway v Blaikie Bros* (above n 23) 472 (HL); *Canadian Aero Service Ltd v O'Malley* [1974] SCR 592, 608–10; *Swain v Law Society* [1982] 1 WLR 17, 29. Indeed, there can be a breach of fiduciary duty even when it is clear that the fiduciary has acted to his principal's benefit.

[46]   *Bray v Ford* [1896] AC 44, 51.

[47]   See, eg, *Lacey* (above n 6) 630 (LC); *Hamilton v Wright* (above n 45) 124; *Bray v Ford (ibid)* 48 and 52; *Regal (Hastings) v Gulliver* (above n 45) 137, 143–44, 145, 151, 153 and 154; *Boardman v Phipps* (above n 16) 104, 105 and 115; *Swindle v Harrison* [1997] 4 All ER 705, 733 (CA).

[48]   *De Bussche v Alt* (1878) 8 ChD 286, 316 (CA).

out a breach of fiduciary duty: the mere existence of the conflict between duty and interest itself suffices for that purpose. Further, it need not be shown that the conflicting interest actually caused the fiduciary to breach his non-fiduciary duty: a breach of non-fiduciary duty is unnecessary.[49]

Similarly, in the context of conflicts between inconsistent duties, a fiduciary's intention is not relevant when applying the actual and potential conflict rules. A fiduciary automatically breaches his fiduciary duty by acting for two parties with only potentially conflicting interests,[50] irrespective of his state of mind. It would be odd indeed to require intention before fiduciary liability arises when the duties are actually in conflict.[51] As the Full Court said in *Commonwealth Bank of Australia v Smith*, 'nor, of course, is it to the point that the appellants did not act with fraudulent intent.'[52] In contrast, liability under the inhibition principle differs from this general pattern. The question this raises is why has the fiduciary inhibition principle been so formulated?

The inhibition principle is concerned with the reasons for a fiduciary's breach of non-fiduciary duty, which presupposes a breach of duty. Hence, the inhibition principle cannot be understood as providing prophylactic protection against breaches of non-fiduciary duty. Nonetheless, one could conceivably try to argue that it provides subsidiary protection for non-fiduciary duties in the sense that it is concerned with and prohibits situations in which the fiduciary actually succumbs to the temptation identified by Lord Eldon LC in *Bennett*.[53] The inhibition principle might therefore be seen as designed to encourage the proper performance of non-fiduciary duties by requiring that the fiduciary put aside one particular kind of reason for not doing so: *viz* the idea that he ought consciously to prefer the interests of one client over those of the other.

However, this attempt to align the inhibition principle with the other fiduciary principles that have already been considered is strained. In particular, the protective function that the analysis identifies is not distinct from the function served by the protected duties themselves. If the inhibition principle is said to perform a subsidiary protective function because it makes clear to fiduciaries that they ought not to prefer one client over another, thereby encouraging fiduciaries to perform the duties that they owe to both clients, the same can potentially be said of any contractual duty: it is clear from the law of contract that contractual duties ought to be performed, and contract law encourages contracting parties to perform those duties by providing remedies for their breach. This is too glib a response, in that the inhibition principle clearly creates a distinct duty that is separate from the non-fiduciary duty at stake and has distinct prerequisites to its

---

[49] See, eg, *Hamilton v Wright* (above n 45) 123–24; *Aberdeen Railway v Blaikie Bros* (above n 23) 472 (HL).

[50] *Mothew* (above n 1) 18–19.

[51] Cf *Bristol & West v Fancy & Jackson* (above n 25) 615.

[52] *Commonwealth Bank of Australia v Smith* (above n 3) 392–93.

[53] See text accompanying n 18 above.

breach. But it serves to emphasise the difficulty in separating the function served by the inhibition principle from the function served by the underlying non-fiduciary duties. Given that there will be a breach of non-fiduciary duty whenever the inhibition principle is breached, it is unclear what purpose, if any, the inhibition principle serves beyond that already served by non-fiduciary doctrines (like contract and tort law) in the same context.

The inhibition principle is not one to which the law was driven as a matter of inexorable logic, but it can nonetheless be defended as a rational policy decision that responds to the unusual circumstances that obtain where it applies. As such, it is connected to the purposes that fiduciary doctrine serves in general, and its unusual form is explained by the particular circumstances in which it operates.

As has been seen, breach of the inhibition principle occurs in circumstances in which proper performance of both sets of non-fiduciary duties was possible. Fiduciary doctrine prohibits a potential conflict between duties, but that prohibition is lifted when the principals knowingly consent to the situation.[54] The inhibition principle therefore applies in circumstances in which the two principals have consented to the potential conflict of non-fiduciary duties owed by the fiduciary. That consent will have been given with knowledge that the conflict might prevent the fiduciary from performing duties that otherwise would have been imposed,[55] or else it would not be fully informed and would be ineffective to shield the fiduciary from the potential conflict rule. Thus, the inhibition principle is concerned with a situation in which a fiduciary is properly acting for two principals, with duties owed to each that *can* be performed properly, and it strikes at situations in which the fiduciary intentionally and consciously chooses not to perform one set of his non-fiduciary duties in order to favour the interests of his other principal.

The fact that the fiduciary is acting in circumstances in which there is a potential conflict, but that has been authorised by his principals, leaves fiduciary doctrine with a choice: clearly, it will not tolerate action by the fiduciary that involves an actual conflict of duties, but will it consider to be 'disloyal' conduct that falls short of an actual conflict? The inhibition principle represents a policy choice to impose some form of regulation in that middle-ground, adopting proof of intentional favouring of one principal over another as the relevant criterion for disloyalty. This can be understood as an attempt, notwithstanding the principals' authorisation of the potential conflict, to continue to protect proper performance of the two sets of non-fiduciary duties by seeking to eliminate breaches of those duties that are 'attributable to the double employment'[56] in the

---

[54] See, eg, *Mothew* (above n 1) 19; *Tuiara v Frost & Sutcliffe* [2003] 2 NZLR 833 at [49] (HC), overturned on appeal for unrelated reasons: [2004] 1 NZLR 782.

[55] *Clark Boyce v Mouat* [1994] 1 AC 428, 435 (PC); *Taylor v Schofield Peterson* [1999] 3 NZLR 434, 440 (HC).

[56] *Mothew* (above n 1) 19.

sense that the fiduciary's reason for breaching one set of non-fiduciary duties was to advance the interests of the principal to whom he owes the other set.

That this involves a policy choice can be seen from *Grove Darlow & Partners v Rusden*, where, contrary to Millett LJ's assertion that 'there can be no justification for treating an unconscious failure as demonstrating a want of fidelity,'[57] Wallace J held that a solicitor had acted in breach of fiduciary duty when, '*though* [*he*] *did not appreciate it*, he was overinfluenced by [his other client] and failed to give the defendant the advice she needed' (emphasis added).[58] In other words, a subconscious preference of one client over another was held to constitute a breach of fiduciary duty because it was brought about by the fact of double employment.

This follows the same pattern of liability as the inhibition principle, involving a breach of non-fiduciary duty coupled with a mental element, but Wallace J recognised that a fiduciary may be subconsciously affected by inconsistent duties, as well as consciously being so affected.[59] Indeed, this approach is arguably more consistent with fiduciary doctrine's concern about the insidious effect that inconsistent temptations can have on the way that a fiduciary may act when performing his non-fiduciary duties. However, the important point is that *Grove Darlow v Rusden* shows that a policy choice has been made in England to interfere in situations in which double employment brings about breaches of non-fiduciary duty only when the fiduciary has consciously chosen to act in that way.[60] Thus, for example, in *Nationwide Building Society v Richard Grosse & Co*, Blackburne J would not have found a breach of fiduciary duty if the solicitor had been favouring the interests of one client over the interests of another but was unconscious of that fact.[61]

The policy choice is also emphasised if one considers fiduciary duties to be contractual default terms implied into contracts involving fiduciaries.[62] That conceptualisation of fiduciary duties is controversial and is relied on here not because it is necessarily correct[63] but rather because it helps to illustrate the point about judicial policy choices. Following the contractarian conceptualisation of fiduciary duties, the question becomes, which term ought to be implied into

---

[57]   *Ibid*, 21.

[58]   *Grove Darlow & Partners v Rusden* (unreported, High Court of New Zealand, Auckland; 17 Dec 1992, CP 48/91) 30.

[59]   See also *Wan v McDonald* (1992) 105 ALR 473, 493 (FCA); *Stewart v Layton* (above n 30) 709.

[60]   The approach in *Mothew* has been applied in Australia as well, in *Re Moage Ltd* (1998) 153 ALR 711, 718–21 (FCA), and was quoted with approval in *Rigg v Sheridan* (above n 28) [46].

[61]   *Nationwide Building Society v Richard Grosse & Co* [1999] Lloyd's Rep PN 348, 356 (ChD). See also *Nationwide Building Society v JR Jones* [1999] Lloyd's Rep PN 414, 419; *Nationwide Building Society v Vanderpump & Sykes* [1999] Lloyd's Rep PN 422, 431; *Nationwide Building Society v Balmer Radmore* [1999] Lloyd's Rep PN 558, 564.

[62]   See, eg, HN Butler and LE Ribstein, 'Opting Out of Fiduciary Duties: A Response to the Anti-Contractarians' (1990) 65 *Washington Law Review* 1; FH Easterbrook and DR Fischel, 'Contract and Fiduciary Duty' (1993) 36 *Journal of Law & Economics* 425; MJ Whincop, 'Of Fault and Default: Contractarianism as a Theory of Anglo-Australian Corporate Law' (1997) 21 *Melbourne University Law Review* 187.

[63]   The contractarian view of fiduciary duties is considered below in ch 8, section I.

fiduciary contracts? The law could treat the fiduciary as impliedly warranting that he will not intentionally favour one client over the other. Alternatively it could treat the fiduciary as impliedly warranting that he will act even-handedly between the clients, so that subconscious favouring of one client would constitute a breach. The approach adopted by Millett LJ represents a policy choice between those two options.

Millett LJ did not justify that policy choice in *Mothew*, but it is a defensible position for the law to take, notwithstanding that it involves embracing a pattern of liability that is unusual for fiduciary doctrine. The inhibition principle responds to the special circumstances that exist when two principals have knowingly consented to a fiduciary acting with duties owed to each that are potentially (but not actually) inconsistent. Clients perceive there to be economic advantages in permitting dual retainers in such situations.[64] Clients are not necessarily always correct in that economic calculus, but the law respects their autonomous right to make it[65] and so respects the principals' fully informed consent to retainers that would otherwise fall foul of the potential conflict rule (unless and until an actual conflict arises). If dual retainers are to be permitted, it is important that the preconditions to any liability imposed on a fiduciary acting in such a situation be cast so as not to render dual retainers too unpalatable to fiduciaries. It might have been more consistent with the rest of fiduciary doctrine for the inhibition principle to have focused on subconscious favouring of one client over another, but that approach would have cast a considerable pall over fiduciaries who act in such situations: it would have been an invitation to claimants to litigate over the subconscious influences that might have affected their fiduciary's conduct. And it would have required very subtle and difficult distinctions to be drawn between subconscious preferences, when there would be a breach of fiduciary duty, and mere negligence, when there would not.

A choice could have been made that fiduciary doctrine would not regulate situations involving potentially conflicting duties once the principals have consented to them. However, recognising the delicacy of such situations, while also respecting the principals' decision to allow the dual retainer, the choice that has been made is to impose the fiduciary inhibition principle as a specific form of protection moulded to the circumstances in which it operates. In order to ensure that it does not regulate authorised dual retainers out of existence while nonetheless balancing the permission of such retainers with its fundamental protective purpose, English fiduciary doctrine has rejected the subconscious approach of *Grove Darlow v Rusden*, thus according fiduciaries greater freedom of action.[66]

Seen in this light, both the need for a breach of non-fiduciary duty and the mental element in the inhibition principle can be understood as consistent with

---

[64] *Taylor v Schofield Peterson* (above n 55) 439. See also *Spector v Ageda* (above n 33) 47.

[65] *Brusewitz v Brown* [1923] NZLR 1106, 1109.

[66] See also RC Nolan, 'Multiple Duties and Multiple Employment' [1997] *Cambridge Law Journal* 39, 41.

fiduciary doctrine's concern to protect non-fiduciary duties from situations that might lead to their breach. The principals' consent precludes fiduciary doctrine from taking its normal strict approach, but there remains cause for concern about the inconsistent motivations to which such situations can give rise, and fiduciary doctrine intervenes when those motivations have caused the fiduciary consciously to forsake the non-fiduciary duties owed to one of his principals.

Thus, the two main fiduciary doctrines that apply when a fiduciary owes multiple sets of conflicting duties—the potential conflict rule and the actual conflict rule—both exhibit fiduciary doctrine's core concern to provide a prophylactic and subsidiary form of protection for the non-fiduciary duties that the fiduciary has undertaken. The third principle—the inhibition principle—cannot be explained directly in those terms as it is predicated on a breach of non-fiduciary duty as well as a mental element, neither of which feature in other forms of fiduciary regulation. However, the inhibition principle is a rational response to an unusual set of circumstances in which fiduciary doctrine's ordinary modes of regulation would run the risk of being so repressive as to destroy the likelihood of fiduciaries being able to act in such situations at all. The inhibition principle has a rational basis in the fundamentally protective function that fiduciary doctrine serves as a whole. It ought not on its own to be allowed to detract from the general and core understanding of fiduciary doctrine as protective of non-fiduciary duties.

III. Remedies

Like the principle governing conflicts between duty and interest, the rules regarding conflicts between multiple duties are also intended to serve a protective function vis-à-vis non-fiduciary duties. What remains to be addressed, however, are the practical consequences of breach of those rules. In contrast with the powerful remedies available for breach of the duty-interest principle, the remedies available for breach of the duty-duty principle seem relatively weak and are unclear in a number of respects. This final part of the chapter addresses those various remedies with a view to assessing the degree of protection actually provided by the duty-duty principle and offering suggestions as to the resolution of some of the areas of uncertainty. In so doing, some of the practical implications of understanding fiduciary duties in the way this book suggests become apparent.

A. Stopping Further Action

A principal who discovers that his fiduciary is acting for, and owes potentially inconsistent duties to, another principal can terminate his relationship with the fiduciary. This avoids the conflict between duties, but it will often be unattractive to the principal as it leaves the fiduciary free to act for the competitor principal, unless the fiduciary holds confidential information that requires protection.[67]

Alternatively, therefore, when there is a reasonable apprehension[68] of a potential conflict or an actual conflict, the principal can seek an injunction to prevent the fiduciary from continuing to act for the other principal.[69] An injunction of that sort gives direct effect to fiduciary doctrine's protective function. However, the fact of double employment is frequently not realised until after a particular transaction has taken place, by which stage an injunction to prevent the fiduciary from acting comes too late.

B. Rescission of Resultant Transaction

The principal may be able to rescind a transaction that was entered into in circumstances involving a fiduciary acting with an unauthorised conflict between duties. However, the mere existence of conflicting obligations owed by the fiduciary does not render the transaction invalid, nor necessarily voidable: it must be shown that the counterparty to the transaction, against whom rescission is sought, had notice of the double employment.[70]

As has already been seen,[71] when a fiduciary is personally involved in a transaction with his client, he has a conflict between duty and interest, and the transaction can be rescinded on that basis, without needing to resort to fiduciary doctrine's duty-duty principles. And, as was also seen earlier, even when the fiduciary is not a party to the transaction, rescission can nonetheless be available if the fiduciary had a different form of interest in the transaction, such as when he received a bribe or secret commission in connection with the transaction.[72] In such a case the party seeking to rescind 'must establish that they were deprived of

---

[67] For the principles regarding protection of confidential information in these circumstances, see, eg, *Bolkiah v KPMG* (above n 16); *Young v Robson Rhodes* [1999] 3 All ER 524 (ChD); *Halewood International v Addleshaw Booth & Co* [2000] PNLR 788 (ChD); *Koch Shipping Inc v Richards Butler* [2002] EWCA Civ 1280, [2002] 2 All ER (Comm) 957; *British American Tobacco Australia Services Ltd v Blanch* [2004] NSWSC 70; *Gus Consulting GmbH v LeBoeuf Lamb Green & MacRae* [2006] EWCA Civ 683, [2006] PNLR 587; *PCCW-HKT Telephone Ltd v Aitken* [2009] HKCFA 11. For an early example, see *Davies v Clough* (1837) 8 Sim 262 (59 ER 105). The doctrine of confidence is discussed below in ch 8, section III-B.

[68] *Re Baron Investments* (above n 28) 282–84; *Marks & Spencer plc v Freshfields Bruckhaus Deringer* [2004] EWHC 1337 (Ch) at [15], [2004] 1 WLR 2331 (affirmed: [2004] EWCA Civ 741); *Conway v Ratiu* [2005] EWCA Civ 1302 at [59], [2006] WTLR 101 (also partially reported at [2006] 1 All ER 571n).

[69] See, eg, *Marks & Spencer plc v Freshfields Bruckhaus Deringer* [2004] EWHC 1337 (Ch) at [26], [2004] 1 WLR 2331.

[70] See generally, PD Finn, *Fiduciary Obligations* (Sydney, Law Book Co, 1977) [586]; RC Nolan, 'Conflicts of Interest, Unjust Enrichment, and Wrongdoing' in WR Cornish, RC Nolan, J O'Sullivan and GJ Virgo (eds), *Restitution: Past, Present and Future* (Oxford, Hart, 1998) 87, 98.

[71] See above ch 4, section III-A.

[72] See *ibid*.

the disinterested advice of their agent by or at least to the knowledge of' the counterparty against whom rescission is sought.[73]

But the basis for rescission in such situations is the fiduciary's conflict between duty and interest. It is unclear from the cases whether rescission can also be claimed on the basis that a fiduciary acted in breach of the duty-duty principle. Some dicta hint at the idea that a fiduciary is incapable of entering into a second inconsistent retainer without consent from the first principal,[74] but more recent cases indicate that this is not a true incapacity.[75] If the second retainer is not invalid, there is no basis for arguing that anything done pursuant to that retainer is a nullity. As Donaldson J said in *North & South Trust Co v Berkeley*,

> Fully informed consent apart, an agent cannot lawfully place himself in a position in which he owes a duty to another which is inconsistent with his duty to his principal, but if nevertheless he does so, his action is not a nullity. It is to be accepted as a fact with all the special consequences flowing from its unlawful nature.[76]

Importantly, Donaldson J added that 'if the agent has been employed to make a contract between his true principal and another for whom he is unlawfully also acting as agent, the true principal can avoid the resulting contract.'[77]

However, as with the duty-interest principle, it seems that rescission is only possible against a counterparty who is not the fiduciary if that counterparty knew of the agency.[78] In *Transvaal Lands Co*,[79] both the court and counsel proceeded on the basis that such notice was necessary for rescission, but the extent to which the other party must have been privy to the fiduciary's breach of duty has not been examined in much detail in the case law.[80]

There is no good reason for equity to apply a different rule when the fiduciary's misdemeanour involves having acted with a conflict between duties rather than between duty and interest. When there has been an unauthorised double employment, an innocent principal ought to be able to set aside the consequent transaction as against the counterparty if the counterparty knew of the double employment, but

---

[73] *Logicrose Ltd v Southend United Football Club Ltd* [1988] 1 WLR 1256, 1261 (ChD).

[74] eg, *Fullwood v Hurley* (above n 2) 502; *Boulting v Association of Cinematograph, Television & Allied Technicians* [1963] 2 QB 606, 626 (CA).

[75] *Newcastle United plc v Commissioners for Revenue & Customs* [2007] EWHC 612 (Ch) at [29], [2007] Simon's Tax Cases 1330; FMB Reynolds, *Bowstead & Reynolds on Agency*, 18th edn (London, Sweet & Maxwell, 2006) [2–013].

[76] *North & South Trust v Berkeley* (above n 2) 484–85. See also *Boulting v ACTAT* (above n 74) 640.

[77] *North & South Trust v Berkeley* (above n 2) 485.

[78] *Ibid.*

[79] *Transvaal Lands Co* (above n 12).

[80] RW Parsons, 'The Director's Duty of Good Faith' (1967) 5 *Melbourne University Law Review* 395, 404.

if both [principals] are unaware of the double employment, neither should be able to avoid a contract effected between them. As both have been victims of [the fiduciary's] wrongdoing neither should have the right to undo the transaction against the wishes of the other.[81]

Allowing rescission of a transaction that has resulted from a fiduciary acting in breach of the double employment rule, but only if the counterparty against whom rescission is sought was privy to the unauthorised double employment, gives effect to the protective function that fiduciary doctrine serves: it allows a wronged principal the chance to consider afresh whether the transaction ought to be entered into, because the transaction ought not to have been brought about by the ministration of a fiduciary who owed conflicting duties, while at the same time recognising that it is inappropriate for a claimant to be able to force that on another of his fiduciary's principals unless that other principal were privy to the fiduciary's wrongdoing.

C. Forfeiture of Fees and Other Profits

A principal may also wish to forfeit any fees the fiduciary may have earned from the engagement he undertook in breach of the duty-duty principle. It is important here to separate analysis of fees paid or payable to the fiduciary by the claimant principal from fees paid by the other principal.

i. Fees Paid by the Non-claimant Principal

Unauthorised remuneration taken by a fiduciary from a party other than his principal is a secret profit and clearly constitutes a breach of fiduciary duty.[82] As such, it can be stripped from the fiduciary.[83] Thus, if the principal is unaware that his fiduciary is acting in the same transaction for another party, any fees received by the fiduciary from that other party constitute a secret profit and can be recovered from the fiduciary by the first principal,[84] irrespective of whether the

---

[81] Finn, *Fiduciary Obligations* (above n 70) [586]. See also *Jones v Canavan* [1971] 2 NSWLR 243, 247; Reynolds (above n 75) [2–013]. It is inappropriate for the purposes of rescission in this context for the fiduciary's knowledge of the dual retainer to be imputed to the two principals if they are in fact unaware of it: cf D O'Sullivan, S Elliott and R Zakrzewski, *The Law of Rescission* (Oxford, Oxford University Press, 2008) [8.48]. It is arbitrary and unjust to permit rescission at the behest of whichever of the two equally innocent principals happens to claim it against the wishes of the other.

[82] *Rhodes v Macalister* (1923) 29 Com Cas 19, 29 (CA); Finn, *Fiduciary Obligations* (above n 70) [585]; JA McGhee (gen ed), *Snell's Equity*, 31st edn (London, Sweet & Maxwell, 2005) [7–109]–[7–113].

[83] See, eg, *Andrews v Ramsay & Co* [1903] 2 KB 635, 636 (Div Ct); *Salford v Lever* [1891] 1 QB 168 (CA).

[84] If the principal is aware of the other retainer and accepts its existence, which is a question of fact, he will generally be taken to have consented to the fiduciary being paid by the other party, extinguishing any complaint of duty-interest conflict: see, eg, *Re Haslam & Hier-Evans* [1902] 1 Ch 765, 769 (CA); *Moiler v Forge* (1927) 27 SR (NSW) 69, 71–72; *Wade v Poppleton & Appleby* [2003] EWHC 3159 (Ch) at [149], [2004] 1 BCLC 674.

bribe affected the terms of the transaction.[85] But the reason these fees can be recovered, as with all secret profits, is that they create a personal interest that is inconsistent with the fiduciary's duty to his principal[86] and so fall foul of the duty-interest principle.[87] In other words, they are not stripped because of the duty-duty conflict. Thus, a claimant need not show that his fiduciary undertook legally binding (and hence conflicting) *duties* to a briber to strip the bribe—it suffices that the fiduciary's *interest* in the bribe conflicts with the duty he owes the claimant.[88]

ii. Fees Paid by the Claimant Principal

The situation is less clear regarding fees paid or payable by the claimant principal. Such fees might be forfeited on grounds unrelated to fiduciary doctrine, such as when the fiduciary's performance has been so poor as to constitute no performance at all[89] so that there is a total failure of consideration.

However, a principal may also be able to forfeit a fiduciary's fees on fiduciary grounds,[90] although the cases are difficult to reconcile. In *Keppel v Wheeler*, for example, Atkin LJ said that 'if an agent . . . has been proved to be guilty of some breach of fiduciary duty, in practically every case he would forfeit any right to remuneration at all.'[91] And in *Rhodes v Macalister*, Bankes LJ held that an agent for a purchaser who took a secret commission from the vendor was not entitled to the fees that he had agreed with the purchaser:

> [This] is not a matter of damages at all; an agent who commits a breach of his duty is not entitled to any remuneration arising out of the transaction in which he has so failed to recognise what his duty to his employer is.[92]

---

[85]   *Shipway v Broadwood* [1899] 1 QB 369, 373 (CA); *Re a Debtor* [1927] 2 Ch 367, 373 (CA).

[86]   *Re Haslam & Hier-Evans* (above n 84) 772.

[87]   *Oceanic Life Ltd v HIH Casualty & General Insurance Ltd* [1999] NSWSC 292 at [42], (1999) 10 ANZ Ins Cases 74,968.

[88]   *Boston Deep Sea Fishing & Ice Co v Ansell* (1888) 39 ChD 339, 363–64 (CA).

[89]   See, eg, *Heywood v Wellers* [1976] QB 446, 458 (CA); *Thornton Hall & Partners v Wembley Electrical Appliances Ltd* [1947] 2 All ER 630, 634 (CA). See also, possibly, *Bulfield v Fournier* (1894) 11 TLR 62 (QBD).

[90]   See, eg, *Rhodes v Macalister* (above n 82) 25; *Imageview Management Ltd v Jack* [2009] EWCA Civ 63 at [50] , [2009] 2 All ER 666; *Premium Real Estate Ltd v Stevens* [2009] NZSC 15 at [12], [30]–[31] and [89]–[90], [2009] 2 NZLR 384.

[91]   *Keppel v Wheeler* [1927] 1 KB 577, 592 (CA).

[92]   *Rhodes v Macalister* (above n 82) 25; see also p 27. And see *Jones v Canavan* (above n 81) 244 (CA). Similarly, in *Salomons v Pender* (above n 5) (Exch) an agent was refused commission on a sale because he had sold the property to a company of which he was a shareholder and director, although that case can also be explained on the basis that the agent had contravened the genuine transaction rule so that there was no sale such as would attract a commission.

However, in *Kelly v Cooper*,[93] Lord Browne-Wilkinson said that a fiduciary only forfeits his fees following a breach of fiduciary duty if he acted dishonestly, although the narrowness of that proposition has since been doubted.[94]

A fiduciary who acts dishonestly will forfeit his right to fees,[95] but he will also forfeit his fees if he takes a secret profit (even if honestly) that is directly related to performance of the duty for which the fees were payable,[96] even if the principal has benefited from performance.[97] Again, the purpose of such forfeiture is to deter fiduciaries from acting disloyally.[98]

Most of the cases that discuss the conditions for forfeiture of fees payable by the claimant have been based on this conflict between duty and interest in the form of fees received from another party in the transaction, rather than conflicts between multiple inconsistent duties. Nonetheless, if a fiduciary forfeits his fees when his personal interest in a transaction is directly related to the duty for which the fees were payable, there seems little good reason for allowing the fiduciary to retain fees when he has undertaken a (gratuitous) duty to a third-party principal that is directly inconsistent with the duty for which the claimant owed him fees. Recognition of that proposition would give deterrent effect to fiduciary doctrine's duty-duty principles in that the potential loss of remuneration if he acts with an impermissible conflict between duties will make it less financially attractive for a fiduciary to act in such circumstances. However, again, the overwhelming importance of the duty-interest principle is apparent here: any such duty-duty rule will 'have a relatively narrow legal compass'[99] given the fiduciary will often be paid for his inconsistent retainer, thereby breaching the duty-interest principle.

---

[93] *Kelly v Cooper* [1993] AC 205, 216 (PC). See also *Nitedals Taendstikfabrik v Bruster* [1906] 2 Ch 671, 674–75; *Harrods v Lemon* [1931] 2 KB 157 (KBD & CA); *Eric V Stansfield (a Firm) v South East Nursing Home Services Ltd* [1986] 1 Estates Gazette Law Rep 29, 32 (QBD).

[94] *The Peppy* [1997] 2 Lloyd's Rep 722, 728–29 (QBD).

[95] *Andrews v Ramsay* (above n 83) 638; *Hippisley v Knee Brothers* [1905] 1 KB 1, 8 (Div Ct); *Nitedals Taendstikfabrik v Bruster* (above n 93) 674–75; *Robinson Scammell & Co v Ansell* [1985] 2 Estates Gazette Law Rep 41, 43–44 (CA); *Premium Real Estate v Stevens* (above n 90) [31], [89]–[94] and [109]. It may be that the dishonest breach of fiduciary duty justifies a *deemed* total failure of consideration: P Watts, 'Restitution and Conflicted Agents' (2009) 125 *Law Quarterly Review* 369, 370.

[96] *Hippisley v Knee Brothers* (*ibid*) 8 and 9; *Nitedals Taendstikfabrik v Bruster* (above n 93) 674–75; *Price v Metropolitan House Investment & Agency Co Ltd* (1907) 23 TLR 630, 631 (CA); *The Peppy* (above n 94) 729; *Imageview Management Ltd v Jack* [2009] EWCA Civ 63 at [44] and [46], [2009] 2 All ER 666.

[97] *Rhodes v Macalister* (above n 82) 27; *Imageview Management Ltd v Jack* [2009] EWCA Civ 63 at [47]–[50], [2009] 2 All ER 666.

[98] *Premium Real Estate v Stevens* (above n 90) [89] and [107].

[99] Finn, *Fiduciary Obligations* (above n 70) [581].

D. Equitable Compensation

Finally, a principal might seek equitable compensation for loss caused by his fiduciary having acted in breach of one of fiduciary doctrine's duty-duty conflict rules.

i. Availability and Function

As has already been seen above in chapter four,[100] notwithstanding commentators' arguments that the courts have no jurisdiction to award equitable compensation for loss following a breach of fiduciary duty, the courts have repeatedly asserted and exercised such a jurisdiction. Several of the statements to that effect have been made in cases concerning conflicts between multiple duties.

Thus, for example, in *Commonwealth Bank of Australia v Smith*,[101] a bank manager had, in the circumstances,[102] undertaken a fiduciary role as the claimants' investment adviser when they bought a hotel business from another client of the bank. The manager was negligent in the advice he gave but also acted in breach of fiduciary duty:

> [E]ven if [he] had disclosed . . . that he was acting for the vendor . . . he would still have been placed in an impossible position when the [claimants] sought his advice on the merits of the transaction, and inquired whether they should offer less than the vendor's asking price. He could give no answer on these matters without running into conflict with his duty to at least one side in the negotiations.[103]

This, the court said, 'leads equity to afford its remedies for breach of duty, including that of compensation'.[104] English authorities are to the same effect.[105]

As has already been seen in connection with the duty-interest conflict principle,[106] the existence of a jurisdiction to compensate for loss following a breach of fiduciary duty is consistent with the protective function of fiduciary doctrine. It provides some level of deterrence against fiduciaries acting in breach of fiduciary principles. Indeed, in the duty-duty context, where the deterrence that profit-stripping remedies provide will be less important—in that, if the fiduciary has made a profit it will more easily be stripped by application of the duty-interest principle without any need of the duty-duty principle—the compensatory jurisdiction may have greater importance as a potential deterrent and remedy than it

---

[100] See above ch 4, section III-B(i).

[101] *Commonwealth Bank of Australia v Smith* (above n 3).

[102] Bankers do not ordinarily owe fiduciary duties to their clients: *Foley v Hill* (1848) 2 HLC 28, 36 and 43 (9 ER 1002); *Lloyds Bank Ltd v Bundy* [1975] QB 326, 341–42; *Commonwealth Bank of Australia v Finding* [2001] 1 QdR 168 at [9]–[10] (CA).

[103] *Commonwealth Bank of Australia v Smith* (above n 3) 393.

[104] *Ibid*, 394.

[105] See, eg, *Bristol & West v Daniels* (above n 24) 326–27; *Nationwide Building Society v Balmer Radmore (Introductory Sections)* [1999] Lloyd's Rep PN 241, 262 (ChD).

[106] See above ch 4, section III-B(iii).

has elsewhere. In addition to the deterrence that it provides, the jurisdiction to award equitable compensation also ensures that a remedy is available when a breach of fiduciary duty has caused loss to the principal that would otherwise be left insufficiently remedied.

It is important, therefore, to be clear about how the jurisdiction might operate when there have been breaches of the duty-duty principle. It can be difficult to identify what loss might be said to have been caused by such a breach, particularly if the aim is to identify a loss that is distinct from losses caused by breaches of non-fiduciary duties committed in the same circumstances. In turn, that raises important questions about the relationship between fiduciary and non-fiduciary breaches in this context and about whether concepts such as contributory fault might allow a fiduciary to reduce the amount of compensation that he has to pay.[107] The remainder of this chapter seeks to answer those questions.

ii. Identifying Loss

When a principal seeks compensation on the basis that his fiduciary has acted in breach of one of fiduciary doctrine's duty-duty rules, Paul Finn noted that 'the fiduciary's breach of duty will often be simply a technical one with the consequence that the aggrieved beneficiary will not be able to show that he has suffered more than nominal damage.'[108] This is true, but the more fundamental question is whether such a breach of fiduciary duty can ever be said to have caused loss. That question is most profitably tackled by considering separately each of the three rules that comprise fiduciary doctrine's regulation of situations involving inconsistent duties: the actual conflict rule, the inhibition principle and the potential conflict rule.

When there is an *actual conflict* between the non-fiduciary duties that a fiduciary owes, by definition he cannot perform both sets of duties: performance of one will necessarily involve breach of the other. If the fiduciary continues to act, in breach of the actual conflict rule, he will breach his non-fiduciary duty to one principal, who will be able to claim compensation for breach of that non-fiduciary duty. The question that matters here, however, is whether the breach of *fiduciary* duty can be said to have caused any loss. In this context, Paul Finn said:

> If he fails to discharge fully the duties he owes to his respective beneficiaries he will be liable to such of them as suffer any loss as a consequence—for damages, if the duty

---

[107] This issue can be very important practically: in *Duke Group Ltd v Pilmer* [1999] SASC 97 at [888] and [1080], (1999) 31 ACSR 213 (FC), for example, the court contemplated a 35% reduction for contributory fault that would have reduced the plaintiff's compensatory award by almost AUD$41m. Ultimately, it was held that there was no fiduciary relationship and no breach of fiduciary duty: *Pilmer v Duke Group Ltd* [2001] HCA 31, (2001) 207 CLR 165.

[108] Finn, *Fiduciary Obligations* (above n 70) [591].

breached is a legal one, for compensation, if an equitable one. The courts, furthermore, will not allow the fiduciary to justify his wrong to one beneficiary by reference to a conflicting duty owed to another.[109]

Finn's differentiation between the fiduciary being liable in 'damages' if the breach is of a legal duty, as opposed to being liable for 'compensation' if the breach is of an equitable duty, suggests that here he was discussing liability for breach of *non*-fiduciary duty rather than for breach of fiduciary duty: if he were discussing liability for breach of fiduciary duty, one would expect him to have referred only to equitable compensation.

One possibility is that the real effect of breach of the actual conflict rule is to preclude any attempt by the fiduciary to defend a claim for breach of non-fiduciary duty by reference to the competing non-fiduciary duty. Undoubtedly, a fiduciary cannot rely on the existence of a competing duty as a defence to a claim for breach of his other duties.[110] But if this is all that the actual conflict rule does—if it merely precludes that type of defence—then it adds nothing to a normal common law analysis: even at common law, it is no defence to a claim for breach of contract to argue that the contract was breached because of another obligation that the defendant had undertaken.[111] Thus, for example, in *Hilton v Barker Booth & Eastwood*, a firm of solicitors who had undertaken 'irreconcilable duties' to two clients could not avoid liability for breach of those duties by referring to the inconsistent duties they had undertaken, but the claimant did not need to rely on any fiduciary principles to achieve that result: it pursued its claim (successfully) in contract alone.[112]

The cases do contain suggestions that compensation could potentially be claimed to the extent that duties owed by a fiduciary to one client 'inhibited the proper performance of their duties towards [the other client]'.[113] However, recent English case law tends to treat the breach of fiduciary duty as causing no loss. In *Mahoney v Purnell*,[114] for example, a solicitor who acted for two clients in the same transaction was acting 'with a plain conflict of interest . . . and was skating on thin ice',[115] particularly when he was asked to advise as to whether the proposed transaction was fair. 'The ice broke'[116] when the solicitor failed to

---

[109] *Ibid*, [588].

[110] See, eg, *Moody v Cox & Hatt* (above n 11) 81, 85 and 91; *North & South Trust v Berkeley* (above n 2) 485; *Mothew* (above n 1) 19; *Premium Real Estate v Stevens* (above n 90) [71].

[111] A prior obligation could be relevant when considering whether a later inconsistent obligation ever actually arose: *Newcastle United plc v Commissioners for Revenue & Customs* [2007] EWHC 612 (Ch) at [29], [2007] Simon's Tax Cases 1330. However, applying the objective theory of contract, this would normally require the second obligee to have some reason to know of the first set of (inconsistent) obligations. The points discussed in the text concern situations in which it is found that inconsistent obligations have been created.

[112] *Hilton v Barker Booth & Eastwood* [2005] UKHL 8 at [30], [2005] 1 WLR 567.

[113] *North & South Trust v Berkeley* (above n 2) 486.

[114] *Mahoney v Purnell* [1996] 3 All ER 61 (QBD).

[115] *Ibid*, 93.

[116] *Ibid*, 94.

provide adequate advice because of the conflict, and damages were awarded, but these appear to have been damages for the solicitor's negligence rather than for his breach of fiduciary duty.[117] Similarly, in *Ball v Druces & Attlee*,[118] solicitors engaged to assist with the creation of the Eden Project negligently failed to advise the founders that operating the project through a trust could adversely affect their expectation of personal reward. Furthermore, after the trust had been created, the solicitors proceeded to advise the trust regarding the founders' claims for personal reward. Nelson J concluded that 'there was a breach of fiduciary duty both in relation to the negotiations and in relation to the Chancery action ... they should not have continued to act.'[119] However, he held that these breaches did not justify any award of compensation, as the claimant's losses had already been fully compensated under his negligence claim: the claimant 'cannot establish any further loss attributable to the Defendants acting for the Trust and Eden Project Limited'.[120]

This contrasts with the approach taken by the Federal Court of Australia in *Commonwealth Bank of Australia v Smith*,[121] where a bank manager acted in breach of fiduciary duty by advising two of his customers regarding a sale and purchase transaction between them. The measure of equitable compensation payable for the breach of fiduciary duty was *the same* as the measure of damages payable for the manager's negligence.[122]

Questions of causation and loss are generally answered in the light of the scope and purpose of the duty that has been breached.[123] The mere existence of an actual conflict between duties does not itself force the fiduciary to breach his duty to the claimant, but if the fiduciary continues to act in such a situation then he must breach at least one duty. The very reason for the existence of the fiduciary prohibition on acting with an actual conflict of duties is to avoid such breaches of non-fiduciary duties. Compensation is made available, following a breach of the actual conflict rule, for the 'loss resulting from the [fiduciary's] inability, due to the conflict of duties, fully to discharge his duty to that principal'.[124] The effect of the fiduciary's inability fully to discharge his non-fiduciary duty to the claimant principal is breach of that duty, which explains why the loss that flows from the breach of fiduciary duty is the same as the loss that flows from the breach of

---

[117] *Ibid*, 95–96.
[118] *Ball v Druces & Attlee* [2004] EWHC 1402 (QB), [2004] PNLR 745.
[119] *Ibid* at [340].
[120] *Ibid*.
[121] *Commonwealth Bank of Australia v Smith* (above n 3).
[122] *Ibid*, 395–96.
[123] *O'Halloran v RT Thomas & Family Pty Ltd* (1998) 45 NSWLR 262, 274–75 (CA); *Environment Agency v Empress Car Co (Abertillery) Ltd* [1999] 2 AC 22, 31–32; *Caparo Industries plc v Dickman* [1990] 2 AC 605, 627; *South Australia Asset Management Corp v York Montague Ltd* [1997] AC 191, 211–12; *Platform Home Loans Ltd v Oyston Shipways Ltd* [2000] 2 AC 190, 208–10; *Swindle v Harrison* (above n 47) 734; *Youyang Pty Ltd v Minter Ellison Morris Fletcher* [2003] HCA 15 at [44], (2003) 212 CLR 484.
[124] *North & South Trust v Berkeley* (above n 2) 485.

non-fiduciary duty. The protective purpose of the actual conflict rule can justify an award of equitable compensation for its breach, even if that award is the same in measure as an award at common law (or in equity[125]) for the breach of non-fiduciary duty.

A breach of the *inhibition principle* seems more naturally to support a claim for equitable compensation for loss, in that the element of intention or consciousness involved in a breach of the inhibition principle differentiates that breach from a mere breach of non-fiduciary duty. However, the position is not so straightforward. The element of intention differentiates the fiduciary cause of action from the non-fiduciary claim, but the non-fiduciary breach remains a necessary element in the breach of fiduciary duty, and so it will always be present as a part of the fiduciary breach, notwithstanding that the breach of fiduciary duty has additional prerequisites that give it a separate character. Furthermore, the element of intention that completes the fiduciary breach is not what causes the claimant's loss—mere intentions do not cause loss. Hence, although the fiduciary's intention or consciousness means he also commits a breach of fiduciary duty when he breaches his non-fiduciary duty, the loss caused to the claimant is the same. Thus, for example, in *Nationwide Building Society v Goodwin Harte*[126] and in *Nationwide Building Society v Richard Grosse & Co*,[127] Blackburne J held solicitors to have acted in breach of their common law (non-fiduciary) duties and also to have breached the inhibition principle. But his analysis of what loss had been *caused* by those distinct breaches was conducted together, without differentiating between the causes of action, on the basis that in either case the court had to determine what loss had been caused by reference to the question how the claimants would have acted if the defendants had conducted themselves properly.[128] Similarly, in cases in which the inhibition principle was breached in a way that involved dishonesty, Blackburne J held that the common law's more generous approach to causation where dishonesty is proven[129] should also be made available in equity.[130] Again, therefore, as with the actual conflict rule, the prima facie assessment of the quantum of loss will not differ between liability for breach of non-fiduciary duty and for breach of the inhibition principle.

When a claimant complains of a breach of the *potential conflict* rule, some decisions suggest that the breach causes the principal no loss. For example, in *Bristol & West Building Society v Daniels & Co*,[131] solicitors acted in breach of

---

[125] Breaches of non-fiduciary duty will generally be breaches of common law obligations, but not exclusively: a trustee's breach of trust is a breach of non-fiduciary duty despite the obligation being equitable rather than legal.

[126] *Nationwide Building Society v Goodwin Harte* (above n 41) 344–45.

[127] *Nationwide Building Society v Richard Grosse* (above n 61) 354–56.

[128] See also *Nationwide Building Society v Balmer Radmore* (above n 105) 270–79 (ChD).

[129] See, eg, *Smith New Court Securities Ltd v Citibank NA* [1997] AC 254.

[130] *Nationwide Building Society v Balmer Radmore* (above n 105) 278 (ChD).

[131] *Bristol & West v Daniels* (above n 24).

fiduciary duty by acting for the vendor, the purchaser and the lender in a property transaction.[132] The judge granted summary judgment for breach of fiduciary duty with compensation to be assessed, depending upon the outcome of an analysis of causation but added:

> [The] causal link [between breach and loss] may not be present in the present case in that it has not been established to me, at least, that the instruction by the vendor of the same solicitors, or rather the retention by the Building Society of the same solicitors as the vendor had previously instructed, has caused the loss which the Building Society is seeking to recover in the present case.[133]

Similarly, in *Bristol & West Building Society v Fancy & Jackson*,[134] a firm of solicitors acted in breach of fiduciary duty when it failed to inform its lender client that it was also acting for the borrower and for an intermediate vendor in a sub-sale transaction, but the breach of fiduciary duty had little remedial impact at all. Chadwick J also found that the firm had breached its retainer, which sounded in damages. In calculating those damages, he applied common law principles,[135] without reference to any equitable principles[136] and added that he was 'not persuaded that [the breach of fiduciary duty] assists the society in the circumstances I have to consider'.[137] And in *Gilbert v Shanahan*, a solicitor had advised both a lessee and the guarantor of the lease. Her advice was negligent, but the guarantor also alleged breach of fiduciary duty, the particulars of which included '(a) Acting for both [the lessee] and the plaintiff'.[138] The Court of Appeal of New Zealand observed that 'it can be said immediately that particular (a) cannot be regarded as causative of [the guarantor's] loss.'[139] However, the court in *Gilbert v Shanahan* also found that the same loss 'would have occurred even if the breach had not occurred'[140] because the guarantor would have continued to retain the solicitor even if full disclosure of the conflict and its ramifications had been made. Thus, *Gilbert v Shanahan* establishes only that loss cannot be recovered by reason of a breach of fiduciary duty when the client would have acted in the same way if there had been no breach of fiduciary duty.[141] In none of these cases is there a positive holding that breach of the fiduciary rule regarding potential conflict between inconsistent duties can *never* generate loss.

---

[132] The lender knew the solicitors were acting for itself and the purchaser but did not know they were also acting for the vendor.

[133] *Bristol & West v Daniels* (above n 24) 328.

[134] *Bristol & West v Fancy & Jackson* (above n 25) 614.

[135] *Ibid*, 620–21, applying *South Australia Asset Management v York Montague* (above n 123).

[136] Chadwick J treated cases regarding equitable principles of causation dismissively, apparently considering *Swindle v Harrison* (above n 47) unhelpful because it 'was concerned with damages arising from breach of fiduciary duty': *Bristol & West v Fancy & Jackson* (above n 25) 620.

[137] *Bristol & West v Fancy & Jackson* (above n 25) 615.

[138] *Gilbert v Shanahan* [1998] 3 NZLR 528, 532 (CA).

[139] *Ibid*.

[140] *Ibid*, 536.

[141] See also *Rawleigh v Tait* [2008] NZCA 525 at [35], upheld on appeal: [2009] NZSC 11.

If the claimant would have acted differently had the fiduciary complied with his fiduciary duties, and would consequently have avoided suffering a loss, the loss can be said to have occurred as a consequence of the breach of fiduciary duty and so ought to be recoverable as equitable compensation. In particular, when a fiduciary owes duties to two principals which *may* conflict (as opposed to his acting with an actual conflict of duties), the fiduciary's failure to obtain fully informed consent to the conflict may cause the principal to lose the opportunity of obtaining independent representation. If the fiduciary had made proper disclosure of the potential conflict between duties and had sought the principal's consent, he would have had to explain the potential effect of the conflict on performance of the non-fiduciary duties he owed to his principal.[142] If such an explanation is not provided, so that the principal's fully informed consent to the double employment is not obtained, the principal may be able to argue that he was deprived of the chance to retain another fiduciary who was not labouring under the potential difficulties that the conflict created.[143]

The question that arises at this juncture is whether that sort of analysis is appropriate in a claim for equitable compensation, given that it effectively adopts common law notions of loss of a chance.[144] Loss of a chance analysis has been applied recently in *Také Ltd v BSM Marketing Ltd*[145] as the appropriate method for assessing loss caused by a breach of fiduciary duty, although the parties appear to have accepted this as the appropriate methodology without argument. It is, however, a developed mechanism for determining what would have happened had there been no breach of duty. In the light of the discussion offered earlier, concerning the 'but for' approach to causation when equitable compensation is claimed,[146] this seems a satisfactory approach when determining what loss a breach of the potential conflict rule has caused: if a court must consider what the claimant would have done but for the breach of fiduciary duty, it seems incongruous not to allow the principal to try to prove that he was deprived of the chance to retain another fiduciary who was not labouring under the difficulties that a potential conflict creates.

However, it will be rare for such loss to arise without, or to differ from, loss caused by breach of non-fiduciary duties in the same circumstances. This results from the application of two basic principles. When liability for loss of a chance

---

[142] See, eg, *Clark Boyce v Mouat* (above n 55) 435; *Taylor v Schofield Peterson* (above n 55) 440.

[143] See, eg, *Day v Mead* [1987] 2 NZLR 443, 468 (CA).

[144] It was not unknown historically for common law principles to influence the development of equitable doctrine. For example, Lord Nottingham LC, who is recognised as 'the father of modern equity' (WS Holdsworth, *Some Makers of English Law* (Cambridge, Cambridge University Press, 1938) 150; DEC Yale, *Lord Nottingham's Chancery Cases*, vol 1 (London, Selden Society, vol 73, 1957) xlv), drew upon common law principles in framing equitable doctrine: see Yale (above) lii. See also RP Meagher, JD Heydon and MJ Leeming, *Meagher, Gummow & Lehane's Equity: Doctrines and Remedies*, 4th edn (Chatswood, Butterworths LexisNexis, 2002) [3–040].

[145] *Také Ltd v BSM Marketing Ltd* [2007] EWHC 2031 (QB) at [8] and [2009] EWCA Civ 45 at [4]. See also *Premium Real Estate v Stevens* (above n 90) [42].

[146] See above ch 4, section III-B(ii).

arises as a result of the defendant's omission, the court must answer the hypothetical question 'what would the claimant have done if the defendant had complied with its duty?'[147] However, when the claimant's loss depends on the hypothetical action of a third party, the claimant need only show a substantial chance that the third party would have acted in a way that would have conferred the benefit sought or avoided the liability suffered.[148]

Thus, in the context of a claim brought under the potential conflict rule, if the court concludes that the principal would not have obtained independent representation if the fiduciary had acted properly, then it is impossible to conclude that the double employment has itself caused any loss, as in *Gilbert v Shanahan*.[149] It seems likely that this will cover the vast bulk of cases involving double employment of solicitors in run-of-the-mill transactions: the reasons why two parties to the same transaction choose to retain the same solicitor seem likely, for most people, to outweigh concerns about reduced effectiveness in that representation. Nonetheless, if the court concludes, on the balance of probabilities, that the claimant would have obtained independent representation, the analysis turns to the hypothetical question whether there is a substantial chance that an independent solicitor would have acted differently from the defendant. As Paul Finn noted, 'in many cases, and particularly where the conflict lies only in an undisclosed double employment, the aggrieved beneficiary's position would often not be one bit different if he in fact had the advantage of a fiduciary with undivided loyalties.'[150] If that is so, the defendant's breach of fiduciary duty again cannot be said to have caused any loss. However, if there is a substantial chance that an independent solicitor would have acted differently, then loss may be recoverable on the basis that the undisclosed double employment has in fact made a difference to the claimant's position because he would have taken independent advice that would have been different.

It therefore becomes apparent that loss of this sort will normally only be caused when there has been negligence (or some other breach of non-fiduciary duty) on the part of the solicitor: if the claimant shows that he would have taken advice from a separate solicitor, the court then needs to consider how an alternative solicitor would have conducted himself, which will normally lead it to consider what a reasonable solicitor would have done in the circumstances. A reasonable solicitor's conduct would most commonly differ from the way in which the defendant conducted himself when the defendant has acted negligently or otherwise in breach of non-fiduciary duty. When that is so, the loss caused by the breach of fiduciary duty again does not seem particularly distinct from the alternative claim for breach of non-fiduciary duty, in this case negligence.

---

[147] *Allied Maples Group Ltd v Simmons & Simmons* [1995] 1 WLR 1602, 1610.
[148] *Ibid*, 1611.
[149] *Gilbert v Shanahan* (above n 138) 535–36. See also *Rawleigh v Tait* (above n 141) [35]. See similarly, in the duty-interest context, *Swindle v Harrison* (above n 47) 718, 728 and 735.
[150] Finn, *Fiduciary Obligations* (above n 70) [591].

Still, it is possible, though likely to be very rare, that a principal could convince the court that he would have taken independent advice if the fiduciary had complied with his fiduciary duty and that such advice would have been of greater advantage to him than the fiduciary's advice was, even though the fiduciary did not act negligently when providing the advice that he gave. That is consistent with the fact that fiduciary doctrine's protection of non-fiduciary duties is not dependent on establishing breach of those non-fiduciary duties before fiduciary liability can arise. A situation in which this might possibly be made out is when the claimant can show that he would have retained a particular, identified alternative fiduciary and that particular fiduciary generally gives better, more valuable, advice. It will, however, be rare because it will be unusual for a court to feel able to conclude that hypothetical alternative advice would have been given and would have been more valuable to the principal than the *non*-negligent advice he received from the defendant.

iii. Contributory Fault

Thus, one can identify loss following a breach of fiduciary doctrine's rules regarding conflicts between inconsistent duties, particularly breaches of the actual conflict rule and the inhibition principle, but the loss seems indistinct from loss caused by breaches of non-fiduciary duty in the same circumstances. An important practical question that arises out of that conclusion is whether a fiduciary should be permitted to plead contributory fault in order to reduce a compensatory award made against him following a breach of fiduciary duty, as a defendant can with claims for negligence or for breaches of contract when liability is co-extensive with liability in tort such that it would have been actionable independently of the contract.[151] This could be rationalised in one of two ways: either by (*i*) accepting the existence of concurrent liability (for breach both of non-fiduciary duty and of fiduciary duty) but rendering inapplicable any defence of contributory fault to the fiduciary claim; or by (*ii*) recognising the loss as sounding only in a claim for breach of non-fiduciary duty but holding that the breach of fiduciary duty renders inapplicable any claim of contributory fault that might otherwise apply in respect of the non-fiduciary claim.

The first interpretation might be thought to be more conceptually sound, in that it does not involve equity negating the effect of a statutory defence of

---

[151] *Forsikringsaktieselskapet Vesta v Butcher* [1989] AC 852, 860, 866–67 and 875; *Barclays Bank plc v Fairclough Building Ltd* [1995] QB 214, 228–29 and 233 (CA); AM Dugdale and MA Jones (gen eds), *Clerk & Lindsell on Torts*, 19th edn (London, Sweet & Maxwell, 2006) [3–48]. Reductions for contributory fault were not possible at common law in Australia where the claim was brought in contract (*Astley v Austrust Ltd* [1999] HCA 6 at [2], [41]–[42] and [62]–[70], (1999) 197 CLR 1), but that has been changed by statute: see, eg, Law Reform (Miscellaneous Provisions) Act 1965 (NSW), ss 8 and 9 (as amended).

contributory fault:[152] if the claims are concurrent, the claimant can simply choose to rely on the one that is not subject to a defence of contributory fault. However, the second interpretation is also conceptually coherent, in that a breach of fiduciary duty can provide a reason for the court to exercise its statutory discretion against the defendant's assertion of contributory fault with respect to the non-fiduciary claim.[153] The difference between the alternatives seems to be of little practical importance.[154] Either way, establishing a breach of fiduciary duty will be more lucrative to claimants.

While the statutory regime that permits reduction of compensatory awards for contributory fault does not extend to breaches of fiduciary duty,[155] that does not answer the question whether equity ought to develop an analogous limitation on compensation claims for breach of fiduciary duty. The point has already been made above in chapter two that the rules of equity have been established over time, as opposed to having existed since time immemorial.[156] Contributory fault is not relevant when a fiduciary is asked to account for his stewardship of property,[157] but not all fiduciaries can be held to account for property. In New Zealand, fiduciaries have been permitted to argue contributory fault to reduce the level of compensation awarded for breach of fiduciary duty,[158] although that position may now be under review.[159] In contrast, the High Court of Australia has indicated that contributory fault will not avail a fiduciary there when the liability is for breach of fiduciary duty.[160]

---

[152] Under the Law Reform (Contributory Negligence) Act 1945. As to equity's inability to disregard a statute, see *Tito v Waddell (No 2)* [1977] Ch 106, 239 (VC); *Cubillo v Commonwealth of Australia* [2001] FCA 1213 at [465], (2001) 112 FCR 455.

[153] Law Reform (Contributory Negligence) Act 1945, s 1(1).

[154] Claimants have a slender practical advantage under the first interpretation, in that they can elect to pursue only their fiduciary claims, whereas the second alternative would require them to prove liability for breach of both kinds of duty in order to achieve the practical result of avoiding a contributory fault defence. The limitation period appears to be the same, whichever form of claim is brought: *Gwembe Valley Development Co Ltd v Koshy* [2003] EWCA Civ 1048 at [90]–[91] and [111], [2004] 1 BCLC 131.

[155] *Standard Chartered Bank v Pakistan National Shipping Corp (Nos 2 and 4)* [2002] UKHL 43 at [12], [2003] 1 AC 959; C Hollander and S Salzedo, *Conflicts of Interest*, 3rd edn (London, Sweet & Maxwell, 2008) [9–022].

[156] See above ch 2, section II-B(ii).

[157] *Beaumont v Boultbee* (1800) 5 Ves 485, 492 (31 ER 695) (LC); *Shropshire Union Railways & Canal Co v R* (1875) LR 7 HL 496, 507–8; *Re Vernon Ewens & Co* (1886) 33 ChD 402, 410, 412 and 413 (CA); *De Beer v Kanaar & Co* [2002] EWHC 688 (Ch) at [92]; *Alexander v Perpetual Trustees WA Ltd* [2004] HCA 7 at [44], (2004) 216 CLR 109.

[158] *Day v Mead* (above n 143) 451 and 462.

[159] The New Zealand Supreme Court appears recently to have reversed this rule for fiduciary claims, although the status of its comment remains unclear as it was made in a mere footnote and without reference to *Day v Mead*, let alone any analysis of the earlier decision: see *Amaltal Corp Ltd v Maruha Corp* [2007] NZSC 40 at [23] (fn 17), [2007] 3 NZLR 192. See also *Bank of New Zealand v New Zealand Guardian Trust Co Ltd* [1999] 1 NZLR 664, 688 (CA), which suggested that breaches of fiduciary duty would attract a stricter approach than wrongs that amounted to negligence or breach of contract.

[160] *Pilmer v Duke Group Ltd* [2001] HCA 31 at [86] and [165]–[173], (2001) 207 CLR 165.

In England, a fiduciary who has acted in breach of fiduciary duty in a way that involved *conscious* disloyalty, such as when the claim is for breach of the inhibition principle, cannot rely on the claimant's want of care for its own interests to reduce any compensation payable for loss caused by that breach.[161] However, the decision that established that proposition was based on the fiduciary's intentional disloyalty in inhibition cases and was expressly limited to such cases.[162] Intention is not a necessary element in making out breach of the fiduciary rules regarding potential or actual conflicts between duties, and whereas the unavailability of contributory fault in inhibition claims indicates the possibility that it is also unavailable in fiduciary claims based on *non-conscious* disloyalty, it does not settle that issue.

Fiduciary doctrine's actual and potential conflict rules are protective of the non-fiduciary duties that the fiduciary owes and which are in conflict. Allowing a claimant's contributory fault to reduce compensation awards in such cases would undermine the protective function that fiduciary doctrine seeks to achieve, irrespective of whether the breach of fiduciary duty involves conscious disloyalty.

When there is an *actual conflict* between two sets of non-fiduciary duties owed by the same fiduciary, the concern that warrants the intervention of fiduciary doctrine is the risk that one or other set of non-fiduciary duties will be breached: the fiduciary is acting in a situation in which there is a strong likelihood that he will fail properly to perform the duties he owes to his two principals. If a fiduciary continues to act in such a situation, thereby necessarily breaching non-fiduciary duties owed to at least one principal, that principal ought to be able to sue for the loss suffered without any reduction for contributory fault. The loss has been caused by precisely the sort of conduct, and is itself precisely the result, against which fiduciary doctrine seeks to protect, and the fiduciary's failure to abide by that protective regulation removes any justification for a reduction in the award on the basis of contributory fault: it is inconsistent with the protective function served by fiduciary doctrine to require a principal to be as vigilant in respect of his own interests as he would need to be without fiduciary doctrine's protection.

Taylor v Schofield Peterson[163] helps to illustrate how perverse it can be to allow contributory fault pleas in this context. A solicitor advising two partners regarding dissolution of their partnership advised them to seek independent advice, but they did not do so. Penlington and Hammond JJ found that the solicitor had not informed the clients sufficiently as to the nature and effect of the conflict of duties, so that they had not given fully informed consent to the conflict. The court awarded the plaintiff compensation for his loss, but the solicitor's liability was reduced by 20 per cent to reflect the plaintiff's failure to take independent

---

[161] *Nationwide Building Society v Balmer Radmore* (above n 105) 281–82 (ChD).
[162] *Ibid*, 281.
[163] *Taylor v Schofield Peterson* (above n 55) (FC).

advice.[164] Yet the fact that the solicitor had failed to explain sufficiently to the plaintiff the need for independent advice and the risks of continuing to retain the plaintiff in a situation in which there was a conflict between the duties that he owed to each of his clients, was the very reason for the court finding that the plaintiff's consent had not been fully informed, such that the solicitor was acting in breach of fiduciary duty.[165] This paradoxical line of reasoning is anathema to the protective function that fiduciary doctrine is designed to perform. The 'introduction of concepts of contributory negligence into that setting inevitably will work a subversion of fundamental principle',[166] as it undermines the very function that fiduciary doctrine serves: the protection of non-fiduciary duties from situations which increase the risk of their breach.

The argument against contributory fault has somewhat less force when the breach of fiduciary duty arises out of a *potential conflict* between duties, as opposed to an actual conflict. When the conflict is only potential, it might be thought that the fiduciary should be allowed greater leeway. However, contributory fault ought not to be allowed in such situations either, largely for the reasons just given regarding actual conflict situations. Fiduciary doctrine is sufficiently concerned about situations involving potential conflicts that it prohibits the fiduciary from acting in such situations unless he has disclosed and explained the conflict so as to obtain fully informed consent from both principals. When that has not been done and loss has been suffered as a result of the conflict, if that loss would not have been suffered had the fiduciary complied with his fiduciary duties, then the loss ought to be recoverable in full. It has already been seen that this is not likely to be common, as it will be rare that a potential conflict actually causes loss.[167] When the loss has been caused by a breach of non-fiduciary duty that is unrelated to the potential conflict, then the normal rules as to contributory fault should apply: there is no justification for altering those rules simply because the breach of duty happened to take place against the coincidental backdrop of a potential conflict between duties. But when the potential conflict has caused loss, that loss ought to be recoverable without reduction for contributory fault. The rationale for the fiduciary duties that apply in situations involving potential conflicts between duties is to reduce the risk of such loss occurring by seeking to avoid situations which increase that very risk.[168] As with actual conflicts, to allow a plea of contributory fault in such cases effectively requires the principal to be on his guard against the fiduciary, subverting the prophylactic and subsidiary form of protection for non-fiduciary duties that fiduciary doctrine is designed to provide. That protection is not lifted unless the fiduciary has

---

[164] *Ibid*, 447–48.

[165] *Ibid*, 445.

[166] WMC Gummow, 'Compensation for Breach of Fiduciary Duty' in TG Youdan (ed), *Equity, Fiduciaries and Trusts* (Toronto, Carswell, 1989) 57, 86. See also KR Handley, 'Reduction of Damages Awards' in PD Finn (ed), *Essays on Damages* (Sydney, LawBook Co, 1992) 113, 127.

[167] See above section III-D(ii).

[168] See above section II-A.

obtained the fully informed consent of his principal. Unless such consent is proven, if the fiduciary has failed to comply with the protective rules, he ought not to be allowed to argue that the principal ought to have been more careful.

Finally, it remains important to pay close attention to the causal analysis in these cases,[169] which is shorthand for the proposition that close attention must be paid to the nature of the breach of fiduciary duty and its relationship to the loss for which the claimant seeks redress.[170] When no link can be shown between a breach of fiduciary duty and a loss, then any liability to compensate for the loss arises solely, if at all, as a result of breach of non-fiduciary duties and is thereby prone to reduction for contributory fault in the ordinary way. The fiduciary's disloyalty has not caused the loss suffered and so is irrelevant to its recovery. When, however, loss has arisen as a result of a breach of fiduciary duty, that loss ought to be recoverable through an award of equitable compensation, which ought not to be reduced for contributory fault.

---

[169] *Nationwide Building Society v Balmer Radmore* (above n 105) 282.

[170] See also *Canson Enterprises Ltd v Boughton & Co* [1991] 3 SCR 534, 551–52; *Corporacion Nacional del Cobre de Chile v Sogemin Metals Ltd* [1997] 1 WLR 1396, 1402–4 (ChD); *Sphere Drake Insurance Ltd v Euro International Underwriting Ltd* [2003] EWHC 1636 (Comm) at [97], [2003] Lloyd's Rep IR 525; RC Nolan and DD Prentice, 'The Issue of Shares: Compensating the Company for Loss' (2002) 118 *Law Quarterly Review* 180, 187; A Underhill and DJ Hayton, *Law Relating to Trusts and Trustees*, 17th edn by DJ Hayton, PB Matthews and CCJ Mitchell (London, LexisNexis Butterworths, 2007) [89.30].

7

Implications

The preceding chapters have explained that fiduciary doctrine offers a subsidiary and prophylactic form of protection to non-fiduciary duties. It makes the proper performance of those non-fiduciary duties more likely by requiring fiduciaries to avoid acting in situations that involve temptations and other influences which create a real, sensible possibility that the fiduciary might breach those duties. The remaining chapters in the book explore the implications of understanding fiduciary doctrine in this way. In particular, this chapter examines a number of propositions that are frequently stated in connection with fiduciary doctrine, with a view to showing that understanding that doctrine as protective of non-fiduciary duties provides an important basis from which to elucidate and evaluate those propositions.

I. Scope of Fiduciary Duties

Courts have frequently observed that 'the scope of the fiduciary duty must be moulded according to the nature of the relationship and the facts of the case.'[1] Thus, 'to say that a man is a fiduciary only begins analysis; it gives direction to further inquiry. To whom is he a fiduciary? What obligations does he owe as a fiduciary?'[2] Statements emphasising that 'the obligation imposed may vary in its

---

[1] *Hospital Products Ltd v United States Surgical Corp* (1984) 156 CLR 41, 102. See also, eg, *Re Coomber* [1911] 1 Ch 723, 729 (CA); *New Zealand Netherlands Society 'Oranje' Inc v Kuys* [1973] 1 WLR 1126, 1129–30 (PC); *Lac Minerals Ltd v International Corona Resources Ltd* [1989] 2 SCR 574, 646; *Kelly v Cooper* [1993] AC 205, 214–15 (PC); *Henderson v Merrett Syndicates Ltd* [1995] 2 AC 145, 206; *Breen v Williams* (1996) 186 CLR 71, 82–83; *Maguire v Makaronis* (1997) 188 CLR 449, 464; *South Australia v Peat Marwick Mitchell & Co* (1997) 24 ACSR 231, 266; *Clay v Clay* [2001] HCA 9 at [46], (2001) 202 CLR 410; *Brandeis (Brokers) Ltd v Black* [2001] 2 All ER (Comm) 980 at [40] (QBD); *Australian Securities & Investments Commission v Citigroup Global Markets Australia Pty Ltd* [2007] FCA 963 at [288], (2007) 160 FCR 35; *Strother v 3464920 Canada Inc* [2007] SCC 24 at [118] and [141], [2007] 2 SCR 177; *Premium Real Estate Ltd v Stevens* [2009] NZSC 15 at [23], [2009] 2 NZLR 384.

[2] *Securities & Exchange Commission v Chenery Corp* 318 US 80, 85–86 (87 L Ed 626) (1943). This statement has been cited with approval on numerous occasions: see, eg, *Re Goldcorp Exchange Ltd*

specific substance depending on the relationship'[3] can be read as suggesting that courts possess discretion to craft and apply fiduciary duties as they see fit. It is important, however, to recognise that the moulding of fiduciary duties to the circumstances of the case is not an unprincipled exercise in judicial discretion. Understanding fiduciary duties as protective of non-fiduciary duties provides a solid theoretical underpinning for this important tenet of fiduciary doctrine. Because fiduciary duties are designed to protect non-fiduciary duties, by removing temptations and incentives that are inconsistent with proper performance of those duties, fiduciary doctrine's response to a particular factual situation must, as a matter of logical necessity, take account of the non-fiduciary duties which are owed in that situation.

Before explaining this point more fully, it is worth noting two other valid explanations for the moulding of fiduciary duties to different situations. The first is of predominantly historical importance and is not relevant to the present understanding of fiduciary duties. As was seen earlier,[4] when the fiduciary concept was used primarily as a vehicle for exporting incidents of the trustee– beneficiary relationship to other similar relationships, duties owed by one kind of fiduciary were modified as necessary to make them appropriate to the context of the new kind of fiduciary to which they were now to be applied. In that context, it is obvious that 'fiduciary relations are of different types, carrying different obligations.'[5]

A second explanation for the moulding of fiduciary duties takes account of the fact that fiduciary duties can be excluded if the principal authorises the fiduciary to act in a way that would otherwise constitute a breach of fiduciary duty.[6] In that sense, the existence of fiduciary obligations is only a presumption, even in cases involving a settled category of fiduciary relationship.[7] Thus, 'the existence and scope of [fiduciary] duties depends upon the terms on which they are acting',[8] and if those terms include permission to act for other clients selling competing products, fiduciary doctrine's prima facie prohibition against so acting is displaced.[9] This is not a matter of judicial discretion but rather gives effect to the arrangements the parties have created.

[1995] 1 AC 74, 98 (PC); *Pilmer v Duke Group Ltd* [2001] HCA 31 at [77], (2001) 207 CLR 165; *Cubillo v Commonwealth of Australia* [2001] FCA 1213 at [462], (2001) 112 FCR 455.

[3] *Lac Minerals v International Corona Resources* (above n 1) 646.

[4] See above ch 2, section II-A; and ch 3, section II.

[5] *Hospital Products Ltd v US Surgical Corp* (above n 1) 69. See also *Re Coomber* (above n 1) 728–29.

[6] This point is discussed further below in section IV.

[7] *Lac Minerals v International Corona Resources* (above n 1) 647.

[8] *Kelly v Cooper* (above n 1) 214. See also *Henderson v Merrett Syndicates* (above n 1) 206.

[9] See, eg, *Ex parte Lacey* (1802) 6 Ves 625, 626 (31 ER 1228); *Ex parte Bennett* (1805) 10 Ves 381, 394 (32 ER 893); *Plowright v Lambert* (1885) 52 LT 646, 653; *Kelly v Cooper* (above n 1) 214–15; *Australian Securities & Investments Commission v Citigroup Global Markets Australia Pty Ltd* [2007] FCA 963 at [324]–[335], (2007) 160 FCR 35; *BBC Worldwide Ltd v Bee Load Ltd* [2007] EWHC 134 (Comm) at [111].

But when fiduciary duties have not been excluded or modified by consent, what requires explanation is why and how fiduciary duties are 'moulded' to a case. In *Aberdeen Railway v Blaikie*, Lord Cranworth LC described the fiduciary conflict principle as 'a rule of universal application'[10] and an 'inflexible' rule,[11] and in *Guinness plc v Saunders*, Lord Templeman said of the profit principle that 'equity has no power to relax its own strict rule further than and inconsistently with the express relaxation contained in the articles of association.'[12] Similarly, in *Breakspear v Ackland*, Briggs J emphasised that 'the court has no discretion' to relieve a trustee from the effects of the self-dealing rule.[13] The reconciliation between such statements and the moulding of fiduciary duties to the circumstances of each case is to be found in the fact that non-fiduciary duties differ from case to case, because it is those non-fiduciary duties to which fiduciary doctrine offers its protection and to which fiduciary doctrine must necessarily respond.

A fiduciary's basic function, be it as solicitor, agent, trustee, company director and so on, will be reflected in and regulated by his non-fiduciary duties. Whatever the source of those duties—whether it be the common law (of contract or torts), equity or statute—they are what 'regulates the basic rights and liabilities of the parties. The fiduciary relationship, if it is to exist at all, must accommodate itself to the terms of'[14] the non-fiduciary duties that exist between the parties. Fiduciary duties are necessarily reactive to non-fiduciary duties because their nature and function is to offer protection to those non-fiduciary duties. The conflict principle, for example, prohibits a fiduciary from acting when there is a conflict between his non-fiduciary duties and his personal interest. By its very terms, therefore, the fiduciary principle 'must accommodate itself' to the non-fiduciary duties to which it refers. Thus, the fiduciary conflict principle can be inflexible in what it requires while at the same time its application depends on the facts of each case. The scope of application of fiduciary duties necessarily depends in each case on the content and scope of the non-fiduciary duties owed in that case because 'the conflicting duty or interests must be identified.'[15] The fiduciary principle remains constant, but the non-fiduciary duties to which it refers are different in each case, which means that application of the fiduciary principle can and must differ from case to case.

Thus, for example, fiduciaries can deal with their principals, notwithstanding the fair-dealing rule, when the transaction does not touch upon the fiduciary

---

[10]   *Aberdeen Railway Co v Blaikie Bros* (1854) 1 Macq 461, 471 (149 RR 32).

[11]   *Ibid*, 472.

[12]   *Guinness plc v Saunders* [1990] 2 AC 663, 692.

[13]   *Breakspear v Ackland* [2008] EWHC 220 (Ch) at [102], [2009] Ch 32.

[14]   *Hospital Products Ltd v US Surgical Corp* (above n 1) 97. This passage has been cited with approval on numerous occasions: see, eg, *Kelly v Cooper* (above n 1) 215; *Global Container Lines Ltd v Bonyad Shipping Co* [1998] 1 Lloyd's Rep 528, 546 (QBD); *Strother v 3464920 Canada Inc* [2007] SCC 24 at [141], [2007] 2 SCR 177. See also *Benedetti v Sawaris* [2009] EWHC 1330 (Ch) at [502].

[15]   *Pilmer v Duke Group Ltd* [2001] HCA 31 at [83], (2001) 207 CLR 165.

relationship between them. The reason such transactions can be upheld is because there is no real, sensible possibility of conflict between the fiduciary's non-fiduciary duties and his personal interest in the transaction. In *Montesquieu v Sandys*, for example, Lord Eldon LC said:

> [T]here is no authority establishing, nor was it ever laid down, that an attorney cannot purchase from his client what was not in any degree the object of his concern as attorney; the client making the proposal, himself proposing the price, no confidence asked or received in that article, and both ignorant of the value. Under such circumstances he is not the attorney *in hac Re*; and therefore, not being under any duty as attorney to advise against the act, he may be the purchaser.[16]

Many other examples of similar statements exist in the case law.[17] If the solicitor is not retained with respect to the sale of the property that he bought, he owes no non-fiduciary duty in connection with the sale of that property. The solicitor's personal interest in such a case is undeniable, but there is no conflict between that interest and his duty—as there is no such duty—and so the fiduciary conflict principle has no effect on the transaction.[18] If, on the other hand, the purchaser were, for example, the managing agent of the property, his non-fiduciary management duties would create a clear conflict between duty and interest if he were to buy the property. In this way, fiduciary duties are moulded to the facts of each case: the non-fiduciary duties that one fiduciary owes in the circumstances of the relationship he has with his principal will differ from the non-fiduciary duties owed by another fiduciary, in a different relationship. Submissions regarding conflict between duty and interest 'make it necessary for the origins of the trustees' various rights and duties to be closely considered'.[19]

The same approach is evident in cases concerning the fiduciary conflict principles that regulate conflicts between inconsistent duties. In *Colyer v Finch*, for example, a mortgagee's solicitor had also acted for the mortgagor in the transaction. Lord Cranworth LC considered this irrelevant to a priority dispute between the mortgagee and a purchaser who bought from the mortgagor after the mortgagee left the title deeds with the mortgagor: the solicitor had only acted

---

[16]   *Montesquieu v Sandys* (1811) 18 Ves 302, 313 (34 ER 331).

[17]   See, eg, *Cane v Allen* (1814) 2 Dow 289, 296 and 297 (3 ER 869) (HL); *Jones v Thomas* (1837) 2 Y & C Ex 498, 519–20 (160 ER 493); *Edwards v Meyrick* (1842) 2 Hare 60, 69–70 (67 ER 25); *Knight v Marjoribanks* (1849) 2 Mac & G 10, 12–13 (42 ER 4) (LC) (also reported at (1849) 2 H & Tw 308 (47 ER 1700)); *Holman v Loynes* (1854) 4 De GM & G 270, 281 (43 ER 510); *McPherson v Watt* (1877) 3 App Cas 254, 270–71. See also *Wood v Downes* (1811) 18 Ves 120, 127 (34 ER 263) (LC); *Hampson v Nicoll* (1827) 6 LJ Ch 22, 22 (MR); *Scott v Dunbar* (1828) 1 Molloy 442, 457; *Austin v Chambers* (1838) 6 Cl & Fin 1, 39 (7 ER 598) (LC); *Nutt v Easton* [1899] 1 Ch 873, 878; *Allison v Clayhills* (1907) 97 LT 709, 711–12 (ChD); *Noranda Australia Ltd v Lachlan Resources NL* (1988) 14 NSWLR 1, 15 (Eq Div).

[18]   Of course, such transactions might still be impugned on other grounds, such as undue influence: see, eg, *Wright v Proud* (1806) 13 Ves 136, 138 (33 ER 246) (LC); *Wood v Downes* (*ibid*) 127; *Hunter v Atkins* (1834) 3 My & K 113, 140 (40 ER 43); *Edwards v Meyrick* (*ibid*) 69–70; *Holman v Loynes* (*ibid*) 283; *Spencer v Topham* (1856) 22 Beav 573, 582 (52 ER 1229) (MR); *McPherson v Watt* (*ibid*) 271; *Wright v Carter* [1903] 1 Ch 27, 50, 53 and 57 (CA).

[19]   *Sargeant v National Westminster Bank plc* (1990) 61 P & CR 518, 522 (CA).

for the mortgagee in drafting the mortgage deed, and 'with regard to the handing over of the documents, [the solicitor] was in no respect the agent or the solicitor of'[20] the mortgagee. So there was no conflict between duties because the mortgagee was acting for himself when handing over the documents, and the solicitor was acting for the mortgagor.

Similarly, in *Clark Boyce v Mouat*, a solicitor acted for both mother and son when the mother mortgaged her home to provide security for a loan made to the son. The son defaulted, leaving the mother liable under the mortgage. The Court of Appeal of New Zealand held the solicitor liable for negligence and for breach of fiduciary duty,[21] but the Privy Council disagreed: 'a fiduciary duty concerns disclosure of material facts in a situation where the fiduciary has either a personal interest in the matter to which the facts are material or acts for another party who has such an interest. It cannot be prayed in aid to enlarge the scope of contractual duties.'[22] Whereas a solicitor's non-fiduciary duties ordinarily would require him to advise on the wisdom of entering into a mortgage transaction,[23] the solicitor in this case had been retained only to carry out the necessary conveyancing and to explain the transaction to the parties—he was not obliged to proffer unsought advice on the wisdom of the transaction.[24] As his only non-fiduciary duty was to ensure that the mortgage documentation was properly executed and registered and to explain the legal implications of the transaction, there was no potential conflict between the non-fiduciary duties that he owed to each of his clients, and so the solicitor committed no breach of fiduciary duty by continuing to act for both of them.

These cases emphasise the critical importance of 'a meticulous examination of the facts of each individual case'[25] when fiduciary claims are made, in order to ascertain precisely what non-fiduciary duties were owed in the circumstances. Only when that is known can one determine how fiduciary doctrine affects a particular case, as only then can one determine whether there was a conflict between the fiduciary's duty and his personal interest, or between inconsistent duties owed by the fiduciary. Determining what non-fiduciary duties are owed in a given case can be a difficult issue, but it is not resolved by fiduciary doctrine itself.[26]

---

[20] *Colyer v Finch* (1856) 5 HLC 905, 930 (10 ER 1159).
[21] *Mouat v Clark Boyce* (1991) 1 NZ Conveyancing Cases 190,917.
[22] *Clark Boyce v Mouat* [1994] 1 AC 428, 437 (PC).
[23] PJ Millett, 'The Husband, the Wife and the Bank' [2001] *Private Client Business* 238, 247.
[24] *Clark Boyce v Mouat* (above n 22) 437. See also *Pickersgill v Riley* [2004] UKPC 14 at [8], [2004] Lloyd's Rep IR 795; and *Dargusch v Sherley Investments Pty Ltd* [1970] Qd R 338, 352 (FC) *per* Kneipp J dissenting. In other words, the solicitor was 'an execution-only solicitor': RC Nolan, 'Conflicts of Duty: Helping Hands from the Privy Council?' (1994) 15 *Company Lawyer* 58, 59.
[25] *Cook v Evatt (No 2)* [1992] 1 NZLR 676, 685 (HC). See also *Re Coomber* (above n 1) 729; *Boardman v Phipps* [1967] 2 AC 46, 125; *Foster Bryant Surveying Ltd v Bryant* [2007] EWCA Civ 200 at [76], [2007] 2 BCLC 239.
[26] RP Austin, 'Fiduciary Accountability for Business Opportunities' in PD Finn (ed), *Equity and Commercial Relationships* (Sydney, Law Book Co, 1987) 141, 148.

The Supreme Court of Canada's split decision in *Strother v 3464920 Canada Inc*[27] provides a powerful illustration of the vital importance of analysing non-fiduciary duties in reaching conclusions about fiduciary liability. A solicitor had advised the claimant regarding a tax shelter investment, which was subsequently rendered ineffective by legislation. Having informed the claimant that he could not see how to avoid the effect of the new legislation, the solicitor later became aware of a possible new scheme, which he exploited to his own personal advantage. A majority of the Supreme Court of Canada held the solicitor liable for breach of fiduciary duty. While accepting that a lawyer does not generally owe a duty to alter past opinions in the light of subsequent changes of circumstances,[28] the majority found that the solicitor's retainer in this case included a duty to explain to the claimant that his earlier advice had been superseded.[29] In contrast, the dissentients considered that the solicitor owed no contractual duty to provide the claimant with unsought advice.[30] Surprising though the majority's conclusion may be, the importance of *Strother* for present purposes is that the success of the claim for breach of fiduciary duty turned on analysis of the *non*-fiduciary duties that comprised the solicitor's retainer. As McLachlin CJ said in dissent:

> [A] conflict arises when a lawyer puts himself or herself in a position of having irreconcilable duties or interests. . . It follows that the first question where conflict of interest is alleged is what duty the lawyer owed to the client alleging the conflict. The second question is whether the lawyer owed a duty to another client, or held a personal interest, that conflicted with the first duty.[31]

McLachlin CJ's first question is a matter of non-fiduciary duty. As she said, 'in a case such as this, *one looks to the contract* between the parties. . . [O]ne begins by asking what the lawyer and the client have agreed the lawyer will do and on what terms' (emphasis added).[32] The solicitor was held to have acted in breach of fiduciary duty only because the majority concluded that he owed a duty to provide further advice to the claimant regarding the new scheme: that duty conflicted with his personal interest in pursuing the new scheme.[33] Absent any such non-fiduciary duty, there would have been no conflict between duty and personal interest, and consequently no breach of fiduciary duty.

These points have particular relevance to cases against solicitors, because the duties owed by solicitors vary with the circumstances of each retainer:

> There is no such thing as a general retainer. . . The expression 'my solicitor' is as meaningless as the expression 'my tailor' or 'my bookmaker' in establishing any general

---

[27] *Strother v 3464920 Canada Inc* [2007] SCC 24, [2007] 2 SCR 177.
[28] *Ibid* at [45].
[29] *Ibid* at [46]–[48].
[30] *Ibid* at [144].
[31] *Ibid* at [132].
[32] *Ibid* at [133]–[134].
[33] *Ibid* at [50], [52] and [70].

duty apart from that arising out of a particular matter in which his services are retained. The extent of his duties depends upon the terms and limits of that retainer and any duty of care to be implied must be related to what he is instructed to do.[34]

Thus, 'whether a conflict between two clients exists is dependent on the scope of the retainer between the lawyer and the client in question. The fiduciary duties owed by the lawyer are molded by this retainer.'[35] As Lord Upjohn said in *Boardman v Phipps*,

> Once it is established that there is [a fiduciary] relationship, that relationship must be examined to see what duties are thereby imposed upon the agent, to see what is the scope and ambit of the duties charged upon him. Having defined the scope of those duties one must see whether he has committed some breach thereof by placing himself within the scope and ambit of those duties in a position where his duty and interest may possibly conflict. It is only at this stage that any question of accountability arises.[36]

Similar points can be made in relation to company directors. Thus, for example, in *In Plus Group v Pyke*, a director was effectively forced out of the company such that, although he remained a director, this was 'entirely nominal'.[37] Consequently, there was no breach of fiduciary duty when one of the company's clients transferred its business to the director's new enterprise, as his effective expulsion from the company 'eliminates the duality of interest or duty which the law seeks to guard against. . . Quite exceptionally, the defendant's duty to the claimants had been reduced to vanishing point'.[38] Just as with the other examples that have been discussed, it is crucial to establish precisely what non-fiduciary duties a director owes in the circumstances of the case at hand, in order to determine whether there is any real, sensible possibility of conflict between those duties and the director's personal interest. The elimination of the director's non-fiduciary duties in *In Plus Group v Pyke* meant that there was no conflict between any such duties and his interest.

---

[34] *Midland Bank Trust Co Ltd v Hett Stubbs & Kemp* [1979] 1 Ch 384, 402. See also *Saffron Walden Second Benefit Building Society v Rayner* (1880) 14 ChD 406, 409 (CA); *Boardman v Phipps* (above n 25) 106 and 126; *Pickersgill v Riley* [2004] UKPC 14 at [7] and [14], [2004] Lloyd's Rep IR 795; *Marplace (Number 512) Ltd v Chaffe Street* [2006] EWHC 1919 (Ch) at [403]. This explains the very careful differentiation of separate retainers conducted by Henderson J in *Winters v Mishcon de Reya* [2008] EWHC 2419 (Ch).

[35] *Strother v 3464920 Canada Inc* [2007] SCC 24 at [118], [2007] 2 SCR 177.

[36] *Boardman v Phipps* [1966] 3 All ER 721, 758 (HL). The All England Report has intentionally been quoted here rather than the official report, because it omits an 'and' that appears in the official report between the words 'thereof' and 'by' in the second sentence quoted above: cf [1967] 2 AC 46, 127. The official report accurately reflects the transcript of Lord Upjohn's speech held in the House of Lords Archives, but the word 'and' in that position renders the sentence grammatically nonsensical.

[37] *In Plus Group Ltd v Pyke* [2002] EWCA Civ 370 at [90], [2002] 2 BCLC 201. He was not allowed access to company information and had no ongoing management role in the company: at [29] and [33].

[38] *Ibid* at [90]. See also *Wilkinson v West Coast Capital* [2005] EWHC 3009 (Ch) at [251], [2007] BCC 717.

Furthermore, just as fiduciary liability will turn on the extent of the non-fiduciary duties owed by the fiduciary, so too it can be important to consider carefully whether the fiduciary has an interest in a transaction said to have been entered into in breach of fiduciary duty. Normally, the fiduciary's interest will be obvious and so requires little thought, but that is not always so:

> [O]ne must regard the realities. If the question is asked: 'Will a sale of trust property by the trustee to his wife be set aside?', nobody can answer it without being told more; for … manifestly there are wives and wives. In one case the trustee may have sold privately to his wife with whom he was living in perfect amity; in another the property may have been knocked down at auction to the trustee's wife from whom he has been living separate and in enmity for a dozen years.[39]

Thus, the moulding of fiduciary duties to the circumstances of each case reflects the critical nature of the factual circumstances when determining what non-fiduciary duties are owed, because it is those non-fiduciary duties that are the reference point when applying the fiduciary principles, and what interest is said to conflict with those duties. The analysis must be done in that order, because it is nonsensical to ask whether there is a conflict between duty and interest if one does not know what non-fiduciary duties are owed or what the fiduciary's interest in the transaction might be.

Jay Shepherd has argued that it is appropriate 'where such flexibility is necessary [for] the courts [to refuse] to treat the rules as completely conclusive'.[40] As an example, Shepherd commends the approach taken in *Holder v Holder*,[41] where the Court of Appeal refused to set aside an executor's purchase of property from the testator's estate because he was only an executor by a technicality, counsel having conceded that his intermeddling in the estate made him an executor, and he had never assumed the duties of an executor. Following that lead, Shepherd argues that 'the court should determine whether on the particular facts of the case, and regardless of whether the fiduciary fits within general labels such as trustee or executor, the case is one of that class of cases in which the generalization upon which the rule is based holds true.'[42] The danger with such an approach is that it can easily descend into a disorderly and unprincipled exercise in judicial discretion as to whether fiduciary liability is appropriate on the facts. The decision in *Holder* could have been reached in a far more principled fashion if the facts had been adequately ventilated. Harman LJ took the unusual step of expressing 'great doubt whether the admission made at the bar was correct, as did the trial judge',[43] and Danckwerts LJ straightforwardly stated that

---

[39] *Tito v Waddell (No 2)* [1977] Ch 106, 240. See also *Newgate Stud Co v Penfold* [2004] EWHC 2993 (Ch) at [234]–[237], [2008] 1 BCLC 46; *Hollis v Rolfe* [2008] EWHC 1747 (Ch) at [181]–[182].

[40] JC Shepherd, *The Law of Fiduciaries* (Toronto, Carswell, 1981) 130.

[41] *Holder v Holder* [1968] 1 Ch 353.

[42] Shepherd (above n 40) 130–31.

[43] *Holder v Holder* (above n 41) 392.

he thought the concession 'was a mistake'.[44] Had the concession not been made, the court could have addressed the true facts, and it seems likely that the court would have concluded that the defendant was not acting as an executor at all. As such, he would not have occupied a fiduciary position vis-à-vis the testator's estate, nor would he have owed non-fiduciary duties that conflicted with his personal interest in purchasing property from that estate. *Holder* is an instance of poor advocacy making a hard case into bad law. Contrary to Shepherd's argument, that does not provide a sound basis on which to analyse fiduciary doctrine.

The more principled approach advocated here has been adopted in other similar cases where the courts have not been hamstrung by inadequate advocacy.[45] As Vinelott J explained in *Re Thompson's Settlement*, 'the reason why the rule did not apply [in *Holder*] was that [the defendant] had never acted as executor in a way which could be taken to amount to acceptance of a duty to act in the interests of the beneficiaries under his father's will.'[46] Without any such duty, the fiduciary conflict principle would not invalidate his purchase of property from the estate.

The moulding of fiduciary duties to the circumstances of each case does ensure an element of flexibility in the way that fiduciary doctrine is applied. However, that flexibility is best understood as an application of the plasticity built into the fiduciary principles themselves, by their response to non-fiduciary duties and factual interests, rather than as a judicial freedom to refuse to reach results that fiduciary duties would otherwise dictate simply because the judge considers those results inappropriate in a particular case. Understanding the moulding of fiduciary duties in this way provides a stable and sustainable doctrinal framework within which judges can work, without the doctrine becoming a byword for unruly judicial discretion.

II. The Vital Nature of Non-fiduciary Duties

A. Consequence of the Protective Function

The protective function that fiduciary doctrine serves vis-à-vis non-fiduciary duties carries a further natural corollary, related to the need to scrutinise carefully the non-fiduciary duties owed in each case. It is vital to the sensible functioning of fiduciary duties that there be non-fiduciary duties owed by the fiduciary: in the absence of any non-fiduciary duties, there is nothing for fiduciary doctrine to protect and thus no sensible function for fiduciary doctrine to serve. In other words, non-fiduciary duties are necessary for the existence of fiduciary duties.

---

[44]   *Ibid*, 397.
[45]   See, eg, *Guest v Smythe* (1870) LR 5 Ch App 551 (LJ). See also *Stacey v Elph* (1833) 1 My & K 195, 199 (39 ER 655) (MR).
[46]   *Re Thompson's Settlement* [1986] 1 Ch 99, 116.

Apparently disagreeing with this view, Paul Finn said of the fiduciary conflict principle:

> The term 'duty' in the rule is used in no technical sense. It does not mean, for example, that the existence of a fiduciary relationship depends upon it being shown that the undertaking given embodies duties of a legally enforceable character.[47]

However, in the same book he also said:

> Until the scope and ambit of the duties assumed by the fiduciary have been ascertained—until the 'subject matter over which the fiduciary obligations extend' has been defined—no question of conflict of duty and interest can arise. You must ascertain what the fiduciary has undertaken to do, before you can say he has permitted his interests to conflict with his undertaking.[48]

As will be apparent, the second of these two passages more closely resembles the argument advanced in this book and, it is suggested, more accurately reflects the state of the law on fiduciary doctrine.[49] Apart from the countless statements of the fiduciary conflict principle that refer to a conflict between duty and interest, it is worth referring also to Lord Young's observation in *Huntington Copper & Sulphur Co Ltd v Henderson*:

> [It is] a large and important principle [that] a person who is charged with the duty of attending to the interest of another shall not bring his own interest into competition with his duty. It is immaterial, as many cases illustrate, what may be the particular relation which raises the duty, provided only it raises a duty, as reposed on trust, of which the law takes cognisance.[50]

While the need for non-fiduciary duties is relatively obvious in the context of fiduciary doctrine's various conflict principles, it is perhaps less obvious whether the profit principle is consistent with the view that non-fiduciary duties are essential to the operation of fiduciary doctrine. Peter Birks said that 'in *almost* every case, the rule against conflicts defines the profits that may not be taken' (emphasis added).[51] It is true that cases in which that is not so will be few in number, but Birks' approach leaves unanswered the question what happens when the conflict rule does not define the profits that may not be taken. As was

---

[47] PD Finn, *Fiduciary Obligations* (Sydney, Law Book Co, 1977) [471].
[48] *Ibid*, [541].
[49] The reason for the difference between Finn's two statements seems to lie in a concern in the first passage to include within fiduciary doctrine situations such as gratuitous agency, wherein it is unclear whether any positive duties to act can be enforced against the fiduciary. However, even in such situations, enforceable non-fiduciary duties can arise apart from positive duties to act: see generally FMB Reynolds, *Bowstead & Reynolds on Agency*, 18th edn (London, Sweet & Maxwell, 2006) [6–001], [6–005] and [6–026]; FE Dowrick, 'The Relationship of Principal and Agent' (1954) 17 *Modern Law Review* 24, 25–28.
[50] *Huntington Copper & Sulphur Co Ltd v Henderson* (1877) 4 SC (4th Series) 294, 299 (OH), approved on appeal: pp 304, 305, 306 and 308.
[51] PBH Birks, 'The Content of Fiduciary Obligation' (2000) 34 *Israel Law Review* 3, 10 (fn 18).

discussed earlier,[52] the profit principle grew out of the conflict principle as a prophylactic extension to that fundamental principle. At its foundation, therefore, it reflects the same sort of protective function as the conflict principle. When a fiduciary is found accountable under the profit principle alone, he will have had a function to perform, and he will have been in a fiduciary relationship. Such functions give rise to non-fiduciary duties with which the fiduciary must comply. Thus, although the profit principle does not on its own terms require the identification of a duty that conflicts with the fiduciary's interest in a transaction, it still reflects fiduciary doctrine's protective function and operates only when there are non-fiduciary duties owed to the principal. As Lord MacMillan explained in *Regal (Hastings) v Gulliver*, the directors in that case were accountable 'for any profit which they made, if it was by reason and in virtue of their fiduciary office as directors that they entered into the transaction'.[53] Or as Lord Russell of Killowen put it in the same case, 'having obtained these shares by reason and only by reason of the fact that they were directors of Regal and in the course of the execution of that office, [they] are accountable for the profits which they have made out of them.'[54] The importance of these statements is that they make clear that the liability to account for unauthorised profits only arises 'if a person in a fiduciary relationship makes a secret profit out of the relationship'.[55] The 'relationship' is itself defined by and embodied in non-fiduciary duties.

Thus, non-fiduciary duties are vital to fiduciary liability. Without non-fiduciary duties one cannot make sense of the fiduciary concept of loyalty as it has been developed and applied in the case law: fiduciary duties are conceptually separate and distinct from non-fiduciary duties but practically cannot exist without non-fiduciary duties. In Peter Birks' terminology, 'while the obligation of care can exist on its own, the obligation of disinterestedness cannot.'[56] Hence, Birks described the fiduciary duty as 'parasitic'[57] on the non-fiduciary duty. While this highlights the need for a non-fiduciary duty in order that the fiduciary duty exist and survive, the parasitic metaphor is apt to mislead as it suggests a relationship quite opposite to the true protective function served by fiduciary doctrine.

---

[52] See above ch 5, section III-B.
[53] *Regal (Hastings) Ltd v Gulliver* [1967] 2 AC 134n, 153.
[54] *Ibid*, 149.
[55] *Ibid*, 154; see also pp 144 and 159. And see *Williams v Barton* [1927] 2 Ch 9, 13; *Re Macadam* [1946] 1 Ch 73, 82; *Attorney-General for Hong Kong v Reid* [1994] 1 AC 324, 338 (PC); *Warman International Ltd v Dwyer* (1995) 182 CLR 544, 557.
[56] Birks (above n 51) 28–29.
[57] *Ibid*, 29, 31 and 33.

B. Potential Counter-examples

The vast bulk of the case law is consistent with the view that non-fiduciary duties are necessary in order for there to be fiduciary liability, but some cases appear to contradict that argument. These therefore need to be addressed.

i. Preventing Circumvention of Fiduciary Protection

In *Bolkiah v KPMG*, Lord Millett observed that the 'fiduciary relationship which subsists between solicitor and client comes to an end with the termination of the retainer.'[58] Similarly, the Court of Appeal said in *Attorney-General v Blake*:

> We do not recognise the concept of a fiduciary obligation which continues notwith-standing the determination of the particular relationship which gives rise to it. Equity does not demand a duty of undivided loyalty from a former employee to his former employer... [T]hese duties last only as long as the relationship which gives rise to them lasts.[59]

These comments are consistent with the view that has just been advanced, in that they indicate that a fiduciary relationship is dependent upon the continued existence of an underlying relationship involving duties: once that underlying relationship has been terminated, the basis for the imposition of fiduciary duties is gone, in that the termination means there are no longer any non-fiduciary duties owed and hence nothing that requires protection.

However, fiduciary doctrines are sometimes applied after the fiduciary relationship has been terminated. The explanation for these cases is that they are instances in which a fiduciary has sought to circumvent fiduciary doctrine's protection, for example by retiring from his position. Fiduciary doctrine is alive to the possibility of fiduciaries seeking to skirt around its protective principles and does what it can to prevent such tactics from being effective. However, these mechanisms for preventing the avoidance of fiduciary doctrine's protection do not contradict the need for non-fiduciary duties to exist in order that fiduciary duties make sense. The application of fiduciary doctrine in this way can be rationalised in two alternative ways, both of which indicate the important relationship between fiduciary and non-fiduciary duties.

First, on pragmatic grounds,[60] and consistently with equity's general concern with intention and substance over form,[61] fiduciary doctrine will not permit a fiduciary to retire from a fiduciary relationship in order to purchase property if

---

[58] *Bolkiah v KPMG* [1999] 2 AC 222, 235.

[59] *Attorney-General v Blake* [1998] Ch 439, 453–54. See also *CMS Dolphin Ltd v Simonet* [2001] 2 BCLC 704 at [95] (ChD); *Foster Bryant Surveying Ltd v Bryant* [2007] EWCA Civ 200 at [8] and [68], [2007] 2 BCLC 239.

[60] *Foster Bryant Surveying Ltd v Bryant* [2007] EWCA Civ 200 at [76], [2007] 2 BCLC 239.

[61] See RP Meagher, JD Heydon and MJ Leeming, *Meagher, Gummow & Lehane's Equity: Doctrines and Remedies*, 4th edn (Chatswood, Butterworths LexisNexis, 2002) [3–160]–[3–200].

that would not have been permitted while the relationship still subsisted.[62] Similarly, a fiduciary cannot sell property to a third party when there is an 'understanding or agreement in honour, or in any other shape'[63] that the fiduciary will repurchase it from the third party once the property is no longer subject to the fiduciary relationship, if it is effectively a sale to the third party on behalf of the fiduciary.[64] Nor can a trustee arrange a transaction and then resign in order to put the transaction into effect if the transaction could not have been entered into while the trustee remained in post.[65] In each case, fiduciary doctrine is being applied to stifle the fiduciary's attempt to elude fiduciary doctrine's protection of non-fiduciary duties. In that sense, one can say that 'fiduciary duties may survive the termination of the relationship that first called those duties into being,'[66] but 'it must . . . be borne in mind that the rationale here is to *prevent* the use of resignation as a device to evade strict fiduciary obligations.'[67] Hence, when the fiduciary did not resign from his fiduciary position with a view to exploiting an otherwise impermissible opportunity, fiduciary doctrine does not intervene. As Buckley J said of a former trustee in *Re Boles & British Land Co's Contract*:

> [I]f he retired with a view to becoming a purchaser so as to put himself in a position to do what would otherwise be a breach of trust, that will not do. But if he has retired and there is nothing to shew that at the time of the retirement there was any idea of a sale, and in fact there is no sale for twelve years after his retirement, is there anything to prevent him from becoming a purchaser? I think not.[68]

---

[62] *Ex parte James* (1803) 8 Ves 337, 352 (32 ER 385) (LC); *Re Boles & British Land Co's Contract* [1902] 1 Ch 244, 246; *Spincode Pty Ltd v Look Software Pty Ltd* [2001] VSCA 248 at [56], (2002) 4 VR 501. (See also *Cholmondeley v Clinton* (1815) 19 Ves 261, 276 (34 ER 515), although that decision appears to have been based on confidentiality of information.) Of course, as with all fiduciary principles, the principal's consent in such a situation will absolve the fiduciary from liability but only if it is fully informed. Thus, for example, Cooley's attempts to gain his company's consent to the termination of his fiduciary directorship in *Industrial Development Consultants Ltd v Cooley* [1972] 1 WLR 442, so that he could personally take up a lucrative contract with another company, EGB, were wholly ineffective because he lied to his company about his health in order to gain his release, thereby avoiding telling the company that he was actually seeking to enter into the contract with EGB.
[63] *Re Postlethwaite* (1888) 37 WR 200, 202 (CA).
[64] *McPherson v Watt* (above n 17) 263, 266 and 272; *Re Postlethwaite (dec'd)* (1888) 59 LT 58, 60 (ChD); *Re Postlethwaite* (*ibid*) 202.
[65] *Spring v Pride* (1864) 4 De GJ & S 395 (46 ER 971) (LJJ); *Wright v Morgan* [1926] AC 788, 796 (PC). See also *Industrial Development Consultants v Cooley* (above n 62).
[66] *Edmonds v Donovan* [2005] VSCA 27 at [56], (2005) 12 VR 513. See also *Longstaff v Birtles* [2001] EWCA Civ 1219 at [1], [2002] 1 WLR 470. The incoherence of the reasoning in *Longstaff v Birtles* is addressed below: see text accompanying nn 84–89.
[67] P Koh, 'Once a Director, Always a Fiduciary?' [2003] *Cambridge Law Journal* 403, 417; see also pp 421 and 423.
[68] *Re Boles & British Land Co's Contract* (above n 62) 246–47. See also *Island Export Finance Ltd v Umunna* [1986] BCLC 460, 482–83 (QBD); *Hunter Kane Ltd v Watkins* [2003] EWHC 186 (Ch) at [25] and [27]; *Foster Bryant Surveying Ltd v Bryant* [2007] EWCA Civ 200 at [87] and [89], [2007] 2 BCLC 239.

Pursuant to this first rationalisation, fiduciary doctrine's prophylactic protection of non-fiduciary duties can be said to extend beyond the formal termination of the underlying relationship, but only when the purpose of the termination is to circumvent the protection that fiduciary doctrine would otherwise provide. As has been seen, that protection is of non-fiduciary duties. The fact that fiduciary doctrine extends in this way beyond the formal termination of the retainer in order to ensure that its protection of those non-fiduciary duties is not emasculated does not mean that fiduciary duties materialise out of thin air without any need for or reference to non-fiduciary duties.

Secondly, one can also rationalise these cases as applications of the normal fiduciary conflict and profit principles. For example, a director who resigns will nonetheless be liable under the profit principle 'if, after his resignation, he uses for his own benefit property of the company or information which he has acquired while a director'.[69] The profit principle only applies when the unauthorised profit arose within the 'scope' of the fiduciary relationship, which means that there must be some connection between the profit and the non-fiduciary duties that comprised the relationship before it came to an end. Thus, the profit principle is inherently linked to the relationship itself and thereby to the duties that comprise that relationship. Furthermore, the conflict principle can also apply to the fiduciary's conduct after he has resigned his fiduciary position because 'the fact that he retires in order to effect that purpose means that the decision to effect that purpose has been taken during the period of his trusteeship when he was actually performing the duties of a trustee.'[70] In other words, in taking the decision to retire in order to take an opportunity that fiduciary doctrine would otherwise deny to him, the fiduciary acted with a conflict between his non-fiduciary duties and his personal interest.[71]

Whichever of these two rationalisations is adopted, the mechanisms by which fiduciary doctrine prevents the undermining of its protective function do not themselves undermine the view that fiduciary doctrine is dependent on the existence of non-fiduciary duties.

ii. Solicitors Cases

In *McMaster v Byrne* the Privy Council held that a solicitor acted in breach of duty when he exercised an option over shares held by the claimant and traded them profitably without disclosing all material facts within his knowledge to the claimant. This was so, notwithstanding that the solicitor was not acting as solicitor for the claimant in the disputed transaction, on the basis that there was

---

[69] *Ultraframe (UK) Ltd v Fielding* [2005] EWHC 1638 (Ch) at [1309].
[70] *Gould v O'Carroll* [1964] NSWR 803, 805.
[71] See also *Foster Bryant Surveying Ltd v Bryant* [2007] EWCA Civ 200 at [69], [2007] 2 BCLC 239; Companies Act 2006 (UK), s 170(2).

an ongoing relationship of confidence arising from the fact that the solicitor had acted for the claimant in respect of several matters in the past.[72]

The difficulty that arises is in explaining the precise basis for the liability in *McMaster v Byrne*. One possibility is that an ongoing relationship between a solicitor and client (or another fiduciary and principal) might create an expectation that the solicitor will provide assistance as and when the client brings issues to the solicitor. This might give rise to some form of contractual or tort-based obligation to provide such assistance, or at least to act carefully when providing it. That would then provide the requisite non-fiduciary duty in relation to which fiduciary liability might arise if the solicitor has a conflicting interest. As the Privy Council said in *Demerara Bauxite v Hubbard*, 'whether in any particular transaction any duty exists which makes the relationship between the parties that of solicitor and client, will depend upon all the circumstances of the particular case.'[73] However, there is no 'office' of solicitor, so that a solicitor's retainer ordinarily lasts only for the length of the particular business for which he is retained.[74] Hence, this explanation will rarely work.

Alternatively, a conflict might arise between, on the one hand, the solicitor's duty to use 'special knowledge' that he obtained during the currency of his retainer only for the benefit of the client[75] and, on the other hand, his personal interest in a transaction in which that information is relevant. This possibility is suggested by *Allison v Clayhills*,[76] which was relied upon in *McMaster* for the proposition that 'the duty of the solicitor may continue after the relationship of solicitor and client in its strict sense has been discontinued.'[77] In *Allison v Clayhills*, Parker J observed that the conflict principle could apply, even after the solicitor was no longer strictly retained as such, but only if the solicitor continued to owe some form of recognisable non-fiduciary duty that relates to the transaction:

> [W]hen the relationship is of such a nature that it does not impose on the solicitor any duty towards his client in the particular transaction, then the principle has no application. . . [T]he test appears to me to be . . . whether *in the particular transaction, he owes his client any duty in the contemplation of a court of equity.* If he owes his client any duty in the particular transaction . . . the solicitor is, I think, solicitor *in hac re* within the meaning of the decisions although not retained to act as solicitor in the transaction or, indeed, in any pending transaction at all. Thus, if a solicitor is actually engaged to conduct or is conducting for his client an action, say, for slander, and, while that action is pending, meets his client in the hunting field and bargains and buys from him a horse, each party relying upon his own knowledge of horseflesh, that transaction will stand on the same footing as a transaction between strangers, because the matter is

---

[72] *McMaster v Byrne* [1952] 1 All ER 1362, 1367–68 (PC).
[73] *Demerara Bauxite Co Ltd v Hubbard* [1923] AC 673, 676 (PC).
[74] See text accompanying n 34 above.
[75] See, eg, *Carter v Palmer* (1842) 8 Cl & Fin 657, 705–6 and 707 (8 ER 256) (HL).
[76] *Allison v Clayhills* (above n 17).
[77] *McMaster v Byrne* (above n 72) 1368.

entirely outside any confidential relationship between the parties and, the solicitor owes his client no duty whatever in the particular matter (emphasis added).[78]

Thus, in *Allison v Clayhills*, Parker J recognised the importance of identifying a connection between the solicitor's non-fiduciary duty and the transaction in question before applying the fiduciary conflict principle. That was lost sight of by the Privy Council in *McMaster v Byrne*.

Paul Finn described *McMaster v Byrne* as a 'significant development' in ensuring that fiduciary doctrine's rules are not too easily defeated by, for example, fiduciaries retiring.[79] As has been seen already, that concern can justify fiduciary principles being applied in a way that appears to involve their extension beyond the formal cessation of a retainer,[80] but the extension ought to be limited to situations in which there is a real risk that the fiduciary might have been attempting to circumvent the protection offered by fiduciary doctrine.

An alternative explanation for *McMaster v Byrne*, which fits more satisfactorily with the relevant legal principles, is for it to be understood as a case resting on a presumption of undue influence.[81] Solicitors are presumed to have influence over their clients,[82] and the doctrine of undue influence can apply beyond the termination of the solicitor's retainer itself, because the influence that arises out of a relationship does not necessarily cease simply because the solicitor's formal duties have ceased.[83]

The Court of Appeal's decision in *Longstaff v Birtles*[84] vividly illustrates the incoherence of applying fiduciary duties in the absence of any non-fiduciary duties. The Longstaffs sought to purchase a particular pub and instructed Mr Birtles to act as their solicitor. The negotiations to purchase the pub failed, and Birtles suggested that they invest in a partnership that owned and ran another pub, without revealing that he was one of the partners. The Longstaffs did so, but the partnership failed. The Court of Appeal held that there was neither a general retainer, nor any assumption of responsibility such as would ground a duty of care after the solicitor's retainer had ended when the negotiations to buy the first pub failed.[85] However, notwithstanding that conclusion, Mummery LJ held that

there was a relationship of trust and confidence [which] did not cease on the termination of the retainer in respect of the intended purchase of the Moorcock Inn; that during the course of that relationship a personal business opportunity presented itself to the solicitors; that the solicitors took advantage of that opportunity to propose that the Longstaffs buy into the partnership of the Castle Hotel at Brough; that in the

---

[78] *Allison v Clayhills* (above n 17) 711–12.

[79] Finn, *Fiduciary Obligations* (above n 47) [443]–[444].

[80] See above section II-B(i).

[81] See, eg, *Boardman v Phipps* (above n 25) 126.

[82] See, eg, *Wright v Carter* (above n 18); *Royal Bank of Scotland plc v Etridge (No 2)* [2001] UKHL 44 at [18], [2002] 2 AC 773. See also *Newman v Payne* (1793) 2 Ves Jun 199 (30 ER 593) (LC).

[83] *Wright v Proud* (above n 18) 138. See also *Wright v Carter* (above n 18) 53.

[84] *Longstaff v Birtles* [2001] EWCA Civ 1219, [2002] 1 WLR 470.

[85] *Ibid* at [33].

context of the relationship the proposal gave rise to a situation in which the *duty* of the solicitors might conflict with their interest; and that they acted in breach of fiduciary duty in continuing to deal with the Longstaffs, in a situation of conflict of *duty* and interest (emphasis added).[86]

Laws LJ added:

I am firmly of the view that the basis on which the claimants are entitled to succeed is and is only that . . . the defendant solicitors are shown to have been in breach of a duty of trust and confidence imposed on them by equity, as Mummery LJ has explained. The suggestion that they might owe an additional duty, arising at common law in tort, is to my mind the fifth wheel of the coach: confusing and unnecessary.[87]

Notwithstanding its later commendation by Auld LJ in *Conway v Ratiu* as 'an authoritative illustration of the readiness of the courts, regardless of the precise issue involved, to draw back the corporate veil to do justice when common-sense and reality demand it',[88] the court's reasoning in *Longstaff v Birtles* was incoherent and reveals it to be another instance of hard cases making bad law.[89] Having concluded, as Mummery LJ did, that the solicitors owed *no* non-fiduciary duty, it is impossible to reach his conclusion that there was a 'conflict between *duty* and interest'. Contrary to Laws LJ's view that non-fiduciary duties are 'the fifth wheel of the coach', they are fundamentally necessary to its coherent operation. Neither *Longstaff v Birtles* nor *McMaster v Byrne* provides any compelling reason to think that non-fiduciary duties are not essential to the existence and operation of fiduciary doctrine.

Another context, again involving solicitors, in which the issue of fiduciary duties surviving beyond the termination of the formal retainer has arisen is when a solicitor seeks to act for a client against the interests of a former client. The House of Lords rejected the possibility of fiduciary duties applying in that situation in England in *Bolkiah v KPMG*.[90] Specifically, once the retainer has ended, fiduciary duties do not prevent a fiduciary from acting against a former client, although the doctrine protecting confidential information may do so.[91]

However, building on the proposition that fiduciary principles are in some circumstances applied beyond the termination of the retainer, *stricto sensu*, some

---

[86] *Ibid* at [35].

[87] *Ibid* at [39].

[88] *Conway v Ratiu* [2005] EWCA Civ 1302 at [75], [2006] 1 All ER 571n. It is entirely unclear why Auld LJ considered the 'corporate veil' at all relevant to *Longstaff v Birtles*, given no corporations were involved in that case.

[89] Mummery LJ himself observed that 'the facts are redolent of some famous judgments of Lord Denning MR': *Longstaff v Birtles* [2001] EWCA Civ 1219 at [3], [2002] 1 WLR 470. Furthermore, the fiduciary argument only surfaced during the course of the appeal hearing.

[90] *Bolkiah v KPMG* (above n 58).

[91] *Ibid*, 235. See also *Foster Bryant Surveying Ltd v Bryant* [2007] EWCA Civ 200 at [8] and [68]–[69], [2007] 2 BCLC 239; *Winters v Mishcon de Reya* (above n 34) [86] and [88]. While the retainer remains *current*, fiduciary principles will apply: *Bolkiah v KPMG* (above n 58) 234–35; *UTi (Aust) Pty Ltd v Piper Alderman* [2008] NSWSC 219 at [30]–[38].

Australian decisions have taken a broader view than that adopted in *Bolkiah*. In *Spincode v Look Software*, for example, Brooking JA endorsed in obiter dicta 'the wider view . . . that the equitable obligation of "loyalty" is not observed by a solicitor who acts against a former client in the same matter'.[92] Other Australian cases have followed suit.[93] Even in Australia, however, this fiduciary approach to the question has not met with uniform acceptance, and the weight of authority favours the approach in *Bolkiah* over that suggested in *Spincode*.[94] Given that one must distort fiduciary principles in order to make them cover such situations, it is preferable for a court in such cases to 'intervene in the exercise of its general jurisdiction over solicitors as officers of the court'[95] if it wishes to control solicitors acting against former clients. Approaching the matter in that way better reflects the true objection to solicitors acting in such situations, while at the same

---

[92] *Spincode Pty Ltd v Look Software Pty Ltd* [2001] VSCA 248 at [53], (2002) 4 VR 501.

[93] See, eg, *Sent v John Fairfax Publication Pty Ltd* [2002] VSC 429 at [98]–[104]; *Disctronics Ltd v Edmonds* [2002] VSC 454 at [168]–[171]; *Australian Liquor Marketers Pty Ltd v Tasman Liquor Traders Pty Ltd* [2002] VSC 324 at [17]; *Wagdy Hanna & Associates Pty Ltd v National Library of Australia* [2004] ACTSC 75 at [55], (2004) 185 FLR 367; *Pinnacle Living Pty Ltd v Elusive Image Pty Ltd* [2006] VSC 202 at [13]; *Adam 12 Holdings Pty Ltd v Eat & Drink Holdings Pty Ltd* [2006] VSC 152 at [40]; *Main-Road Property Group Pty Ltd v Pelligra & Sons Pty Ltd* [2007] VSC 43 at [65]; *Commonwealth Bank of Australia v Kyriackou* [2008] VSC 146 at [10].

[94] See, eg, *Bureau Interprofessionnel Des Vins De Bourgogne v Red Earth Nominees Pty Ltd* [2002] FCA 588 at [17]–[18]; *PhotoCure ASA v Queen's University at Kingston* [2002] FCA 905 at [48] and [55], (2002) 56 Intellectual Prop Rep 86; *Rothschild v Mullins* [2002] TASSC 100 at [12]; *Belan v Casey* [2002] NSWSC 58 at [15]–[21]; *British American Tobacco Australia Services Ltd v Blanch* [2004] NSWSC 70 at [97]–[104]; *Durban Roodepoort Deep Ltd v Reilly* [2004] WASC 269 at [58]; *Anton v PKB Veterinary Supplies Pty Ltd* [2004] WASC 107 at [22]; *Blythe v Northwood* [2005] NSWCA 221 at [195], (2005) 63 NSWLR 531; *Kallinicos v Hunt* [2005] NSWSC 1181 at [76], (2005) 64 NSWLR 561; *Asia Pacific Telecommunications Ltd v Optus Networks Pty Ltd* [2005] NSWSC 550 at [54]; *Zalfen v Gates* [2006] WASC 296 at [64] and [69]; *Ismail-Zai v Western Australia* [2007] WASCA 150 at [23], (2007) 34 WAR 379; *Styles v O'Brien* [2007] TASSC 13 at [15]–[19]; *Styles v O'Brien* [2007] TASSC 67 at [14]–[19], (2007) 16 Tas R 268; *Salfinger v Niugini Mining (Australia) Pty Ltd* [2007] FCA 470 at [28]; *Asia Pacific Telecommunications Ltd v Optus Networks Pty Ltd* [2007] NSWSC 350 at [31]; *Qihua Zhao v Sheng Yu Zhang* [2007] NSWSC 891 at [26]–[28]; *Billington v Billington (No 2)* [2008] FamCA 409 at [35].
Several cases decided before *Spincode* also followed *Bolkiah*: see, eg, *Beach Petroleum NL v Abbott Tout Russell Kennedy* [1999] NSWCA 408 at [204]–[205], (1999) 48 NSWLR 1; *Newman v Phillips Fox* [1999] WASC 171 at [20], (1999) 21 WAR 309; *A v Law Society of Tasmania* (2001) 10 Tas R 152 at [46]–[58].

[95] *Winters v Mishcon de Reya* (above n 34) [94]. See also *Grimwade v Meagher* [1995] 1 VR 446, 452; *Oceanic Life Ltd v HIH Casualty & General Insurance Ltd* [1999] NSWSC 292 at [48], (1999) 10 ANZ Ins Cases 74,968; *Pott v Jones Mitchell* [2004] QSC 48 at [21], [2004] 2 Qd R 298; *Kallinicos v Hunt* [2005] NSWSC 1181 at [66] and [76], (2005) 64 NSWLR 561; *Geelong School Supplies Pty Ltd v Dean* [2006] FCA 1404 at [26]; *Re Westgate Wool Co Pty Ltd* [2006] SASC 372 at [48], (2006) 206 FLR 190. And see *Davies v Clough* (1837) 8 Sim 262, 267 (59 ER 105) (VC); *Kooky Garments Ltd v Charlton* [1994] 1 NZLR 587, 590.
This is not a 'duty to the former client' and so is not ruled out by *Bolkiah v KPMG* (above n 58) 235. The jurisdiction clearly includes the power to enjoin a solicitor from acting, but it also includes a power to award compensation, at least where the malfeasance takes place 'in a matter in which the Court has seizin': *Marsh v Joseph* [1897] 1 Ch 213, 245 (CA). See also *Dixon v Wilkinson* (1859) 4 De G & J 508, 522–23 (45 ER 198) (LJJ); *Re Dudley* (1883) 12 QBD 44, 47 (CA); *Batten v Wedgwood Coal & Iron Co* (1886) 31 ChD 346, 349; *Re Grey* [1892] 2 QB 440, 443 and 447–48 (CA).

time ensuring that fiduciary doctrine is not stretched too far out of shape in the pursuit of an objective that is not one of its core purposes.

iii. Negotiations towards Joint Ventures

Joint ventures are not, in Anglo-Australian law,[96] a recognised category of fiduciary relationship.[97] As Toulson LJ explained in *BBC Worldwide v Bee Load*,

> it is perfectly common for commercial entities to want to enter into cooperative arrangements for a specific purpose, involving a share of profits, but without intending to follow the route of mutual agency and the court should give effect to their intentions.[98]

Nonetheless, when parties have arranged a joint venture in such a way that a mutual agency has been created between them, fiduciary duties can arise.[99] When that is the case, the joint venture arrangements will involve duties owed between the parties, in respect of which fiduciary doctrine can sensibly perform its protection function.

In some cases, however, the courts have found that parties owe one another fiduciary duties in circumstances in which they have been negotiating towards a formal joint venture agreement. In *United Dominions Corp v Brian*,[100] for example, the High Court of Australia held that one of three parties negotiating the terms of a joint venture agreement committed a breach of fiduciary duty by using joint venture property as security for a loan that it owed in respect of matters wholly unrelated to the joint venture. Mason, Brennan and Deane JJ observed that 'a fiduciary relationship can arise and fiduciary duties can exist between parties who have not reached, and who may never reach, agreement upon the consensual terms which are to govern the relationship between them.'[101] This seems to suggest that fiduciary duties can arise in the absence of non-fiduciary duties.

However, as always, it is important to understand this comment in the context of the case in which it was uttered.[102] The parties were in negotiations towards

---

[96]   The position is apparently different in the United States: see, eg, *Meinhard v Salmon* 164 NE 545, 546 (1928).

[97]   See, eg, *Global Container Lines v Bonyad Shipping* (above n 14) 546–47; *Explora Group plc v Hesco Bastion Ltd* [2005] EWCA Civ 646 at [51]; *Gibson Motorsport Merchandise Pty Ltd v Forbes* [2006] FCAFC 44 at [2], (2006) 149 FCR 569; *Button v Phelps* [2006] EWHC 53 (Ch) at [59]–[61]; *Ross River Ltd v Cambridge City Football Club Ltd* [2007] EWHC 2115 (Ch) at [197], [2008] 1 All ER 1004.

[98]   *BBC Worldwide v Bee Load* (above n 9) [107].

[99]   See, eg, *United Dominions Corporation Ltd v Brian Pty Ltd* (1985) 157 CLR 1, 7–8, 12–13 and 16; *Fawcett v Whitehouse* (1829) 1 Russ & M 132, 148 (39 ER 51); *Nathan v Smilovitch* [2002] EWHC 1629 (Ch) at [8]–[12]; *Murad v Al-Saraj* [2004] EWHC 1235 (Ch) at [325]–[341], not challenged on appeal on this issue: [2005] EWCA Civ 959, [2005] WTLR 1573; *Chirnside v Fay* [2006] NZSC 68, [2007] 1 NZLR 433.

[100]   *United Dominions Corp Ltd v Brian Pty Ltd* (1985) 157 CLR 1.

[101]   Ibid, 12. See also *Fraser Edmiston Pty Ltd v AGT (Qld) Pty Ltd* [1988] 2 Qd R 1, 9.

[102]   *Boardman v Phipps* (above n 25) 125.

the creation of a partnership, but they had already 'acted upon the proposed agreement'.[103] As Sundberg and Emmett JJ said in *Gibson Motorsport v Forbes*, 'a fiduciary relationship, with attendant fiduciary obligations, may exist between prospective partners who have embarked upon the conduct of the partnership, business or venture before the precise terms of the partnership agreement have been settled.'[104] Indeed, in most of the cases that have found fiduciary duties to exist prior to a formal joint venture agreement being reached the parties had already embarked upon the venture.[105] Thus, in *Goose v Wilson Sandford & Co*,[106] the Court of Appeal distinguished *UDC v Brian* and held that no fiduciary relationship had arisen between proposed joint venturers, on the basis that the parties had not yet embarked on the venture.

The importance of this in the present context is that when the venture has been embarked upon, courts will frequently find that the parties owe obligations to one another, notwithstanding that those non-fiduciary duties might subsequently be superseded by a more detailed and comprehensive partnership or joint venture agreement if one is entered into.[107] This is so when the court concludes that the parties did not intend their arrangement to be completely legally unregulated.[108] Importantly for present purposes, it shows that non-fiduciary duties can be owed in such situations, even though the parties are still negotiating towards a final agreement, based on the parties' conduct and preliminary arrangements.

The connection between embarking on the venture and the legal duties that can attend such conduct was drawn by Giles JA in *Cassis v Kalfus (No 2)*, when he explained:

---

[103]   *United Dominions v Brian* (above n 100) 16; see also p 7.

[104]   *Gibson Motorsport Merchandise Pty Ltd v Forbes* [2006] FCAFC 44 at [75], (2006) 149 FCR 569. See also *United Dominions v Brian* (above n 100) 12.

[105]   See, eg, *Schipp v Cameron* [1998] NSWSC 997 at [720], not disturbed on appeal as to this point: *Harrison v Schipp* [2001] NSWCA 13 at [65]; *Burger King Corp v Hungry Jack's Pty Ltd* [2001] NSWCA 187 at [567]–[573], (2001) 69 NSWLR 558; *Chirnside v Fay* [2006] NZSC 68 at [52], [71], [90] and [92], [2007] 1 NZLR 433.

[106]   *Goose v Wilson Sandford & Co* [2001] Lloyd's Rep PN 189 at [83] and [85].

[107]   As to the possibility of contractual duties arising, even when the arrangements appear incomplete, when the parties have embarked upon a venture, see, eg, *G Percy Trentham Ltd v Archital Luxfer Ltd* [1993] 1 Lloyd's Rep 25, 29–30 (CA); *First Energy (UK) Ltd v Hungarian International Bank Ltd* [1993] 2 Lloyd's Rep 194, 205 (CA); *Khan v Miah* [2000] 1 WLR 2123, 2127–28 (HL). See also HG Beale (ed), *Chitty on Contracts*, 30th edn (London, Sweet & Maxwell, 2008) [2–113]–[2–114]; and see [2–005], [2–028] and [2–030]–[2–031].

[108]   Thus, when preliminary agreements are expressly made 'subject to contract', the possibility of arguing that obligations have arisen is severely diminished, on the basis that the parties have chosen consciously to proceed without any legally binding obligations in place: see, eg, *Ramsden v Dyson* (1866) LR 1 HL 129, 145–46 and 170; *Attorney-General of Hong Kong v Humphreys Estate (Queen's Gardens) Ltd* [1987] AC 114, 127–28; *Cobbe v Yeoman's Row Management Ltd* [2008] UKHL 55 at [25], [53] and [61], [2008] 1 WLR 1752. For the same reason, it will also be very hard in such cases to show that fiduciary duties are owed: *Cobbe v Yeoman's Row Management Ltd* [2008] UKHL 55 at [81], [2008] 1 WLR 1752.

A fiduciary relationship may arise during negotiations for a partnership or a joint venture, before any partnership or joint venture agreement has been finally concluded, if the parties have acted upon the proposed agreement, or have acted on an informal arrangement to become partners or joint venturers and taken steps to establish or implement the partnership or joint venture. . . If partnership is not involved, whether there is such a relationship depends upon the nature of the particular joint venture *and the content of the obligations which the parties to it have undertaken* (emphasis added).[109]

Comments that suggest fiduciary duties can apply when no non-fiduciary duties exist must therefore be treated with caution.

iv. Bare Trusts

Bare trusts present something of a curiosity when considering whether fiduciary duties can apply in the absence of non-fiduciary duties. The orthodox view is that fiduciary duties do not apply to a bare trustee,[110] which would mean they are irrelevant to the question whether fiduciary duties are dependent on the existence of non-fiduciary duties. However, the authorities cited for that view are not as clear as the leading texts suggest, and there is some authority in support of the contrary view. If bare trustees do owe fiduciary duties, a question then arises as to whether any non-fiduciary duties exist in such circumstances.

Of the cases cited by the leading texts, there are statements in *Parkes v White*,[111] *Sutton v Jones*[112] and Kindersley VC's first instance decision in *Pooley v Quilter*[113] that a trustee to preserve contingent remainders is able to purchase from the beneficiary, which seems to mean such trustees are exempt from fiduciary doctrine's conflict principle, although these cases did not discuss the position of bare trustees in terms.

Several of the other cases cited by the leading texts are irrelevant to the question. *Naylor v Winch*, for example, concerned a transaction entered into by someone in his personal capacity as a residuary legatee, though he also happened to be an executor.[114] *Denton v Donner* involved a straightforward application of the fair-dealing rule. Romilly MR did refer to a 'mere trustee for sale'[115] but only in order to differentiate the fair-dealing rule from the self-dealing rule, both of

---

[109] *Cassis v Kalfus (No 2)* [2004] NSWCA 315 at [11].

[110] See, eg, A Underhill and DJ Hayton, *Law Relating to Trusts and Trustees*, 17th edn by DJ Hayton, PB Matthews and CCJ Mitchell (London, LexisNexis Butterworths, 2007) [59.35]; J Mowbray, L Tucker, N Le Poidevin, E Simpson and and J Brightwell, *Lewin on Trusts*, 18th edn (London, Sweet & Maxwell, 2008) [20–85]; Finn, *Fiduciary Obligations* (above n 47) [424]; DM Fox, *Property Rights in Money* (Oxford, Oxford University Press, 2008) [6.61]. See also EB Sugden, *Vendors and Purchasers of Estates*, 3rd edn (London, J Butterworth, 1808) 434; EA Swan, *Law Relating to Vendors and Purchasers* (London, Sweet & Maxwell, 1912) 166; WA Jolly and CHS Fifoot, *Seaborne's Vendors and Purchasers*, 9th edn (London, Butterworth & Co, 1926) 76 (fn q).

[111] *Parkes v White* (1805) 11 Ves 209, 226 (32 ER 1068) (LC).

[112] *Sutton v Jones* (1809) 15 Ves 584, 587 (33 ER 875) (LC).

[113] *Pooley v Quilter* (1858) 4 Drew 184, 189 (62 ER 71). The leading texts do not mention that Kindersley VC's decision was overturned on appeal: (1858) 2 De G & J 327 (44 ER 1016) (LJJ).

[114] *Naylor v Winch* (1824) 1 Sim & St 555, 567 (57 ER 219).

[115] *Denton v Donner* (1856) 23 Beav 285, 290 (53 ER 112).

which are applications of the fiduciary conflict principle. And *Guest v Smythe* concerned a purchase of property in a mortgagee foreclosure by someone who happened to be a solicitor but who had not acted as solicitor for the mortgagees or for the claimants. The parties for whom he had acted could have bought the property, and 'if they were not precluded from purchasing, why should their solicitor be precluded, this application being not by them against their own solicitor.'[116] None of these support the view that fiduciary duties do not apply to bare trustees.

The clearest authority in support of the orthodox view, albeit that its reasoning is rather conclusory, is *Sinnett v Darby*, where the court held that the fair-dealing rule did not apply because the defendants were 'bare dry trustees of the legal estate with no duty to the plaintiff other than to assign to her or as she should direct'.[117] As the Full Court put it, 'we think that relation, whatever title may be applied to it, is not a relation of trustee and *cestui que trust* within the meaning of the rule forbidding a trustee from buying from his *cestui que trust*.'[118] However, *Sinnett v Darby* appears not to have been cited or applied judicially since it was decided,[119] and some other more recent cases suggest the contrary.

In *Brown v Inland Revenue Commissioners*,[120] for instance, a solicitor who held money on behalf of his clients, which normally entails a bare trust,[121] was held to be 'in a fiduciary relationship to his client, and if and when he is entrusted with his client's money he can make no profit out of it'.[122] However, the fiduciary nature of the solicitor–client relationship itself provides a basis for stripping any unauthorised profits made by the solicitor, irrespective of whether there was a bare trust.

Similarly, in *China National Star Petroleum v Tor Drilling*, Lord Drummond Young noted:

> [T]he fiduciary, the defender, cannot place itself in a position where its own interest and its duty to the pursuer as beneficiary may conflict. . . In the event of such a conflict, the fiduciary must invariably yield to the instructions of the beneficiary. That is clearly illustrated in a case such as the present where the trustee holds property under a nominee relationship or bare trust.[123]

---

[116]   *Guest v Smythe* (above n 45) 557.
[117]   *Sinnett v Darby* (1887) 13 VLR 97, 99.
[118]   *Ibid*, 108.
[119]   The *Australian Case Citator* has no mention of *Sinnett v Darby* between the date it was decided and February 2009. Searches on electronic databases have also produced no citations of the decision.
[120]   *Brown v Inland Revenue Commissioners* [1965] AC 244.
[121]   See, eg, *Target Holdings Ltd v Redferns* [1996] AC 421, 436; P Matthews, 'All About Bare Trusts: Part 1' [2005] *Private Client Business* 266, 267.
[122]   *Brown v IRC* (above n 120) 265.
[123]   *China National Star Petroleum Co v Tor Drilling (UK) Ltd* [2002] SLT 1339 at [27]. Scottish and English law on fiduciary duties do not differ in any material respects: see, eg, *Aberdeen Railway v Blaikie Bros* (above n 10) 473–74 (HL); *McPherson v Watt* (above n 17) 270; *Brown v IRC* (above n 120) 265.

However, the comment was made to justify the view that a nominee must act in accordance with his principal's instructions, which can be justified on straight-forward contractual agency or non-fiduciary trust principles, without necessarily applying fiduciary principles. In *Persey v Bazley*, the Court of Appeal held that transferees of property who were

> bare trustees were effectively the nominee for the transferor. They were bound to do what they were told by the beneficial owners and only what they were told. The relationship between the transferors and the transferees was analogous to, if not the same as that between principal and agent, which be it remembered, is in any event of itself a fiduciary one.[124]

And in *Re Brooke Bond & Co Ltd's Trust Deed*, Cross J said of the fiduciary conflict principle, 'I can see no sound reason for saying that the rule does not apply to a custodian trustee as much as to an ordinary trustee.'[125] Again, however, the role of custodian trustee is defined by statute,[126] and distinctions have been drawn in other cases between the duties owed by custodian trustees and bare trustees.[127]

Hence, the position remains unclear. 'The mere separation of the legal and beneficial ownership does not ipso facto create a fiduciary relationship,'[128] but it is unclear whether an expressly created bare trusteeship or nomineeship carries with it the fiduciary conflict and profit principles. If the orthodox position is correct, and the fiduciary conflict principle does not apply to bare trustees and nominees, then such situations are not relevant to the question whether non-fiduciary duties can always be identified when fiduciary duties are enforced. On the other hand, if fiduciary principles can be applied to bare trustees, the question arises whether any non-fiduciary duties exist to which those fiduciary principles offer some form of protection.

That question is difficult to answer, in large part because the concept of 'bare trusteeship' is itself not a clear one. Some cases suggest that its defining charac-teristic is the trustee's lack of beneficial interest,[129] but the more modern view is that this is a necessary but insufficient qualification for bare trusteeship.[130] Thus, in *Herdegen v Federal Commissioner of Taxation*, Gummow J observed:

> Today the usually accepted meaning of 'bare' trust is a trust under which the trustee or trustees hold property without any interest therein, other than that existing by reason of

---

[124] *Persey v Bazley* (1984) 47 P & CR 37, 44 (CA).

[125] *Re Brooke Bond & Co Ltd's Trust Deed* [1963] 1 Ch 357, 365.

[126] Public Trustee Act 1906, s 4.

[127] See, eg, *Inland Revenue Commissioners v Silverts Ltd* [1951] Ch 521, 526 and 530–31 (CA).

[128] *R v Chester & North Wales Legal Aid Area Office (No 12), ex parte Floods of Queensferry Ltd* [1998] 1 WLR 1496, 1500 (CA). See also *Westdeutsche Landesbank Girozentrale v Islington London Borough Council* [1996] AC 669, 706–7.

[129] See, eg, *Lysaght v Edwards* (1876) 2 ChD 499, 506 (MR); *Loke Yew v Port Swettenham Rubber Co Ltd* [1913] AC 491, 506 (PC).

[130] See, eg, *Christie v Ovington* (1875) 1 ChD 279, 281; *Morgan v Swansea Urban Sanitary Authority* (1878) 9 ChD 582, 585–86 (MR); *Re Cunningham & Frayling* [1891] 2 Ch 567, 572.

the office and the legal title as trustee, and without any duty or further duty to perform, except to convey it upon demand to the beneficiary or beneficiaries or as directed by them.[131]

These decisions have generally considered the concept of bare trusteeship in the context of determining whether discrete statutory provisions were applicable,[132] which can affect the interpretation given to the concept,[133] but they do support the view that a bare trustee owes *some*, albeit minimal, duties to his beneficiaries: 'the very notion of a trustee is that there are some duties attached to the office.'[134] As Meagher JA said in *Corumo Holdings v C Itoh*, 'a "bare trust" is one in which the trustee has no active duties to perform and is usually contrasted with a trust where there are such active duties. . . But, as a matter of strict logic, almost no situation can be postulated where a trustee cannot in some circumstances have active duties to perform.'[135] As such, one can conceive of situations in which fiduciary principles could coherently offer their protection to the non-fiduciary duties owed by bare trustees.

A bare trustee owes, at the minimum, a duty to hold on to the trust property so as to be in a position to convey it to the beneficiary on demand or as the beneficiary directs. A conflict between that duty and the fiduciary's personal interest is not as obvious as it is in the cases that have been considered elsewhere in the book, but it is not unimaginable. Particularly when the trust property is money, the trustee will ordinarily deposit the funds.[136] One would expect the

---

[131] *Herdegen v Federal Commissioner of Taxation* (1988) 84 ALR 271, 281.

[132] eg, s 5, Vendor and Purchaser Act 1874 (*Christie v Ovington*); s 48, Land Transfer Act 1875 (*Christie v Ovington, Morgan v Swansea Urban Sanitary Authority* and *Re Cunningham & Frayling*); s 7, Registration of Titles Regulation 1891 and s 3, Specific Relief Enactment 1903 (Selangor) (*Loke Yew v Port Swettenham Rubber Co Ltd*); s 5(5), Taxation (Unpaid Company Tax) Assessment Act 1982 (Cth) (*Herdegen v Federal Commissioner of Taxation*). See also *Corumo Holdings Pty Ltd v C Itoh Ltd* (1991) 24 NSWLR 370, considering ss 8(8)(a)(iii)(B) and 230(1)(a)(iiia), Companies (New South Wales) Code 1981.

[133] See *Herdegen v Federal Commissioner of Taxation* (above n 131) 283; *Corumo Holdings v C Itoh* (*ibid*) 398; *CPT Custodian Pty Ltd v Commissioner of State Revenue* [2005] HCA 53 at [14]–[15], (2005) 224 CLR 98; *Kennon v Spry* [2008] HCA 56 at [52], [89], [154] and [162], (2008) 83 ALJR 145. See also *Yearworth v North Bristol NHS Trust* [2009] EWCA Civ 37 at [28], [2009] 2 All ER 986.

[134] *Morgan v Swansea Urban Sanitary Authority* (above n 130) 584. See also *Armitage v Nurse* [1998] Ch 241, 253 (CA); *Hulbert v Avens* [2003] EWHC 76 (Ch) at [62], [2003] WTLR 387; cf *Cowan de Groot Properties Ltd v Eagle Trust plc* [1992] 4 All ER 700, 765 (ChD). Indeed, even trustees to preserve contingent remainders owed enforceable duties: see L Bonfield, *Marriage Settlements 1601–1740* (Cambridge, Cambridge University Press, 1983) 56 and 58.

[135] *Corumo Holdings v C Itoh* (above n 132) 398. See also *Lake v Bayliss* [1974] 1 WLR 1073, 1076 (ChD); Mowbray, et al (above n 110) [1–21] and [34–03].

[136] *Hulbert v Avens* [2003] EWHC 76 (Ch) at [54], [2003] WTLR 387. The increasing 'de-physicalisation' of money means that some form of deposit is not merely a matter of safekeeping but more a matter of necessity: corporeal money has been all but totally replaced by incorporeal money (see Fox (above n 110) [1.135]–[1.140]), and for practical reasons, the trustee's receipt of such money will involve a deposit. The fact that a trustee owes no active *duty* to invest does not mean that he is without *power* to do so: P Matthews, 'All about Bare Trusts: Part 2' [2005] *Private Client Business* 336, 343; Mowbray, et al (above n 110) [1–25]–[1–26].

trustee to exercise care in his choice as to where to deposit the funds,[137] but one can also see room for the operation of fiduciary principles when, for example, the trustee is offered a bonus or commission for depositing the funds with a particular institution. An account of that profit could be rationalised on the basis of the fiduciary profit principle, as in *Brown v Inland Revenue Commissioners*,[138] or on the basis of the fiduciary conflict principle. To borrow a phrase from Arden MR's judgment in *Lonsdale v Church*, 'not being accountable for interest would be a temptation to receivers not to be ready to pay money due from them when demanded.'[139] *Lonsdale v Church* concerned a receiver of harbour duties, who appears not to have occupied a position of bare trusteeship, but the dictum is useful in that it indicates a coherent reason why the fiduciary conflict principle might be applied in the case of a bare trustee, notwithstanding the minimal non-fiduciary duties owed by such a trustee, in that it identifies an intelligible situation of conflict between those minimal duties and the trustee's personal interest.

In any event, what matters most for the purposes of the analysis advanced in the book is that bare trusts do not present a reason for rejecting the understanding of fiduciary doctrine as protective of non-fiduciary duties.

III. Proscriptive Duties

Conceiving of fiduciary doctrine as protective of non-fiduciary duties also provides a solid basis from which to explain the prevailing Anglo-Australian view that fiduciary duties are proscriptive in nature, rather than prescriptive.[140] Following a prescriptive view of fiduciary duties, the Supreme Court of Canada

---

[137] Trustee Act 2000, s 2 and Sch 1(1).
[138] *Brown v IRC* (above n 120).
[139] *Lonsdale v Church* (1789) 3 Bro CC 41, 45 (29 ER 396).
[140] See, eg, *Breen v Williams* (above n 1) 95, 113 and 137–38; *Attorney-General v Blake* (above n 59) 455 (CA), not discussed on appeal: [2001] 1 AC 268; *Pilmer v Duke Group Ltd* [2001] HCA 31 at [74] and [127], (2001) 207 CLR 165; *Aequitas v AEFC* [2001] NSWSC 14 at [284], (2001) 19 ACLC 1,006; *Youyang Pty Ltd v Minter Ellison Morris Fletcher* [2003] HCA 15 at [41], (2003) 212 CLR 484; *Brooker v Friend* [2006] NSWCA 385 at [26]; *Gibson Motorsport Merchandise Pty Ltd v Forbes* [2006] FCAFC 44 at [12], (2006) 149 FCR 569; *P & V Industries Pty Ltd v Porto* [2006] VSC 131 at [12] and [23], (2006) 14 VR 1; *Dresna Pty Ltd v Linknarf Management Services Pty Ltd* [2006] FCAFC 193 at [132], (2006) 156 FCR 474; *Australian Securities and Investments Commission v Citigroup Global Markets Australia Pty Ltd (No 4)* [2007] FCA 963 at [290], (2007) 160 FCR 35; *Motor Trades Association of Australia Superannuation Fund Pty Ltd v Rickus (No 3)* [2008] FCA 1986 at [70]; *Bell Group Ltd v Westpac Banking Corp (No 9)* [2008] WASC 239 at [4540]–[4544]; *Friend v Brooker* [2009] HCA 21 at [84]; cf *Trevorrow v South Australia* [2007] SASC 285 at [1002] and [1006]–[1007].
See also PD Finn, 'The Fiduciary Principle' in TG Youdan (ed), *Equity, Fiduciaries and Trusts* (Toronto, Carswell, 1989) 1, 25 and 28–29; RC Nolan, 'A Fiduciary Duty to Disclose?' (1997) 113 *Law Quarterly Review* 220, 222; JK Maxton, 'Contract and Fiduciary Obligation' (1997) 11 *Journal of Contract Law* 222, 237–38; PJ Millett, 'Equity's Place in the Law of Commerce' (1998) 114 *Law Quarterly Review* 214, 222–23; A Abadee, 'A Fiduciary's Obligation to Disclose in a Commercial Setting' (2001) 29 *Australian Business Law Review* 33, 42–43; TM Carlin, 'Fiduciary Obligations in Non-traditional Settings: An Update' (2001) 29 *Australian Business Law Review* 65, 70; AF Mason,

held in *McInerney v MacDonald* that a doctor owes his patient a positive fiduciary duty 'to grant access to the information the doctor uses in administering the treatment'.[141] In direct contrast, the High Court of Australia held in *Breen v Williams*[142] that no such fiduciary duty exists.

In an early observation, Dan Prentice noted in 1972 that 'in the past the fiduciary duties imposed on directors have been negative in nature'.[143] The point was developed much further by Paul Finn, who argued that fiduciary duties are proscriptive rather than prescriptive, in that they are concerned with maintaining fidelity to the principal rather than with whether the fiduciary is in fact serving the principal's interests.[144] That reflects the function served by fiduciary doctrine, at least as it has developed within Anglo-Australian law, but the proscriptive nature of fiduciary duties is further explained if one understands that the 'maintenance of fidelity' is more specifically concerned with the protection of non-fiduciary duties.

Fiduciary doctrine seeks to enhance the likelihood that the fiduciary will properly perform his non-fiduciary duties by removing temptations, such as inconsistent interests or duties, which have a tendency to sway the fiduciary away from proper performance of those non-fiduciary duties. The removal of such influences is an essentially negative task, so that it is only natural that the fiduciary duties which are designed to achieve that result will themselves generally be proscriptive in nature: they prohibit the fiduciary from taking opportunities or from allowing his personal interest or other duties to conflict with the underlying—non-fiduciary—duties that he owes. As the Court of Appeal put it in *Attorney-General v Blake*, fiduciary doctrine 'tells the fiduciary what he must not do. It does not tell him what he ought to do.'[145] The fiduciary's positive duties—those that tell him what he ought to do—comprise the underlying

'Fusion' in S Degeling and J Edelman (eds), *Equity in Commercial* Law (Pyrmont, Lawbook Co, 2005) 11, 16; Underhill and Hayton (above n 110) [1.55] and [33.9]. And see R Cooter and BJ Freedman, 'The Fiduciary Relationship: Its Economic Character and Legal Consequences' (1991) 66 *New York University Law Review* 1045, 1054.

It is doubtful that Austin J called this state of the law into question by his decision in *ENT Pty Ltd v Sunraysia Television Ltd* [2007] NSWSC 270, (2007) 61 ACSR 626: cf R Teele Langford, 'ENT Pty Ltd v Sunraysia Television Ltd: A Positive Fiduciary Duty of Disclosure' (2008) *Companies & Securities Law Journal* 470. In *ENT v Sunraysia*, Austin J recognised that company directors owe a duty to make full disclosure when recommending a course of action to their shareholders, and described this as a fiduciary duty. However, the fiduciary descriptor added nothing to the analysis of the duty to give clear notice of the purpose of shareholder meetings (which has long been recognised: see, eg, RP Austin, HAJ Ford and IM Ramsay, *Company Directors: Principles of Law and Corporate Governance* (Chatswood, LexisNexis Butterworths, 2005) [12.16]), and nothing in Austin J's decision suggests that he was setting out to challenge the authority of the High Court of Australia's decision in *Breen v Williams*, or indeed of his own earlier decision in *Aequitas v AEFC*.

[141]   *McInerney v MacDonald* [1992] 2 SCR 138, 150.

[142]   *Breen v Williams* (above n 1).

[143]   DD Prentice, 'Directors' Fiduciary Duties: The Corporate Opportunity Doctrine' (1972) 50 *Canadian Bar Review* 623, 626.

[144]   Finn, 'The Fiduciary Principle' (above n 140) 25 and 28–29.

[145]   *Attorney-General v Blake* (above n 59) 455 (CA).

undertaking between fiduciary and principal. In other words, the positive duties are the non-fiduciary duties that comprise the fiduciary's undertaking, and those positive duties are protected by proscriptive fiduciary duties. It is therefore unnecessary for fiduciary duties to be positive in nature because when positive duties are appropriate to the relationship they will be identified in the form of non-fiduciary duties. Fiduciary duties, in contrast, are concerned with preventing the fiduciary from acting in a way that might cause the fiduciary to breach his non-fiduciary duties, whatever they may be, and so are fundamentally negative or proscriptive in nature.

This explains the validity of the proscriptive view of fiduciary doctrine. However, it is also worth noting that some degree of caution should be exercised in attaching importance to the proscriptive maxim. The maxim can undoubtedly be important, as it was in *Breen v Williams*,[146] in explaining that certain duties cannot be fiduciary duties because they are prescriptive in nature rather than proscriptive. Thus, the proscriptive–prescriptive dichotomy provides guidance when determining whether a particular duty is fiduciary: the proscriptive nature of fiduciary duties operates as an 'excluder' when determining whether duties are properly classified as fiduciary duties or under some other genus. But the true determinant of whether a particular 'fiduciary' duty exists ought to be whether the duty serves part of fiduciary doctrine's protective function vis-à-vis other, non-fiduciary duties, rather than merely whether it is positive or negative—it is the *reasons* for the proscription that ought to be the focus of attention. The importance of that point is emphasised when it is borne in mind that there can be difficulty in differentiating positive from negative acts and obligations[147] (although the distinction is drawn and is important in a number of legal contexts[148]) and that other legal duties are proscriptive in effect and yet not fiduciary, such as the torts of deceit and trespass. What sets fiduciary duties apart from other kinds of duties is the function that they serve in protecting other, frequently positive, non-fiduciary duties and the manner in which they serve that function. It is their subsidiary and prophylactic nature that differentiates them from other duties rather than the mere fact that they are proscriptive.

---

[146] *Breen v Williams* (above n 1).

[147] *Pilmer v Duke Group Ltd* [2001] HCA 31 at [128], (2001) 207 CLR 165; J Getzler, 'Rumford Market and the Genesis of Fiduciary Obligations' in A Burrows and A Rodger (eds), *Mapping the Law* (Oxford, Oxford University Press, 2006) 577, 580 (fn 15).

[148] RC Nolan and DD Prentice, 'The Issue of Shares: Compensating the Company for Loss' (2002) 118 *Law Quarterly Review* 180, 183. In tort law, 'the distinction between acts and omissions is not watertight,' but it remains important: T Weir, *An Introduction to Tort Law*, 2nd edn (Oxford, Oxford University Press, 2006) 13 and 54. See also *Stovin v Wise* [1996] AC 923, 930–32 and 943–44; *Brodie v Singleton Shire Council* [2001] HCA 29 at [14] and [16], (2001) 206 CLR 512; WVH Rogers, *Winfield & Jolowicz on Tort*, 17th edn (London, Sweet & Maxwell, 2006) [5–21]. The importance of the distinction may be diminishing in Australian tort law: see, eg, *Brodie v Singleton Shire Council* [2001] HCA 29 at [85], (2001) 206 CLR 512.

IV. Authorisation

As has already been mentioned,[149] a fiduciary can avoid liability for what would otherwise be a breach of fiduciary duty if his conduct has been properly authorised. Such authorisation can come in the form of a court sanction[150] but is far more commonly obtained from the fiduciary's principal[151] or from the person who created the fiduciary relationship at the outset.[152] Such consent insulates the fiduciary from liability because the difficulty that a fiduciary faces when acting with a conflict between duty and interest is not with the substantive content of the transaction but with the fiduciary character in which he acts.[153] The principal's consent means that the fiduciary 'shakes off the character'.[154]

To achieve this when a fiduciary relationship has arisen, the 'relation must be in some way dissolved: or, if not, the parties must be put so much at arm's length, that they agree to take the characters of purchaser and vendor.'[155] The principal may bring an end to the fiduciary relationship completely,[156] thereby releasing the former fiduciary from the strictures of the fiduciary conflict principle, or the principal may alter the fiduciary's non-fiduciary duties in respect of a particular transaction so that, for that specific transaction, there is no longer any conflict

---

[149]   See above section I.

[150]   See, eg, *Campbell v Walker* (1800) 5 Ves 678, 681 (31 ER 801) (MR); *Farmer v Dean* (1863) 32 Beav 327 (55 ER 128) (MR); *Tennant v Trenchard* (1869) LR 4 Ch App 537, 547 (LC); *Re Brooke Bond & Co Ltd's Trust Deed* (above n 125) 365; *Holder v Holder* (above n 41) 398 and 402 (CA). See also *Re Drexel Burnham Lambert UK Pension Plan* [1995] 1 WLR 32, 41–42 (ChD).

[151]   *Gibson v Jeyes* (1801) 6 Ves 266, 270–71 and 277 (31 ER 1044); *Downes v Grazebrook* (1817) 3 Mer 200, 208 (36 ER 77); *Regal (Hastings) Ltd v Gulliver* (above n 53) 150 and 157; *Brown v IRC* (above n 120) 262, 263, 265, 266 and 267; *Boardman v Phipps* (above n 25) 109; *Queensland Mines Ltd v Hudson* (1978) 52 ALJR 399, 403 (PC); *Quarter Master UK Ltd v Pyke* [2004] EWHC 1815 (Ch) at [70], [2005] 1 BCLC 245; *Australian Securities & Investments Commission v Citigroup Global Markets Australia Pty Ltd* [2007] FCA 963 at [278]–[280] and [293], (2007) 160 FCR 35.

[152]   Ie, authorisation can come from the trust deed or other documents that constitute the fiduciary relationship, such as a company's articles of association: *Costa Rica Railway Co Ltd v Forwood* [1901] 1 Ch 746, 757–58 (CA); *Dale v Inland Revenue Commissioners* [1954] AC 11, 27; *Brown v IRC* (above n 120) 256; *Guinness plc v Saunders* (above n 12) 689, 692 and 700; *Re Beatty (dec'd)* [1990] 1 WLR 1503, 1506 (ChD); *Edge v Pensions Ombudsman* [2000] Ch 602, 621–22 (CA). For companies, see now Companies Act 2006 (UK), ss 175(4)–(5), 177 and 180.

Authorisation can also be *implied* where a settlor appoints a trustee *knowing* that the trustee would thereby be placed in a situation of conflict between duty and interest: *Tempest v Lord Camoys* (1888) 58 LT 221, 223 (ChD); *Hordern v Hordern* [1910] AC 465, 475 (PC); *Hobkirk v Ritchie* (1933) 29 Tas LR 14, 48, approved on appeal: see p 57; *Princess Anne of Hesse v Field* [1963] NSWR 998, 1009–10 (SC); *Jones v Firkin-Flood* [2008] EWHC 2417 (Ch) at [266]–[267]. But the settlor's authorisation will not be implied where the settlor was *unaware* of the potentially conflicting interest: *Peyton v Robinson* (1823) 1 LJ (OS) 191, 194 (ChD).

[153]   *Aberdeen Railway v Blaikie Bros* (above n 10) 472 (HL).

[154]   *Ex parte James* (above n 62) 348.

[155]   *Gibson v Jeyes* (above n 151) 277 (LC); see also pp 270–71. And see *Downes v Grazebrook* (above n 151) 208 (LC).

[156]   See, eg, *Ex parte Lacey* (above n 9) 626 (LC); *Ex parte Bennett* (above n 9) 394 (LC); *Plowright v Lambert* (above n 9) 653 (ChD).

between those non-fiduciary duties and the fiduciary's personal interest.[157] Either way, the effect is the same,[158] in that the fiduciary is then free to enter into the transaction immune from the consequences that fiduciary doctrine would otherwise attach to his acting in that way.

However, 'nothing short of fully informed consent'[159] on the part of the principal to relaxation of the fiduciary's liability will suffice to protect the fiduciary from liability once a fiduciary relationship has arisen.[160] The consent will 'be watched with infinite and the most guarded jealousy'[161] in the sense that there must be clear evidence[162] that it was given after the fiduciary made 'full and frank disclosure of all material facts'.[163]

The requirement that the fiduciary make full disclosure of all material facts, in order to obtain a fully informed consent and thereby be insulated from liability for breach of fiduciary duty, stands in contrast to the level of consent that applies in ordinary contract law: 'the general rule of the common law is that a person contemplating entering a contract with another is under no duty to disclose information to that other.'[164] Thus, 'ordinarily the failure to disclose a material fact which might affect the mind of a prudent contractor does not give the right to avoid the contract.'[165]

Understanding fiduciary doctrine as providing a form of protection for non-fiduciary duties provides a natural explanation for why a more exacting standard of conduct is demanded in the fiduciary context. Absent a requirement that there be fully informed consent before a fiduciary is exempted from

---

[157] See, eg, *Robinson v Randfontein Estates Gold Mining Co Ltd* [1921] AD 168, 178 (S Africa); *Movitex Ltd v Bulfield* [1988] BCLC 104, 118 (ChD).

[158] *Queensland Mines v Hudson* (above n 151) 403–4.

[159] *Boardman v Phipps* (above n 25) 109. See also *Re Haslam & Hier-Evans* [1902] 1 Ch 765, 770 (CA); *Maguire v Makaronis* (above n 1) 466.

[160] The requirement that consent to what would otherwise be a breach of fiduciary duty must be fully informed does not apply when no fiduciary relationship has yet arisen: *Australian Securities & Investments Commission v Citigroup Global Markets Australia Pty Ltd* [2007] FCA 963 at [345]–[346], (2007) 160 FCR 35. When, however, some other fiduciary relationship already exists in the context of which a new fiduciary relationship is being created (eg, possibly, when a solicitor who is to become a trustee provides professional advice on the drafting of the trust deed and includes a generous trustee charging clause), the pre-existing fiduciary relationship may mean that fully informed consent is necessary: see the discussion in *Bogg v Raper* (1998) 1 ITELR 267, 284–87 (CA).

[161] *Ex parte Lacey* (above n 9) 626 (LC).

[162] *Barr Leary & Co v Hall* (1906) 26 NZLR 222, 225 (SC); *York & North-Midland Railway Co v Hudson* (1845) 16 Beav 485, 491 (51 ER 866) (MR); *Coles v Trecothick* (1804) 9 Ves 234, 246–47 (32 ER 592) (LC).

[163] *Oranje* (above n 1) 1132.

[164] J Beatson, *Anson's Law of Contract*, 28th edn (Oxford, Oxford University Press, 2002) 236. See also MP Furmston, *Cheshire, Fifoot & Furmston's Law of Contract*, 15th edn (Oxford, Oxford University Press, 2007) 335–36; WE Peel, *Treitel's Law of Contract*, 12th edn (Oxford, Oxford University Press, 2007) [9–123]; Beale (above n 107) [6–014].

[165] *Bell v Lever Brothers Ltd* [1932] AC 161, 227. See also *Norwich Union Life Insurance Co Ltd v Qureshi* [1999] 2 All ER (Comm) 707, 717 (CA); *Agnew v Länsförsäkringsbolagens AB* [2001] 1 AC 223, 265.

fiduciary liability, it would be too easy for fiduciaries to circumvent the protection that fiduciary doctrine seeks to provide by extracting an ordinary contractual agreement from the principal authorising the relevant conduct. The fiduciary requirement that the principal's consent be fully informed ensures that the principal is provided with the means of fully understanding the risk that the transaction carries, so that the principal is placed in a position to determine for himself 'that he would rather run the risk'.[166] In other words, fiduciary doctrine affords its prophylactic protection against the risk of breach of non-fiduciary duty, but that protection is removed if the principal has made an informed decision to permit the transaction to proceed despite the risk.

Both the common law and equity have always accorded a high degree of respect to the right of *sui iuris* legal actors to exercise autonomous distributive power over their assets. Consistently with that, fiduciary doctrine protects non-fiduciary duties from inconsistent temptations that might cause their breach, but it respects a principal's decision to forgo that protection:

> The reason why the law permits the rule to be relaxed is obvious. . . If the person entitled to the benefit of the rule is content with that position and understands what are his rights in the matter, there is no reason why he should not relax the rule, and it may commercially be very much to his advantage to do so.[167]

In allowing the fiduciary principle to be relaxed, equity balances the principle of respect for autonomous decisions with the protective function that fiduciary doctrine serves. Autonomy outweighs that protective function, but only when it is reasonable to believe that the principal truly understands the implications of his decision. It would very substantially undermine the protective function that fiduciary doctrine serves if its protection were to be lifted in response to a consent granted by the principal without the benefit of full disclosure of all material facts (in other words, consent at the ordinary contractual level) because such consent would not ensure that the principal understood the risk that he was thereby running. This explains why 'what is required for a fully informed consent is a question of fact in all the circumstances of each case'[168] and 'the sufficiency of disclosure can depend on the sophistication and intelligence of the persons to whom disclosure must be made.'[169] The sophistication and intelligence of the principal are important in determining whether the principal's consent has been sufficiently well informed to constitute a truly autonomous decision, which the court will respect, to forgo the protection that fiduciary doctrine would provide

---

[166] *Christophers v White* (1847) 10 Beav 523, 524 (50 ER 683) (MR). See also *Rawleigh v Tait* [2008] NZCA 525 at [20], upheld on appeal: [2009] NZSC 11.

[167] *Boulting v Association of Cinematograph Television & Allied Technicians* [1963] 2 QB 606, 637 (CA).

[168] *Maguire v Makaronis* (above n 1) 466. See also *Premium Real Estate v Stevens* (above n 1) [72].

[169] *Farah Constructions Pty Ltd v Say-Dee Pty Ltd* [2007] HCA 22 at [107], (2007) 230 CLR 89. See also *Gray v New Augarita Porcupine Mines Ltd* [1952] 3 DLR 1, 14 (PC); *Australian Securities & Investments Commission v Citigroup Global Markets Australia Pty Ltd* [2007] FCA 963 at [296], (2007) 160 FCR 35.

and to proceed with the transaction notwithstanding the risks involved. In the absence of such autonomous consent, the protective function served by fiduciary doctrine is not outweighed, and its protection remains in place. Fiduciary doctrine respects an autonomous decision to waive its protection, but only if the consent that has been obtained to that decision is consistent with the protective function that it seeks to serve.

In this way, fiduciary doctrine performs its protective function in two ways. First, as has been seen, it protects non-fiduciary duties from the heightened possibility of breach of those duties caused by temptations, such as inconsistent interests or duties, that have a tendency to cause breach of the protected duties. And secondly, it ensures that the protection it provides is not defeated or circumvented unless the principal fully understands and accepts the consequences of waiving that protection.

A related question that arises in this context is whether there are any fiduciary duties the protection of which a principal cannot consent to losing. Some have suggested that there are circumstances in which fiduciary duties cannot be abrogated by consent. Julie Maxton has argued, for example, that 'in some situations, the whole point of fiduciary doctrine is its ability to override contractual stipulations.'[170] Similarly, in *Farrington v Rowe McBride & Partners*, Richardson J suggested that some fiduciary duties can not be removed, even by informed consent:

> A solicitor's loyalty to his client must be undivided. . . If there is a conflict in his responsibilities . . . he must ensure that he fully discloses the material facts to both clients and obtains their informed consent to his so acting. . . And there will be some circumstances in which it will be impossible, notwithstanding such disclosure, for any solicitor to act fairly and adequately for both.[171]

Richardson J 'no doubt had in mind a situation where one client sought advice on a matter which would involve disclosure of facts detrimental to the interests of the other client'.[172] But even when there is an actual conflict between the duties a solicitor owes to his clients, it is not clear that consent cannot operate effectively, provided the solicitor adequately explains that his acting for another client means he cannot advise fully because of the duties owed to the other client. If the client whose consent is sought agrees to that, such consent should suffice to alter the solicitor's non-fiduciary duties so there is no longer any actual conflict of duties.[173] The solicitor undoubtedly occupies an extremely precarious position in that his non-fiduciary duties respond to the reasonable expectations of the client

---

[170] Maxton (above n 140) 229. See also D Bayliss, 'Breach of Confidence as a Breach of Fiduciary Obligations: A Theory' (2002) 9 *Auckland University Law Review* 702, 715.

[171] *Farrington v Rowe McBride & Partners* [1985] 1 NZLR 83, 90 (CA). See also *3464920 Canada Inc v Strother* [2005] BCCA 35 at [17], (2005) 7 ITELR 748

[172] *Clark Boyce v Mouat* (above n 22) 436.

[173] There would, of course, remain a potential conflict between the duties, and so the solicitor would need to get fully informed consent from his original client, which may not be forthcoming.

in the circumstances, which means they can change over time: 'a role which was limited when originally assumed may, by reason of conduct in the performance of the role, be expanded so as to extend the duty.'[174] Such amendments to the retainer can catch a solicitor unawares, as they need not necessarily be formally agreed with the client[175] and can thus create again an actual conflict of duties. But that is because the changed circumstances have given rise to an actual conflict, in spite of the solicitor's attempts to avoid that, rather than because the principal's consent was ineffective when it was given. There is no a priori reason why consent, if it has been properly obtained, cannot cure any breach of fiduciary duty.

In summary, fiduciary doctrine's subsidiary and prophylactic protection for non-fiduciary duties can be relaxed by the principal. However, such relaxation will only be effective when it has been provided in circumstances that are consistent with the protection that fiduciary doctrine seeks to provide. Only when it is clear that the principal has made a truly autonomous decision to forgo fiduciary doctrine's protection by consciously accepting the risks of the relevant transaction will fiduciary doctrine's protection be withdrawn.

V. Critiques of Fiduciary Doctrine

Finally, fiduciary doctrine is often criticised, particularly in the way it controls the commercial activities of company directors, large firms of solicitors, and professional trustees. Critical evaluation of the doctrine is valuable, but some of the criticism misunderstands the content of fiduciary doctrine, and, more importantly in the context of this book, a large proportion of it proceeds without understanding the purpose that fiduciary doctrine, as currently formulated, is designed to serve. It is important to bear in mind that fiduciary doctrine seeks to provide protection against situations in which there is an increased risk of breach of non-fiduciary duties when the formulation of that doctrine is critically appraised.

The most common critique of fiduciary doctrine calls for its strictness to be eased, especially when it is applied in commercial contexts. Rosemary Teele, for example, has argued that it is essential to reformulate the conflict principle because 'an unmodified, strict fiduciary duty to avoid a conflict of duties is, arguably, increasingly inappropriate'[176] in the regulation of solicitors' conduct: 'modification of the original fiduciary notion is therefore necessary to keep the

---

[174] *Beach Petroleum NL v Abbott Tout Russell Kennedy* [1999] NSWCA 408 at [195], (1999) 48 NSWLR 1. See also *Farrington v Rowe McBride & Partners* (above n 171) 97.

[175] See, eg, *Kitchen v Burwell Reed & Kinghorn Ltd* [2005] EWHC 1771 (QB) at [16]. See also *Mahoney v Purnell* [1996] 3 All ER 61, 71 and 93 (QBD).

[176] R Teele, 'The Necessary Reformulation of the Classic Fiduciary Duty to Avoid a Conflict of Interest or Duties' (1994) 22 *Australian Business Law Review* 99, 105.

law in step with changes in society.'[177] Similarly, debating the appropriateness of permitting solicitors and other fiduciaries to act for multiple clients to whom conflicting duties are owed, Andrew Mitchell has argued:

> [T]he emergence of large firms is a response to client needs. There are some matters that only large firms have the necessary resources and expertise to handle. Further, such disqualification rules may limit the scope for multi-disciplinary practices, seen by some consumers of legal services as the way of the future.[178]

And in the context of company law, John Lowry and Rod Edmunds have argued that 'as commercial enterprise becomes more complex, the strict rule exemplified by *Regal* does not hold the tension between capitalist principles which encourage profit-making and equity's strict rules governing liability.'[179] According to them, what is needed is recognition that

> whilst it may not be open to the fiduciary to earn a profit from business opportunities which in fairness belong to the company, there is the possibility that other opportunities may be available for his or her personal development, provided they fall outside the company's maturing line of business... [W]hat is required is some connection between the business of the company and the alleged wrongdoing.[180]

This reveals a misunderstanding of the way that fiduciary doctrine already is applied in the cases.[181] Courts already do focus closely, and have done so for a long time, on the facts of each case to determine whether there is any real, sensible possibility of conflict between a fiduciary's personal interest and the non-fiduciary duties that he owes to his principal.[182] Moreover, a fiduciary's liability to account for profits only arises as regards profits made 'in the course of the execution of that office',[183] which again depends on a careful analysis of the fiduciary's undertaking and the way the profit came to him.[184]

One can properly evaluate whether fiduciary doctrine is 'in need of substantive modernisation'[185] only in the light of a proper appreciation of its current content and reach. Further, particularly when the argument is that fiduciary doctrine has failed to keep pace with commercial developments and 'the sophistication of

---

[177] *Ibid*, 111.

[178] AD Mitchell, 'Chinese Walls in Brunei: *Prince Jefri Bolkiah v KPMG*' (1999) 22 *University of New South Wales Law Journal* 243, 254.

[179] J Lowry and R Edmunds, 'The Corporate Opportunity Doctrine: The Shifting Boundaries of the Duty and its Remedies' (1998) 61 *Modern Law Review* 515, 517. See also LS Sealy, *Company Law and Commercial Reality* (London, Sweet & Maxwell, 1984) 38–40.

[180] Lowry and Edmunds, 'The Corporate Opportunity Doctrine' (*ibid*) 518.

[181] For further criticism of the arguments advanced by Lowry and Edmunds, see R Flannigan, 'The Strict Character of Fiduciary Liability' [2006] *New Zealand Law Review* 209, 220–31.

[182] See above section I. In other words, Rosemary Teele is wrong to say that close factual examination in fiduciary cases is a recent phenomenon: Teele (above n 176) 102.

[183] *Regal (Hastings) Ltd v Gulliver* (above n 53) 149; see also pp 139, 153 and 158.

[184] See also *O'Donnell v Shanahan* [2009] EWCA Civ 751 at [60]; *Byrne v Hoare* [1965] Qd R 135, 151 (FC).

[185] J Lowry and R Edmunds, 'The No Conflict–No Profit Rules and the Corporate Fiduciary: Challenging the Orthodoxy of Absolutism' [2000] *Journal of Business Law* 122, 123.

modern society',[186] it is important that sight not be lost of the function that fiduciary doctrine was designed to serve, because critiques of fiduciary doctrine can only be sustained by analysing the effectiveness and appropriateness of that function in the context of modern commercial life.

Debates about whether, and if so how, fiduciary doctrine should be altered to accommodate modern developments can only proceed at an impoverished level of sophistication, and ultimately therefore of relevance, if they fail to engage with the fundamental nature of and the function served by fiduciary doctrine in its present form. Analysing fiduciary doctrine as serving a protective function does not show that it ought not to be altered, as that is ultimately a question of public policy. But understanding that fiduciary doctrine serves to protect non-fiduciary duties from situations involving heightened risk of their being breached does militate against too readily altering fiduciary doctrine so as to sanction recent developments in commercial practice. When that protective function is borne squarely in mind, and taking into account recent experiences with companies such as Enron, WorldCom and numerous others, the comments made by Norris JA in his dissenting judgment in *Peso Silver Mines Ltd v Cropper*, still seem particularly apposite:

> [T]he complexities of modern business are a very good reason why the rule should be enforced strictly in order that such complexities may not be used as a smoke screen or shield behind which fraud might be perpetrated... The history today of the activities of many corporate bodies has disclosed scandals and loss to the public due to failure of the directors to recognize the requirements of their fiduciary position.[187]

Contrary to the picture presented by many critics, the courts have not ignored the question whether fiduciary doctrine should be changed in order to match current commercial practice. In *North & South Trust Co v Berkeley*,[188] for example, Donaldson J was faced with the common practice of insurance brokers acting for both insured and insurer. The propriety or not of that practice was fundamental to his decision,[189] and he ultimately condemned it because of the risk that it created of breaches of duty:

> What course of action can possibly be adopted which does not involve some breach of the duty to one principal or the other? I yield to no one in my admiration for the skill and honesty of insurance brokers and other men of business of the City of London, but neither skill nor honesty can reconcile the irreconcilable.[190]

---

[186] C Hollander and S Salzedo, *Conflicts of Interest and Chinese Walls*, 2nd edn (London, Thomson, 2004) [2–02].

[187] *Peso Silver Mines Ltd v Cropper* (1965) 56 DLR (2d) 117, 139 (BCCA).

[188] *North & South Trust Co v Berkeley* [1971] 1 WLR 470 (QBD).

[189] *Ibid*, 478.

[190] *Ibid*, 483. See also *Gillett v Peppercorne* (1840) 3 Beav 78, 83–84 (49 ER 31) (MR); *Anglo-African Merchants Ltd v Bayley* [1970] 1 QB 311, 323–24.

Far from ignoring the exigencies of commercial life, the courts have weighed those pressures against the protective function that fiduciary doctrine has traditionally served vis-à-vis non-fiduciary duties and have concluded that no case has been shown for eroding that protection. Importantly, while it is exacting in what it requires of fiduciaries, fiduciary doctrine itself provides a mechanism for its strictures to be lifted, if a fiduciary obtains fully informed consent from his principal.[191] Norris JA noted in *Peso Silver Mines Ltd v Cropper* that 'no great hardship is imposed on directors by the enforcement of the rule, as a very simple course is available to them which they may follow'[192] in that they can seek authorisation.[193]

John Langbein has recently advanced a more sophisticated case for modifying the fiduciary conflict principle, arguing that it imposes too high a cost as it prohibits transactions that are beneficial to the fiduciary's principal as well as non-beneficial transactions.[194] In developing that argument he offers a cost-benefit analysis of the conflict principle which, he suggests, shows that fiduciaries ought to be able to argue that a transaction was objectively in the best interests of the beneficiaries, even if the fiduciary acted with a conflict between duty and interest. Langbein's analysis could also find support in the suggestions in *Murad v Al-Saraj* that 'it may be that the time has come when the court should revisit the operation of the inflexible rule of equity in harsh circumstances.'[195] Any relaxation of the rule in England would require a decision of the House of Lords, but the question that remains is whether Langbein's cost-benefit analysis provides a sufficient justification for that happening. With respect, his argument is insufficiently compelling to justify departure from the longstanding orthodoxy.[196]

Langbein's cost-benefit analysis is skewed to his purpose. He argues:

> [The] preoccupation with prophylaxis follows naturally enough from the two suspect assumptions . . . that when a trustee has a conflict it must be harmful to trust beneficiaries, and that a conflicted trustee can easily conceal wrongdoing. . . The

---

[191] See above section IV.
[192] *Peso Silver Mines v Cropper* (above n 187) 139. See also *Anglo-African Merchants v Bayley* (above n 190) 323–24.
[193] See also M Waller, 'Book Review: *Conflicts of Interest and Chinese Walls*' (2001) 117 *Law Quarterly Review* 335, 338.
[194] JH Langbein, 'Questioning the Trust Law Duty of Loyalty: Sole Interest or Best Interest?' (2005) 114 *Yale Law Journal* 929.
[195] *Murad v Al-Saraj* [2005] EWCA Civ 959 at [82], [2005] WTLR 1573; see also at [83] and at [121]–[122]. And see *John Taylors v Masons* [2001] EWCA Civ 2106 at [41] *per* Arden LJ, [2005] WTLR 1519, although cf at [44] *per* Morland J. Cf also *Lindsley v Woodfull* [2004] EWCA Civ 165 at [30], [2004] 2 BCLC 131 *per* Arden LJ.
[196] For other criticisms of Langbein's argument, see MB Leslie, 'In Defense of the No Further Inquiry Rule: A Response to Professor John Langbein' (2005) 47 *William & Mary Law Review* 541; Flannigan (above n 181) 231–41.

counterargument, of course, is that in cost-benefit terms, the value of beneficiary-regarding conduct now foreclosed under the sole interest rule outweighs any losses that might arise from changing the force of the presumption of wrongdoing from conclusive to rebuttable.[197]

There are a couple of problems with this analysis. First, the justification for the fiduciary conflict principle is not that allowing a fiduciary to act with a conflict between duty and interest 'must' be harmful to the principal but rather that there is a *risk* that the fiduciary 'might' act in that way. That risk is the target at which fiduciary doctrine is aimed.

Secondly, and more importantly, Langbein's assessment of the cost imposed by the conflict principle—that its absolute terms prohibit much 'beneficiary-regarding conduct'—fails to take account of the fiduciary's ability to obtain authorisation for such conduct, whether in the trust instrument or equivalent, from a court, or by obtaining the fully informed consent of his principal. As Langbein himself admits later in the same article, 'the exclusions and the categoric exemptions from the sole interest rule . . . make it increasingly fictional to continue to treat the sole interest rule as the baseline norm.'[198]

The relevant 'baseline norm' for a cost-benefit analysis is the principle that a fiduciary cannot act when his personal interest conflicts with his non-fiduciary duty *unless* that has been properly authorised. The very fact that a fiduciary thinks a transaction involving a conflict is justified but has nonetheless chosen not to seek authorisation either from the court or from his principal, raises serious questions as to the wisdom of sustaining that transaction—all too often 'secrecy is the badge of fraud.'[199] Only in a minuscule number of cases will obtaining one or other of those forms of authorisation present any form of difficulty for an honest fiduciary, in which cases all the fiduciary need do is abstain. From this perspective, the costs of the conflict principle are relatively low when compared with the benefit that it provides.

The benefit side of the cost-benefit analysis comes in the form of the protection that fiduciary doctrine provides against situations involving temptations to act in breach of non-fiduciary duty. The courts have refused to hear arguments that the fiduciary has acted objectively in the best interests of the principal because the possibility that courts might countenance such arguments will do nothing to reduce the temptation that a fiduciary faces in situations in which there is conflict between his personal interest and the non-fiduciary duties he owes. Fiduciary doctrine is based on a fundamentally cynical view of human nature. It is prophylactic, both in nature and in methodology, because 'human nature being what it is, there is danger . . . of the person holding the fiduciary

---

[197] Langbein (above n 194) 951.
[198] *Ibid*, 980.
[199] *Agip (Africa) Ltd v Jackson* [1990] Ch 265, 294. See also *Fawcett v Whitehouse* (above n 99) 148 (LC).

position being swayed by interest rather than by duty.'[200] Allowing fiduciaries to argue that they have not in fact succumbed to such temptations actually increases the temptation they face, by making the possibility of personal profit more accessible, thereby decreasing the level of protection that fiduciary doctrine manages to provide.[201] As Robert Flannigan has observed,

> Particularly where they are sophisticated, fiduciaries are able to structure and document intentions, events, and opportunities so as to erect a façade of regularity. Where they do so effectively, ex ante or ex post, others will not perceive or comprehend the operation of their self-interest.[202]

Allowing fiduciaries to argue that an impugned transaction was nonetheless in the best interests of their principals, notwithstanding that there was a conflict between duty and interest, would undermine the protection that fiduciary doctrine provides. It would create an incentive for fiduciaries to seek to engineer situations in which they could make such an argument. It undermines the internal logic and the fundamentally protective function of fiduciary doctrine for courts to be willing to hear such arguments. There is only a minute cost involved in abstention in the small number of cases where an honest fiduciary finds it impractical to obtain proper authorisation for conduct that falls foul of the conflict principle when compared with the benefit of the subsidiary and prophylactic protection for non-fiduciary duties that fiduciary doctrine has successfully provided for over two hundred years.

The argument that Langbein has sought to advance ought to be rejected. It subverts the fundamentally protective function that fiduciary doctrine has been, and still is, designed to perform. The benefit which that protection has provided over centuries is not outweighed by the need to avoid the very small cost incurred as a result of fiduciary doctrine leaving honest fiduciaries with no real option but to forgo potentially profitable opportunities in a very small number of cases.

---

[200] *Bray v Ford* [1896] AC 44, 51.
[201] See also above ch 4, sections II-B and IV.
[202] Flannigan (above n 181) 210.

8

Conceptual Affinities

The previous chapter considered a number of the implications of understanding fiduciary loyalty as a subsidiary and prophylactic form of protection for non-fiduciary duties. In so doing, attention was focused on the doctrinal relationship between fiduciary and non-fiduciary duties. This chapter now focuses attention on that relationship at a more theoretical level. In particular, it addresses the conceptual similarities and differences between fiduciary duties and other duties such as contractual obligations and torts. Notwithstanding some degree of affinity with these other kinds of obligations, fiduciary doctrine serves a distinct purpose that usefully distinguishes it and justifies its existence as a discrete set of doctrine.

I. Contract and Fiduciary Doctrine

There is no doubt that fiduciary duties can be altered or relaxed if the fiduciary's principal gives his fully informed consent to that happening. As has been seen, this phenomenon sits comfortably with the protective understanding of fiduciary doctrine.[1] Other commentators, particularly law and economics scholars, have argued instead that the fact that fiduciary duties can be altered by the principal shows that 'fiduciary obligations are a gap-filling device. They are no more or less than contractual implied terms.'[2] Thus, Henry Butler and Larry Ribstein have described fiduciary duties as 'legally enforceable standard-form provisions that reduce transaction costs by making it unnecessary for the parties to draft for remote contingencies. . . [F]iduciary duties are not distinct from the contract but are simply one of many drafting alternatives.'[3] This section of the chapter subjects such 'contractarian' claims to scrutiny and shows that they inadequately reflect the true nature and function of fiduciary doctrine.

---

[1] See above ch 7, section IV.

[2] AJ Duggan, 'Is Equity Efficient?' (1997) 113 *Law Quarterly Review* 601, 624.

[3] HN Butler and LE Ribstein, 'Opting Out of Fiduciary Duties: A Response to the Anti-Contractarians' (1990) 65 *Washington Law Review* 1, 29.

In its positive or descriptive form, the contractarian view of fiduciary doctrine holds that 'fiduciary duties are fundamentally gap-filling default rules'[4] in contracts between fiduciaries and their principals. Thus, 'to the economist, the starting point for an analysis of fiduciary duty is the theory, such as it is, of incomplete contracting.'[5] According to this theory, 'because it is difficult to spell out what particular commitments over behaviour will achieve joint welfare maximisation [a] contract is incomplete',[6] and fiduciary doctrine 'provides efficient terms to fill gaps in the contracts.'[7] In other words, 'default rules fill the gaps in incomplete contracts; they govern unless the parties contract around them. Immutable rules cannot be contracted around; they govern even if the parties attempt to contract around them.'[8]

It is incontestable that fiduciary duties are default rules, in the sense that the parties can contract around them.[9] This has been clear since the start of the nineteenth century, if not earlier.[10] However, there are dangers in adopting wholesale a contractarian view of fiduciary duties, for two reasons. First, there are difficulties with the descriptive accuracy of some contractarian theories of fiduciary doctrine. Secondly, there is a risk that descriptive analysis may slide imperceptibly and ill-advisedly into normative arguments that fiduciary doctrine ought to operate differently. This elision often loses sight of the unique function that fiduciary duties were designed to perform. These difficulties can potentially be overcome within the confines of a contractarian analysis, but in order to do so the idea of fiduciary duties as 'no more or less than contractual implied terms'[11] requires considerable revision. Consequently, it is preferable to treat fiduciary duties as a distinct kind of duty, so as not to lose sight of their unique nature and function.

The descriptive deficiencies of contractarian theories of fiduciary doctrine are addressed first. Frank Easterbook and Daniel Fischel have argued that 'the duty of loyalty replaces detailed contractual terms, and courts flesh out the duty of loyalty by prescribing the actions the parties themselves would have preferred if

[4] MJ Whincop, 'Of Fault and Default: Contractarianism as a Theory of Anglo-Australian Corporate Law' (1997) 21 *Melbourne University Law Review* 187, 207.
[5] GK Hadfield, 'An Incomplete Contracting Perspective on Fiduciary Duty' (1997) 28 *Canadian Business Law Journal* 141, 141.
[6] *Ibid*, 142.
[7] Whincop (above n 4) 189. See also R Cooter and BJ Freedman, 'The Fiduciary Relationship: Its Economic Character and Legal Consequences' (1991) 66 *New York University Law Review* 1045, 1046–47 and 1048–49; Duggan (above n 2) 623; cf H Hansmann and U Mattei, 'The Functions of Trust Law: A Comparative Legal and Economic Analysis' (1998) 73 *New York University Law Review* 434, 447–48.
[8] I Ayres and R Gertner, 'Filling Gaps in Incomplete Contracts: An Economic Theory of Default Rules' (1989) 99 *Yale Law Journal* 87, 87.
[9] The argument that it is impossible to contract around some fiduciary duties was rejected earlier: see above ch 7, section IV.
[10] Eg, *Ex parte Bennett* (1805) 10 Ves 381, 394 (LC) ; *Ex parte Lacey* (1802) 6 Ves 625, 626 (31 ER 1228) (LC).
[11] Duggan (above n 2) 624.

bargaining were cheap and all promises were enforced.'[12] In other words, in this positive, descriptive formulation, the contractarian argument is that fiduciary duties are obligations that the parties would themselves have chosen had they been able, or had it not been too costly to try, to foresee all the situations in which they might be needed. Thus, fiduciary doctrine is simply one form of implied term, like other terms implied into contracts when the parties would have assented to them had they thought about it.[13]

The trouble with this approach is twofold. First, courts do not generally approach the issue of fiduciary duties by asking whether the parties in each individual case would have considered those duties to be an obvious part of their arrangements. Secondly, insofar as the contractarian analysis is based on the claim that parties to fiduciary relationships would in general opt for such terms, proponents of the theory have provided no empirical evidence to support that claim, nor have they engaged in the process of applying a hypothetical bargaining model.[14] For example, Gillian Hadfield has simply asserted that 'had identification and negotiation over the precise contingencies . . . been possible, it is very likely . . . that the parties would have negotiated something like a fiduciary obligation.'[15] But it is far from clear that this is the case. One can readily understand why principals in fiduciary relationships would wish to contract for the sort of protection that fiduciary doctrine provides for the proper performance of their fiduciary's obligations, but it is not so clear that fiduciaries would be keen to accede to such requests. The difficulties of predicting what fiduciaries would agree to are illustrated by two statements of John Langbein. In one article he argued:

> A crucial consideration in understanding why trustees, especially expert professional trustees such as corporate fiduciaries, willingly accept the potential liability of trust fiduciary law with every trust deal is that compliance with trust fiduciary law is ordinarily not onerous. . . . The duty of loyalty, though it threatens draconian prophylactic liabilities for breach, is also easy enough to obey in ordinary cases. It says to the trustee, 'You are left with the entire universe of investment possibilities as outlets for your entrepreneurial impulses; you are required only to stay away from the trust assets when you seek your own fortune'.[16]

---

[12] FH Easterbook and DR Fischel, 'Contract and Fiduciary Doctrine' (1993) 36 *Journal of Law & Economics* 425, 427.

[13] For the position in contract law generally, see, eg, *The Moorcock* (1889) 14 P 64, 68 and 70 (CA); *Shirlaw v Southern Foundries (1926) Ltd* [1939] 2 KB 206, 227 (CA), affirmed on appeal: [1940] AC 701; *Luxor (Eastbourne) Ltd v Cooper* [1941] AC 108, 137; *BP Refinery (Westernport) Pty Ltd v President, Councillers and Ratepayers of the Shire of Hastings* (1977) 180 CLR 266, 282–84 (PC); WE Peel, *Treitel's Law of Contract*, 12th edn (Oxford, Oxford University Press, 2007) [6–029]–[6–030].

[14] For the process of and difficulties with conducting a hypothetical bargaining model, see BR Cheffins, *Company Law: Theory, Structure and Operation* (Oxford, Oxford University Press, 1997) ch 6.

[15] Hadfield (above n 5) 147.

[16] JH Langbein, 'The Contractarian Basis of the Law of Trusts' (1995) 105 *Yale Law Journal* 625, 657.

However, ten years later, in arguing that the fiduciary conflict principle ought to be altered to permit fiduciaries to argue that their conduct was actually in the best interests of their beneficiaries,[17] he described the conflict principle in these terms:

> What the sole interest rule does in such a case is to identify some conceivable but conjectural evil and then conclusively presume that this farfetched plot actually transpired, by refusing to let the putative evildoer prove that no such thing happened.[18]

If that were so, then contrary to what Hadfield suggested, it seems far from 'very likely' that fiduciaries would willingly accede to such obligations were they to negotiate the issue with their principals. In other words, it is quite unclear how fiduciaries would react if their principals were openly to ask them to be bound by fiduciary obligations when the fiduciary relationship is first created. Fiduciaries would not necessarily refuse such a request in every case, as many fiduciaries agree to take on their roles with full knowledge of the legal obligations that entails. But it is difficult to accept the bare assertion made by Easterbrook, Fischel and Hadfield that such obligations are self-evidently those to which principals and, particularly, fiduciaries would generally agree.[19]

A further deficiency in the descriptive accuracy of this form of contractarian model is the way that it treats fiduciary duties as equivalent to any other form of contractual obligation. To quote Easterbrook and Fischel again, 'fiduciary duties are not special duties; they have no moral footing; they are the same sort of obligations, derived and enforced in the same way, as other contractual undertakings.'[20]

For the reasons that have already been given above in chapters four and five, Easterbrook and Fischel are right to reject the view that fiduciary duties have a moral footing. However, the view that fiduciary duties are 'the same sort of obligations . . . as other contractual undertakings' runs the risk of misrepresenting fiduciary doctrine in two respects. First, fiduciary duties are not 'enforced in the same way' as other contractual obligations. In particular, the powerful profit-stripping remedies that fiduciary doctrine makes available following a breach of fiduciary duty—in the form of equities to rescind, accounts of profits and proprietary constructive trusts—are a long way from the compensatory damages that ordinarily follow a breach of contract.[21] Profit-stripping remedies

---

[17]   This argument has been addressed above in ch 7, section V.

[18]   JH Langbein, 'Questioning the Trust Law Duty of Loyalty: Sole Interest or Best Interest?' (2005) 114 *Yale Law Journal* 929, 953.

[19]   In a trust situation, the analysis is further complicated by the fact that it is normally the settlor rather than the beneficiaries who is the party to the bargain with the trustee. Presumably the settlor will act in what he considers to be the beneficiaries' best interests when he settles the trust, but the beneficiaries might have a different view of how the relationship between them (as ultimate principals in the fiduciary relationship) and the trustee (as fiduciary) ought to be arranged.

[20]   Easterbook and Fischel (above n 12) 427.

[21]   See also PD Finn, 'Contract and the Fiduciary Principle' (1989) 12 *University of New South Wales Law Journal* 76, 83.

are potentially available for a breach of contract, at least in the form of an account of profits, but 'only in exceptional circumstances'.[22] In contrast, an account of profits follows a breach of fiduciary duty essentially as a matter of right: 'the basic principle remains that a principal who so elects is *entitled* to an account of profits' (emphasis added).[23]

Easterbrook and Fischel attempt to save the contractarian model of fiduciary duties from this descriptive deficiency by arguing that even in contract cases, profit-stripping remedies are 'the remedy the parties would have selected had they bargained in advance without transaction costs' because 'the profits remedy induces the parties to contract explicitly. It is a contract-inducing, not a contract-frustrating, approach.'[24] The difficulty with this argument is that it again depends on hypothetical bargaining analysis, without any clear evidence to support it, and again it cannot be considered unarguably correct. Indeed, it seems contrary to what one would normally expect contracting parties to agree to if they were to think about what remedies should be available in the event that the contract is breached.

The second problem with Easterbrook and Fischel's statement that fiduciary duties are the 'same sort of obligations . . . as other contractual undertakings' is that it creates a danger that fiduciary duties will be seen as amenable to alteration by mere contract. As has already been seen, fiduciary duties can be altered if the principal consents, but such consent must be fully informed, which requires the fiduciary to make full disclosure of all material facts.[25] The manner in which such consent is obtained is thus quite distinct from the way in which consent to the alteration of ordinary contractual obligations can be obtained: 'valid consent by a beneficiary requires meeting considerably more rigorous conditions than does comparable consent by parties to contracts (or other species of contract).'[26] The source of the difficulty in Easterbrook and Fischel's observation lies in the conception of 'contract' that contractarians adopt. Henry Butler and Larry Ribstein, for example, have said that 'if the parties can choose the terms by either accepting them or contracting around them, the result of this choice is a contract.'[27] On that basis, almost *all* private law obligations ought to be treated as contractual in nature: liability for most, if not all, torts can also be contracted around. If that is so, the concept of contract loses any analytical value that it

---

[22] *Attorney-General v Blake* [2001] 1 AC 268, 285.

[23] *Warman International Ltd v Dwyer* (1995) 182 CLR 544, 560. The account of profits is, like other equitable remedies, discretionary. However, this discretion is exercised according to settled principles and so the starting position is that a claimant is entitled to elect an account if it so chooses: see *Ultraframe (UK) Ltd v Fielding* [2005] EWHC 1638 (Ch) at [1579]; *Warman International Ltd v Dwyer* (1995) 182 CLR 544, 559–60.

[24] Easterbook and Fischel (above n 12) 444.

[25] See above ch 7, section IV.

[26] V Brudney, 'Contract and Fiduciary Duty in Corporate Law' (1997) 38 *Boston College Law Review* 595, 605; see also pp 625–26.

[27] Butler and Ribstein (above n 3) 29. See also FH Easterbrook and DR Fischel, 'The Corporate Contract' (1989) 89 *Columbia Law Review* 1416, 1428.

might otherwise have, because it simply means, or comes very close to meaning, 'civil obligations, however created'. It is dangerous to conclude from this premise that all such obligations can be contracted around in the same manner. It simply is not the case that fiduciary duties can be contracted around in the same way as can other forms of civil obligation.

The last point leads to the second main criticism of contractarian theory, which concerns its normative implications. Contractarian analysis of fiduciary duties often slides between a positive analysis of how the doctrine is, towards a normative analysis of how the doctrine ought to be. For example, Butler and Ribstein have argued that 'the fundamentally contractual nature of fiduciary duties means that they *should* be subject to the same presumption in favor of private ordering that applies to other contracts' (emphasis added).[28] Insofar as this is an argument that fiduciary duties ought to be able to be excluded by mere contractual assent, it runs counter to centuries of fiduciary jurisprudence. As such, it requires more justification than the mere observation that fiduciary duties are contractual, if all that is meant by 'contractual' is that they can be modified by consent.

Tamar Frankel has observed that even if one accepts, as she does, that 'most fiduciary rules constitute default rules',[29] it does not follow that they are or should be altered in the same way as ordinary contractual terms. The cases make clear that that is not so with fiduciary duties, and it is dangerous to slide from the observation that fiduciary duties are alterable with the principal's consent, to the conclusion that they ought to be alterable with consent of the same kind as is sufficient in other contexts. As Victor Brudney remarked,

> To cut through substance to form (ie, to characterize the fiduciary relationship and its traditional strictures as a form of contract) and then to invoke the form as a fulcrum on which to ratchet down the substantive restrictions uses the term 'contract' as an undistributed middle in a problematic syllogism.[30]

However, an alternative form of contractarian analysis of fiduciary duties has been proposed, which is not subject to all of the deficiencies that have just been mentioned. The alternative analysis is built on the idea of '*penalty* default rules', as opposed to rules that the parties would allegedly have chosen for themselves. Ian Ayres and Robert Gertner have explained:

> [E]fficient defaults would take a variety of forms that at times would diverge from the 'what the parties would have contracted for' principle. . . Penalty defaults are designed to give at least one party to the contract an incentive to contract around the default rule and therefore to choose affirmatively the contract provision they prefer. . . [P]enalty

---

[28] Butler and Ribstein (above n 3) 32.
[29] T Frankel, 'Fiduciary Duties as Default Rules' (1995) 74 *Oregon Law Review* 1209, 1211–12.
[30] Brudney (above n 26) 597.

defaults are purposefully set at what the parties would not want—in order to encourage the parties to reveal information to each other or to third parties (especially the courts).[31]

Michael Whincop has usefully shown that penalty default analysis more accurately describes fiduciary duties than the other form of contractarian analysis that has been advanced.[32] A penalty default analysis need not show that the parties would have chosen the default rule because the very point of the analysis is that the rule would not be chosen by one party. This is consistent with the observation made earlier that of the two parties in a typical fiduciary relationship, fiduciaries seem unlikely to be wholeheartedly in favour of adopting fiduciary obligations as the terms of that relationship. The penalty default analysis suggests that the point of those default terms is to provide fiduciaries with an incentive to contract around their fiduciary obligations if they so wish. The penalty default analysis also explains why a fiduciary must make full disclosure of all material facts to his principal before the default fiduciary obligation is effectively contracted around: the disclosure of information is seen as the very reason for the fiduciary obligation being imposed. A penalty default analysis can also presumably accommodate fiduciary doctrine's remedial regime, by arguing that the powerful profit-stripping remedies are a further incentive to the fiduciary to make full disclosure of all material facts. And finally, the penalty default analysis does not slide between description and normative arguments, because it accepts that the principal's consent will be obtained in a manner different from that normally involved in the alteration of contractual terms. Again, the point of the rule from the penalty default perspective is to encourage parties to reveal information, which is not the ordinary contractual model.

Thus, in terms of its functional effect, fiduciary doctrine can be understood as a penalty default. However, this is an unusual form of contractual term—the very point of the penalty default analysis is to identify a default term that performs a function different from that performed by ordinary contractual terms, because its object is to encourage disclosure of information. If one were designing regulation of fiduciaries from the ground up, in a legislative fashion, the fact that such terms can be incorporated in that regulation could be important.

However, it is not clear that the penalty default analysis accurately reflects the reasons why the courts created fiduciary doctrine in the way that they did. In particular, judicial decisions—through which fiduciary doctrine was first developed, before legislators adopted and altered some of its ideas—suggest that fiduciary doctrine was created in order to provide a subsidiary and prophylactic form of protection for non-fiduciary duties. It was not created with disclosure of information in mind as the primary objective: full disclosure of all material facts was a side effect of the protection that fiduciary doctrine created, which would

---

[31] Ayres and Gertner (above n 8) 91.
[32] Whincop (above n 4) 199–200 and 208–15.

come about only if the parties to the fiduciary relationship sought to alter or contract around the protection itself. Similarly, the remedial regime that fiduciary doctrine has imposed for centuries, particularly in the form of its potentially swingeing profit-stripping awards, was designed to deter fiduciaries from entering into transactions that carried the heightened risk of breach of non-fiduciary duties against which fiduciary doctrine fought, rather than in order to promote greater disclosure of information in such transactions.

The protective understanding of fiduciary doctrine that is advanced in this book is not inconsistent with a penalty default analysis of fiduciary duties. But it is easier to explain the doctrines that have developed by reference to the justifications given in the case law itself than it is to impose an order on those doctrines by reference to reasons external to the development of the doctrine.

The conclusions to be drawn from this discussion of contractarian analyses of fiduciary doctrine are as follows. Contractarian views of fiduciary duties which hold that they are 'the same sort of obligations, derived and enforced in the same way, as other contractual undertakings'[33] are inadequate and need to be approached with considerable caution. In contrast, penalty default contractarian analyses of fiduciary duties are not untenable, but they do not accurately reflect the function and the purpose of fiduciary duties. Insofar as legislators wish to adapt those functions and purposes—or, indeed, to adopt them and continue them for the future, but from a statutory basis—the penalty default analysis can be instructive if legislators are seeking to identify efficient information disclosure schemes. But it would be wise for legislators considering such action also to bear in mind the original purposes of fiduciary doctrine. This will enable them to make an informed decision as to whether the traditional protective purpose, function and operation of fiduciary duties are things that they wish to adopt (in whole or in part) or to alter in their new statutory systems.[34]

In short, the methods by which fiduciary doctrine has traditionally operated are linked to the protective function that it was designed to serve. That function may or may not be appropriate in a new statutory regime. That protective function stands in contrast to the highly facilitative function served by ordinary contract law, which in turn explains the different forms of consent relevant to each of those kinds of doctrine.

II. Torts and Fiduciary Doctrine

In contrast to the contractarian view of fiduciary doctrine, other commentators have presented alternative conceptualisations of fiduciary doctrine, arguing that

---

[33] Easterbrook and Fischel (above n 12) 427.

[34] See, eg, the new statutory statement of directors' duties for the United Kingdom, which states the duties themselves but simply adopts the remedial regime from the common law: Companies Act 2006 (UK), ss 170–77 (duties) and s 178 (civil consequences).

it is better understood by reference to the law of torts. In particular, some have argued that fiduciary duties are inherently linked to duties of care, whereas others have argued that fiduciary duties can be understood as surrogates for torts.

A. Fiduciary Doctrine and Negligence

Peter Birks' view that a trustee's duty of care is a fiduciary duty, albeit one that is not 'especially fiduciary', has already been discussed and criticised.[35] However, Birks' analysis is again relevant at this juncture in that he argued that there is an inexorable link between fiduciary duties and duties of care:

> [C]are in the affairs of the beneficiary is the very heart of the trustee's obligation. . . There is a fine distinction between saying that a trustee's duty of care is not a fiduciary obligation and saying that it is a fiduciary obligation but is not, as such, distinguishable from any contractual or non-contractual duty of care. . . [O]nly the latter saves one from having to deny that a trustee's central obligation is, and always has been, with due care and skill, and disinterestedly, to promote and preserve the interests of the beneficiary.[36]

Birks' concern here was to defend the notion of fiduciary duties as exporters of duties from trustees to other similar actors. But even in that context, although fiduciaries have generally been held liable to act with due care and skill, trustees can be exempted from liability for acting carelessly,[37] which makes it odd to describe duties of care as the *central* trustee-like obligation. As has been explained in the previous chapter,[38] fiduciary duties are nonsensical without non-fiduciary duties, but Birks erred in insisting that it is a duty of care that must accompany fiduciary duties. The inexorable link between fiduciary and non-fiduciary duties is not an inexorable link between fiduciary duties and duties of care. A trustee whose duty of care has been abrogated does not thereby necessarily owe no fiduciary duties.

In order to advance his view of duties of care as fiduciary duties, Birks altered what Millett LJ had said in *Bristol & West Building Society v Mothew*[39] in an attempt to make it more consistent with what Lord Browne-Wilkinson had said in *Henderson v Merrett Syndicates Ltd.*[40] To understand the area correctly, the reverse is necessary. As was seen earlier,[41] in *Henderson v Merrett* Lord Browne-Wilkinson referred to the 'liability of a fiduciary for the negligent transaction of

---

[35] See above ch 3, section II.

[36] PBH Birks, 'The Content of Fiduciary Obligation' (2000) 34 *Israel Law Review* 3, 36–37.

[37] *Armitage v Nurse* [1998] Ch 241, 253–54 (CA); Trustee Act 2000 (UK), s 2 and Sch 1 para 7.

[38] See above ch 7, section II-A.

[39] Birks' subheading was 'Adapting the Approach of Millett LJ': Birks, 'The Content of Fiduciary Obligation' (above n 36) 33.

[40] *Henderson v Merrett Syndicates Ltd* [1995] 2 AC 145.

[41] See above ch 3, section II.

his duties'[42] and said that this was not a separate head of liability but the paradigm of the general duty to act with care when acting for or advising others. This might be taken to mean that the duty of care is a fiduciary duty, or might suggest that fiduciary duties are concurrent with duties of care and therefore cede to the tort-based obligation.[43] But the better understanding of what Lord Browne-Wilkinson meant is that a duty of care does not become a fiduciary duty merely because it is owed by a fiduciary—it is the same kind of duty as the duty of care owed by persons who do not owe fiduciary duties. Hence, he thought it 'misconceived'[44] to plead a breach of such a duty as a breach of fiduciary duty: entirely consistently with what Millett LJ held in *Mothew*, a fiduciary is generally liable for the 'negligent transaction of his duties' but does not by that fact alone act in breach of fiduciary duty. There is no necessary connection between peculiarly fiduciary duties and duties of care, and it is preferable if they are treated as wholly separate kinds of duties to reflect the quite distinct purpose that fiduciary duties serve in providing subsidiary and prophylactic protection to non-fiduciary duties.

A different argument about the necessary connection between fiduciary duties and negligence is presented by Steven Elliott, who has argued that negligence by a solicitor (and presumably other fiduciaries) is also a breach of *fiduciary* duty when it is aggravated by a conflicting interest or adverse fiduciary engagement.[45] The concept of 'aggravation' employed here is not explained, but it appears from Elliott's citation of *Nocton v Ashburton*[46] as a prime example of the phenomenon that the mere presence of a conflicting interest or duty transforms what would otherwise merely be negligent conduct into a breach of fiduciary duty.[47]

Nocton was a solicitor who had a personal interest in his client's release of a mortgage,[48] and he negligently misrepresented to the client that a valuer's report showed there would be sufficient security remaining for the client's debt. Thus, there was both negligence and a conflicting interest, and Nocton was held liable for breach of fiduciary duty. However, as Lord Devlin recognised in *Hedley Byrne v Heller*, 'it is not at all easy to determine exactly what [*Nocton v Ashburton*] decided,'[49] and it is far from clear that the Lords considered Nocton's personal interest in the transaction to be relevant to his liability. Viscount Haldane LC did mention once the fact of a solicitor entering into a financial transaction with his

---

[42] *Henderson v Merrett* (above n 40) 205.

[43] See, eg, JD Heydon, 'The Negligent Fiduciary' (1995) 111 *Law Quarterly Review* 1, 3–4.

[44] *Henderson v Merrett* (above n 40) 205.

[45] S Elliott, 'Fiduciary Liability for Client Mortgage Frauds' (1999) 13 *Trust Law International* 74. This argument is said to have 'considerable force' in RP Meagher, JD Heydon and MJ Leeming, *Meagher, Gummow & Lehane's Equity: Doctrines and Remedies*, 4th edn (Chatswood, Butterworths LexisNexis, 2002) [5–325].

[46] *Nocton v Ashburton* [1914] AC 932.

[47] Elliott (above n 45) 79.

[48] The release promoted a mortgage in which Nocton had an interest to the status of first mortgage.

[49] *Hedley Byrne & Co Ltd v Heller & Partners Ltd* [1964] AC 465, 520.

client as a basis for courts of equity to scrutinise the solicitor's actions[50] but did not mention it again, and the other Lords did not seem to treat that point as having any particular importance. Indeed, Lord Parmoor emphasised that the client was well aware of Nocton's interest in the transaction,[51] and Lord Shaw mentioned Nocton's conflict between duty and interest as an aside, in parentheses, which meant that Nocton should have declined to act at all.[52] As Lord Dunedin put it,

> [The solicitor] may have put himself in a fiduciary position, and that fiduciary position imposes on him the duty of making a full and not a misleading disclosure of facts known to him when advising his client. He fails to do so. Equity will give a remedy to the client.[53]

In other words, the importance of the fiduciary relationship between Nocton and his client was simply that it provided a basis for concluding that Nocton owed a duty to be careful in his statements.[54] As Viscount Haldane himself said not two years after *Nocton v Ashburton* was decided,

> I think, as I said in *Nocton's* case, that an exaggerated view was taken by a good many people of the scope of the decision in *Derry v Peek*. The whole of the doctrines as to fiduciary relationships, as to the duty of care arising from implied as well as express contracts, as to the duty of care arising from other special relationships which the Courts may find to exist in particular cases, still remains, and I should be very sorry if any word fell from me which should suggest that the Courts are in any way hampered in recognising that the duty of care may be established when such cases really occur.[55]

At the time *Nocton* was decided, the distinction drawn in *Mothew* between fiduciary duties that are peculiar to fiduciaries, and duties that fiduciaries owe in common with others,[56] was not drawn anywhere nearly as sharply as it has been over the last two decades. Indeed, an ordinary fiduciary conflict analysis would not depend on Nocton having misrepresented anything at all: if Nocton's interest in the transaction was in conflict with the non-fiduciary duty that he owed his client, that conflict would suffice to found fiduciary liability without need of any negligence on Nocton's part. The crucial question in that analysis is whether

---

[50]   *Nocton v Ashburton* (above n 46) 956.

[51]   *Ibid*, 974. Nocton's own partners had told the client of Nocton's interest and had warned the client against entering into the loan transaction at the outset: *ibid*, 936.

[52]   *Ibid*, 969.

[53]   *Ibid*, 965.

[54]   See *ibid*, 947, 948, 957, 958, 964–65, 967, 969, 972 and 977–78. The practical importance of treating this as a claim for breach of fiduciary duty was to avoid the fact that the claim had been inadequately pleaded as a claim only for fraud. At first instance, Neville J had dismissed the action on the basis that although Nocton had fallen short of the duty that he owed as a solicitor, his conduct did not amount to fraud: see *ibid*, 939. Treating the claim as a claim for breach of fiduciary duty allowed the House of Lords to treat it as a claim based on equitable fraud, thereby bringing it within the original pleading.

[55]   *Robinson v National Bank of Scotland Ltd* 1916 SC (HL) 154, 157; see also p 155 *per* Earl Loreburn. And see *Candler v Crane Christmas & Co* [1951] 2 KB 164, 187, 191–92 and 198 (CA).

[56]   *Bristol & West Building Society v Mothew* [1998] Ch 1, 16 (CA).

Nocton owed any relevant duty to his client. When *Nocton* was decided, duties to be careful in statements were not found as frequently as they are now, but the fiduciary relationship provided a basis for holding that Nocton owed such a duty. His liability turned on the fact that in breach of that duty of care, he had misrepresented the level of security that would remain following the release, rather than because Nocton had (or had misrepresented) a personal interest in the release.

In modern terms, therefore, the liability in *Nocton v Ashburton* is best understood as based on a breach of Nocton's duty of care, rather than on a breach of fiduciary duty. Hence, the case provides a shaky foundation for the recognition of a modern liability for breach of *fiduciary* duty when a fiduciary acts negligently and, coincidentally, with a conflict between duty and interest.

Elliott also cited a number of other cases as supporting his claim. The relevance to the argument of several of these is difficult to discern. In *Todd v Wilson*,[57] for example, a solicitor claimed fees for work done for a trust of which he was also a trustee. In doing so without proper authorisation, he committed a clear breach of the fiduciary conflict principle, but there is no suggestion that he was negligent. In *Cleland v Leech*,[58] the plaintiff lent money to a solicitor's brother-in-law after the solicitor gave an assurance that his brother-in-law was capable of repaying the loan. The solicitor was held liable, despite not having acted dishonestly, because if he had discharged his duty properly he would have realised his representation was untrue. Again, this is liability for negligent misstatement and is not based on any conflict between duty and interest or between duties. In *Chapman v Chapman*,[59] Stuart VC stated in an obiter dictum[60] that a solicitor could be held liable for loss caused by negligence in the discharge of his duty both at law and also in equity, but the latter jurisdiction was not said to be based on any conflict.

More relevant is *Bulkley v Wilford*,[61] which seems to suggest that a fiduciary is liable for negligence committed in a situation of conflict, although the decision is difficult to analyse. A solicitor who was the presumptive heir to a landowner advised the landowner to levy a fine over the entire estate, rather than merely the part the landowner was trying to sell, without explaining that this would revoke the landowner's will. Thus, when the landowner died, the remaining part of the landowner's estate was lost to the intended devisee and passed instead to the solicitor as heir. Analysis of the case is complicated by the fact that the jury found the solicitor had been fraudulent in concealing the effect of the fine.[62] However, the Lords proceeded by assuming that the non-disclosure was the result of mere

---

[57] *Todd v Wilson* (1846) 9 Beav 486, 489 (50 ER 431) (MR).
[58] *Cleland v Leech* (1856) 5 Ir Ch Rep 478, 489 (LC) (also reported as *Clelland v Leech* (1856) 8 Ir Jur 193).
[59] *Chapman v Chapman* (1870) LR 9 Eq 276, 294.
[60] See *British Mutual Investment Co v Cobbold* (1875) LR 19 Eq 627, 630–31 (VC).
[61] *Bulkley v Wilford* (1834) 2 Cl & Fin 102, 177 (6 ER 1094) (HL).
[62] Ibid, 180–81 and 189.

ignorance, rather than fraud, and held that a solicitor, like a trustee,[63] is unable to take advantage of his own professional ignorance.[64] Thus, the case can potentially be analysed as involving liability in equity for professional negligence, independent of fraud, if the defendant made a profit from that negligence. However, analysis of the older cases in this area is beset with difficulties because the concept of negligence was only slowly being worked out, and equity was making a significant contribution to that process, using the fiduciary relationship to justify imposition of a duty of care in situations in which it otherwise would not have been recognised. *Bulkley v Wilford* is better understood as an application of the fiduciary conflict and profit principles.[65] In providing the advice that he did, the solicitor acted with a conflict between the duty he owed to the landowner and his personal interest as presumptive heir to the estate. Rather than providing the basis for his liability, the solicitor's negligence provided the court with a reason to ignore his protestations that he was unaware that he was the presumptive heir because, as a solicitor, he should have known that. This also fits with the remedial consequence of the solicitor's conduct: he was held to take the estate as a constructive trustee for the intended devisee. A profit-stripping remedy of that sort is readily explained as an application of ordinary fiduciary conflict and profit principles without needing to invent a fiduciary wrong of negligence which happened to be committed against the backdrop of a conflict.

The other cases cited by Elliott are also based upon contravention of the fiduciary conflict principle, rather than upon negligence becoming a breach of fiduciary duty when it is 'aggravated' by a conflict. In *Segrave v Kirwan*, the next of kin successfully challenged an executor's claim that he was entitled to the undisposed of personal estate. The executor had acted as the testator's solicitor when the will was drawn up and had failed to explain to the testator that he would benefit personally as executor if the personal estate were not disposed of in the will.[66] Again, the case therefore concerns the conflict between the solicitor's duty when advising about the will and his personal interest in the undisposed of personal estate. The solicitor's conflict between duty and interest readily explains why the executor was stripped of his unauthorised profit and thus held the personal estate on trust for the next of kin.[67]

Similarly, in *Bayly v Wilkins*,[68] a solicitor gave informal advice, which was followed by its recipient, thereby benefiting the solicitor personally without making it clear that he would benefit in that way. Sugden LC mentioned *Bulkley v*

---

[63] *Ibid*, 181.

[64] *Ibid*, 177, 181 and 183.

[65] In addition to the reasons given in the text, see also the point made below in n 67. And see FW Maitland, *Equity*, 2nd edn rev by J Brunyate (Cambridge, Cambridge University Press, 1936) 80–82.

[66] *Segrave v Kirwan* (1828) Beatty 157, 166.

[67] *Ibid*, 170. Indeed, in *Bulkley v Wilford*, Lord Eldon discussed *Segrave v Kirwan* as an illustration of the relevant principle, which further supports the view that this is the true basis of the decision in *Bulkley v Wilford* as well: see *Bulkley v Wilford* (above n 61) pp 177–78.

[68] *Bayly v Wilkins* (1846) 3 Jones & La Touche 630 (LC(I)).

Wilford in reaching his conclusion that the solicitor ought to have revealed that he would be the primary person to benefit from the transaction, and he would not be heard to say that he was unaware that this would be the effect.[69] Again, negligence or ignorance is no defence to a fiduciary's responsibility under the general fiduciary conflict principle.

The evidence in support of Elliott's claim is therefore not strong. It becomes complicated when one tries to reconcile it with a more modern understanding of the way in which the doctrine of negligence operates and relates to the doctrines that regulate fiduciaries. In *Mothew*, the Court of Appeal rejected the argument that negligence would constitute a breach of fiduciary duty merely by virtue of having been committed in the context of a conflict situation. As Staughton LJ said,

> [I]n this particular case the building society were not the sole clients of Mr Mothew. . . That is said to make all the difference, because Mr Mothew then became under a fiduciary duty to the building society. . . It seems to me wrong that a breach of contract or tort should become a breach of fiduciary duty in that way. . . In my judgment, Mr Mothew was in breach of a duty of care and nothing more. True he was in a situation where he owed duties to two clients, and those duties might conflict with each other. But he did not prefer the interest of one client to that of another; at most he was guilty of negligence which had that unintended effect.[70]

The cases relied upon by Elliott do not show that statement to have been a mistake.

The one context where Elliott's argument is potentially successful is when a solicitor (or other fiduciary) is acting for two clients, owing potentially conflicting duties to each, and has acted in breach of non-fiduciary duty, intending in so doing to favour the interests of one client over those of the other. As has been discussed above in chapter six, that constitutes a breach of the fiduciary inhibition principle identified by Millett LJ in *Mothew*,[71] but even there, liability does not arise simply because there has been a breach of non-fiduciary duty in a conflict situation: the element of intention to prefer one client over the other adds a further criterion, beyond the mere breach of non-fiduciary duty, before fiduciary liability is made out.[72]

Contrary to the arguments advanced by Birks and Elliott, the cases do not reveal any special link between negligence and fiduciary duties that would justify treating the former as an instance of the latter. It invites confusion to understand negligence as a kind of fiduciary duty.

---

[69] *Ibid*, 635–36.
[70] *Mothew* (above n 56) 26.
[71] *Ibid*, 19.
[72] See above ch 6, section II-C(i).

B. Surrogacy for Tort Law Generally

The arguments that have just been addressed attempt to treat some instances of negligence as breaches of fiduciary duty, thereby connecting fiduciary doctrine to the law of torts. A related but distinct connection between fiduciary doctrine and the law of torts is advanced by other commentators, who argue that fiduciary duties are themselves torts, or alternatively can be understood as surrogates for torts.

i. Cause of Action Surrogacy

Paul Finn once commented that 'the recent revitalization of the jurisdiction to award damages for breach of fiduciary duty . . . presages the development of what is, in effect, a surrogate tort of negligence.'[73] It is not entirely clear what he meant by the surrogacy concept, but his reference to the procedural and remedial advantages of a claim for equitable compensation providing 'a particularly potent, fiduciary-based, surrogate "tort"'[74] suggests that what he envisaged was fiduciary liability somehow replicating liability in tort and so providing an alternative, or 'surrogate', cause of action to tort claims that might otherwise be brought on the same set of facts. Thus, he thought that compensatory claims for breach of fiduciary duty are 'progressively displacing negligence-based ones in "same-matter" conflicts and in conflict of duty and interest cases',[75] creating the potential for the surrogate fiduciary claim to eclipse tort-based claims.

Two comments should be made about this argument. First, when two forms of liability might arise on the same set of facts, one more favourable to claimants than the other, if there is nothing in the circumstances of the case to show that either form of liability has legitimately been excluded by the parties, then there is nothing objectionable in a claimant being entitled to elect to pursue the more advantageous of the two (or more) claims.[76]

Secondly, and more importantly in the context of the arguments advanced in this book, it will not generally be the case that a claim for breach of fiduciary duty offers a true alternative or surrogate for whatever other non-fiduciary claims may be available. In other words, while it is not objectionable for the same set of facts to generate two different kinds of liability, it is important to bear in mind that a cause of action for breach of fiduciary duty is not normally generated by the same facts as a claim for non-fiduciary liability. It is true enough that the same factual setting can give rise to liability both for breach of fiduciary duty and for torts (or other breaches of non-fiduciary duty), but it is critically important to bear in mind that different facts must be shown in order to make out each form

---

[73] PD Finn, 'Fiduciary Law and the Modern Commercial World' in E McKendrick (ed), *Commercial Aspects of Trusts and Fiduciary Obligations* (Oxford, Oxford University Press, 1992) 7, 7.
[74] *Ibid*, 40.
[75] *Ibid*, 41.
[76] *Henderson v Merrett* (above n 40) 194.

of liability. A cause of action comprises 'every fact which it would be necessary for the plaintiff to prove, if traversed, in order to support his right to the judgment of the Court'.[77] As has been emphasised throughout the book, the facts that make out a cause of action for breach of fiduciary duty are not identical to those that make out a cause of action in tort. Indeed, in most cases concerning breach of fiduciary duty it is entirely unnecessary to show any breach of the law of torts or of any other non-fiduciary obligations: the very point of fiduciary duties is to provide a subsidiary and prophylactic form of protection for non-fiduciary duties, so that breach of fiduciary duty is not dependent on establishing a breach of non-fiduciary duty. Even under the inhibition principle, the requisite elements for breach of the fiduciary duty differ from what must be shown to establish a breach of the non-fiduciary duty: a breach of non-fiduciary duty must be coupled with an intention to prefer one client over the other before there is a breach of the fiduciary inhibition principle.

Thus, claims for breach of fiduciary duty are not straightforward surrogates or substitutes for tort-based claims: the facts that constitute a cause of action in fiduciary doctrine are not the same as those that generate liability for breach of contract or for torts or for breach of non-fiduciary equitable duties. Thus, even with the revived recognition that equitable compensation can be awarded for breaches of fiduciary duty, fiduciary claims may arise concurrently with claims based on torts or other breaches of non-fiduciary duties, but they do not create a surrogate for them.

ii. Civil Wrongs

An alternative understanding of the surrogacy concept is that instead of fiduciary duties potentially replacing one or other torts, they can be understood as themselves being a form of tort, in that they involve compensatory remedies for non-consensual wrongs. In that sense, fiduciary duties might be described as surrogate torts, as opposed to surrogates for torts.

This view of the surrogacy concept has more in common with Birks' arguments that the common law ought to be reorganised according to a fourfold taxonomy, than it does with Finn's scholarship regarding fiduciary doctrine. As is well-known, Birks argued that 'all rights are either (by jurisdictional origin) legal or equitable . . . and all such rights arise from wrongs, from consent, from unjust enrichment or from other causative events.'[78] The category of 'wrongs' was so called to reflect Birks' view that history alone, rather than any rational principle, had divided common law rights and wrongs from equitable rights and wrongs. Thus, the concept of 'wrongs' could encompass common law wrongs, such as

---

[77] *Read v Brown* (1888) 22 QBD 128, 131 (CA).
[78] PBH Birks, 'Equity in the Modern Law: An Exercise in Taxonomy' (1996) 26 *University of Western Australia Law Review* 1, 9. See also PBH Birks, 'The Concept of a Civil Wrong' in DG Owen (ed), *Philosophical Foundations of Tort Law* (Oxford, Oxford University Press, 1995) 31; PBH Birks, *Unjust Enrichment*, 2nd edn (Oxford, Oxford University Press, 2005) 21–22.

torts, but also equitable wrongs,[79] which the 'books on tort have made a habit of ignoring'.[80] Hence, he preferred 'to speak of civil wrongs generally and, except where the context otherwise makes clear, [used] "tort" to denote all civil wrongs, whatever their jurisdictional root'.[81] On that basis and notwithstanding that his fourfold classification of rights intentionally included what he admitted was a 'sort of cheat'[82] in the form of the 'other causative events' category,[83] Birks placed breach of fiduciary duty within the category of wrongs.[84] Thus, at times he referred to them as 'meta-torts' but argued that 'there is no real difference between tort and meta-tort'.[85]

Andrew Burrows has taken a similar stance. He has argued that 'equitable wrongs, such as breach of fiduciary duty . . . are analogous to torts but differ because of their historical roots in the Court of Chancery rather than the common law courts'[86] and has said that 'in the long-term, one can hope that such equitable wrongs will be absorbed as torts,'[87] although he recognises that 'at the present time, one cannot simply call these equitable wrongs "torts". They should be seen as alongside, rather than as within, the law of tort.'[88] Following Birks and Burrows, *Clerk and Lindsell* also now addresses breach of fiduciary duty as part of the discussion of torts while accepting that 'strictly speaking, they cannot be regarded as torts.'[89]

Bearing in mind the deficiencies that have been identified earlier in contractarian analyses of fiduciary duties, the question that falls to be addressed here is whether such duties should instead be understood as torts, or at least 'alongside' torts. Again, there are reasons to be cautious before conceptualising fiduciary duties in this way. First, Burrows' view that fiduciary duties sit comfortably alongside torts is premised on the idea that 'although restitution can readily be awarded, the main remedy for these wrongs is "equitable compensation", which

---

[79] Birks, 'The Concept of a Civil Wrong' (*ibid*) 34–35; Birks, *Unjust Enrichment* (*ibid*) 21.
[80] PBH Birks 'Definition and Division: A Meditation on *Institutes* 3.13' in PBH Birks (ed), *The Classification of Obligations* (Oxford, Oxford University Press, 1997) 1, 14.
[81] Birks, 'The Concept of a Civil Wrong' (above n 78) 35.
[82] Birks, 'Equity in the Modern Law' (above n 78) 9.
[83] The need for such a category 'points to the limitations of this kind of diagrammatic classification': S Waddams, *Dimensions of Private Law* (Cambridge, Cambridge University Press, 2003) 11.
[84] PBH Birks, 'Rights, Wrongs, and Remedies' (2000) 20 *Oxford Journal of Legal Studies* 1, 31.
[85] Birks 'Definition and Division' (above n 80) 14.
[86] A Burrows, *Understanding the Law of Obligations* (Oxford, Hart, 1998) 14.
[87] *Ibid*. See also A Burrows, 'We Do This at Common Law but That in Equity' (2002) 22 *Oxford Journal of Legal Studies* 1, 9.
[88] Burrows, *Understanding the Law of Obligations* (above n 86) 14. See also PH Winfield and JA Jolowicz, *Winfield & Jolowicz on Tort*, 17th edn by WVH Rogers (London, Sweet & Maxwell, 2006) [1.11]; J Edelman and J Davies, 'Torts and Equitable Wrongs' in A Burrows (ed), *English Private Law*, 2nd edn (Oxford, Oxford University Press, 2007) ch 17, [17.03].
[89] AM Dugdale and MA Jones (eds), *Clerk and Lindsell on Torts*, 19th edn (London, Sweet & Maxwell, 2006) [1–06]; and see [10–20]–[10–30]. The previous edition devoted an entire chapter to breach of fiduciary duty: AM Dugdale (ed), *Clerk and Lindsell on Torts*, 18th edn (London, Sweet & Maxwell, 2000) ch 28.

seeks to put the plaintiff into as good a position as if no wrong had occurred.'[90] *Clerk and Lindsell* adopts the same view.[91] Naturally, fiduciary doctrine appears close to tort law when it is approached on that footing. But the premise is false. Equitable compensation for loss is not the 'main remedy' for breach of fiduciary duty. Were it so, one would not expect it to have 'languished apparently unnoticed'[92] for a considerable period.[93]

Secondly, it is far from clear that categorising fiduciary duties as falling within or without the concept of a 'civil wrong' is particularly instructive. As Birks himself accepted, it is not easy to be clear about whether rights arising under contracts (or other expressions of consent) merit a category separate from civil wrongs such as torts:

> Arguably modern common law still deals in category (1) obligations (primary obligations from contract) where fixed sums of money are promised—that is, in respect of contractual debts—and where the contract is regarded as specifically performable. For the rest, it appears to deal only in category (2) obligations (secondary obligations arising out of the primary wrong of breach of contract). In other words the correct conclusion must be that for most purposes the common law approaches contract through the wrong of breach of contract. In effect it adds breach of contractual duty to the list of torts.[94]

The idea that the common law understands most breaches of contract as torts shows the difficulty in applying the concept of a 'civil wrong'. There is an analogous difficulty in debates about the nature of fiduciary duties, in that some commentators consider that fiduciary duties arise primarily as a result of agreement between the parties,[95] which might suggest that they fit most comfortably within Birks' 'consent' category,[96] whereas others consider fiduciary duties

---

[90] Burrows, *Understanding the Law of Obligations* (above n 86) 14. See also A Burrows, 'Limitations on Compensation' in A Burrows and WE Peel (eds), *Commercial Remedies* (Oxford, Oxford University Press, 2003) 27, 44.

[91] Dugdale and Jones (eds), 19th edn (above n 89) [1–06].

[92] Finn, 'Fiduciary Law and the Modern Commercial World' (above n 73) 40. See also CEF Rickett, 'Equitable Compensation: The Giant Stirs' (1996) 112 *Law Quarterly Review* 27, 29.

[93] Furthermore, one would not expect other commentators to have argued that equitable compensation is not available as a remedy for breach of fiduciary: see, eg, PBH Birks, *An Introduction to the Law of Restitution*, rev edn (Oxford, Oxford University Press, 1989) 332; S Worthington, 'Fiduciaries: When is Self-Denial Obligatory?' [1999] *Cambridge Law Journal* 500, 507; S Worthington, 'Corporate Governance: Remedying and Ratifying Directors' Breaches' (2000) 116 *Law Quarterly Review* 638, 664–65. As was seen above in ch 4, section III-B(i), those arguments are inconsistent with the case law, but the fact that they have even been made indicates that equitable compensation cannot be the *main* remedy for breach of fiduciary duty.

[94] Birks, 'The Concept of a Civil Wrong' (above n 78) 51.

[95] Eg, CEF Rickett, 'Compensating for Loss in Equity: Choosing the Right Horse for Each Course' in PBH Birks and FD Rose (eds), *Restitution and Equity: Resulting Trusts and Equitable Compensation*, vol 1 (London, Mansfield Press, 2000) 173, 180.

[96] Eg, *Harris v Digital Pulse Pty Ltd* [2003] NSWCA 10 at [36], (2003) 56 NSWLR 298 *per* Spigelman CJ.

are more correctly understood as imposed by equity,[97] suggesting perhaps an analogy 'closer to tort law'.[98] The truth probably lies somewhere in between, in the sense that the fiduciary will have voluntarily undertaken the role (and hence the non-fiduciary duties that fiduciary duties protect) that generates the fiduciary duties but does not normally expressly undertake the fiduciary duties themselves. The latter are more readily seen as having been imposed in order to protect proper performance of the non-fiduciary duties that the fiduciary undertook to perform.

But what matters most in the present context is that arguments about whether fiduciary duties are best characterised as 'civil wrongs' are not terribly illuminating as to the purpose and function that those duties serve. As Birks himself said,

> Because the concept of a civil wrong is broad and abstract, its explanatory power is weak. To say that a consequence follows certain conduct because the conduct is a breach of a primary duty is to offer a formal explanation but not a satisfying one. The real explanation has to be completed in every case from the policies and values underlying the recognition of the primary duty which is in question.[99]

The core of the 'policies and values' that support and justify the recognition of fiduciary duties is best understood as a concern to provide a subsidiary and prophylactic form of protection for non-fiduciary duties.

This indicates the third and greatest reason to be cautious before equating fiduciary duties with tort law generally, which is that protection of non-fiduciary duties is not a function commonly reflected in the policies and values underlying the recognition of torts. In the main, tort obligations are concerned with requiring a defendant to take such care as is reasonable in the circumstances to avoid acts or omissions that will reasonably foreseeably cause injury to others,[100] and with prohibiting direct physical interference with basic bodily or proprietary rights.[101] Negligence 'tells us when a person has to pay compensation for harm he has caused without meaning to',[102] while trespass is concerned 'to protect and vindicate the basic rights of the citizen against deliberate, even well-meaning,

---

[97]   Eg, FE Dowrick, 'The Relationship of Principal and Agent' (1954) 17 *Modern Law Review* 24, 31; Brudney (above n 26) 598 and 628–29; A Underhill and DJ Hayton, *Law Relating to Trusts and Trustees*, 17th edn by DJ Hayton, PB Matthews and CCJ Mitchell (London, LexisNexis Butterworths, 2007) [1.51]; *Beach Petroleum NL v Abbott Tout Russell Kennedy* [1999] NSWCA 408 at [192], (1999) 48 NSWLR 1; *Chirnside v Fay* [2006] NZSC 68 at [72], [2007] 1 NZLR 433.

[98]   PD Finn, 'The Fiduciary Principle' in TG Youdan (ed), *Equity, Fiduciaries and Trusts* (Toronto, Carswell, 1989) 1, 54. See also *Harris v Digital Pulse Pty Ltd* [2003] NSWCA 10 at [184]–[185], (2003) 56 NSWLR 298 *per* Mason P; J Glover, 'The Identification of Fiduciaries' in PBH Birks (ed), *Privacy and Loyalty* (Oxford, Oxford University Press, 1997) 269, 275. Yet others have argued that some aspects of fiduciary doctrine are 'best understood and explained as actions to reverse unjust enrichment': RC Nolan, 'Conflicts of Interest, Unjust Enrichment and Wrongdoing' in WR Cornish, RC Nolan, J O'Sullivan and GJ Virgo (eds), *Restitution: Past, Present and Future* (Oxford, Hart Publishing, 1998) 87, 99.

[99]   Birks, 'The Concept of a Civil Wrong' (above n 78) 51.

[100]   T Weir, *An Introduction to Tort Law*, 2nd edn (Oxford, Oxford University Press, 2006) ch 2.

[101]   *Ibid*, ch 9.

[102]   *Ibid*, 133.

invasion, whether or not any damage is caused'.[103] Neither of these functions is concerned with the protection of other duties from situations that carry a heightened risk of breach of those other duties. Liability for negligence arises as a direct response to the infliction of harm, rather than as a subsidiary and prophylactic protection against other possible harms, and tort law doctrines such as trespass and conversion are, at least insofar as they relate to property, partly *constitutive* of the property holder's *rights* far more than they are *protective* of the proper performance of other *duties*.[104]

Some of the doctrines of tort law are designed to protect other duties. The doctrine of inducing breaches of contract, in particular, provides some form of protection for contractual undertakings,[105] by imposing (secondary) accessory liability when a breach of contract has been intentionally brought about by the non-contracting defendant.[106] This presupposes that the contract was breached,[107] which differs from most fiduciary doctrines. However, the doctrine is similar to the fiduciary inhibition principle, as is the requisite mental element for the tort, namely that the defendant knew of the contract and intended to interfere with its performance.[108]

There are, of course, differences between the tort and the inhibition principle, the most obvious of which is that the tort concerns the defendant inducing a third party to breach his contract,[109] whereas the inhibition principle concerns the fiduciary himself breaching his own non-fiduciary duties.[110] Further, whereas the inhibition principle applies only to fiduciaries, the tort applies when any person procures breach of any kind of contract.[111] Thus, the two doctrines are

---

[103]   *Ibid*, 133.

[104]   The tort duties are correlative to claim rights held by the property holder (WN Hohfeld, 'Some Fundamental Legal Conceptions as applied in Judicial Reasoning' (1913) 23 *Yale Law Journal* 16, 32), which rights in turn are part of the complex bundle of relations that comprise the property holder's 'property': WN Hohfeld, 'Fundamental Legal Conceptions as applied in Judicial Reasoning' (1917) 26 *Yale Law Journal* 710, 746; J Waldron, *The Right to Private Property* (Oxford, Oxford University Press, 1988) 28; JW Harris, *Property and Justice* (Oxford, Oxford University Press, 1996) 129. See also AM Honoré, 'Ownership' in AG Guest (ed), *Oxford Essays in Jurisprudence* (Oxford, Oxford University Press, 1961) 107.

[105]   H Carty, *An Analysis of the Economic Torts* (Oxford, Oxford University Press, 2001) 43.

[106]   *OBG Ltd v Allan* [2007] UKHL 21 at [5], [32] and [172], [2008] 1 AC 1; *Credit Lyonnais Bank Nederland NV v Export Credits Guarantee Dept* [2000] 1 AC 486, 496; Carty (*ibid*) 54; P Sales, 'The Tort of Conspiracy and Civil Secondary Liability' [1990] *Cambridge Law Journal* 491, 503 and 504.

[107]   *OBG Ltd v Allan* [2007] UKHL 21 at [5], [2008] 1 AC 1; Dugdale and Jones (eds), 19th edn (above n 89) [25–22] and [25–31]; Carty (above n 105) 45 and 54.

[108]   Dugdale and Jones (eds) (*ibid*) [25–16].

[109]   *Ibid*, [25–15].

[110]   Accessory liability in the fiduciary context is governed by the doctrine of dishonest assistance: see *Royal Brunei Airlines Sdn Bhd v Tan* [1995] 2 AC 378 (PC); *Twinsectra Ltd v Yardley* [2002] UKHL 12, [2002] 2 AC 164; *Barlow Clowes International Ltd v Eurotrust International Ltd* [2005] UKPC 37, [2006] 1 WLR 1476; *Abou-Rahmah v Abacha* [2006] EWCA Civ 1492, [2007] 1 Lloyd's Rep 115.

[111]   Dugdale and Jones (eds) (above n 89) [25–15]; Carty (above n 105) 42–43; SF Deakin, AC Johnston and B Markesinis, *Markesinis & Deakin's Tort Law*, 6th edn (Oxford, Oxford University Press, 2008) 576.

not identical, but the similarities between them raise the question whether fiduciary doctrine should perhaps be categorised within the field of torts.

The similarities between the inhibition principle and the tort of inducing breaches of contract ought not to be allowed to overshadow the more fundamental distinctions between torts and the way fiduciary doctrine operates generally. The inhibition principle is but one part of fiduciary doctrine's general response to situations in which a fiduciary acts with potentially inconsistent duties owed to more than one principal, which itself is only one of the types of situations in which fiduciary doctrine is troubled by heightened risks of breach of non-fiduciary duties. The inhibition principle must be taken in context, so as not to distort understanding of the other duties that fiduciary doctrine imposes to regulate conflicts between inconsistent duties or duty and interest. Fiduciary doctrine does not generally require proof of a knowing and intentional breach of non-fiduciary duty. Indeed, it does not normally require proof of a breach of non-fiduciary duty at all. In contrast, fault is perhaps a more natural aspect of tort law, in that tortfeasors are as a class generally strangers to the victim who are more legitimately entitled (than are fiduciaries[112]) not to have to exhibit concern for the economic interests of others unless they deliberately damage those interests.[113]

So, it would be wrong to conclude from the resemblance between the inhibition principle, which is only one part of fiduciary doctrine—and a part that responds to a quite restricted set of circumstances[114]—and one part of the law of torts, that fiduciary doctrine generally resembles the law of torts. No single theory provides a unitary explanation of the various purposes served by the Anglo-Australian law of torts.[115] As *Winfield and Jolowicz* puts it, 'it is perhaps unkind to call tort the dustbin of the law of obligations, but it is certainly the great residuary category. No one theory explains the whole of the law.'[116] Thus, 'there is no *general* principle in English law to tell us when conduct is tortious . . . and when it is not.'[117] Without any general governing principle, it is impossible to rebut conclusively the argument that fiduciary duties can be understood as part

---

[112] Fiduciaries are far from strangers vis-à-vis their principals: M Conaglen, 'Public–Private Intersection: Comparing Fiduciary Conflict Doctrine and Bias' [2008] *Public Law* 58, 78.

[113] Even those who deliberately damage the economic interests of others are not necessarily liable in tort: *Allen v Flood* [1898] AC 1.

[114] See above ch 6, section II-C(ii).

[115] See, eg, JG Fleming, *The Law of Torts*, 9th edn (Sydney, Law Book Company, 1998) 8; R Goff, 'The Search for Principle' reprinted in W Swadling and GH Jones (eds), *The Search for Principle* (Oxford, Oxford University Press, 1999) 313, 324–25; P Cane, *The Anatomy of Tort Law* (Oxford, Hart, 1998) 21–22; *Furniss v Fitchett* [1958] NZLR 396, 401 (SC).

[116] Winfield and Jolowicz, 17th edn (above n 88) [1–2]. Notwithstanding this acknowledgement, the same book seeks to advance as a unifying theory of torts 'the principle that unjustifiable harm is tortious': at [1–16]. That, however, is 'question begging, because [it] avoid[s] facing the crucial problem of what the law will recognise as "justification"': Fleming (*ibid*) 8. The position may differ in America, where a 'prima facie tort theory' has been adopted: see Winfield and Jolowicz, 17th edn (above n 88) [1–15].

[117] Weir, *An Introduction to Tort Law* (above n 100) 11.

of the series of obligations that we refer to as 'torts'. However, while the concept of a civil wrong is not necessarily inapt to describe fiduciary duties, it is inadvisable to think of them simply as torts. Similarly to the points made already regarding the contractarian view of fiduciary doctrine, the main consideration weighing against treating fiduciary duties as part of the law of torts is the danger, inherent in that approach, that sight will be lost of the distinctive protective function of fiduciary doctrine.

Notwithstanding its lack of a governing principle, it can fairly be said that the law of torts is generally marked out by the fact that it is 'looking for behaviour which can be castigated'.[118] That approach to liability stands in stark contrast to fiduciary doctrine's subsidiary and prophylactic concern to prevent breaches of non-fiduciary duty from arising. Fiduciary doctrine has very little consonance with any of the vast number of doctrines contained within the 'ragbag'[119] of the law of torts, the overwhelming majority of which do not exhibit the same subsidiary and prophylactic protective function as that served generally by fiduciary doctrine.

The whole point of classification is that it 'promotes understanding'.[120] When terms are as devoid of real meaning as the concepts of 'tort' or 'civil wrong', it is not difficult to shoe-horn within them doctrines such as fiduciary duties. However, it is unhelpful to do that because of the tendency it generates to treat fiduciary duties as no different from the indistinct range of wrongs that comprise the law of torts. Fiduciary doctrine has an identifiable and clear purpose that is distinct from that served by torts generally, which is to provide subsidiary and prophylactic protection for non-fiduciary duties. Further, the range of remedies that is made available for a breach of fiduciary duty is consonant with and gives effect to that purpose. And treating fiduciary duties as providing a distinct form of protection for non-fiduciary duties promotes understanding of the relationship between fiduciary duties and other kinds of duties.

Attempts to fold fiduciary duties into other legal concepts engender no real clarity of thought about their nature and function, and instead run the risk that their true purpose will be subverted by their being analysed and applied as somehow similar to entirely unrelated doctrines. It is preferable for fiduciary doctrine to be understood on its own terms, as a discrete set of duties that serve a purpose which usefully distinguishes them from the law of torts and from contract.

---

[118] T Weir, *Economic Torts* (Oxford, Oxford University Press, 1997) 32.

[119] Weir, *An Introduction to Tort Law* (above n 100) ix.

[120] Birks, 'Equity in the Modern Law' (above n 78) 3.

III. Undue Influence and Confidence

The final section of this chapter addresses a slightly different aspect of the conceptual implications of understanding fiduciary duties as a subsidiary and prophylactic form of protection for non-fiduciary duties. The question is whether the doctrines of undue influence and confidence, which are frequently treated as fiduciary in nature, ought to be so understood.

When they are compared carefully, the doctrines of undue influence and breach of confidence can be seen to perform functions quite different from that served by fiduciary doctrine's concept of 'loyalty'. However, before advancing the analysis which supports that conclusion, it must be acknowledged that the argument is necessarily somewhat tentative. As was explained above in chapters two and three, the task undertaken in the book is to identify the nature and function of fiduciary doctrine by reference to the duties that comprise its core, 'distinguishing'[121] obligation of loyalty. That approach is made possible, and indeed necessary, by the fact that the courts have refused to define the fiduciary concept. As such, there is no pure or universal ideal of 'fiduciary' to which one can refer in determining whether a duty is or is not fiduciary in nature. One is forced to adopt a more empirical course, as this book has sought to do, of observation of the case law, identifying which duties are owed peculiarly by fiduciaries and then seeking to derive an understanding of the nature and function of those duties. However, it is inherent in such a process that any theory that is developed on the basis of those observations is prone to need alteration if the observations turn out not to have been correct. Thus, if undue influence and confidence are peculiar in their application to fiduciaries, then an analysis of them ought to have been offered earlier in the book, when the nature and function of fiduciary doctrine was addressed. After all, the peculiarity of fiduciary duties has been the basis of the analysis and argument offered in this book. In respect of each of the doctrines of undue influence and confidence, therefore, it is necessary to consider first whether they apply peculiarly to fiduciaries before addressing their content to see whether they perform functions like that performed by fiduciary doctrine's concept of loyalty.

A. Undue Influence

There is considerable overlap between the situations in which claims of undue influence arise and those in which fiduciary duties arise, particularly when the claim is based on so-called presumed undue influence. Hence, some have conflated the two doctrines, arguing that influence is the basis of the fiduciary

---

[121] *Mothew* (above n 56) 18.

conflict principles.[122] Alternatively, Rick Bigwood has presented a refined analysis of the doctrine of presumed undue influence that argues that it is best understood as an instantiation of the fiduciary conflict principle.[123] There are a number of reasons not to accept these arguments.

First, while there is overlap in the situations to which the two doctrines can be applied, the degree of overlap is less than at first appears. As Lord Scarman said in *National Westminster Bank plc v Morgan*, 'there are plenty of confidential relationships which do not give rise to the presumption of undue influence ... and there are plenty of non-confidential relationships in which one person relies upon the advice of another.'[124] Thus, for example, the relationship between solicitor and client is presumed to be one of influence,[125] and solicitors clearly owe fiduciary duties to their clients. But while company directors undoubtedly owe fiduciary duties, they are not presumed to have influence over the conduct of their companies of the sort relevant to application of the doctrine of undue influence.[126] Further, trustees clearly owe fiduciary duties to the trust beneficiaries, but it is less clear that they are presumed to have influence over the beneficiaries: some of the cases suggest that trustees are presumed to have that form of influence,[127] but doubts have been raised.[128] As Lord Cranworth said in *Smith v Kay*, 'it is only a particular sort of trusteeship that gives the influence.'[129] One would have expected that a 'fiduciary' doctrine would apply without any doubt to the paradigm class of fiduciary actors.

The doctrine of undue influence can also apply when fiduciary duties are not owed. By way of example, solicitors whose retainers have come to an end are no longer bound by fiduciary duties,[130] and yet the influence that they have over their clients may remain, with the consequence that the doctrine of undue influence is still applicable.[131] Indeed, the doctrine of undue influence applies to *anyone*, irrespective of whether they owe any other fiduciary duties, who 'has acquired over another a measure of influence, or ascendancy, of which the

---

[122] See, eg, *Holman v Loynes* (1854) 4 De GM & G 270, 283 (43 ER 510) *per* Turner LJ; *O'Sullivan v Management Agency & Music Ltd* [1985] QB 428, 448–49 (CA) *per* Dunn LJ. See also *Tate v Williamson* (1866) LR 2 Ch App 55, 61 (LC).

[123] R Bigwood, *Exploitative Contracts* (Oxford, Oxford University Press, 2003) ch 8.

[124] *National Westminster Bank plc v Morgan* [1985] AC 686, 703. See also *Re Estate of Brocklehurst* [1978] Ch 14, 41 (CA); *Goldsworthy v Brickell* [1987] Ch 378, 401 (CA); *Cowen v Piggott* [1989] 1 Qd R 41, 44–45 (FC); *Barkley v Barkley-Brown* [2009] NSWSC 76 at [136]; G Spencer Bower, *Actionable Non-Disclosure*, 2nd edn by AK Turner and RJ Sutton (London, Butterworths, 1990) [16.06]–[16.08]; Meagher, Heydon and Leeming (above n 45) [15–100]; Bigwood, *Exploitative Contracts* (*ibid*) 427.

[125] See, eg, *Royal Bank of Scotland plc v Etridge (No 2)* [2001] UKHL 44 at [18], [2002] 2 AC 773.

[126] LS Sealy, 'The Director as Trustee' [1967] *Cambridge Law Journal* 83, 90.

[127] See Bigwood, *Exploitative Contracts* (above n 123) 432 (fn 300).

[128] See, eg, PD Finn, *Fiduciary Obligations* (Sydney, Law Book Co, 1977) [176]; Meagher, Heydon and Leeming (above n 45) [15–095]; WHD Winder, 'Undue Influence and Fiduciary Relationship' (1940) 4 *Conveyancer (New Series)* 274.

[129] *Smith v Kay* (1859) 7 HLC 750, 771 (11 ER 299).

[130] See above ch 7, section II-B(ii).

[131] Eg, *Wright v Proud* (1806) 13 Ves 136, 138 (33 ER 246) (LC). See also Meagher, Heydon and Leeming (above n 45) [15–065].

ascendant person then takes unfair advantage'.[132] In other words, the doctrine of undue influence does not apply peculiarly to fiduciaries.

That conclusion is reinforced by differences in the methodologies by which the two doctrines operate. For example, when a claimant seeks to rely on a presumption of undue influence, he must show that he reposed trust and confidence in the defendant, that the defendant had acquired a position of ascendancy or that the case falls within one of the categories in which such influence is presumed.[133] Once that has been established, the claimant is entitled to relief if he can also show that the transaction was manifestly disadvantageous to him, unless the defendant is able to displace the presumption.[134] The important point here is that the court can only infer that the transaction came about as a result of undue influence if the claimant shows not merely a relationship of influence but also 'that the transaction is not readily explicable by the relationship of the parties'.[135] It is the combination of those two factors that justifies the inference that the transaction came about as a result of undue influence.

This approach, which requires the claimant to prove disadvantage to himself, stands in stark contrast to the approach under fiduciary doctrine. In cases in which the self-dealing rule is concerned, for example, the substantive content of the transaction is generally not looked into at all.[136] And even in cases in which a claimant relies on the fair-dealing rule, when it can be relevant to determine whether full value has been paid,[137] the fiduciary bears the onus of proving that fact.[138] In other words, the principal need not establish that any advantage was taken.

Noting the discrepancy between these two approaches, Lord Browne-Wilkinson suggested in *CIBC Mortgages plc v Pitt* that the need for a claimant to show manifest disadvantage in presumed undue influence claims may require reconsideration.[139] However, that possibility has since been rejected in *Royal Bank of Scotland v Etridge*,[140] where it was held that the requirement is a

---

[132] *Royal Bank of Scotland plc v Etridge (No 2)* [2001] UKHL 44 at [8], [2002] 2 AC 773.

[133] *Ibid* at [18] and [21].

[134] *Ibid* at [14] and [21]–[25].

[135] *Ibid* at [21]; see also [25], [156] and [220]. And see *R v Attorney-General for England & Wales* [2003] UKPC 22 at [22].

[136] See above ch 5, section IV-A.

[137] As has been explained above in ch 5, section IV-B, the fairness or otherwise of a fair-dealing transaction goes to the fullness of the fiduciary's disclosure of material facts, but this point does not detract from the methodological differences between the fair-dealing rule and the presumption of undue influence.

[138] *Thomson v Eastwood* (1877) 2 App Cas 215, 236; *Gibson v Jeyes* (1801) 6 Ves 266, 271 and 278 (31 ER 1044) (LC); *Denton v Donner* (1856) 23 Beav 285, 290 (53 ER 112) (MR).

[139] *CIBC Mortgages plc v Pitt* [1994] 1 AC 200, 209. See also *Barclays Bank plc v Coleman* [2001] QB 20 at [57]–[67].

[140] *Royal Bank of Scotland plc v Etridge (No 2)* [2001] UKHL 44 at [24], [2002] 2 AC 773.

necessary limitation on the width of the doctrine because otherwise any trans-action within a relationship of influence, no matter how 'innocuous and inno-cent',[141] would be caught by the presumption that it was caused by an undue exercise of that influence.

The drawing out of these methodological differences is not mere pedantry. The methodological differences are related to and based upon the fundamental function served by each of the doctrines. The 'presumption' of undue influence is an inference reached by the court that the defendant unduly exercised the influence that he had over the claimant to procure the transaction. In other words, 'when a plaintiff succeeds by this route he does so because he has succeeded in establishing a case of undue influence.'[142] In that sense, although it is reached by a different evidential route, the presumption of undue influence is not qualitatively different from a finding that the defendant used actual undue influence:

> A finding of actual undue influence and a finding that there is a presumption of undue influence are not alternatives to one another. The presumption is . . . an evidential presumption. If it applies, and the evidence is not sufficient to rebut it, an allegation of undue influence succeeds.[143]

The importance of this is that claims of undue influence, no matter how they are proven, are concerned with 'unacceptable forms of persuasion'.[144] The use of influence is pervasive within society, 'and all without discredit. It is part of life.'[145] Hence, relief is not given simply because a transaction was brought about by influence[146] but only when there is proof of 'mala fides, or of undue or unfair exercise of the influence'.[147] 'As its name suggests, undue influence . . . involves the wrongful exercise of influence.'[148]

In sharp contrast, fiduciary doctrine is not concerned with the question whether a fiduciary has acted in a morally reprehensible manner. The moral acceptability of a fiduciary's conduct is not a relevant consideration when a claim is brought for breach of fiduciary duty because fiduciary doctrine provides a prophylactic protection for non-fiduciary duties. It concerns situations in which a fiduciary might be tempted not to perform his non-fiduciary duties properly. It seeks to prevent fiduciaries from acting in such situations at all, rather than

---

[141] *Ibid* at [156]. See also *Rhodes v Bate* (1866) LR 1 Ch App 252, 258; *Spong v Spong* (1914) 18 CLR 544, 550; *Watkins v Combes* (1922) 30 CLR 180, 193–94.
[142] *Royal Bank of Scotland plc v Etridge (No 2)* [2001] UKHL 44 at [16], [2002] 2 AC 773.
[143] *Ibid* at [219].
[144] *Ibid* at [7].
[145] Birks, *An Introduction to the Law of Restitution* (above n 93) 173.
[146] *Allcard v Skinner* (1887) 36 ChD 145, 185 *per* Lindley LJ (CA). See also *Lloyds Bank Ltd v Bundy* [1975] QB 326, 336 (CA).
[147] *Rhodes v Bate* (above n 141) 258. See also R Bigwood, 'Undue Influence: "Impaired Consent" or "Wicked Exploitation"?' (1996) 16 *Oxford Journal of Legal Studies* 503, 508–9.
[148] J Cartwright, *Unequal Bargaining* (Oxford, Oxford University Press, 1991) 170; see also p 173. And see *National Westminster Bank v Morgan* (above n 124) 705–6.

seeking to ensure that fiduciaries act in a morally acceptable manner in such situations. Fiduciary doctrine operates 'without imputing fraud' on the basis of 'a general principle of public policy'.[149] In contrast, the principle underlying undue influence 'is not a vague "public policy" but specifically the victimisation of one party by the other'.[150] As the High Court of Australia has said, undue influence 'is concerned with the production by malign means of an intention to act'.[151]

Rick Bigwood has argued that 'the ritualistic raising of a "presumption" of undue influence . . . is but an exercise in applying the conventional conflict rule to the parties' specific relationship and transactional encounter'.[152] This view of undue influence has two flaws: it is based on a misapplication of the fiduciary conflict principle, and it is based on a misunderstanding of the nature and function served by that principle.

As to the first point, Bigwood has argued that the requirement that a claimant show manifest disadvantage when he seeks to rely on the presumption of undue influence is 'an exercise in applying, *mutatis mutandis*, to transactions that occur within the context of influential relationships (as specially defined), the conflict of interest and duty rule that operates more generally in wider fiduciary law'.[153] A defendant who is found to have exercised undue influence will have 'preferred his own interests'[154] and can be said, as Bigwood puts it, to have been engaged in self-dealing: 'it is, of course, not self-dealing in the "purest" sense . . . but it is "self-dealing" nonetheless (that is, to the extent that the fiduciary's influence may causally operate to control both sides of the transaction)'.[155] But those two points only establish half of the analysis necessary to make out a breach of the fiduciary conflict principle. The fact that a fiduciary acts in a 'self-regarding' way does not necessarily mean that there was a relevant conflict:[156] 'the self-dealing rule is an application of the wider principle that a man must not put himself in a position where *duty* and interest conflict or where his *duty* to one conflicts with his *duty* to another' (emphasis added).[157]

The difficulty with treating the undue influence doctrine as an application of the fiduciary conflict principle is that while the defendant's interest in the transaction is clear, it is far from clear that there is any conflicting duty owed to the claimant that conflicts with that interest. The analysis might be saved from this flaw by arguing that the doctrine of undue influence imposes a duty not to take unfair advantage of the weaker party in the relationship, which is then

---

[149] *Gibson v Jeyes* (above n 138) 271.

[150] *National Westminster Bank v Morgan* (above n 124) 705. See also *Allcard v Skinner* (above n 146) 182–83 (CA); *Re Estate of Brocklehurst* (above n 124) 41 (CA).

[151] *Tanwar Enterprises Pty Ltd v Cauchi* [2003] HCA 57 at [23], (2003) 217 CLR 315.

[152] Bigwood, *Exploitative Contracts* (above n 123) 449.

[153] *Ibid*, 445; see also p 424.

[154] *Royal Bank of Scotland plc v Etridge (No 2)* [2001] UKHL 44 at [14], [2002] 2 AC 773.

[155] Bigwood, *Exploitative Contracts* (above n 123) 444.

[156] Cf *ibid*, 426.

[157] *Re Thompson's Settlement* [1986] 1 Ch 99, 115.

opposed to the defendant's interest. However, like the flawed analysis that treats the fiduciary conflict principle as concerned with preventing conflicts between fiduciary duties and interest,[158] this understanding of undue influence collapses in on itself: the undue influence principle then itself provides both the duty that is not permitted to conflict with the defendant's interest and also the duty not to allow that duty (itself) to conflict with interest.[159]

Secondly, Bigwood's argument that undue influence is an application of the fiduciary conflict principle is based on a misunderstanding of the nature of the latter principle. He rightly points out that the presumption of undue influence 'is not that D *might* have abused his special influence, but rather that he *did* in fact do so'[160] and then argues that this is an application of the fiduciary conflict principle that operates on the basis that 'when fiduciaries are proven to have conflicting motives, *they are assumed to have done the worst.*'[161] The first proposition—regarding undue influence—is correct, but the second is not. Fiduciary doctrine does not operate on the basis of assuming that the fiduciary has acted in breach of non-fiduciary duty but rather is concerned with the risk that the fiduciary might be tempted not to perform his non-fiduciary duties properly. It is the risk against which the doctrine strikes, which explains why it applies irrespective of whether that risk was, in Bigwood's terminology, 'actualized'.[162]

In short, it is preferable for the doctrine of undue influence to be kept separate from fiduciary doctrine in order that the distinct conceptual underpinnings of the two doctrines are not confused.

B. Confidence

An involved debate has continued for many years as to whether breach of confidence ought properly to be understood as an instance of breach of fiduciary duty. Several commentators have suggested that is so,[163] as has some of the case

---

[158] See the discussion above in ch 4, section II-A.

[159] A further problem with this attempt to save the conflict analysis of undue influence is that the doctrine of undue influence is not itself a duty: *Agnew v Länsförsäkringsbolagens AB* [2001] 1 AC 223, 265.

[160] Bigwood, *Exploitative Contracts* (above n 123) 388.

[161] *Ibid*, 388–89; see also p 471. Bigwood attributes the statement to Lord Herschell's speech in *Bray v Ford* [1896] AC 44, 52, but that is an error.

[162] Bigwood, *Exploitative Contracts* (above n 123) 388 and 471.

[163] Eg, DR Klinck, '"Things of Confidence": Loyalty, Secrecy and Fiduciary Obligation' (1990) 54 *Saskatchewan Law Review* 73, 92–93; JL McDougall, 'The Relationship of Confidence' in DWM Waters (ed), *Equity, Fiduciaries and Trusts* (Scarborough, Carswell, 1993) 157, 164–65 and 168; Law Commission, *Fiduciary Duties and Regulatory Rules* (Law Com 236, 1995) [1.4]; PJ Millett, 'Equity's Place in the Law of Commerce' (1998) 114 *Law Quarterly Review* 214, 219–20; D Bayliss, 'Breach of Confidence as a Breach of Fiduciary Obligations: A Theory' (2002) 9 *Auckland University Law Review* 702; R Flannigan, 'The Boundaries of Fiduciary Accountability' (2004) 83 *Canadian Bar Review* 35, 46, 71 and 87–88; GJ Virgo, *The Principles of the Law of Restitution*, 2nd edn (Oxford, Oxford

law,[164] whereas other commentators[165] and yet further cases[166] have taken the opposite view.

It is preferable to treat breach of confidence as conceptually distinct and hence separate from fiduciary doctrine. As with undue influence, the reasons are again twofold: the doctrine of confidence is not peculiar in its application to fiduciaries, and it performs a function quite distinct from that performed by fiduciary doctrine.

First for consideration is the question of peculiarity. While there is a large degree of overlap in the application of fiduciary duties and obligations of confidence,[167] the latter are not peculiar in their application to fiduciaries. The doctrine of confidence owes something in terms of its early development to analogies drawn with trusts and with property held for another,[168] as did the foundations for the development of fiduciary doctrine.[169] However, the doctrine of confidence has developed considerably since that time. Notwithstanding contrary suggestions,[170] the prevailing modern view is that the foundation of the doctrine of confidence no longer rests in the protection of property[171] but rather in the 'obligation of conscience arising from the circumstances in or through which the information was communicated or obtained'.[172] Furthermore, those 'obligations of conscience' are not limited in their application to fiduciary

University Press, 2006) 267–69; R Flannigan, 'The Fiduciary Accountability of Ordinary Employees' (2007) 13 *Canadian Labour & Employment Law Journal* 375, 380 and 389.

[164] Eg, *Schering Chemicals Ltd v Falkman Ltd* [1982] QB 1, 27–28 (CA); *Attorney-General v Blake* [1998] Ch 439, 454 (CA) and [2001] 1 AC 268, 292.

[165] Eg, RG Hammond, 'Is Breach of Confidence Properly Analysed in Fiduciary Terms?' (1979) 25 *McGill Law Journal* 244, 251; RP Austin, 'The Corporate Fiduciary: *Standard Investments Ltd v Canadian Imperial Bank of Commerce*' (1986) 12 *Canadian Business Law Journal* 96, 97; J Glover, 'Is Breach of Confidence a Fiduciary Wrong? Preserving the Reach of Judge-Made Law' (2001) 21 *Legal Studies* 594, 594–95 and 613; Meagher, Heydon and Leeming (above n 45) [41–035]; HW Tang, 'Confidence and the Constructive Trust' (2003) 23 *Legal Studies* 135, 142–46; P Koh, 'Once a Director, Always a Fiduciary?' [2003] *Cambridge Law Journal* 403, 429–30.

[166] Eg, *Indata Equipment Supplies Ltd v ACL Ltd* [1998] FSR 248, 256 and 262 (CA); *Maclean v Arklow Investments Ltd* [1998] 3 NZLR 680, 690 (CA); *Arklow Investments Ltd v Maclean* [2000] 1 WLR 594, 600 (PC); *Lac Minerals Ltd v International Corona Resources Ltd* [1989] 2 SCR 574, 600–1.

[167] *Oceanic Life Ltd v HIH Casualty & General Insurance Ltd* [1999] NSWSC 292 at [43], (1999) 10 ANZ Ins Cases 74,968.

[168] See, eg, the connection identified in early confidence cases with the trust concept: *Abernethy v Hutchinson* (1825) 1 H & Tw 28, 37 (47 ER 1313) (LC); *Prince Albert v Strange* (1849) 1 Mac & G 25, 44 (41 ER 1171) (LC); *Morison v Moat* (1851) 9 Hare 241, 255 (68 ER 492) (VC).

[169] See above ch 2, section II-A.

[170] Eg, *Boardman v Phipps* [1967] 2 AC 46, 107 and 115; S Ricketson, 'Confidential Information: A New Proprietary Interest? Part II' (1978) 11 *Melbourne University Law Review* 289; J Birch, 'Breach of Confidence: Dividing the Cause of Action along Proprietary Lines' (2007) 81 *Australian Law Journal* 338.

[171] *Moorgate Tobacco Co Ltd v Philip Morris Ltd (No 2)* (1984) 156 CLR 414, 438; *OBG Ltd v Allan* [2007] UKHL 21 at [275], [2008] 1 AC 1.

[172] *Moorgate Tobacco v Philip Morris (No 2)* (ibid) 438. See also *Boardman v Phipps* (above n 170) 89–90, 102 and 127–28; *Breen v Williams* (1996) 186 CLR 71, 81, 91, 111–12 and 129; *Cadbury Schweppes Inc v FBI Foods Ltd* [1999] 1 SCR 142 at [48]; *Douglas v Hello! Ltd (No 3)* [2005] EWCA Civ 595 at [119] and [126], [2006] QB 125; WR Cornish and D Llewelyn, *Intellectual Property: Patents, Copyright, Trade Marks and Allied Rights*, 6th edn (London, Sweet & Maxwell, 2007) [8–50]–[8–54].

relationships: they can be owed by anyone who receives information in circumstances in which it is clear that it ought to be kept confidential, regardless of whether that person owes any fiduciary duties.

In *Ocular Sciences v Aspect Vision*, Laddie J commented that 'in most, if not all, cases where obligations of confidence arise, it will be in circumstances where the court will find that a fiduciary relationship exists also.'[173] However, the courts have since shied away from that view. In *Indata v ACL*, the Court of Appeal unanimously considered that 'the mere fact that a confidant has received confidential information does not create a fiduciary relationship so as to create fiduciary obligations.'[174] While there will be numerous instances when fiduciary duties and duties of confidence coexist, that is because it is common for confidential information to be disclosed in fiduciary relationships, rather than because the disclosure of confidential information necessarily creates a fiduciary relationship:

> The fact that confidential information is obtained and misused does not itself create a fiduciary relationship, though communications in confidence may be an incidence of such a relationship. The obligations of loyalty and fidelity arising from that relationship continue only so long as the relationship itself.[175]

Even in the absence of any fiduciary relationship or fiduciary duties, obligations of confidence can nonetheless be owed,[176] indicating that they are not peculiar to fiduciaries.

Secondly, the doctrine of confidence performs a function very different from that performed by fiduciary duties. Whereas fiduciary doctrine is concerned with providing a subsidiary and prophylactic form of protection for non-fiduciary duties, obligations of confidence do not protect the proper performance of other obligations. They exhibit neither the prophylactic nor the subsidiary character of fiduciary duties. In contrast to the subsidiary function performed by the fiduciary conflict and profit principles, obligations of confidence are primary obligations that protect confidential information from disclosure or other forms of misuse. Thus, 'it is essential not to confuse the claimed [fiduciary] duty [of

---

[173] *Ocular Sciences Ltd v Aspect Vision Care Ltd* [1997] RPC 289, 413.

[174] *Indata Equipment Supplies v ACL* (above n 166) 262; see also at pp 256 and 264. And see *Lac Minerals v International Corona Resources* (above n 166) 601 and 603.

[175] *MacLean v Arklow Investments* (above n 166) 690.

[176] *AB Consolidated Ltd v Europe Strength Food Co Pty Ltd* [1978] 2 NZLR 515, 520; *Boardman v Phipps* (above n 170) 128–29; *Oceanic Life Ltd v HIH Casualty & General Insurance Ltd* [1999] NSWSC 292 at [44], (1999) 10 ANZ Ins Cases 74,968; *Hadid v Lenfest Communications Inc* [1999] FCA 1798 at [815]–[819]; *Bolkiah v KPMG* [1999] 2 AC 222, 235; *Halewood International v Addleshaw Booth & Co* [2000] PNLR 788, 791 (ChD); *Také Ltd v BSM Marketing Ltd* [2006] EWHC 1085 (QB) at [45]. Hence, all of the judges in *Lac Minerals* held that there had been a breach of confidence (*Lac Minerals v International Corona Resources* (above n 166) 614, 630, 631 and 635), notwithstanding that only La Forest and Wilson JJ thought that fiduciary duties had been breached (pp 630 and 666). Similarly, in *Cadbury Schweppes* (above n 172), there was a breach of confidence, but the facts did not disclose a relationship that justified fiduciary protection: [1] and [32].

loyalty] with the separate duty to respect confidential information.'[177] As the Supreme Court of New Zealand said in *Paper Reclaim v Aotearoa,* 'the obligation not to misuse or disclose confidential information . . . has different characteristics from the quite separate obligations of trust and loyalty between fiduciaries.'[178]

This explains why obligations of confidence are capable of surviving after a fiduciary relationship has ended.[179] Obligations of confidence are primary obligations, which are designed to protect information rather than to protect other non-fiduciary duties, and so they continue in force until the information is no longer confidential or some other defence arises.[180] As such, they differ from fiduciary duties, which come to an end when the fiduciary relationship ceases, because cessation of the relationship will mean there is no remaining non-fiduciary undertaking between the parties and so nothing for fiduciary duties to protect.

Hence, it is preferable for obligations of confidence, as well as the doctrine of undue influence, to be segregated from fiduciary loyalty. It should be emphasised that the argument is not that it is somehow impossible or illogical to treat confidence and undue influence as fiduciary doctrines. Rather, the argument in favour of keeping them separate is that the fiduciary 'concept' will be lacking in practical and analytical utility if it is applied to a wide variety of doctrines that do not share common features.[181] The doctrines of undue influence and confidence both apply in circumstances in which no other fiduciary duties are applied, so that they are not peculiar to fiduciaries, and they serve purposes quite different from the purpose served by the duties that are peculiarly applied to fiduciaries. They should be kept separate from fiduciary doctrine, in order that they can be understood and explained in a manner more directly related to the concerns they are designed to address and to the manner in which they do so. The fiduciary concept of loyalty is best understood as a unified concept that gives subsidiary and prophylactic protection to non-fiduciary duties in certain circumstances. What those circumstances are is the question addressed in the next chapter.

---

[177]   *Arklow Investments v Maclean* (above n 166) 600.
[178]   *Paper Reclaim Ltd v Aotearoa International Ltd* [2007] NZSC 26 at [32], [2007] 3 NZLR 169. See also *Attorney-General v Blake* [1998] Ch 439, 454 (CA); *Neil v R* [2002] SCC 70 at [17], [2002] 3 SCR 631.
[179]   Eg, *Bolkiah v KPMG* (above n 176) 235.
[180]   Eg, if a 'public interest' defence can be made out: see *Attorney-General v Observer Ltd* [1990] 1 AC 109, 282.
[181]   *Mothew* (above n 56) 16 and see above ch 2, section II-B(ii).

9

The Incidence of Fiduciary Duties

This book has sought to address the nature and function of fiduciary doctrine. It has developed and considered the consequences of an analysis of what fiduciary duties do when they exist, rather than focusing on the question of when fiduciary duties exist. It is now necessary to address the question of when fiduciary duties arise. The primary difficulty in answering that question stems from the fact that

> the courts have come up with many different formulations in trying to capture the essence of the fiduciary relationship, usually with the cautionary notes that it is either unwise or impossible to do so and that the categories are not closed.[1]

Thus, mere analysis of the case law alone produces little fruit in this context. For that reason, it is proposed instead to consider the strengths and weaknesses of several of the more prominent theories that have been advanced by academic commentators before assessing the degree to which those theories have been adopted in the cases.

The protective view of fiduciary doctrine advanced in the earlier chapters of this book does not magically identify when fiduciary duties can be expected to arise. It does, however, have some relevance for that topic. As Robert Flannigan has said, 'the starting point is necessarily the social function of fiduciary responsibility. The proper contours of regulation are determined by the nature of that function.'[2] The view that fiduciary doctrine offers a subsidiary and prophylactic form of protection for non-fiduciary duties clarifies what the various principles of fiduciary doctrine are concerned to achieve, which is important in considering whether it is appropriate for fiduciary doctrine to apply. The view that fiduciary duties are protective of other non-fiduciary duties indicates the need for non-fiduciary duties to exist in order that fiduciary doctrine can serve its protective function vis-à-vis those non-fiduciary duties.[3] However, beyond that, the protective thesis does not itself identify when it is or is not appropriate for non-fiduciary duties to be protected in this way.

---

[1] *Bell Group Ltd v Westpac Banking Corp (No 9)* [2008] WASC 239 at [4532].
[2] R Flannigan, 'The Boundaries of Fiduciary Accountability' (2004) 83 *Canadian Bar Review* 35, 36.
[3] See above ch 7, section II.

I. Academic Commentators

The discussion in this section is organised according to the themes of the arguments advanced by the various commentators, rather than chronologically, as it is those themes that have been applied in the cases.

A. Acting on Behalf of Another

One of the earliest contributions to the debate about when fiduciary duties arise was made by Austin Scott, who said 'a fiduciary is a person who undertakes to act in the interest of another person.'[4] Little more was said by Scott, as his purpose was to begin analysis of the principles that apply to such actors at a time when those principles were not a main focus for academic investigation, and his description was sufficient to that end. The difficulty with Scott's description, if one seeks to do more with it than he intended and use it as a basis for determining when fiduciary duties will apply, is that it is too broad. The notion of acting in the interests of another person could encompass most contractual arrangements, in the sense that each contracting party is acting in his own interests but is also (presumptively) agreeing to do something in the interests of the contractual counterparty.[5] Hence, the law implies into contracts an obligation that the parties will do the things necessary to ensure that the other party to the contract can take its intended benefit and not hinder the fulfilment of the purpose of the contract.[6] That obligation can be excluded, as it is 'implied, in the sense of attributed to the contractual intention of the parties, unless the contrary appears on a proper construction of their bargain'.[7] But the point is that the obligation is designed to ensure that both parties are able to enjoy the respective benefits that each contracted to provide to the other.

Rather than seeking to isolate a single definition that would identify all fiduciary relationships, Len Sealy offered instead a set of four categories of fiduciary relationships: (*i*) situations in which 'one person has control of property which . . . in the view of a court of equity is the property of another';[8] (*ii*) situations in which a person 'has undertaken or is under an obligation (not necessarily contractual) to act on another's behalf or for another's benefit, or is

---

[4] AW Scott, 'The Fiduciary Principle' (1949) 37 *California Law Review* 539, 540.

[5] SA Smith, *Contract Theory* (Oxford, Oxford University Press, 2004) 110; RA Posner, *Economic Analysis of Law*, 6th edn (New York, Aspen, 2003) 99; EA Posner, 'Economic Analysis of Contract Law after Three Decades: Success or Failure?' (2003) 112 *Yale Law Journal* 829, 832; LD Smith, 'The Motive, Not the Deed' in J Getzler (ed), *Rationalizing Property, Equity and Trusts* (London, LexisNexis, 2003) 53, 64; AB Laby, 'The Fiduciary Obligation as the Adoption of Ends' (2008) 56 *Buffalo Law Review* 99, 131.

[6] *Peters (WA) Ltd v Petersville Ltd* [2001] HCA 45 at [36], (2001) 205 CLR 126; *Mackay v Dick* (1881) 6 App Cas 251, 263; *Service Station Association Ltd v Berg Bennett & Associates Pty Ltd* (1993) 45 FCR 84, 93–94.

[7] *Byrne v Australian Airlines Ltd* (1995) 185 CLR 410, 449.

[8] LS Sealy, 'Fiduciary Relationships' [1962] *Cambridge Law Journal* 69, 74–75.

deemed in equity to have done so';[9] (*iii*) situations in which 'persons with limited or partial interests in property'[10] are treated as holding accretions to that property in an equally limited fashion; and (*iv*) situations involving undue influence, particularly when that is presumed. The merits of treating undue influence as a fiduciary doctrine have been discussed earlier,[11] and the relevance of limited property rights as an indicator of fiduciary relationships will be addressed later.[12] For the moment, the point of greatest interest lies in Sealy's second category and the reference to acting 'on another's behalf', which helps to identify more clearly the significant aspect of Scott's reference to undertaking to act in the interest of another: a fiduciary will normally be acting more in a representative capacity—acting *for* another rather than merely acting in a way that will benefit another.

Paul Finn also advanced this view of fiduciary relationships in his influential book, essentially adopting what Sealy had said, albeit in a slightly modified form:

> For a person to be a fiduciary he must first and foremost have bound himself in some way to protect and/or to advance the interests of another. This is perhaps the most obvious of the characteristics of the fiduciary office for Equity will only oblige a person to act in what he believes to be another's interests if he himself has assumed a position which requires him to *act for or on behalf* of that other in some particular matter (emphasis added).[13]

This view of fiduciary relationships has been influential with the judiciary.

B. Discretion and Power

Ernest Weinrib offered an alternative view of when fiduciary duties arise:

> [F]iduciary obligation is the law's blunt tool for the control of ... discretion. ... Two elements thus form the core of the fiduciary concept and these elements can also serve to delineate its frontiers. First, the fiduciary must have scope for the exercise of discretion, and, second, this discretion must be capable of affecting the legal position of the principal.[14]

It is difficult to imagine fiduciary relationships that do not involve some element of discretion on the fiduciary's part, and that discretion will inevitably be capable of affecting the legal position of the fiduciary's principal. In large part, that follows from the idea of the fiduciary acting for and on behalf of another: in that capacity, the fiduciary will inevitably be acting in a way that affects the legal interests of that other person and is likely to have discretion as to how he does so.

[9] *Ibid*, 76.
[10] *Ibid*, 77.
[11] See above ch 8, section III-A.
[12] See below section I-D.
[13] PD Finn, *Fiduciary Obligations* (Sydney, Law Book Co, 1977) [15].
[14] EJ Weinrib, 'The Fiduciary Obligation' (1975) 25 *University of Toronto Law Journal* 1, 4.

This view of fiduciary relationships also sits well with the view that fiduciary doctrine serves a protective function in respect of non-fiduciary duties: when there is discretion that affects the interests of others, the discretion is generally regulated by duties that control its exercise, and the presence of inconsistent interests or duties carries with it a heightened risk of breach of those non-fiduciary duties. Frequently, therefore, when there is discretion fiduciary duties may also exist in order to eliminate temptations that are inconsistent with the proper exercise of the discretion, so as to increase the chance of the discretion being exercised in accordance with those non-fiduciary duties. Thus, the presence or absence of wide discretion can be helpful in determining whether fiduciary duties might exist. As Scott said, 'the greater the independent authority to be exercised by the fiduciary, the greater the scope of his fiduciary duty.'[15]

However, the presence or absence of discretion is insufficient on its own to discriminate between fiduciary and non-fiduciary relationships in all cases. Many contractual arrangements effectively allow the parties a choice—discretion—as to the mode of performance they adopt, where differing modes can be more or less beneficial to the performing party, and yet it is not suggested that they owe fiduciary obligations as a result. It is relatively clear why not all relationships in which there is discretion are circumscribed with fiduciary duties: if the parties have autonomously contracted for something to be done without specifying how that will be achieved, that contractual agreement sets certain bounds within which the party must perform its obligations, but within those bounds the party is free. The parties' autonomous decision to allow that latitude is respected. In contrast, when fiduciary duties apply that latitude is restricted by further obligations, such as the conflict and profit principles. The mere presence of discretion is an insufficient explanation for why fiduciary doctrine circumscribes the conduct of some actors and not others.

The question is which discretions attract regulation by fiduciary doctrine and which are left to be regulated by ordinary doctrines of contract law. Seeking to answer that question, Gordon Smith has suggested that a 'unified theory of fiduciary duty'[16] can be achieved if one approaches the issue on the basis that 'fiduciary relationships form when one party (the "fiduciary") acts *on behalf of* another party (the "beneficiary") while exercising *discretion* with respect to a *critical resource* belonging to the beneficiary.'[17]

Smith's theory therefore combines the representational idea that Scott, Sealy and Finn advanced, of acting for and 'on behalf of another', with the presence of a discretion, as Weinrib suggested, but it is apparently limited by the discretion being related to a 'critical resource' of the principal. The innovative aspect of this theory lies in its reference to the principal's critical resources, as opposed to more

---

[15] Scott (above n 4) 541.
[16] DG Smith, 'The Critical Resource Theory of Fiduciary Duty' (2002) 55 *Vanderbilt Law Review* 1399, 1400.
[17] *Ibid*, 1402.

tangible interests of the principal, such as his property. This rightly reflects the fact that not all fiduciaries act in respect of their principals' property, but it is not clear that the critical resource concept provides any real limitation on the element of discretion as the identifier of fiduciary relationships. Any discretion held by someone who is acting on behalf of another party will inevitably affect some interest of that other party or it is simply unimportant. Those interests can be called 'critical resources', but that does not change the fact that all that has really been identified is a discretion held by someone acting on behalf of another. Smith's theory offers no clear guidance on which discretions implicate 'critical' resources, as opposed to other resources, so as to trigger the application of fiduciary duties.

Related to Weinrib's emphasis on discretion, Jay Shepherd argued that fiduciary relationships arise whenever there has been a transfer of 'encumbered power':

> A fiduciary relationship exists whenever any person acquires a power of any type on condition that he also receive with it a duty to utilize that power in the best interests of another, and the recipient of the power uses that power.[18]

Again, this theory focuses on discretion (although Shepherd emphasised the concept of 'power' instead of discretion in order for his theory to encompass both formal and informal transfers of power[19]), in that it is concerned with the ability of the donee of the power to choose to affect the interests of another. Shepherd differentiates discretions—or 'powers'—that are held in a fiduciary capacity from other discretions by reference to the question whether the power was received on condition that it be used in the best interests of another, which again brings the analysis back to the idea of acting on behalf of another. Shepherd's analysis does not advance much further the ability to discriminate between fiduciary and non-fiduciary relationships: it is easy enough to apply when it is clear that a power has been granted on condition that it is to be used in the best interests of another, but when that is not clear (as it will not be in many cases) the difficulty remains in identifying whether any such condition governs the use of the power.

C. Reasonable Expectations

Building on the idea of acting for another, Finn advanced a further description of when fiduciary duties arise in a later article:

> A person will be a fiduciary in his relationship with another when and insofar as that other is entitled to expect that he will act in that other's or in their joint interest to the exclusion of his own several interest.[20]

---

[18] JC Shepherd, *The Law of Fiduciaries* (Toronto, Carswell, 1981) 96.

[19] *Ibid*, 99–100.

[20] PD Finn, 'The Fiduciary Principle' in TG Youdan (ed), *Equity, Fiduciaries and Trusts* (Toronto, Carswell, 1989) 1, 54; see also p 46. And see Finn, *Fiduciary Obligations* (above n 13) [400].

This approach adopts the idea of acting for and on behalf of another but develops it by indicating that the court must determine whether it is legitimate to expect that the actor will put aside his own interests and act solely in the interests of the other party. This helps to explain why not all contractual discretions are subject to fiduciary regulation, because a fiduciary relationship will only arise when it is reasonable to expect that the person who is said to be a fiduciary will act to the exclusion of his own interest. That expectation is not normal in contracts, because contracting parties are ordinarily expected to be looking out for and acting in their own interests.[21]

Similarly, Deborah DeMott has argued that 'the law applicable to fiduciary duty can best be understood as responsive to circumstances that justify the expectation that an actor's conduct will be loyal to the interests of another'[22] but has argued:

> Assessing whether a plaintiff's expectations of loyalty are justifiable is related to, but not identical to, assessing whether they are reasonable. Focusing on justifiability reinforces the point that fiduciary duties, although necessarily shaped by or related to any contract between the parties or their conduct more generally, are imposed by the law. Moreover, a plaintiff's expectation of loyal conduct may be justifiable even when the plaintiff has some basis to doubt whether an actor will fulfil that expectation.[23]

This is but a minor modification of Finn's analysis, if indeed it is any modification at all. Finn himself said that the circumstances 'may generate an actual expectation that the other's interests are being served. . . But equally, the expectation may be a judicially prescribed one because the law itself ordains it to be that other's entitlement.'[24] Thus, a court can determine that a claimant was '*entitled* to expect'[25] (emphasis added) that the other actor would act in the claimant's best interests to the exclusion of his own, even if the claimant subjectively had some doubt as to whether the defendant would comply with that expectation.

Finn's focus on legitimate expectations of loyalty is only a subtle shift from Shepherd's argument that fiduciary duties exist when power has been granted subject to fiduciary controls. The question remains: when is it reasonable to expect that a person will put aside his own interest and act solely in the interests of the other party? Notwithstanding that, the approach advocated by Finn has

---

[21] *Canson Enterprises Ltd v Boughton & Co* [1991] 3 SCR 534, 554; *Norberg v Wynrib* [1992] 2 SCR 226, 272; *Pilmer v Duke Group Ltd* [2001] HCA 31 at [71], (2001) 207 CLR 165; *Cubillo v Commonwealth of Australia* [2001] FCA 1213 at [462], (2001) 112 FCR 455.

[22] DA DeMott, 'Breach of Fiduciary Duty: On Justifiable Expectations of Loyalty and Their Consequences' (2006) 48 *Arizona Law Review* 925, 926.

[23] *Ibid*, 938. See also T Frankel, 'Fiduciary Duties as Default Rules' (1995) 74 *Oregon Law Review* 1209, 1228: 'fiduciaries should be *trustworthy*, not necessarily *trusted.*'

[24] Finn, 'The Fiduciary Principle' (above n 20) 47. See also PD Finn, 'Fiduciary Law and the Modern Commercial World' in E McKendrick (ed), *Commercial Aspects of Trusts and Fiduciary Obligations* (Oxford, Oxford University Press, 1992) 7, 9, 10 and 38.

[25] See text accompanying n 20 above.

become influential in the case law. Suggestions will be made in the final section of this chapter as to how it can be practically implemented.

D. Limited Access

One of the categories of fiduciary relationship identified by Sealy was situations in which people with only 'limited or partial interests in property'[26] are treated as holding accretions to that property in a limited fashion. More recently, Flannigan has advanced a theory of fiduciary relationships that, like the theory proffered by Smith, expands the idea of limited access to assets beyond the idea of access to property alone:

> The boundaries of fiduciary accountability appear to be unsettled. That is an illusion. Though currently obscured by a layer of confusion, the conventional boundaries remain intelligible and unchanged. Those who have access for a defined or limited purpose are subject to fiduciary regulation; those with open access are not.[27]

There are two difficulties with this approach. First, it is not clear that it differs in any important way from the expectation analysis advanced by Finn. Secondly, insofar as it is intended to differ from that analysis, it is flawed in that it fails accurately to capture the difference between fiduciary and non-fiduciary situations.

As to the first point, Flannigan himself has said that 'the physical arrangement that attracts fiduciary regulation is limited access or, in traditional terms, the undertaking to act wholly or partly in the interest of another.'[28] The link between the concept of 'limited access' and Finn's notion of legitimate expectations of loyalty becomes apparent from a consideration of Flannigan's category of 'open access' arrangements, where fiduciary duties do not arise. Flannigan argues that self-regarding opportunism is only possible when there is limited access,[29] because when access is given on an 'open' basis no constraint is imposed on freedom to exploit the resource.[30] As Flannigan has put it, 'if the access is open, rather than limited, consumption or exploitation does not amount to objectionable self-regard.'[31] Hence, it seems that access is given on an 'open' basis if the recipient can use it as he sees fit, for his own benefit and in a self-regarding

---

[26] Sealy (above n 8) 77.

[27] Flannigan, 'The Boundaries of Fiduciary Accountability' (above n 2) 88–89. See also R Flannigan, 'The Fiduciary Obligation' (1989) 9 *Oxford Journal of Legal Studies* 285, 310; R Flannigan, 'Fiduciary Obligation in the Supreme Court' (1990) 54 *Saskatchewan Law Review* 45, 48; R Flannigan, 'Commercial Fiduciary Obligation' (1998) 36 *Alberta Law Review* 905, 906; R Flannigan, 'Fiduciary Duties of Shareholders and Directors' [2004] *Journal of Business Law* 277, 281; R Flannigan, 'The Strict Character of Fiduciary Liability' [2006] *New Zealand Law Review* 209, 209–10; R Flannigan, 'The Economics of Fiduciary Accountability' (2007) 32 *Delaware Journal of Corporate Law* 393, 393.

[28] Flannigan, 'The Boundaries of Fiduciary Accountability' (above n 2) 36–37.

[29] *Ibid*, 37.

[30] *Ibid*, 38.

[31] *Ibid*, 37; see also pp 38–39.

fashion. Thus, 'open access' arrangements can be described in terms of the legitimate expectations of the parties: access is given on an 'open' basis if there is no legitimate expectation on the part of the donor that the recipient will use it only in the donor's best interests to the exclusion of the recipient's own interests. Therefore, in contrast with the idea of open access, the notion of 'limited access' appears to reflect the idea that the donor expects that the recipient will not make use of the access other than in the donor's best interests: 'the limited access abstraction identifies those arrangements where self-service will not be tolerated.'[32] Seen in this light, the limited access criterion seems more like a label for the conclusion that the expectation of fiduciary loyalty is legitimate in the circumstances, rather than a separate criterion for analysing when that will be the case.

However, Flannigan intends the 'limited access' concept to provide a mechanism for translating the policy underlying fiduciary doctrine into 'analytical criteria'[33] for determining when fiduciary obligations will arise. Thus, he has criticised the legitimate expectation test as illegitimately indeterminate[34] and has argued that it is unnecessary to draw analogies with other fiduciary relationships because 'the analogy approach is necessarily displaced by the recognition and direct application of the limited access principle.'[35] The difficulty with this is that the limited access concept does not accurately predict which relationships will be held to involve fiduciary duties and which will not. For example, mortgagees have access to the property of their mortgagors that is limited, in the form of powers to take possession of and to sell the property to recoup the outstanding debt. Courts have repeatedly emphasised that a mortgagee's powers must be exercised consistently with the fact that its interest in the mortgagor's property is granted only 'as a security for the payment of a debt or the discharge of some other obligation for which it is given'.[36] Yet, the mortgagee does not owe fiduciary duties with respect to the exercise of its powers over the mortgagor's property, notwithstanding that his is 'always a qualified and limited right'[37] of access to the property: 'it never remains in his hands cloathed with any fiduciary duty.'[38]

The reason for this is better explained by the legitimate expectation approach than it is by the limited access concept: 'while a mortgagee owes a duty to the mortgagor to exercise his power of sale fairly, he is entitled to have regard to his

---

[32] *Ibid*, 39.
[33] Flannigan, 'Fiduciary Obligation in the Supreme Court' (above n 27) 50.
[34] Flannigan, 'The Boundaries of Fiduciary Accountability' (above n 2) 74; see also p 84.
[35] *Ibid*, 48.
[36] *Santley v Wilde* [1899] 2 Ch 474, 474 (CA). See also *Noakes & Co Ltd v Rice* [1902] AC 24, 28, 30 and 32–33; *Swiss Bank Corp v Lloyds Bank Ltd* [1982] AC 584, 595 (CA).
[37] *Cholmondeley v Clinton* (1820) 2 Jac & W 1, 183 (37 ER 527) (MR) (cited favourably in *Farrar v Farrars Ltd* (1888) 40 ChD 395, 411 (CA)).
[38] *Cholmondeley v Clinton* (*ibid*) 185. See generally RE Megarry and HWR Wade, *The Law of Real Property*, 7th edn by C Harpum, S Bridge and MJ Dixon (London, Sweet & Maxwell, 2008) [25–018]. Further authorities to this effect are collected above in ch 3, section II.

own interests'[39] because 'every mortgage confers upon the mortgagee the right to realize his security and to find a purchaser if he can.'[40] Despite the fact that the mortgagee's rights and powers give him only limited access to the mortgagor's property, they are 'given to him for his own benefit, to enable him the better to realize his debt',[41] such that it would be unrealistic for the mortgagor to expect them to be exercised solely in the mortgagor's interest to the exclusion of the mortgagee's own self interest.[42]

Indeed, that is so for any proprietary security interest:

> A proprietary interest provided by way of security entitles the holder to resort to the property *only* for the purpose of satisfying some liability due to him. . . [W]hatever the form of the transaction, the owner of the property retains an equity of redemption to have the property restored to him when the liability has been discharged (emphasis added).[43]

Thus, for example, when goods are pledged as security for an obligation, the recipient of the pledged goods obtains a security interest in those goods but has 'only a special property'[44] in them. If that limited right of access to the pledgor's property were the true determinant of fiduciary accountability, one would expect the fiduciary conflict principle to prevent the pledgee from being able in his own interest to pledge the goods to another party as security for obligations owed by the pledgee to that third party. And yet in *Donald v Suckling*[45] four judges of the Court of Queen's Bench upheld such a transaction as a valid exercise of the limited rights held by the pledgee.

Further, even when there is no proprietary security interest, a creditor who obtains a writ of *fieri facias*[46] is not prevented from purchasing his debtor's property when it is sold.[47] Similarly, holders of easements—a paradigm example

---

[39] *Movitex Ltd v Bulfield* [1988] BCLC 104, 122 (ChD).

[40] *Farrar v Farrars* (above n 37) 411.

[41] *Warner v Jacob* (1882) 20 ChD 220, 224. See also *Pendlebury v Colonial Mutual Life Assurance Society Ltd* (1912) 12 CLR 676, 699; *Downsview Nominees Ltd v First City Corp Ltd* [1993] AC 295, 312–15 (PC).

[42] If the answer to this objection to the limited access analysis is that a mortgagee has 'open access' for these purposes, the weak analytical value of the limited access concept is thereby further revealed.

[43] *Re Bank of Credit and Commerce International SA (No 8)* [1998] AC 214, 226. As *Santley v Wilde* (above n 36) shows, this is the case even for traditional mortgages, whereby title to the mortgaged property is transferred to the mortgagee such that the mortgagor might be said no longer to be the 'owner' of the property.

[44] *Babcock v Lawson* (1880) 5 QBD 284, 286 (CA).

[45] *Donald v Suckling* (1866) LR 1 QB 585. See also *Mores v Conham* (1609) Owen 123, 124 (74 ER 946) (CP).

[46] Now a 'writ of control' in England and Wales: Tribunals, Courts and Enforcement Act 2007, s 62(4)(a).

[47] *Stratford v Twynam* (1822) Jac 418, 421–22 (37 ER 908) (MR).

of limited rights of access to the assets of another—do not owe fiduciary duties to the owner of the servient tenement by virtue of that fact alone. Nor do co-owners owe one another fiduciary duties.[48]

The concept of limited access is helpful insofar as it focuses attention on the purpose for which access has been given, but it fails to provide a criterion that accurately predicts whether fiduciary duties will be owed in a given situation.[49] To answer that question more accurately, the limited access analysis seems to utilise, whether tacitly or not, the idea of legitimate expectations.

II. Turning Theory into Practice

A. Judicial Applications

The courts themselves have acknowledged that no one theory or definition of the fiduciary concept has met with wide judicial consensus[50] and indeed have said that it would be undesirable for them to attempt to provide such a definition.[51] They have preferred 'instead to develop the law in a case by case approach'.[52] A complete review of those thousands of cases is far beyond the capacity of a book like this. Instead, what is offered here is a review of some of the more prominent of those cases in which the theories advanced by academic commentators have been addressed. By considering a combination of the theories that have been advanced by the academic commentators coupled with the cases that have applied them, a picture emerges of when fiduciary duties will be recognised outside of the settled categories of cases (in other words, outside of the situations in which fiduciary duties are applied without any question) and of the sorts of considerations that courts take into account in making that decision.

In her dissenting judgment in *Frame v Smith*, Wilson J acknowledged that 'there has been a reluctance throughout the common law world to affirm the

---

[48] *Kennedy v De Trafford* [1896] ChD 762, 774 and 775–76 (CA); *Kennedy v De Trafford* [1897] AC 180, 186–89; *Re Biss* [1903] 2 Ch 40, 57 (CA). As Romer LJ explained in *Re Biss*, *Palmer v Young* (1684) 1 Vern 276 (23 ER 468) does not establish that joint tenants are, by that fact alone, fiduciaries for one another: see [1903] 2 Ch 40, 62–64.

[49] This undermines Flannigan's argument that car mechanics owe fiduciary duties: see R Flannigan, 'Fiduciary Mechanics' (2008) 14 *Canadian Labour & Employment Law Journal* 25; Flannigan, 'Commercial Fiduciary Obligation' (above n 27) 909 and 911. If the limited access criterion does not accurately predict whether other actors owe fiduciary duties, it cannot confidently be used to do that with respect to mechanics.

[50] Eg, *MacLean v Arklow Investments Ltd* [1998] 3 NZLR 680, 691 (CA); *Frame v Smith* [1987] 2 SCR 99, 135.

[51] Eg, *Lloyds Bank Ltd v Bundy* [1975] QB 326, 341 (CA).

[52] *Hospital Products Ltd v United States Surgical Corp* (1984) 156 CLR 41, 96.

existence of and give content to a general fiduciary principle.'[53] But she sought to resist that trend and proffered a description of when fiduciary duties will be recognised:

[T]here are common features discernible in the contexts in which fiduciary duties have been found to exist and these common features do provide a rough and ready guide to whether or not the imposition of a fiduciary obligation on a new relationship would be appropriate and consistent. Relationships in which a fiduciary obligation have been imposed seem to possess three general characteristics: (1) The fiduciary has scope for the exercise of some discretion or power. (2) The fiduciary can unilaterally exercise that power or discretion so as to affect the beneficiary's legal or practical interests. (3) The beneficiary is peculiarly vulnerable to or at the mercy of the fiduciary holding the discretion or power.[54]

In terms of the themes that have been identified in the various academic theories, Wilson J's approach is closest to Weinrib's argument that fiduciary duties are concerned with the control of discretion,[55] particularly in Wilson J's first characteristic. The second characteristic also reflects the point later made by Smith and Flannigan, that the fiduciary may affect the principal's legal interests by the exercise of discretion, but such an exercise might also affect the practical interests of the principal.[56] However, Wilson J appears to have sought to limit the width of Weinrib's discretion analysis by insisting that the discretion be capable of unilateral exercise by the fiduciary and that the principal be 'peculiarly vulnerable to or at the mercy of' the fiduciary.

It is not clear, however, that Wilson J's second and third characteristics provide any real limit on the first. The second characteristic is little more than a restatement of the first, in that powers and discretions are generally exercised unilaterally by their holders.[57] And the third characteristic also seems to fold back into the first, in that the principal's 'vulnerability' to the fiduciary arises *because* the fiduciary has the ability to exercise a discretion or power that will affect the principal's interests in some way.[58]

---

[53] *Frame v Smith* (above n 50) 135.

[54] *Ibid*, 136.

[55] The connection between the analyses of Weinrib and Wilson J was explicitly recognised by Sopinka J in *Lac Minerals Ltd v International Corona Resources Ltd* [1989] 2 SCR 574, 599–600.

[56] *Frame v Smith* (above n 50) 136–37.

[57] The discretion may of course need to be exercised by a *group* of fiduciaries, as in the case of trustees who must act unanimously to exercise their powers: see generally A Underhill and DJ Hayton, *Law Relating to Trusts and Trustees*, 17th edn by DJ Hayton, PB Matthews and CCJ Mitchell (London, LexisNexis Butterworths, 2007) [56.1]–[56.14]. Wilson J does not appear to have meant to exclude such cases from being fiduciary (which would be odd indeed) but rather seems to have meant that the fiduciary can exercise the power or discretion without the *principal's* concurrence.

[58] See also RP Meagher and A Maroya, 'Crypto-Fiduciary Duties' (2003) 26 *University of New South Wales Law Journal* 348, 350. Indeed, even when there is little or no discretion, a contracting party is vulnerable to non-performance by her counterparty: Posner, *Economic Analysis of Law* (above n 5) 94.

Wilson J dissented in *Frame v Smith*, but her approach to the question of when fiduciary duties arise was adopted shortly thereafter by a majority of the Supreme Court of Canada in *Lac Minerals v Corona*.[59] However, in the later decision of *Hodgkinson v Simms*,[60] a differently constituted majority of the same court emphasised that 'the concept of vulnerability is not the hallmark of fiduciary relationship though it is an important *indicium* of its existence. Vulnerability is common to many relationships in which the law will intervene to protect one of the parties.'[61] In place of the vulnerability criterion, La Forest J said:

> The presence of loyalty, trust, and confidence distinguishes the fiduciary relationship from a relationship that simply gives rise to tortious liability. . . [T]he special elements of trust, loyalty, and confidentiality that obtain in a fiduciary relationship give rise to a corresponding duty of loyalty.[62]

The cases have for a long time referred to fiduciary duties as arising when there is a relationship of 'trust and confidence',[63] but as La Forest J's statement shows, this does not advance our understanding of when fiduciary duties arise very far: the presence of loyalty generates a duty of loyalty.

Perhaps for that reason, the more recent Anglo-Australian cases have often supplemented the concept of trust and confidence with other aspects of the academic theories that have been discussed. Thus, for example, in *Mothew*, Millett LJ said, in a statement that has since been applied in many cases,[64] that 'a fiduciary is someone who has undertaken to act for or on behalf of another in a particular matter in circumstances which give rise to a relationship of trust and

---

[59]   *Lac Minerals* (above n 55) 598–99.
[60]   *Hodgkinson v Simms* [1994] 3 SCR 377.
[61]   *Ibid*, 405. In dissent, Sopinka J (who had led the majority in *Lac Minerals*) re-emphasised vulnerability and the approach advocated by Wilson J in *Frame v Smith*: see *Hodgkinson v Simms* (*ibid*) 462 and 466–67.
[62]   *Hodgkinson v Simms* (above n 60) 405.
[63]   See, eg, *Re Agriculturist Cattle Insurance Co* (1870) LR 5 Ch App 725, 733 (LJJ); *Furs Ltd v Tomkies* (1936) 54 CLR 583, 590; *United Dominions Corp Ltd v Brian Pty Ltd* (1985) 157 CLR 1, 12; *Day v Mead* [1987] 2 NZLR 443, 458 (CA); *Marr v Arabco Traders Ltd* (1987) 1 NZBLC 102,732, 102,743–45 (HC); *Murad v Al-Saraj* [2004] EWHC 1235 (Ch) at [328] and [332], not challenged on appeal: [2005] EWCA Civ 959 at [4], [2005] WTLR 1573; *Chirnside v Fay* [2006] NZSC 68 at [85], [2007] 1 NZLR 433.
[64]   See, eg, *Global Container Lines Ltd v Bonyad Shipping Co* [1998] 1 Lloyd's Rep 528, 546 (QBD); *Arklow Investments Ltd v Maclean* [2000] 1 WLR 594, 599 (PC); *Brandeis (Brokers) Ltd v Black* [2001] 2 All ER (Comm) 980 at [32] (QBD); *Hooper v Gorvin* [2001] WTLR 575, 590 (ChD); *Re Papadimitriou* [2004] WTLR 1141 at [57] (IOM); *Daraydan Holdings Ltd v Solland International Ltd* [2004] EWHC 622 (Ch) at [55], [2005] Ch 119; *Conway v Ratiu* [2005] EWCA Civ 1302 at [57], [2006] WTLR 101 (also partially reported at [2006] 1 All ER 571n); *Button v Phelps* [2006] EWHC 53 (Ch) at [58]–[60]; *Fenwick v Trustees of Nga Kaihautu O Te Arawa Executive Council* [2006] NZHC 392 at [89]; *Haines v Carter* [2006] NZHC 566 at [30]; *Sinclair Investment Holdings SA v Versailles Trade Finance Ltd* [2007] EWHC 915 (Ch) at [78], [2007] 2 All ER (Comm) 993; *JD Wetherspoon plc v Van de Berg & Co Ltd* [2009] EWHC 639 (Ch) at [74]. See also *Oceanic Life Ltd v HIH Casualty & General Insurance Ltd* [1999] NSWSC 292 at [74], (1999) 10 ANZ Ins Cases 74,968. And see *Amaltal Corp Ltd v Maruha Corp* [2007] 1 NZLR 608 at [138] (CA), which was overturned on appeal, but without casting doubt on the authority of *Mothew*: [2007] NZSC 40, [2007] 3 NZLR 192.

confidence.'[65] This reflects the idea advanced by Scott, Sealy and Finn, that a fiduciary is someone acting for and on behalf of another in a 'representative character', which has been influential in many cases.[66] The same idea, linked with the points that have been made about discretion and vulnerability, underpins Mason J's observations in *Hospital Products v United States Surgical Corp*:

> The critical feature of these relationships is that the fiduciary undertakes or agrees to act for and on behalf of or in the interests of another person in the exercise of a power or discretion which will affect the interests of that other person in a legal or practical sense. The relationship between the parties is therefore one which gives the fiduciary a special opportunity to exercise the power or discretion to the detriment of that other person who is accordingly vulnerable to abuse by the fiduciary of his position. The expressions 'for', 'on behalf of', and 'in the interests of' signify that the fiduciary acts in a 'representative' character in the exercise of his responsibility.[67]

Similarly, as has been seen earlier,[68] Gummow J observed in *Breen v Williams* that 'fiduciary obligations arise (albeit perhaps not exclusively) in various situations where it may be seen that one person is under an obligation to act in the interests of another.'[69] Gaudron and McHugh JJ made the same point in their judgment in *Breen v Williams*,[70] and Mason J pointed out elsewhere in his judgment in *Hospital Products* that the 'obligation to act in the interests of another . . . is the foundation of the fiduciary relationship.'[71]

Similarly conspicuous in attracting judicial adherence, particularly relatively recently, is Finn's argument that fiduciary duties arise when it is legitimate to expect that they will apply. In several cases, this comes as no surprise given that the decisions are themselves judgments of Finn J. Thus, for example, in *Australian Securities Commission v AS Nominees Ltd*, he explained:

> Securities is so circumstanced vis-à-vis the beneficiaries of the various trusts of ASN and Ample that the beneficiaries of each individual trust are entitled to expect that Securities will act in the interests of those beneficiaries to the exclusion of its own or any third party's interests, in its dealings for or on behalf of that trust.[72]

---

[65]   *Bristol & West Building Society v Mothew* [1998] Ch 1, 18 (CA).
[66]   See also *South Australia v Peat Marwick Mitchell & Co* (1997) 24 ACSR 231, 265 (SASC); *Peskin v Anderson* [2001] 1 BCLC 372 at [34] (CA); *Kyrris v Oldham* [2003] EWCA Civ 1506 at [142], [2004] 1 BCLC 305; *Brooker v Friend* [2006] NSWCA 385 at [149] (reversed on appeal without reference to this issue: [2009] HCA 21); *Australian Securities and Investments Commission v Citigroup Global Markets Australia Pty Ltd (No 4)* [2007] FCA 963 at [272], (2007) 160 FCR 35.
[67]   *Hospital Products v US Surgical Corp* (above n 52) 96–97. See also *Schipp v Cameron* [1998] NSWSC 997 at [697], not questioned on appeal: *Harrison v Schipp* [2001] NSWCA 13; *Brooker v Friend* (*ibid*) [149] (reversed on appeal without reference to this issue: [2009] HCA 21); *Trinkler v Beale* [2009] NSWCA 30 at [45].
[68]   See above ch 3, section VII.
[69]   *Breen v Williams* (1996) 186 CLR 71, 137.
[70]   *Ibid*, 113.
[71]   *Hospital Products v US Surgical Corp* (above n 52) 99.
[72]   *Australian Securities Commission v AS Nominees Ltd* (1995) 133 ALR 1, 17. See also *Hughes Aircraft Systems International v Air Services Australia* (1997) 76 FCR 151, 237; *Gibson Motorsport Merchandise Pty Ltd v Forbes* [2006] FCAFC 44 at [12], (2006) 149 FCR 569.

But other judges and courts have approached the issue in that way as well. In *Glandon v Strata Consolidated*, Cripps JA expressly adopted Finn's description of when fiduciary duties arise, 'with its emphasis on the appropriate expectation as the hallmark of the relationship',[73] as did Handley JA in *Brunninghausen v Glavanics*.[74] The Federal Court did the same in *News Ltd v Australian Rugby Football League Ltd*,[75] as did Jacobson J in *ASIC v Citigroup*.[76] And Toulson J expressly applied Finn's legitimate expectations approach in England, in *Brandeis (Brokers) Ltd v Black*.[77]

The approach has also been applied in cases without reference to Finn's academic writing. Thus, for example, in *Imperial Group Pension Trust v Imperial Tobacco*, Browne-Wilkinson VC explained that an employer company's power to give or withhold consent to amendments to the company's pension scheme was not held in a fiduciary capacity because that would run counter to the expectations of all involved: 'if this were a fiduciary power the company would have to decide whether or not to consent by reference only to the interests of the members, disregarding its own interests. *This plainly was not the intention*' (emphasis added).[78] In *DHL v Richmond*, the Court of Appeal of New Zealand said that 'the fiduciary duty arises where one party to the relationship (A) is reasonably entitled to expect of the other (B) that B will act in the interests of A, not in the interests of B.'[79]

In *Hospital Products*, a majority of the High Court of Australia held that a distributor of surgical equipment did not owe fiduciary duties to the manufacturer. The distributor was obliged (contractually) to exercise its best efforts to promote the sale of the manufacturer's products,[80] but there was no fiduciary obligation owed because it was clear that the whole purpose of the arrangement involved the distributor acting in its own interests, in order to make a profit for itself.[81] Mason J dissented, on the basis that the distributor owed a limited fiduciary duty with regard to the manufacturer's goodwill,[82] but he too agreed that there was no general fiduciary relationship in the case because it was 'unrealistic'[83] to suggest that the distributor would not make decisions by reference to its own financial interests. The unrealistic nature of that suggestion

---

[73] *Glandon Pty Ltd v Strata Consolidated Pty Ltd* (1993) 11 ACSR 543, 557 (NSWCA).

[74] *Brunninghausen v Glavanics* [1999] NSWCA 199 at [100]–[101], (1999) 46 NSWLR 538.

[75] *News Ltd v Australian Rugby Football League Ltd* (1996) 64 FCR 410, 541 (FC).

[76] *Australian Securities and Investments Commission v Citigroup Global Markets Australia Pty Ltd (No 4)* [2007] FCA 963 at [273]–[274], (2007) 160 FCR 35.

[77] *Brandeis (Brokers) v Black* (above n 64) [36]–[37].

[78] *Imperial Group Pension Trust Ltd v Imperial Tobacco Ltd* [1991] 1 WLR 589, 596. See also *Re Courage Group's Pension Schemes* [1987] 1 WLR 495, 514 (ChD); *National Grid Co plc v Laws* [1997] Occupational Pensions Law Rep 207, 227 (ChD).

[79] *DHL International (NZ) Ltd v Richmond Ltd* [1993] 3 NZLR 10, 23.

[80] *Hospital Products v US Surgical Corp* (above n 52) 63–64.

[81] Ibid, 72–73, 122–24 and 144–46.

[82] Ibid, 101.

[83] Ibid, 94.

meant the manufacturer could not legitimately expect the distributor would act only in the best interests of the manufacturer or, of the two parties combined, to the exclusion of the distributor's own several interest. The distributor's 'capacity to make decisions and take action in some matters by reference to its own interests is inconsistent with the existence of a general fiduciary relationship'.[84]

The same approach underlies Rix J's conclusion in *Global Container Lines v Bonyad* that a shipping joint venture between Global and Bonyad did not prevent Global from operating its pre-existing shipping operations, even if they competed with the joint venture. Rix J found that Bonyad was aware of and made no complaint about Global's shipping operations,[85] explaining:

> If the parties' relationship has been premised ... on the possibility of competition within such areas, then I do not see how, in those respects at any rate, the parties can owe to one another the full range of fiduciary duties.[86]

These cases are all consistent with Finn's proposition that the existence or otherwise of fiduciary duties depends on whether it is legitimate in all the circumstances of the case for one party (the principal) to expect that the other (the fiduciary) will act to the exclusion of his own several interest.[87] Fiduciary doctrine requires that a fiduciary put aside all possibility of personal benefit from the transaction, unless the contrary has been properly authorised. When it is not legitimate for one party to expect that the other will comply with the strict abnegation of self-interest that fiduciary doctrine insists upon, particularly when the circumstances of the case indicate that the parties have always assumed that the contrary will be the case, the courts will not impose any such expectation and consequently will not recognise fiduciary duties.[88] If, in the circumstances, the court considers such an expectation to be legitimate, that expectation provides the foundation for the recognition of fiduciary duties, and hence a fiduciary relationship, between the parties.[89] As the Privy Council said in *Arklow Investments v Maclean,*

> [T]he concept encaptures a situation where one person is in a relationship with another which gives rise to a legitimate expectation, which equity will recognise, that the fiduciary will not utilise his or her position in such a way which is adverse to the interests of the principal.[90]

---

[84] *Ibid,* 98.

[85] *Global Container Lines v Bonyad Shipping* (above n 64) 543.

[86] *Ibid,* 545.

[87] See also *Paper Reclaim Ltd v Aotearoa Ltd* [2007] NZSC 26 at [31], [2007] 3 NZLR 169.

[88] See, eg, *Global Container Lines v Bonyad Shipping* (above n 64) 545–46 (QBD); *Hadid v Lenfest Communications Inc* [1999] FCA 1798 at [816]–[817]; *Nottingham University v Fishel* [2000] Industrial Relations Law Reports 471 at [97] (QBD); *Sinclair Investment Holdings SA v Versailles Trade Finance Ltd* [2007] EWHC 915 (Ch) at [85]–[88], [2007] 2 All ER (Comm) 993.

[89] See, eg, *Waxman v Waxman* (2004) 7 ITELR 162 at [512] (Ont CA).

[90] *Arklow Investments v Maclean* (above n 64) 598. See also *R v Neil* [2002] SCC 70 at [16], [2002] 3 SCR 631; *Chirnside v Fay* [2006] NZSC 68 at [78]–[80], [2007] 1 NZLR 433; *Hageman v Holmes* [2009] EWHC 50 (Ch) at [52].

The cases also support the point made by DeMott and Finn, that this expectation need not be held subjectively by the principal:

> [A]n actual relation of confidence—the fact that one person subjectively trusted another—is neither necessary for nor conclusive of the existence of a fiduciary relationship; on the one hand, a trustee will stand in a fiduciary relationship to a beneficiary notwithstanding that the latter at no time reposed confidence in him, and on the other hand, an ordinary transaction for sale and purchase does not give rise to a fiduciary relationship simply because the purchaser trusted the vendor and the latter defrauded him.[91]

There is thus considerable support within the case law for the view, associated most closely with Finn but also with the theories advanced by Scott and Sealy, that fiduciary duties arise when it is legitimate to expect that the fiduciary will 'act for and on behalf of' the other party to the relationship—'in the interests' of that party—and will do so to the exclusion of his own interest.

B. Relevant Considerations

The difficulty with the legitimate expectations approach is that it is not particularly illuminating in practical terms. It works well as a theory, but in large measure that is because it operates at such a high level of abstraction: in effect, the legitimate expectations approach states little more than that fiduciary duties arise whenever it is appropriate for them to apply. The issue that remains is how to determine whether an expectation of fiduciary duties is legitimate in the circumstances.

Flannigan has criticised the legitimate expectations approach because it 'confers an uncontrolled discretion that courts may employ to find fiduciary responsibility wherever they please'.[92] As Kirby J observed in *Pilmer v Duke Group Ltd*, the approach 'can be criticised as tautologous and subjective', although he also considered that it nonetheless 'represents the best attempt to express what is involved'.[93] The cases discussed above show that the judiciary consider it to be a helpful description of when fiduciary duties arise, so that it cannot simply be rejected out of hand. Indeed, the courts' repeated refusals to define or describe the fiduciary concept, and their insistence on retaining flexibility as to when

---

[91] *Hospital Products v US Surgical Corp* (above n 52) 69; see also p 147. And see *Glandon Pty v Strata Consolidated Pty* (above n 73) 557; *Liggett v Kensington* [1993] 1 NZLR 257, 290 (CA); *News v Australian Rugby Football League* (above n 75) 544; *South Australia v Peat Marwick Mitchell & Co* (above n 66) 265; *Brunninghausen v Glavanics* [1999] NSWCA 199 at [87] and [101], (1999) 46 NSWLR 538; *Hooper v Gorvin* (above n 64) 591 (ChD); *3464920 Canada Inc v Strother* [2005] BCCA 35 at [17], (2005) 7 ITELR 748; *Gibson Motorsport Merchandise Pty Ltd v Forbes* [2006] FCAFC 44 at [11], (2006) 149 FCR 569. Cf *Chirnside v Fay* [2006] NZSC 68 at [85], [2007] 1 NZLR 433. The fact that the expectation is or is not held subjectively by the principal must, however, be a *relevant* factor when the court considers whether such an expectation was legitimate in all the circumstances.

[92] Flannigan, 'The Boundaries of Fiduciary Accountability' (above n 2) 74.

[93] *Pilmer v Duke Group Ltd* [2001] HCA 31 at [136], (2001) 207 CLR 165.

fiduciary duties arise, tend to mean that the legitimate expectations approach is the only one likely to be accurate, in that any attempt at a more restrictive definition or description is highly unlikely to match the cases. The legitimate expectations approach may not be the most intellectually satisfying conclusion, but it seems likely to be the most accurate reflection of the case law.

Furthermore, the difficulties inherent in applying any standard that is based on the 'reasonableness' or 'legitimacy' of expectations are not necessarily fatal to the theory. For example, in parallel with fiduciary doctrine, 'the categories of negligence are never closed',[94] and a series of decisions has 'emphasised the inability of any single general principle to provide a practical test which can be applied to every situation to determine whether a duty of care is owed and, if so, what is its scope'.[95] And notwithstanding that a duty of care is recognised when damage is reasonably foreseeable, when there is a relationship of proximity between the parties and when it is fair, just and reasonable for the duty to be imposed[96]—all of which are 'fairly blunt tools'[97] that tend to the merge in the final element of fairness, justice and reasonableness[98]—courts have persevered with the concept, and the skies have not fallen. It is, of course, not the case that the doctrine of negligence is a paragon of principled virtue in this regard. The crucial point is that the legitimate expectations view of the fiduciary concept may be, as Finn himself acknowledged, 'no more precise than a description of the tort of negligence',[99] but it is still plausible for the courts to adopt such an approach, as the cases themselves show.

The remainder of this chapter seeks to enumerate some of the considerations that can assist in determining whether the fiduciary expectation is legitimate in the circumstances. Whatever observations can be made must necessarily be broad, as it is not possible in such a short space to consider in detail the individual circumstances of cases that have been held to engender fiduciary duties. Nevertheless, a number of related points can be made that are not so much criteria for determining whether expectations are legitimate as they are modes of analysis that can be brought to bear when approaching that question.

Understanding that fiduciary doctrine provides subsidiary and prophylactic protection for non-fiduciary duties clarifies what the various fiduciary principles are concerned to achieve. However, that does not assist greatly in determining whether it is legitimate for one party in a relationship to expect that the other will meet the obligations that those principles impose.

---

[94] *Donoghue v Stevenson* [1932] AC 562, 619.
[95] *Caparo Industries plc v Dickman* [1990] 2 AC 605, 617; see also p 628.
[96] *Ibid*, 617–18; *Customs & Excise Commissioners v Barclays Bank plc* [2006] UKHL 28 at [53], [2007] 1 AC 1. See also PH Winfield and JA Jolowicz, *Tort*, 17th edn by WVH Rogers (London, Sweet & Maxwell, 2006) [5–7]; SF Deakin, AC Johnston and B Markesinis, *Markesinis & Deakin's Tort Law*, 6th edn (Oxford, Oxford University Press, 2008) 128.
[97] *Customs & Excise Commissioners v Barclays Bank plc* [2006] UKHL 28 at [71], [2007] 1 AC 1.
[98] *Ibid* at [36]; Winfield and Jolowicz (above n 96) [5–8]–[5–9] and [5–14]–[5–15].
[99] Finn, 'Fiduciary Law and the Modern Commercial World' (above n 24) 9.

The first point that can be made about whether that expectation might be legitimate flows naturally from the nature of common law analysis in general: the reasonableness or legitimacy of expectations regarding legal obligations is related, at least in part, to pre-existing patterns of judicial behaviour as to the application of those obligations. Thus, for example, it is clearly legitimate to expect that a trustee will not act in a way that involves a conflict between his personal interests and the duties he owes as a trustee because the courts have recognised and enforced such a requirement for centuries. That example is based on a settled category of fiduciary relationship, and in that context the legitimate expectations approach is not applied because the conclusion is preordained by the nature of the relationship itself.

However, pre-existing patterns of judicial behaviour can be relevant in two ways when the legitimate expectations approach comes to be applied in cases that do not fall within one of the settled categories of fiduciary relationship. First, the similarities and differences between the facts of the case in question and those involved in other cases that did not involve settled categories of fiduciary relationship can provide guidance. Secondly, comparison between the facts of the case in question and the kinds of facts that obtain in the settled classes of fiduciary relationships will assist any determination of the issue. In other words, analogies with settled categories of fiduciary relationship—where the legitimacy of the fiduciary expectation is beyond doubt—can assist courts in determining whether that expectation is legitimate in the circumstances of the case before them.

Hence, courts have considered it useful, in determining whether fiduciary duties are owed, to consider the degree to which the facts are similar to the relationship between trustee and beneficiary. In *Benson v Heathorn*, Knight Bruce VC said that 'trustees and all parties whose character and responsibilities are similar (for there is no magic in the word)'[100] are precluded from making a profit from their position. As has been seen, that analogical process was used in the early cases that determined that directors owed fiduciary duties because of the similarity between their position and that of trustees.[101] Company directors are of course now themselves a settled category of fiduciary relationship, but that same process of analogical reasoning—assessing the degree to which the facts of a given case are similar to or different from those involved in settled categories of fiduciary relationships—can be applied to the facts of individual cases outside the settled categories of fiduciary relationships. Thus, for example, while company directors are a settled category of fiduciary in the sense that they clearly owe fiduciary duties to the company, they do not ordinarily owe such duties to the shareholders.[102] However, it is possible for a fiduciary relationship to arise

---

[100] *Benson v Heathorn* (1842) 1 Y & CCC 326, 342 (62 ER 909).
[101] See, eg, the cases discussed above in ch 2, section II-A.
[102] See, eg, *Percival v Wright* [1902] 2 Ch 421, 425–26; *Re Chez Nico (Restaurants) Ltd* [1992] BCLC 192, 208 (VC); *Peskin v Anderson* (above n 66) [28].

between directors and shareholders, as Mummery LJ put it in *Peskin v Anderson*, 'in special circumstances which replicate the salient features of well-established categories of fiduciary relationships'.[103]

While the drawing of analogies can be criticised, it has the advantage here of allowing developments to take place 'incrementally and by analogy with established categories',[104] rather than by reference to some broad principle that does not accurately reflect what has been done in previous cases.

Another observation about the process by which the courts reach the conclusion that the fiduciary expectation is or is not legitimate, albeit one not often acknowledged by the courts themselves, may be that there is societal value in protecting the integrity of the performance of obligations in that relationship and in others of its kind. Thus, Finn suggested:

> [T]he fiduciary principle . . . is, itself, an instrument of public policy. It has been used, and is demonstrably used, to maintain the integrity, credibility and utility of relationships perceived to be of importance in a society. And it is used to protect interests, both personal and economic, which a society is perceived to deem valuable.[105]

In other words, the judges whose job it is to determine whether any given circumstances generate a legitimate expectation such as will beget fiduciary duties reach the conclusion that fiduciary duties are appropriate in certain types of relationship not because those who occupy the 'fiduciary' position are inherently suspect but because the institutions themselves have societal importance and are therefore deserving of added protection, beyond that provided by other legal mechanisms. Institutions with control over property have often fallen within that category, but not every societal institution concerning property is considered sufficiently important to generate such protection,[106] nor are all service relationships necessarily fiduciary. Car mechanics provide a useful and recurrent example. As Finn said:

> [I]t is a rather large step to take to say that every such relationship of service is also a confidential one. Suppose that B ordinarily has his car serviced by S, a mechanic. After some years B intimates to S that he is thinking of selling it. S with full knowledge of the condition of the car offers to purchase it. Could B have the contract set aside if the sale

---

[103] *Peskin v Anderson* (above n 66) [34].

[104] *Sutherland Shite Council v Heyman* (1985) 157 CLR 424, 481 (quoted with approval in *Caparo Industries v Dickman* (above n 95) 618). See also *Stovin v Wise* [1996] AC 923, 949.

[105] Finn, 'The Fiduciary Principle' (above n 20) 26. See also Weinrib (above n 14) 15; T Frankel, 'Fiduciary Law' (1983) 71 *California Law Review* 795, 802–4; T Frankel, *Fiduciary Law* (Anchorage, Fathom Publishing, 2008) 29–30.

[106] The very concept of 'property' is itself a social construct, created by the law as a metaphysical reaction to societal instincts regarding the significance of certain rights when compared with others: M Arnold, 'Copyright' (1880) 159 *Fortnightly Review (New Series)* 319, 323; J Bentham, *Theory of Legislation*, 5th edn by R Hildreth (London, Trübner & Co, 1887) 113; Weinrib (above n 14) 10–11; C Rotherham, 'The Conceptual Structure of Restitution for Wrongs' [2007] *Cambridge Law Journal* 172, 194–95.

was at an undervalue? S has been entrusted with B's property and has performed services for B in relation to it. But can it be said that his position is a confidential one.[107]

One way of understanding why car mechanics are generally thought not to owe fiduciary duties, despite the fact that they have (limited) access to the car owner's property and that their work can potentially be a matter of life or death for the owner (something not often the case for fiduciaries generally), is that their work is not considered of sufficient societal importance to engender the specially protective rules that attend a fiduciary relationship: contractual and tort-based obligations suffice. Thus, whereas between solicitors and their clients, 'loyalty to the client . . . is regarded as necessary if the integrity and credibility of these socially important service relationships are to be maintained,'[108] the same cannot be said of car mechanics.

The relevance of considering the societal importance of protecting obligations in particular institutions is not often openly acknowledged by the judiciary. But it has been referred to in *Lac Minerals v Corona*[109] and in *Hodgkinson v Simms*, where La Forest J observed that 'the desire to protect and reinforce the integrity of social institutions and enterprises is prevalent throughout fiduciary law.'[110] Similarly, discussing the strict standard exacted by fiduciary doctrine's conflict principle, Finn J said in *Hughes v Air Services Australia*:

> There are discernible public policy reasons for imposing such a standard, not the least of which is the need to maintain public confidence in the integrity and utility of a range of socially important relationships in which loyal service is properly to be expected.[111]

Thus, societal interests can be a relevant consideration when determining whether the fiduciary expectation is a legitimate one in a given case, particularly when analogies with other fiduciary relationships are being addressed. As Julius Stone said of the process of drawing analogies generally, 'the crucial decision is then as to *relevant* similarities and differences, and this necessarily involves advertence to factors of justice and social policy, transcending any mere syllogistic relation to or among rules of law formally enounced in the available cases.'[112] In the fiduciary context, therefore, 'policy supplies the direction in which fiduciary analogies are formed. Social purposes external to the system are served.'[113] This also means that the line between fiduciary and non-fiduciary relationships is capable of moving 'as perceptions of social interest and values change'.[114]

---

[107] Finn, *Fiduciary Obligations* (above n 13) [399].
[108] Finn, 'The Fiduciary Principle' (above n 20) 47.
[109] *Lac Minerals* (above n 55) 672.
[110] *Hodgkinson v Simms* (above n 60) 422; see pp 420–22 generally.
[111] *Hughes Aircraft Systems International v Air Services Australia* (above n 72) 237.
[112] J Stone, *Legal System and Lawyers' Reasonings* (London, Stevens & Sons, 1964) 316.
[113] J Glover, 'The Identification of Fiduciaries' in PBH Birks (ed), *Privacy and Loyalty* (Oxford, Oxford University Press, 1997) 269, 277.
[114] Finn, 'The Fiduciary Principle' (above n 20) 26.

A related way of approaching the question whether the fiduciary expectation is legitimate in a given case is to ask from an external perspective whether it was reasonable to expect the person claiming fiduciary doctrine's protection to use the legal mechanisms already at their disposal, particularly in the form of the law of contract, to try to control the risks that fiduciary doctrine would address. As Tamar Frankel has argued, 'the risk of abuse which all fiduciary relations pose for the entrustors is the main feature which triggers the application of fiduciary law, *when the protective mechanisms outside of fiduciary law cannot adequately eliminate this risk*' (emphasis added).[115]

This attitude towards the legitimate expectations question is particularly relevant when the person alleged to be a fiduciary has been accorded considerable discretion and it is difficult to define in advance how that discretion ought to be exercised. Contractual mechanisms will not always provide adequate controls on that discretion, for a variety of reasons. First, the objects of the discretion may not themselves have conferred the discretion, such as trust beneficiaries, which limits their ability to place ex ante controls on it. Secondly,

> even if such contractual arrangements were feasible, the transaction costs involved in drawing up a detailed prior agreement covering all possible discretionary uses of power over the life of the relation would not only be enormous, but would also probably exceed the benefits of the proposed relation.[116]

In contrast, in situations in which it is feasible to put in place contractual controls on the conduct of the counterparty, that party's discretion is generally reduced by those controls, and there is consequently less need for fiduciary doctrine's protection. As Richard Nolan has said, again discussing car mechanics:

> Why, for example, is a car mechanic not a fiduciary for his or her customer[?] From the perspective of English law, the answer seems to be that it is possible to control the car mechanic's action through specific, easily contracted duties to perform a set task with a set measure of diligence. There is a bounded task around which parties can contract, not merely in theory, but in practice too: performance of the task can be assessed relatively easily, and consequently it is practicable *ex ante* to stipulate (or to have the law imply) specific constraints on the parties' conduct. In contrast, it is exceptionally difficult to stipulate specifically for the conduct to be undertaken by a trustee managing a trust fund or by a director managing a company, without abolishing managerial freedom: there are so many different circumstances that may arise in the course of conducting the undertaking and so many different, unobjectionable ways of performing the undertaking.[117]

---

[115] Frankel, 'Fiduciary Law' (above n 105) 808.
[116] *Ibid*, 813.
[117] RC Nolan, 'The Legal Control of Directors' Conflicts of Interest in the United Kingdom: Non-executive Directors Following the Higgs Report' (2005) 6 *Theoretical Inquiries in Law* 413, 422–23.

This approach is reflected in one of the points that the majority of the Supreme Court of Canada considered helpful in reaching their decision in *Lac Minerals v Corona*. The majority held that no fiduciary duty arose when one mining company, Corona, revealed confidential information to another mining company showing that substantial mineral deposits might be found on land adjacent to that owned by Corona. As Sopinka J said, 'nothing prevented Corona from exacting an undertaking from Lac that it would not acquire the [adjacent] property unilaterally.'[118]

Like all of the approaches that have been considered in this section, however, application of this approach is not a simple matter. It once again requires the court to assess whether it was practicable and appropriate for the person claiming to be owed fiduciary duties to rely on an expectation of loyalty or instead to take steps to protect his interests through contract. Thus, La Forest J led the dissentients in *Lac Minerals v Corona* in arguing:

> I cannot understand why a claim for breach of confidence is available absent a confidentiality agreement, but a claim for breach of fiduciary duty is not. The fact that the parties could have concluded a contract to cover the situation but did not in fact do so does not, in my opinion, determine the matter. Many claims in tort could be avoided through more prudent negotiation of a contract, but courts do not deny tort liability.[119]

However, the point of asking whether contractual regulation was a viable alternative is not that it necessarily determines that fiduciary duties are inapplicable. Rather, it is *one* of the considerations that help to determine whether a fiduciary expectation was legitimate in all of the circumstances.[120] As La Forest J himself went on to say, 'the existence of an alternative procedure is only relevant in my mind if the parties would realistically have been expected to contemplate it as an alternative.'[121] In other words, the question to be addressed is whether, in all of the circumstances, it was legitimate for the claimant to expect the other party to act in the claimant's interests to the exclusion of its own several interests. All of the various approaches to answering the question that have been considered in this section of the chapter are merely different facets of that one question.

A final facet of that question concerns the appropriateness or legitimacy of finding fiduciary duties to have been owed between commercial actors. Lord Millett said extra-curially that 'it is of the first importance not to impose fiduciary obligations on parties to a purely commercial relationship who deal with each other at arms' length and can be expected to look after their own

---

[118] *Lac Minerals* (above n 55) 607.

[119] *Ibid*, 664.

[120] The last sentence of La Forest J's statement also ignores the difference between the law of torts, which applies prima facie to all legal persons unless it has been contracted away, and fiduciary doctrine, which applies only in some situations. The difficulty lies in identifying those situations.

[121] *Lac Minerals* (above n 55) 664–65.

interests.'[122] Support for that view can also be mustered from the case law. Thus, for example, Bramwell LJ famously said in *New Zealand and Australian Land Co v Watson*:

> I do not desire to find fault with the various intricacies and doctrines connected with trusts, but I should be very sorry to see them introduced into commercial transactions, and an agent in a commercial case turned into a trustee with all the troubles that attend that relation.[123]

However, 'business relationships (leaving aside partnerships) clearly can attract fiduciary obligations',[124] notwithstanding that the context concerns a commercial transaction. Thus, for example, company directors act in a commercial context and yet owe fiduciary duties to the company, and lawyers and agents frequently act in commercial contexts while owing fiduciary duties to their principals. Hence, Mason J observed in *Hospital Products* that 'it is altogether too simplistic, if not superficial, to suggest that commercial transactions stand outside the fiduciary regime as though in some way commercial transactions do not lend themselves to the creation of a relationship in which one comes under an obligation to act in the interests of another.'[125]

The view that fiduciary duties arise when it is legitimate to expect that they will do so provides a means of reconciling these apparently inconsistent perspectives on the appropriateness of fiduciary duties in commercial settings. Fiduciary duties do not commonly arise in commercial settings because it is normally inappropriate to expect a commercial party to put its own interests aside and to act solely in the interests of another commercial party.[126] But if in all the circumstances of the relationship between the parties, that expectation is not inappropriate, then fiduciary duties can and will arise notwithstanding that it is a commercial relationship.

This can create some uncertainty as to the applicability of fiduciary duties in a given relationship, which is always undesirable in commercial transactions. However, this is a consequence of the application of the legitimate expectations standard, as opposed to a clear rule, which itself is a consequence of the courts' refusal to allow the fiduciary concept to be hamstrung by a formal definition. Furthermore, the degree of uncertainty that the legitimate expectations standard produces should not be exaggerated. Fiduciary doctrine is not regularly applied in commercial settings outside of the settled categories of fiduciary relationships,

---

[122] PJ Millett, 'Equity's Place in the Law of Commerce' (1998) 114 *Law Quarterly Review* 214, 217–18.

[123] *New Zealand & Australian Land Co v Watson* (1881) 7 QBD 374, 382 (CA). See also *Cobbe v Yeoman's Row Management Ltd* [2008] UKHL 55 at [81], [2008] 1 WLR 1752.

[124] *News v Australian Rugby Football League* (above n 75) 538. See also *South Australia v Peat Marwick Mitchell & Co* (above n 66) 266.

[125] *Hospital Products v US Surgical Corp* (above n 52) 100. See also *Re Goldcorp Exchange Ltd* [1995] 1 AC 74, 98 (PC).

[126] See also JRF Lehane, 'Fiduciaries in a Commercial Context' in PD Finn (ed), *Essays in Equity* (Sydney, Law Book Co, 1985) 95, 98.

where the fiduciary actors are (or at least should be) well aware of the fiduciary obligations that attend their positions. When it is applied outside of those settled categories, it responds to the legitimate expectations of the parties:

> Certainty, in commercial law is, no doubt, an important value, but it is not the only value. . . In any event, it is difficult to see how giving legal recognition to the parties' expectations will throw commercial law into turmoil. Commercial relationships will more rarely involve fiduciary obligations. That is not because they are immune from them, but because in most cases, they would not be appropriately imposed.[127]

Thus, all things considered, the cases can be seen to support the view, advanced most comprehensively by Paul Finn, that there is no clear rule as to when fiduciary duties arise but rather that they respond to a standard of legitimate expectation. In considering whether that standard has been met in individual cases the courts can, and do, take into account analogies with pre-existing patterns of judicial conduct on that question, while bearing in mind also the need to move cautiously and take into account the societal value placed on the kind of relationship at issue. Courts have also found it helpful to consider whether the parties were able to regulate their relationship by mechanisms other than the protection that fiduciary doctrine provides, particularly when the relationship is a commercial one. These differing approaches all reflect alternative but related facets of the question whether the fiduciary expectation is legitimate in the circumstances. Approaching the question as to when fiduciary duties arise by reference to the legitimacy of expectations to that effect also emphasises the importance of understanding the content of fiduciary doctrine, which has been the predominant focus of this book. What is to be expected of a putative fiduciary must surely have an impact on when it is right to expect that of him.

---

[127] *Lac Minerals* (above n 55) 666–67. See also PD Finn, 'Commerce, the Common Law and Morality' (1989) *Melbourne University Law Review* 87, 98–99.

10

Epilogue

This book has sought to examine what it means to say that an obligation is a fiduciary obligation, as distinct from other kinds of obligation known to law—what distinguishes fiduciary duties from other sorts of duties such that we set them apart from those other types of duties and give them a different name? A partial answer to that question is found in the important observation that 'the distinguishing obligation of a fiduciary is the obligation of loyalty.'[1] That obligation, which is peculiar to fiduciaries, differentiates them from other kinds of actors. However, the observation is only a partial answer in that it raises the further question: what is meant by 'loyalty' in this context? That question has been the focus of attention in this book. The central answer that has been proposed is that the fiduciary concept of loyalty, as it is used in Anglo-Australian legal doctrine, is best understood as the summation of the various doctrines that are applied peculiarly to fiduciaries, rather than as a legal duty that is directly enforceable in its own right. The idea of the fiduciary concept of 'loyalty' is a subsidiary and prophylactic mode of protection for non-fiduciary duties. Its function is to make it more likely that the non-fiduciary duties that comprise the fiduciary's undertaking will be properly performed. It does this by requiring the fiduciary to eschew influences that might sway him away from such proper performance.

No judicial consensus has yet emerged about a general definition to identify when fiduciary duties arise. However, the lack of any such definition does not prevent analysis of fiduciary duties as they have been applied in the cases. Thus, the argument in this book has been developed from the 'bottom up', as opposed to starting with a preconceived notion of what is distinctively 'fiduciary' and proceeding from there. Especially when it is borne in mind that there are a number of settled categories of relationships in which fiduciary duties undoubtedly are owed, there is sufficient material in the cases from which one can extract and develop a theory as to the nature and function of fiduciary doctrine, without needing to resort to 'top-down' reasoning, thus avoiding the profound problems that the latter form of reasoning has in the grounds for and manner of selecting its axioms.

---

[1] *Bristol & West Building Society v Mothew* [1998] Ch 1, 18 (CA).

Furthermore, although the 'fiduciary' concept has been used in the past to justify the extension or export of duties to situations that are analogous to the relationship between trustee and beneficiary, the focus of the analysis provided in this book has been the duties that are peculiar to fiduciaries, rather than all of the duties owed by fiduciaries. This approach has been adopted by Anglo-Australian courts in more recent times, particularly the last two decades. It sharpens the analysis of fiduciary duties by excluding from that concept doctrines that also apply to others who owe no fiduciary duties. It is those peculiarly fiduciary duties that are distinctive of fiduciary status and that constitute the fiduciary concept of loyalty.

When that approach is applied to the cases, the analysis focuses on the fiduciary conflict and profit principles. They enhance the likelihood of fiduciaries properly performing their core functions or undertakings. They require fiduciaries to avoid situations in which there is a real possibility that they will be swayed away from proper performance of those functions. The content of each fiduciary's undertaking is given legal effect in the form of non-fiduciary duties. These necessarily vary from case to case, dependent upon the particular relationship between the fiduciary and the principal and the function that the fiduciary has undertaken to perform. Whatever non-fiduciary duties comprise that core function, the function served by fiduciary duties is to protect the due performance of those non-fiduciary duties by requiring the fiduciary to eschew situations that carry a heightened risk that the non-fiduciary duties will be breached. In so doing, fiduciary duties provide a prophylactic and subsidiary form of protection to non-fiduciary duties.

Fiduciary doctrine is frequently described as prophylactic. Such observations generally refer to and accurately reflect the methodology by which fiduciary doctrine is implemented. In particular, evidential difficulties are treated as a justification for fiduciary doctrine's rules being cast in terms that are broader than might be thought necessary for their purpose. However, the element of prophylaxis in fiduciary doctrine runs deeper than mere methodology. The very nature of fiduciary doctrine is prophylactic in the function that it is intended to serve, in that it is designed to 'prevent rather than cure'. Fiduciary duties are designed to prevent situations from arising that carry an increased or heightened risk that the fiduciary will be drawn away from proper performance of his non-fiduciary duties. By requiring fiduciaries to avoid acting in such situations, the likelihood of them acting in breach of their non-fiduciary duties is reduced. Thus, the very function of fiduciary doctrine is prophylactic, which in turn provides a substantial justification for its rules being implemented in a prophylactic manner.

The protective function that this form of prophylaxis entails also means that fiduciary duties are subsidiary to the non-fiduciary duties that they protect. This does not mean that fiduciary duties are secondary remedial duties that arise consequent upon a primary breach of non-fiduciary duties. Fiduciary doctrine does not simply provide a more powerful remedial regime for breaches of a fiduciary's non-fiduciary duties. Indeed, fiduciary liability can be established without proof of any breach of non-fiduciary duty at all, which again reflects the prophylactic nature of the protection that fiduciary doctrine provides for non-fiduciary duties. Rather than being reliant upon breaches of non-fiduciary duties, fiduciary duties are separate and distinct rules that are born of an attempt to prevent such breaches from occurring. Fiduciary doctrine is subsidiary to those non-fiduciary duties in the sense that it helps to ensure that they are properly performed.

The protective function that fiduciary doctrine serves vis-à-vis non-fiduciary duties is most clearly reflected in the principle that prohibits fiduciaries from acting in situations in which there is a real sensible possibility of conflict between their personal interest in a transaction and their non-fiduciary duties. Fiduciary doctrine requires fiduciaries to avoid such situations because a fiduciary's personal interest in a transaction when he also owes non-fiduciary duties to his principal creates a risk that the fiduciary will be inattentive, or worse, in the performance of his non-fiduciary duties. Fiduciary doctrine thus reduces the risk that the fiduciary will act in breach of non-fiduciary duty by seeking to eliminate temptations towards such breaches. In so doing, fiduciary doctrine cannot guarantee proper performance of the non-fiduciary duties, because such duties can be breached for myriad reasons that can have nothing whatever to do with inconsistent temptations. However, fiduciary doctrine does enhance the likelihood of proper performance by seeking to reduce the risk of breach that the presence of a distracting temptation inherently raises. In this way, the fiduciary conflict principle provides a subsidiary and prophylactic form of protection for the fiduciary's non-fiduciary duties.

This protective function is also evident in the other rules that comprise fiduciary doctrine's distinctive concept of loyalty. The principle that prohibits fiduciaries from receiving unauthorised profits that come to them as a result of their fiduciary positions can be understood as an adjunct to the conflict principle. In other words, the concern that motivates the profit principle is that when a fiduciary makes a profit by reason of his fiduciary position it is highly likely that there is a conflict between the fiduciary's personal interest in making the profit and the non-fiduciary duties that he owes to his principal. The profit principle applies even if a conflict is not formally identified, as a deliberately over-inclusive adjunct to the conflict principle: the conflict principle serves a prophylactic function, which is implemented in a prophylactic fashion so as to generate the profit principle.

Similarly, the fiduciary principles that regulate situations in which a fiduciary acts with multiple sets of inconsistent non-fiduciary duties are also concerned with protecting the proper performance of non-fiduciary duties. In such a situation, the temptation to act in breach of one set of non-fiduciary duties may be less than when there is a personal interest, but there is still sufficient reason for fiduciary doctrine to intervene. The protective function is certainly identifiable in the rule regarding situations in which a fiduciary owes non-fiduciary duties to two or more principals and the performance of those duties may be in some way inconsistent. It is also identifiable in the rule that prohibits a fiduciary from continuing to act when performance of the duties that he owes two or more principals will necessarily involve breach of one or other of those sets of duties. These two rules, the potential and actual conflict rules, have been developed as analogical extensions of the more venerable principle regarding conflicts between duty and interest. The same concern to reduce the likelihood of breaches of non-fiduciary duties is evident in all of them.

The inhibition principle, which prevents a fiduciary who is properly acting for two principals with potentially inconsistent duties from intentionally favouring one client over the other, is unusual for fiduciary doctrine, in that it turns on the reasons for a breach of non-fiduciary duty having occurred. Fiduciary liability ordinarily arises irrespective of whether there has been a breach of non-fiduciary duty and without any regard to the reasons that the fiduciary may have had for acting as he did. Thus, it is harder to explain this principle as providing a subsidiary and prophylactic form of protection for non-fiduciary duties. It is predicated on a breach of non-fiduciary duty having occurred. However, the inhibition principle can be seen to provide a modified form of protection to non-fiduciary duties in the unusual situation that exists when a fiduciary has the fully informed consent of both principals to his acting—so that he is acting 'properly' and not in breach of the potential conflict rule—but is not in breach of the actual conflict rule. The modifications that have been made are a response to the specific circumstances that obtain when the inhibition principle applies and in which it must operate. As such, they do not detract in any serious way from understanding fiduciary doctrine as generally providing a subsidiary and prophy-lactic form of protection for non-fiduciary duties.

Fiduciary doctrine's remedial regime is also consistent with the view that its nature and function are to provide subsidiary and prophylactic protection for non-fiduciary duties. The clearest evidence of this is found in the best known of fiduciary doctrine's remedies, namely the principal's ability to require a fiduciary to disgorge profits he has made in breach of fiduciary duty, whether through rescission of the transaction, an account of profits or a proprietary constructive trust over such profits. These remedies are not simply more powerful remedies for breach of non-fiduciary duty, as no such breach need be shown in order to claim them. Instead, the profit-stripping remedies are part of fiduciary doctrine's attempt to prevent breaches of non-fiduciary duties: profit-stripping remedies remove the fruits of temptation, which is an effective means of reducing the temptation itself. This in turn protects the non-fiduciary duties that are also owed. As Nourse LJ said in *Sargeant v National Westminster Bank*:

> The rule that a trustee must not profit from his trust holds that prevention is better than cure. While it invariably requires that a profit shall be yielded up, it prefers to intervene beforehand by dissolving the connection out of which the profit may be made. At that stage the rule is expressed by saying that a trustee must not put himself in a position where his interest and duty conflict.[2]

---

[2] *Sargeant v National Westminster Bank plc* (1990) 61 P & CR 518, 519 (CA).

Compensatory remedies, which are another recognised option in a principal's remedial armoury following a breach of fiduciary duty, fit less clearly with this protective understanding of fiduciary doctrine but are nonetheless consistent with it. As Nourse LJ's statement in *Sargeant* recognises, even profit-stripping remedies, which are designed to deter a fiduciary from acting in a way that will involve a breach of fiduciary duty, operate only after the fact of disloyalty. When a fiduciary has ignored fiduciary doctrine's protective rules, it is legitimate for the remedies available to strip the fiduciary's profit on the basis that the transaction ought not to have taken place. But it is also legitimate for the remedies to redress any prejudice that the principal might have suffered. Loss-based remedies are therefore available in order to complement the protective function served by fiduciary doctrine.

Understanding fiduciary duties as providing subsidiary and prophylactic protection for non-fiduciary duties affords important insights into a number of aspects of fiduciary doctrine. These are both conceptual and practical. It indicates, for example, that fiduciary doctrine has an instrumental outlook, based on a cynical view of human nature, far more than it represents any moralistic viewpoint. The requirements of fiduciary doctrine are undoubtedly more exacting than those of non-fiduciary doctrines. However, these requirements are adequately explained by the instrumental, protective function served by fiduciary doctrine, rather than because fiduciary doctrine involves some sort of moral exhortation to fiduciaries to do more than would otherwise be required in the performance of their non-fiduciary duties. If fiduciary doctrine truly were based on a moralistic view of how fiduciaries ought to conduct themselves, one would have expected that moralistic view to have become far more developed in the case law than it has been. Fiduciary rules that appear to be based on moral assessments of the fiduciary's conduct, such as the fair-dealing rule and the corporate opportunities doctrine, are best understood as specific implementations of the fiduciary conflict and profit principles, rather than as vehicles by which the law somehow transmits ethical resolve into practice.

Fiduciary doctrine is not based on a moralistic view of how fiduciaries ought to behave. It does not single out fiduciaries and seek to make them into more moral or better people. Its nature is far more functional. It aims to provide subsidiary and prophylactic protection for non-fiduciary duties in situations in which extraneous influences generate a risk of those non-fiduciary duties being breached. The high-handed moral rhetoric that is often associated with fiduciary doctrine distorts understanding of its true function.

The understanding of the protective nature of fiduciary loyalty that has been advanced yields a fuller understanding of the relationship between fiduciary and non-fiduciary duties than has previously been provided. It also provides a concrete theoretical foundation on which to explain many other important tenets of fiduciary doctrine. It explains, for example, how fiduciary duties can be both 'inflexible' but also moulded to the circumstances of each particular case. The 'moulding' of fiduciary duties to the facts of each case is not an unruly discretion given to judges to allow them latitude in the way fiduciary duties are applied in order somehow to do 'justice' in individual cases. Instead, it is a logical consequence of the protective function that fiduciary duties serve vis-à-vis non-fiduciary duties. The fiduciary remains bound to perform his non-fiduciary duties in any event. Fiduciary doctrine does not alter the content of that burden. Rather, the function of fiduciary duties is to avoid temptations that tend to distract the fiduciary from proper performance of his non-fiduciary duties. In order to do that, fiduciary doctrine must take into account what those non-fiduciary duties entail, which will differ from case to case. In this way, it can determine whether temptations are in fact inconsistent with the non-fiduciary duties in a given case.

The requirement that non-fiduciary duties exist before fiduciary liability can arise is important to the theoretical relationship between fiduciary and non-fiduciary duties. It is also significant in practical terms. It emphasises that a meticulous examination of the facts of each case is necessary to ascertain precisely what non-fiduciary duties have arisen in the circumstances of a relationship. That, in turn, is important in determining the way fiduciary duties will apply in the relationship and whether there may have been any breach of those fiduciary duties.

The subsidiary character of fiduciary duties and the protective function they serve vis-à-vis non-fiduciary duties also indicate that there must actually be non-fiduciary duties owed for fiduciary doctrine sensibly to be applied: it is nonsensical to analyse duties that protect non-fiduciary duties if no non-fiduciary duties subsist in the particular relationship and none have ever existed. A number of examples that appear to suggest the contrary are best explained on the basis that they involve different (non-fiduciary) principles, such as the court's ability to control solicitors as officers of the court, or that they are pragmatic extensions of fiduciary principles designed to ensure that fiduciaries cannot circumvent the protection that fiduciary doctrine is designed to provide by, for example, resigning from their fiduciary position in order to act in a way that would otherwise be prohibited by fiduciary doctrine.

Fiduciary duties direct the fiduciary towards proper performance of his non-fiduciary duties by leading him away from temptations that are inconsistent with those non-fiduciary duties. This explains the validity of the proposition that fiduciary duties are predominantly proscriptive in nature rather than prescriptive. That proposition captures the essentially negative function served by fiduciary doctrine in seeking to avoid situations that involve distracting influences. The positive or prescriptive duties that a fiduciary owes are provided by non-fiduciary doctrines. It is those non-fiduciary duties that fiduciary duties protect. The protective function is fundamentally one of negative prohibition or proscription.

The understanding of fiduciary doctrine advanced in this book also explains why the principal's fully informed consent is required, as opposed to mere contractual consent, in order to forgo that level of protection once it has arisen. Fiduciary doctrine's protection can be waived by a principal, but it would seriously undermine the effectiveness of the protection if a mere contractual consent were sufficient to displace it, as that would not ensure that the principal appreciated the risks he was thereby accepting.

A proper appreciation of both the content and fundamental purpose of fiduciary doctrine is indispensable when considering suggestions that fiduciary doctrine ought to be changed because it is somehow no longer 'fit for purpose' in its current form. The fact that the function of fiduciary doctrine is protective does not mean that the doctrine should not be altered. All too often, however, those who advocate such changes fail to address that function so as to explain why it is no longer appropriate.

The protective function of fiduciary doctrine also indicates that awards of equitable compensation for breach of fiduciary duty ought not to be reduced by reference to the principal's contributory fault. If it is shown that loss has actually been caused by a breach of fiduciary duty, which will not always be easy to establish, that loss ought to be compensated in full on the basis that the fiduciary's principal should be able to rely on the protection that fiduciary doctrine is designed to provide.

Understanding fiduciary duties as protective of non-fiduciary duties suggests that caution is warranted before fiduciary duties are treated as default contractual obligations or as torts. Fiduciary duties can be analysed as default contractual terms, particularly as penalty defaults, but this risks losing sight of the special function that fiduciary duties serve vis-à-vis other duties, including contractual duties. It also risks rendering fiduciary duties prone to ordinary contractual alteration, without fully informed consent, which will undermine their protective purpose.

Similarly, fiduciary duties can potentially be conceived of as torts or 'civil wrongs'. However, again there is a risk that the distinguishing nature and function of fiduciary duties will be lost sight of if they are treated in that way. The subsidiary and prophylactic form of protection that fiduciary doctrine provides does not figure in the doctrines that comprise the law of torts. Taxonomical debates are helpful only when they assist with clarity of thought. There is greater danger of confusion if fiduciary doctrine is aligned with other non-fiduciary forms of civil wrong, rather than being understood on its own terms as unique, because the distinctive protective function is too easily ignored in such a setting. The subsidiary and prophylactic nature of the protection provided by fiduciary doctrine also suggests that doctrines that are sometimes considered to be fiduciary in character, such as the doctrines of undue influence and confidence, are best kept separate from the fiduciary concept of loyalty.

This book presents a comprehensive survey of the nature and function of the distinguishing fiduciary concept of loyalty by reference to the duties that are peculiarly owed by fiduciaries. Fiduciary doctrine provides a subsidiary and prophylactic form of protection for non-fiduciary duties. That, however, does not answer every possible question about the law relating to fiduciaries. For example, it does not provide an unambiguous answer to the problematic question of when fiduciary duties arise. The content and purpose of fiduciary doctrine are important in thinking about when such regulation might be appropriate but are not themselves determinative of that question. The most compelling answer that can be gleaned from the cases is that fiduciary duties arise when it is legitimate to expect the abnegation of self-interest upon which fiduciary doctrine insists.

That, of course, is not the only question that could be asked. For example, the historical development of fiduciary doctrine has yet to be examined exhaustively.[3] As was argued in chapter two, fiduciary doctrine has changed in recent years in an attempt to focus analysis more sharply on duties that are peculiar to fiduciaries, as opposed merely to duties that are owed by fiduciaries. Thus, the history may not have answers to the questions that arise in modern fiduciary analysis, but it remains helpful to know where the doctrine came from. Studying the previous incarnations of fiduciary doctrine and the process by which that doctrine has changed can add to our understanding of the current position by illuminating and highlighting the differences that have developed over time. In particular, the issue of why and when certain duties of trustees were exported to other trustee-like actors may help with developing a deeper understanding of when fiduciary duties arise generally.

There is also scope for further analysis of the variety of rules that regulate the exercise of powers held by fiduciaries and the interrelationship between the peculiarly fiduciary and the non-fiduciary aspects of that regulation. In other words, rather than seeking to separate out the peculiarly fiduciary aspects of the regulation of fiduciary actors, attention can be focused instead on the overall regulation of such actors.[4] That then permits a comparison with the overall regulation of powers not held in a fiduciary capacity, with a view to developing a better understanding of the regulation of fiduciary and non-fiduciary decision-makers.

These issues are beyond the scope of this book, which has focused instead on the task of identifying a coherent and compelling account of the distinctive fiduciary obligation of loyalty.

---

[3] See, eg, J Getzler, 'Rumford Market and the Genesis of Fiduciary Obligations' in A Burrows & A Rodger (eds), *Mapping the Law* (Oxford, Oxford University Press, 2006) 577.
[4] See, eg, RC Nolan, 'Controlling Fiduciary Power' [2009] *Cambridge Law Journal* 293.

Index

Lightning Source UK Ltd.
Milton Keynes UK
UKOW05f1203030417
298211UK00004B/305/P

9 781849 462143